BUILDING IN SECURITY AT AGILE SPEED

BUILDING IN SECURITY AT AGILE SPEED

JAMES RANSOME
BROOK S. E. SCHOENFIELD

CRC Press
Taylor & Francis Group
Boca Raton London New York

CRC Press is an imprint of the
Taylor & Francis Group, an **informa** business

AN AUERBACH BOOK

Material in this book is taken from the following books written by one or both of the authors, with permission from Taylor & Francis Group:

Core Software Security: Security at the Source / ISBN: 9781466560956 / 2013
Securing Systems: Applied Security Architecture and Threat Models / ISBN: 9781482233971 / 2015
Secrets of a Cyber Security Architect / ISBN: 9781498741996 / 2019

CRC Press
Taylor & Francis Group
6000 Broken Sound Parkway NW, Suite 300
Boca Raton, FL 33487-2742

© 2021 by Taylor & Francis Group, LLC
CRC Press is an imprint of Taylor & Francis Group, an Informa business

No claim to original U.S. Government works

Printed on acid-free paper

International Standard Book Number-13:
978-0-367-43326-0 (Hardback)
978-1-032-01005-2 (Paperback)
978-1-003-00245-1 (eBook)

Visit the Taylor & Francis Web site at
http://www.taylorandfrancis.com

and the CRC Press Web site at
http://www.crcpress.com

Dedications

This book is dedicated to my parents, who taught me how to think outside the box, and to my teachers at Almond Avenue School, who taught me to both focus and multi-task at the same time, all at a very young age. This has served me well in this journey we call life.

— James Ransome

A succeeding generation (to me) of software security specialists are well into their careers, people like (to name just a sample) Luis Servin, Damilare Fagbemi, Sandeep Kumar Singh, Subir Biswas, François Proulx, Zoe Braiterman, Jonathan Marcil, Kim Wuyts, and including, I'm proud to say, my daughter, Allison Schoenfield. You must carry this work forward, critique it, refine it, recreate it. It is to you, and to those that follow whom you will teach, coach, and mentor, that I dedicate this work. Use what works; throw out what doesn't; reinvent as needed. However you shape and execute your version of software security, you must continue; our digital world is counting on you.

— Brook S. E. Schoenfield

Contents

Foreword

Software is changing the trajectory at which the world operates. From driverless cars to cryptocurrency, software reimagines possibilities. With software standing at the core of everything we do, we find ourselves pushing out code faster than ever. Current estimates show that there are over 111 billion lines of new code written per year. And our fixation on rapidly developing the latest technology has positioned security to be in the way, coming at a "cost."

It's time to redefine the way we view security and see security as a value, not a cost. When we trust software, new economies are created. For example, today's e-commerce market is possible because of cryptographic protocols and software implementations for Transport Layer Security (TLS) to secure our browsers' connections. As a result, today's online economy is the size of Spain's gross domestic product (GDP). Security is an enabler for innovation. You cannot have innovation without security.

Today, however, we're finding ourselves paying the price for neglecting this foundational element for innovation in favor of speed. Headline-worthy breaches and hacking demonstrations remind us of the debt we've accrued and must pay off. Although some may perceive this as a setback, I see the paradigm shift from software development to secure software development pivotal to the new wave of innovation yet to come. I believe that the implementation of DevSecOps as a formal process within organizations will make a mark on history, multiplying not only the scale but also the speed at which we will be able to push out ingenious solutions.

What do organizations who excel at creating trustworthy software do differently? Consider Google Chrome™. Chrome is open source, meaning everyone has complete access to comb through the code to find new vulnerabilities. Chrome is a highly valued target. A single vulnerability could affect millions of users.

Google's Chrome development team has set up security as a *process*, not an end product. There are four fundamental steps:

1. Design your code with security in mind.
2. Find a bug or vulnerability in your code.
3. Fix the vulnerability, testing to make sure the patch is fit for purpose.
4. Field the fix into operations.

Google builds security into Chrome with their sandbox design. Chrome sandboxes limit the ability for any one component, for example, the movie player, to compromise the rest of Chrome. A secure SDLC goes beyond design and includes security testing. Chrome leverages tens of thousands of CPU cores to continuously probe for new vulnerabilities using fuzzing. If a vulnerability is found, they can field a fix to over 90% of the world within 30 days. All automatically, without a user having to click "upgrade."

In *Building In Security at Agile Speed*, Dr. James Ransome and Brook S. E. Schoenfield have distilled down the best security lifecycle practices into one comprehensive book. They show both "the how," as well as "the why." The two juggernauts combine their industry experience to demystify continuous integration and continuous delivery (CI/CD), DevSecOps, and continuous security so that it no longer remains an art that only the elite few know how to implement. The pair share my vision to democratize this knowledge and give back to the software security community that has given so much to us.

The new possibilities of technology hinge on our ability to execute the principles outlined in *Building In Security at Agile Speed*. With the knowledge we need to set forth, the future of technology is within reach, but it remains up to you—all of us—to courageously grasp for it.

I look to the future with confidence as we collaborate together to secure the world's software.

Dr. David Brumley
CEO and Founder
ForAllSecure, Inc.

About David Brumley:

Dr. David Brumley, CEO of ForAllSecure, is a tenured professor at Carnegie Mellon University with an expertise in software security. With over 20 years of cybersecurity experience in academia and practice, Dr. Brumley is the author of over 50 publications in computer security, receiving multiple best paper awards. He is also a founder and faculty sponsor for the competitive hacking team Plaid Parliament of Pwning (PPP), which is internationally ranked and the most winning DEFCON team ever.

Dr. Brumley's honors include being selected for the 2010 DARPA CSSP program and 2013 DARPA Information Science and Technology Advisory Board, a 2010 NSF CAREER award, a 2010 US Presidential Early Career Award for Scientists and Engineers (PECASE) from President Obama (the highest award in the United States for early career scientists), and a 2013 Sloan Foundation award.

Preface

The age of software-driven machines has taken significant leaps over the last few years. Human tasks such as those of fighter pilots, stock exchange floor traders, surgeons, and industrial production and power plant operators that are critical to the operation of weapons systems, medical systems, and key elements of our national infrastructure, have been, or are, rapidly being taken over by software. This is a revolutionary step in the machine whose brain and nervous system is now controlled by software-driven programs, taking the place of complex, nonrepetitive tasks that formerly required the use of the human mind. This has resulted in a paradigm shift in the way the state, military, criminals, activists, and other adversaries can attempt to destroy, modify, or influence countries, infrastructures, societies, and cultures. This is true even for corporations, as we have seen increasing cases of cyber corporate espionage over the years. The previous use of large armies, expensive and devastating weapons systems and platforms, armed robberies, the physical stealing of information, violent protests, and armed insurrection is quickly being replaced by what is called cyber warfare, crime, and activism.

In the end, the cyber approach may have just as profound effects as the techniques used before in that the potential exploit of software vulnerabilities could result in:

- Entire or partial infrastructures taken down, including power grids, nuclear power plants, communication mediums, and emergency response systems
- Chemical plants modified to create large-yield explosions and/or highly toxic clouds
- Remote control, modification, or disablement of critical weapon systems or platforms
- Disablement or modification of surveillance systems
- Criminal financial exploitation and blackmail
- Manipulating financial markets and investments
- Murder or harm to humans through the modification of medical support systems or devices, surgery schedules, or pharmaceutical prescriptions
- Political insurrection and special interest influence through the modification of voting software, blackmail, or brand degradation though website defacement or underlying Web application takedown or destruction

A side effect of the cyber approach is that it has given us the ability to do all of that listed the above at a scale, distance, and anonymity previously unthought of from jurisdictionally protected locations through remote exploitations and attacks. This gives governments, criminal groups, and activists the ability to proxy prime perpetuators to avoid responsibility, detection, and political fallout.

Although there is much publicity regarding network security, the real Achilles heel is the (insecure) software that provides the potential ability for total control and/or modification of a target, as described above. The criticality of software security as we move quickly towards this new age of tasks previously relegated to the human mind and now being replaced by software-driven machines cannot be underestimated. It is for this reason that we have written this book. In contrast and for the foreseeable future, software programs will be written by humans. This also means new software will keep building on legacy code or software that was written prior to security being taken seriously or before sophisticated attacks become prevalent. As long as humans write the programs, the key to successful security for the same is in making the software development program process more efficient and effective.

We, the authors, James and Brook, have spent days drawing on whiteboards, hours sitting in cafés with strategy documents and diagrams spread over a couple of tables (much to the horror of the barista and waitstaff), coffees in hand, trying to divine the most effective methods to deliver software security. We've wondered why some tactic was as successful as it appeared to have been. We've scratched our collective head trying to understand why a method that looked great on paper failed: Was our execution faulty? Were our assumptions false? Was there some as yet undefined cultural element that we hadn't accounted for? Did we just not explain well enough what we believed could work?

This book is surely an update and rework of *Core Software Security: Security at the Source.* As such, some of that book's material has been reprinted as is, or slightly reworked, sometimes with our updating comments surrounding the quoted material. Since writing that book, each of us has continued to write about, present about, and teach our latest understandings. We wanted to pull those single-subject works from each of us into our holistic views on software security. You will see numerous quotes herein pulled from these intervening publications. Worth mentioning up front are two of Brook's books that were published since 2014: *Securing Systems: Applied Security Architecture and Threat Models,*[†] and *Secrets of a Cyber Security Architect.*[‡]

However, this book also includes a great deal of entirely new material. There have been sea changes in software development, architecture, and operation since 2013–2014, during which we were planning, then drafting *Core Software Security.* Furthermore, and perhaps just as importantly, we learned a lot. Our practices have changed to account for the profound changes that were underway in 2014, but which have manifested, in fact, pretty much taken over since then. Some of our methods have been refined. Some have been shifted to new paradigms. In addition, we have a few new tricks up our collective sleeves that we felt needed to be put into print for others to use, or, at least, react to.

James and Brook have never shied away from conflict, so long as the resulting discussion is constructive and in the service of improvement. In many ways, this book is about our striving for "continuous improvement." Hence, what we say in this book should not be taken as the final word, but rather, as our point-in-time reflection on where we are, where we might (should?) go, and how we could get there.

Although this book focuses on people, processes, and technological approaches to software security, we believe that the people element of software security is still the most important part to manage as long as software is developed, managed, and exploited by humans. What follows is a step-by-step process for software security that is relevant to today's technical, operational, business, and development environments with a focus on what humans can do to control and manage the process in the form of best practices and metrics. We will always have security issues, but this book should help to minimize them when software is finally released or deployed. We hope you enjoy our book as much as we have enjoyed writing it.

---

[*] Ransome, J. and Misra, A. (2014). *Core Software Security: Security at the Source.* Boca Raton (FL): CRC Press/ Taylor & Francis Group.

[†] Schoenfield, B. S. E. (2015). *Securing Systems: Applied Security Architecture and Threat Models.* Boca Raton (FL): CRC Press/Taylor & Francis Group.

[‡] Schoenfield, B. (2019). *Secrets of a Cyber Security Architect.* Boca Raton, (FL): Auerbach Publications/Taylor & Francis Group.

Acknowledgments

Without the confidence of CRC Press/Taylor & Francis Group and our editor, John Wyzalek, this book would have been no more than a gleam in the authors' eyes. John found a way to realize our vision. We thank John for his support and for his commitment to the project.

This book could not have been delivered without the guidance and patience of DerryField Publishing Services as we put together this manuscript. Please accept our heartfelt gratitude.

Copyediting, typesetting, and page proofing are key to delivery of any book. Marje Pollack has once again navigated the authors' idiosyncrasies. This book was particularly difficult to typeset due to the interlacing of pieces of other works with new text. We hope that Marje's concepts will create an intuitive flow for its readers. Susan Culligan provided much-needed reviews and critiques.

Theron R. Shreve (Director, DerryField Publishing Services) has once again provided invaluable assistance. We might very well still be struggling through some of the finer points for references if not for his input. Once again, Theron, we've danced the book publishing dance to completion. Thanks for working with us.

— James Ransome and Brook S. E. Schoenfield

I would like to thank all my former employees, co-workers, team members, and business partners who have helped me manage application and product security and keep software secure since 1997. A special thanks to Dr. David Brumley for writing the Foreword for this book on a subject and message for which we both share a passion and want to get out to both practitioners and decision makers alike. And last, but not least, a thanks to my co-author, Brook S. E. Schoenfield, who has joined me on this journey to prove there is another, faster, and efficient way to architect, implement, and manage software security than what is the current status quo. As Will Roper, the Assistant Secretary for Acquisition in the U.S. Air Force so aptly said: "We can build the best airplanes and satellites, but we will lose if we can't update the software at the speed of relevance in this century."[*]

— James Ransome

A book like this cannot, if it is to reflect real-world practice, spring forth from the imaginations of the authors. This work is firmly grounded in each author's extensive experience—in security, in software security, in experience gained from developing and maintaining software, and, most importantly, in

---

[*] Christopherson. A. (2019). "Faster, Smarter: Speed Is Key in Acquisition Reform." Retrieved from https://www.wpafb.af.mil/News/Article-Display/Article/1771763/faster-smarter-speed-is-key-in-acquisition-reform/

experiences derived from working collectively with sometimes thousands of others. That "collective" must be recognized.

The conclusions expressed herein are firmly based upon the experiences and practices of the developers, managers, project managers, Scrum Masters, directors, executives, product managers, product owners, teachers, facilitators, and, of course, security practitioners, who ultimately make up any effective software security program. Software security cannot be imposed. It can only be earned through the inspired and driven efforts of many people from varied roles and specialties working together toward common goals. Failure to acknowledge the universe of contributions would erase enormous amounts of hard work. But it would also paint a false view of reality. A great many of our colleagues have contributed to what you will find here. We will remain eternally grateful for your collaboration. Unfortunately, the list of names could easily fill the pages of the book.

Of particular note are the several hundred security architects with whom we worked at McAfee, Inc. (which became Intel Security, which became McAfee, LLC), who gave their best efforts to execute our Security Development Lifecycle (SDL). These "security champions" delivered, but they also critiqued and helped to refine that SDL, which then was foundational to this SDL.

Mentioned in this book, but worth acknowledging here, are Robert Hale and Catherine Blackadar Nelson. We might have struggled to plumb the software development assumptions that have lain buried beneath extant SDLs if we had not participated in that SDL research at Intel, Inc., in 2015–2016. I did the technical work, yes. But James and the then Vice President of Quality at Intel Security, Noopur Davis, and I thoroughly and regularly analyzed the results from that project as the work proceeded. Much of the foundation of a truly generic SDL springs directly from that effort.

In the years since leaving McAfee, LLC, both of the authors have had opportunities to prove that the work we generated together wasn't a fluke of circumstance. Every software security program that I've been a part of continues to provide validation as well as refinement. My recent teams' contributions also receive our hearty thanks.

No book can be complete without a dash of project management. James is far better at this task than I. Without his keeping us both on task, the book might not have come together quite as quickly and easily as it has. This book represents yet another journey through the trials and tribulations of software security that we've taken together.

Dr. James Ransome has long since earned my enduring appreciation of his skills, insight, determination, and perseverance. I'm incredibly lucky to call James "co-author," and luckier still, "friend."

Importantly, no book can be completed without the support of family. I once again must thank my spouse, Cynthia, for enduring yet one more book on security.

— Brook S. E. Schoenfield

About the Authors

Dr. James Ransome is the Chief Scientist for CyberPhos, an early-stage cybersecurity startup, and continues to do *ad hoc* consulting. He also serves on the Board of Directors for the Bay Area CSO Council. Most recently, Dr. Ransome was the Senior Director, Security Development Lifecycle (SDL) Engineering, in the Intel Product Security and Assurance, Governance and Operations (IPAS GO) Group, where he led and developed a team of SDL engineers, architects, and product security experts that implemented and drove security practices across all of Intel. Prior to that, he was the Senior Director of Product Security and PSIRT at Intel Security and McAfee, LLC. Over a six-year period, he built, managed, and enhanced a developer-centric, self-sustaining, and scalable software security program, with an extended team of 120 software security architects embedded in each product team. All of this was a result of implementing and enhancing the model described in his most recent book, *Core Software Security: Security at the Source*, which has become a standard reference for many corporate security leaders who are responsible for developing their own SDLs. His career is marked by leadership positions in the private and public industries, having served in Chief Information Security Officer (CISO) roles at Applied Materials, Autodesk, and Qwest Communications, and four chief security officer (CSO) roles at Pilot Network Services, Exodus Communications, Exodus Communications—A Cable and Wireless Company, and the Cisco Collaborative Software Group.

Prior to entering the corporate world in 1997, Dr. Ransome retired from 23 years of government service, having served in various roles supporting the U.S. intelligence community, federal law enforcement, and the Department of Defense. Key positions held include Weapons Platoon Sergeant (U.S. Marine Corps), U.S. Federal Special Agent—Foreign Counter-Intelligence (NCIS), Retired Commander and Intelligence Officer, U.S. Navy, Retired Scientist-Geospatial Intelligence Analyst for WMD and DOE Nuclear Emergency Search Team (NEST) Key Leader, and Threat Assessment Analyst at Lawrence Livermore National Laboratory.

Dr. Ransome holds a PhD (https://nsuworks.nova.edu/gscis_etd/790/) in Information Systems, specializing in Information Security; a Master of Science Degree in Information Systems; and graduate certificates in International Business and International Affairs. He developed and tested a security model, architecture, and leading practices for converged wired and wireless network security for his doctoral dissertation. This work became the baseline for the Getronics Wireless Integrated Security, Design, Operations, and Management Solution, of which Dr. Ransome was a co-architect This resulted in an increase of over 45 million USD revenue for Getronics and Cisco within a two-year period.

Building in Security at Agile Speed is Dr. Ransome's 14th book and the 12th on cybersecurity. His last book, *Core Software Security: Security at the Source*, became a standard reference for many corporate security leaders who are responsible for developing their own Security Development Lifecycles and Product Security Programs.

Dr. Ransome was an Adjunct Professor for Nova Southeastern University's Graduate School of Computer and Information Sciences Information Security Program, designated a National Center of Academic Excellence in Information Assurance Education by the U.S. National Security Agency and U.S. Department of Homeland Security, where he taught Applied Cryptography, Advanced Network Security, and Information Security Management. He received the 2005 Nova Southeastern University Distinguished Alumni Achievement Award. Dr. Ransome is a member of Upsilon Pi Epsilon, the International Honor Society for the Computing and Information Disciplines. He is also a Certified Information Security Manager (CISM), a Certified Information Systems Security Professional (CISSP), and a Ponemon Institute Distinguished Fellow.

— James Ransome, PhD, CISSP, CISM

Brook S. E. Schoenfield is the author of *Secrets of a Cyber Security Architect, Securing Systems: Applied Security Architecture and Threat Models,* and Chapter 9: Applying the SDL Framework to the Real World in *Core Software Security: Security at the Source.* He has been published by CRC Press, Auerbach, SANS Institute, Cisco, SAFECode, and the IEEE. Occasionally, he even posts to his security architecture blog, brookschoenfield.com.

Brook helps organizations achieve their software security goals, with a particular focus on secure design. He provides his clients with technical leadership and support and mentorship to client leaders. He has held security architecture leadership positions at high-tech enterprises for 20 years. Previous to security, he held leadership positions for about 10 of his 20-year software development career. He has helped hundreds of people in their journey to becoming security architects. Several thousand people have taken his participatory threat modeling classes.

Brook has presented and taught at conferences such as RSA, BSIMM, OWASP, AppSec, and SANS What Works Summits and guest lectured at universities on subjects within security architecture, including threat models, DevOps security, information security risk, and other aspects of secure design and software security.

Brook lives in the Rocky Mountains of Montana, USA. When he's not thinking about, practicing, writing about, and speaking on secure design and software security, he can be found telemark skiing, hiking, and fly fishing in his beloved mountains, exploring new cooking techniques, or playing various styles of guitar—from jazz to percussive fingerstyle.

Brook is an inveterate and unrepentant Dodgers* fan.

— Brook S. E. Schoenfield, MBA

---

* And baseball, in general.

Chapter 1

Setting the Stage

1.1 Introduction

What we didn't realize while we were drafting *Core Software Security: Security at the Source** was that we were on the cusp of a confluence of a host of software development shifts. At the time, what we dealt with seemed, perhaps, to be disparate threads. But these were, in fact, highly interdependent and interacting strands that would transform software development. It is in the face of this that we've decided to write another software security book.

We understand that there exist a multitude of software security books. In fact, there are many very good ones. Including our own more recent publications, there are books devoted to each and every aspect of secure development—from designing secure software through the testing of it. There are books about the management of software security programs, to be sure. But none of these bring these pieces together into that necessary synthesis that deals with software practices of today and, at the same time, represents a dynamic union of technical, cultural, organizational, and managerial skills.

Trust us, software security requires all of its aspects to be individually successful; however, the aspects aren't independent, but rather are highly interdependent and interactive. Software security is a collection of intersecting, mutually supportive activities, while it also requires cultural change, process, and organizational muscle to succeed in today's heterogeneous environments.

Besides, we've learned a lot in the intervening years about how to build continuous software security programs based upon and natively integrating with Agile methods. This includes the way that these programs are managed, as well as how to build a security development lifecycle (SDL) that doesn't interfere with how people are actually creating and then fielding software. Our aim is for security to be foundational to software creation, as well as for security practices (the SDL) to be a part of the warp and weft of software development.

As Brook's Developer-centric Security Manifesto states:

- Enable development teams to be creative and to innovate
- Ensure that developers have as much specificity as required to "deliver security correctly"

---

* Ransome, J. and Misra, A. (2014). *Core Software Security: Security at the Source*. Boca Raton (FL): CRC Press/Taylor & Francis Group.

1

- Build tools for developers to check for correctness
- Deeply participate such that security earns its "rightful place"
- "Prove the value" of security processes and tools*

The authors are hardly alone among security practitioners focused on working with and empowering development versus imposing security on top of it. At the time of this writing, in talking with our peers, we believe that we still belong to a minority. Enabling development to take charge of security through the support and specialized knowledge of security folks unfortunately remains an emergent practice, rather than the norm.

Many of the tectonic shifts that we've seen in the years since writing *Core Software Security* were already underway. However, none of these shifts had profoundly changed the way that much of software was built. Although some development teams might adopt Agile software practices in order to improve their process, few large organizations were in the process of adopting Agile as an organization-wide standard. It is true that smaller organizations, especially startups, might be fully Agile; however, much of this was seen in the software development world as "boutique."

Continuous integration and continuous delivery (CI/CD) and DevOps were approaches that some cloud native teams were discovering while other teams, focused on other types of targets, were looking on in amazement and wonder at the boost in productivity these enabled. But it wasn't obvious then how these technologies and approaches might be applied in other contexts and toward other software targets.

As Agile became more and more prevalent, or was just in the process of organization-wide adoption, software security practitioners began to take notice. Indeed, during the drafting of *Core Software Security*, two of the authors were engaged in an organizational shift to Agile Scrum. It should be no surprise that Agile and iterative development, in general, deserved some focus in the book. In hindsight, we now believe that the software security program that James and Brook were leading at the time produced one of the industry's first fully Agile SDLs.

Still, much of the software security industry continued building SDLs aligned with Waterfall development methods. The prevalent published SDLs at the time were all linear, conceived in phases, assuming first idea, then requirements, then coding, and followed by testing and other verification, which, if passed, signaled willingness to release. These "phases" follow each other in an orderly fashion, the next not starting until the first has been completed fully. (As we shall see, this tendency towards linearity that does not match how software is actually built continues to plague software security practice.) But that's not how software is built today.

All of the software development practices that we now think of as "normal" and "typical" were emerging when *Core Software Security* was published. At that time, many of these were considered by large organizations as "only for special circumstances or small efforts." Today, we only find Waterfall development confined to particular contexts to which it is well suited: where coding and compilation are expensive and where design misses can be catastrophic (e.g., firmware). Some form of Agile, whether Scrum or another iterative method, has become widespread in organizations large and small, new and old. CI/CD and DevOps methods are also in wide use, even in organizations or contexts that have little to do with cloud development (where these approaches got started). DevOps is a worldwide movement.

Public cloud use is normal for at least some types of applications and data. Although some organizations do maintain private clouds for particular needs, such as compliance or control, those same organizations also use public clouds. Public cloud use is not at all unusual any longer, but rather expected. Long since, most security practitioners have stopped worrying about whether "data are safe in the cloud," and, rather, focus on what data are in the cloud and how will they be secured. That's

---

* First published at http://brookschoenfield.com/?page_id=256; republished in Schoenfield, B. (2019). *Secrets of a Cyber Security Architect.* Boca Raton (FL): Auerbach Publications/Taylor & Francis Group, p. 177.

because just about everybody's data are in a cloud, probably many clouds. It's no longer a matter of "if" or "whether" but rather "where" and "how to secure."

Software development has been seeking its new "normal" for some time. We believe that security must meet and enable that "normal" if we are to stop the seemingly never-ending release of software issues that plague our digital lives. Each of the authors has field-tested the advice and techniques laid out here—both together and individually. We have seen fairly significant improvements unfold through our efforts. Still, taken as a whole, the software industry continues to stumble through issue after issue, allowing compromise after compromise. We know that we can do better. The transformation won't be easy; it will take concerted effort, focused on that which developers can and will do, coupled with significant organizational support, including security and a somewhat shifted security mindset.

1.2 Current Events

Over the last 10 years or so,[*] there has been a profound and revolutionary shift in the way that software is produced, employed, and maintained: This paradigm shift has come to be known as "DevOps"— that is, "development plus (and through) operations" united into as seamless and holistic a practice as can be fostered by those involved.

At the same time, a platform for running code and storing data has matured—that is, "the cloud": public, private, and hybrid. Code still runs on a person's device, be that a phone, a tablet, a laptop, or desktop computer (all of which are still sold and used). But, increasingly, many of the functions that used to stand alone on a device are in some way, and typically, many ways, tied to services and functionality that runs within a cloud, quite often, a public, commercial cloud offering. There are many compelling reasons to structure (architect) functionality in this way, among them:

- On-demand server workloads (expansion and contraction of compute resources based upon need)
- Ease of operating, maintaining, and updating cloud software
- Maturity of cloud services (allowing operators to delegate some portion of maintenance duties to the cloud provider, including maintenance for security)
- Availability and stability
- Global distribution
- Continuity requirements
- High resource computation needs (e.g., artificial intelligence and machine learning)
- Larger data sets and their manipulation
- Minimizing compute resources needed from devices (often using battery power)

There are computer tasks that are handled much better in a cloud than on a constrained device. The nearly "always connected" state of most devices fosters an architecture that can take advantage of the characteristics of each environment while, at the same time, enabling sufficient inter-environment communications to make cloud service integration seem nearly seamless.

In short, the paradigms for producing and operating software, as well as the way that functionality is architected, have been through fairly profound sea changes such that if security is going to be built and then run effectively, security techniques, tools, and operations must match, and, in fact, integrate easily, fully, and relatively painlessly with the ways that software is currently built and run (and on into the foreseeable future, if current trends continue).

---

[*] Patrick Debois is credited with coining the term "DevOps" in 2009 for a conference, DevOpsDays. Kim, G., Humble, J., Debois, P., and Willis, J. (2016). *The DevOps Handbook*. Portland (OR): IT Revolution Press, p. xiii.

DevOps involves a continuation of the Agile Manifesto*: Developers must have control over their work via high trust working environments, coupled to high velocity, rapid delivery tools and methods.

[DevOps is creating]: "safe systems of work and enabling small teams to quickly and independently develop and validate code that can be safely deployed to customers."[†]

DevOps includes a mental and cultural shift toward removing artificial barriers between the various technical specializations:

- Creators
- Designers
- Programmers
- Validators
- Operators
- Monitors

In the past, it was not atypical for creators to toss concepts over to designers who generate plans and specifications that programmers implement and then toss to the "quality people" (validators). Once the software passes its tests, operators are supposed to release the software onto whatever infrastructure may be required (if any), while someone, somewhere, watches feedback data to ensure that the software is running as specified (monitors).

DevOps throws a spanner into the works with the attitude that everyone involved, whatever their specialty skills, has essentially the same goal: good software that provides value to its owners and users. There are dependencies. An idea isn't implementable unless it can fit into existing structures (architecture) and can actually be implemented into working code. Since errors are a very consistent product of building software, implementers and designers provide a significant contribution to the testing of the software. At the same time, testers will have expertise in the most effective validation techniques. Implementers need feedback from operators and monitors so that the software will run effectively, while at the same time, returning clear information about inconsistencies and unintentional behaviors (i.e., "bugs") so that these can be removed. Going forward, each discipline has input to all the others and must incorporate the dependencies from other knowledge domains. Ergo, rid development of "artificial knowledge domain walls."

At the same time, the ability to write code implementing complex deployment and runtime environments has exploded. "Operators" are, increasingly, "coders," not system administrators. The days of specialty administrators grinding through long series of commands to build environments or bring hosts online is long gone. The vast majority of those actions can be coded such that deterministic logical conditions trigger software runs. These runs are often highly elastic, in that as load increases, the virtual runtime environments expand to meet demand, or release resources when no longer needed—that is, the software runs on and utilizes cloud capabilities. This is all coded; no human interaction is required after operations code is considered stable and working.

One set of coders may program architecture documents, whereas another generates functional logic, and another, deploy and run code. "Programmer" no longer solely refers to someone generating functional code; nearly every role may require coding, though the languages and work products differ.

Although DevOps and Agile principles are certainly not adhered to religiously everywhere, even fairly command and control organizations have adopted some of the techniques associated with Agile:

- Small, independently operating development teams.
- Discreet, easily understandable and sizeable tasks.

---

* The Agile Manifesto can be retrieved from https://agilemanifesto.org/principles.html
† Kim, G., Humble, J., Debois, P., and Willis, J. (2016). *The DevOps Handbook*. p. xvi.

- Regular, usually daily, team meetings.
- A queue of work items and some process for choosing what to work on next.
- Relatively short delivery schedules, often a few weeks.
- Distinct and discrete deliverable chunks or items ("Minimum Releasable Increment" or "Minimum Viable Product").
- Teams retain some development process control, at minimum control over who works on what and how algorithms are chosen.
- At the end of a cycle of development, the team reviews the last cycle for challenges and potential improvements to the work and processes. The team then chooses one or a few of the identified improvements to attempt in the next cycle of development.

Our list should not be taken as a definitive expression of an Agile software development process. Please note that we observe these process approaches widely adopted in many organizations. The list above should be viewed as having descended from Agile practices.

Many development organizations are shortening their delivery schedules and making use of DevOps or DevOps-like pipelines to build, release, and run software. Again, we have observed this trend even influencing relatively older software development organizations building legacy applications.

It bears repeating: Software development has and continues to experience a significant paradigm shift.

1.3 The State of Software Security

At the same time, software security industry practices have made relatively incremental improvements. For instance, if one were to survey the published SDLs, there is a strong tendency to represent secure development in a linear fashion—security activities preceding from planning and design through testing and release in an orderly fashion. Even Agile SDL presentations try to flatten out the iteration in an effort to order (and make understandable) what might seem as a relatively chaotic process when viewed from the outside (although there is nothing inherently chaotic about Agile development).

But these attempts to provide order through linearity are, in the authors' opinion, a mistake.

First and foremost, since developers often work on tasks with a lot of parallelism and a lot of feedback between different mini efforts, a linear representation doesn't map to what's actually going on during development. In fact, our experiences suggest that where there is a large discrepancy between the expression of SDL timing and the process by which software is actually developed, developers either outright ignore or give short shrift to the security requirements and tasks because these appear to developers as nonsensical, unimplementable, or worse, completely irrelevant to their development practices.

Second, extant SDLs typically remain coupled to an underlying software development life cycle (SDLC) to which the security activities and their timing are tied. In any environment where more than a single SDLC is employed, some set of developers will feel left out, or worse, alienated, once again leading to a sense of SDL irrelevancy.

The integration lessons expressed in this book have been hard won over many years of building, and then maintaining software security programs. We, the authors, have each built programs independently, as well as two software security programs at two very different organizations together. Our errors, and our ultimate successes, are founded upon the thousands of dedicated developers who've been honest and vulnerable enough to share what works, what doesn't, and their willingness to reach with us for better solutions that both deliver measurable security and are achievable across a gamut of software development practices and styles. Yes, we've made a lot of mistakes. And, equally so, this work is the direct result of identifying solutions not *for* but *with* our engineering partners. We've listened; this work is the result.

We will return to the question of generic SDL below.

Although software development has been undergoing a sea change over the last 10 years, we don't mean to imply that the security industry, and especially security tools, have been standing still. However, the changes in tooling have largely been incremental rather than revolutionary.* The changes in approach and tooling associated with DevOps have been revolutionary: Software is simply not produced, deployed, and then maintained in the same way that it had been in the not very distant past.

Vulnerability analysis of various kinds (Chapter 3 will detail various approaches and technologies) has certainly been improving its reliability, offering developers different analysis options—from analysis as a part of the code-writing process through lengthy, full-build analysis. Vendors have been experimenting with combinations of source code analysis (static) and dynamic analysis† of a running program to improve analysis fidelity. Still, none of these improvements precisely matches continuous delivery and partition/elastic, code-driven load paradigms, as are typically seen in cloud forms of DevOps.

The second problem that needs to be addressed is the continuing SDL to SDLC coupling that we repeatedly find in the published SDLs. Even the SDL that we proposed in *Core Software Security* (Chapter 9 is devoted to it) suffers from implied linearity as well as attempting to cover just Waterfall and Agile SDLCs.

It may be worth noting that we were in the midst of an Agile transformation at our day job while we were drafting *Core Software Security*. We were most certainly thinking hard about security in an Agile context. It is possible that McAfee's Agile SDL was among the first truly Agile SDLs. Perhaps the first?

Still, it was hard for us to divorce ourselves from accounting for the SDLC that lay before us at work: pure Waterfall and every shade of Agile implementation imaginable. But there are more SDLCs than Waterfall and Agile. In addition, looking at Figure 1.1 (reprinted from *Core Software Security*), you will see some progression from design through validation implied, even though we were trying with the circles not to imply a strong linear progression.

But as we shall see in the Agile and, especially, DevOps, activities listed in Figure 1.1 can be happening in parallel with the others; these SDLC methods value the benefits resulting from extreme parallelism. There is simply no benefit derived from forcing all design and planning to occur before a line of code can be generated. Likewise, there isn't an overarching value to waiting until most of the code has been written before performing validations. All can be executing simultaneously, in small increments, and providing feedback to improve each iteration based upon learning gathered from each incremental task.

This is not to suggest that one need plan *nothing* before starting to code. That is an oft-quoted myth: "Planning (or design) is dead. Just code." It remains true that a lack of planning leads to poor architectures that become brittle and fragile, that is, cannot be changed without profound impacts, some of which invariably include security weaknesses.

However, equally untrue is the also oft-implemented security preference (sometimes codified into inflexible policies) that require all *security* planning to be done early, preferably before much coding has occurred. Usually, wherever unchangeable security requirements are delivered all at once, especially in an Agile (iterative development) context, the security requirements will not keep pace with other shifts during development. This nearly always results in requirements left "on the shop floor," unimplemented because the stated requirement no longer matched the realities of what was being built and could no longer be implemented as specified. As we shall see in some detail, security requirements are no different from any other specification: all early specifications benefit from refinement, pivots, and learning that are the result of an iterative approach. Security has no special attribute making it somehow

---

*   Of course, security tool vendors are free to disagree with us: tool evolution vs. revolution. Our intention is not to dismiss the efforts of security tool creators, but rather to direct the reader to a set of problems that we believe need to be addressed, as expressed in this, the first chapter of our book.

†   We return to the various types of security analysis in subsequent chapters.

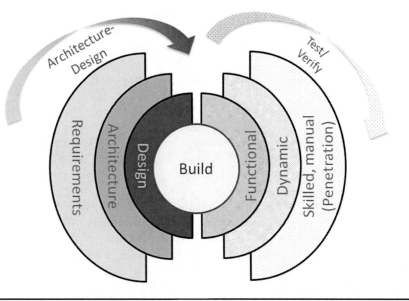

Figure 1.1 Consensus SDL. (*Source:* Reproduced from Schoenfield, B. [2014]. "Applying the SDL Framework to the Real World." In Ransome, J. and Misra, A. *Core Software Security: Security at the Source.* Boca Raton [FL]: CRC Press/Taylor & Francis Group, Ch. 9, Figure 9.1, p. 258, with permission.)

different from other design domains: security can be just as flexible and adaptive as, for instance, usability or performance.

In short, although the world of developers has become ever more iterative, parallel, and continuous, security's processes (SDL, if you will) have remained at least somewhat bound by Waterfall, one-task-at-a-time thinking. Partly, this is a function of trying to express a highly cross-dependent and overlapping set of tasks (SDL consensus) in some understandable manner. Abstractions tend toward the linear for ease of comprehension.

The Microsoft "Simplified" Security Development Lifecycle (SDL):

- Provide Training
- Define Security Requirements
- Define Metrics and Compliance Reporting
- Perform Threat Modeling
- Establish Design Requirements
- Define and Use Cryptography Standards
- Manage the Security Risk of Using Third-Party Components
- Use Approved Tools
- Perform Static Analysis Security Testing (SAST)
- Perform Dynamic Analysis Security Testing (DAST)
- Perform Penetration Testing
- Establish a Standard Incident Response Process[*]

While we were creating the first draft of this book (2020), Microsoft revised their SDL once again (activity names are quoted above).

---

[*] © Microsoft 2020. Retrieved from https://www.microsoft.com/en-us/securityengineering/sdl/practices#practice7

Previous versions (which we were going to quote as examples) retained an implied linearity to SDL activities. The first encounter for the reader with Microsoft's SDL activities on the Microsoft SDL site indicates no overt ordering with respect to SDLC timing or flows. Like our generic SDL, activities are grouped around essential SDLC general tasks, just as DevOps acknowledges that "Planning," that is, what we term "Design," requires some different mental approaches from coding, although the two, as we've noted several times, are intimately related.

Despite the implied grouping (nothing is explained in these terms on the Microsoft site) into design/plan, code generation, and verification activities, no time-bound ordering is implied or explicit. Microsoft SDL no longer makes any assumption about the ordering of the activities in the SDL's presentation. This is in tune with our generic SDL, more closely following today's software development practices. Each security task must be taken in its proper relationship to development activities; assumptions about ordering only serve to reduce developers' creativity while solving problems, be those security, privacy, or otherwise. The activity explanations have been numbered for convenience: 1–12. Our quote, above, removes the numbering as an irrelevant presentation device.

As presented, the various aspects of secure design activities have been placed together. Likewise, verification tasks are grouped. This is useful but does not imply that design precedes coding and verification. It should be obvious to any engineer that one cannot test without code. Furthermore, unless one knows at least something about what one will build (design), it's far more difficult to code it. But, as we've repeated, these are interacting aspects of holistic software development, not discrete, separate activities that must be fully completed before the next "phase" of software development (strict Waterfall SDLC).

Microsoft was one of the first organizations to attempt to create and then implement software security. In our humble opinion, as an organization, Microsoft continues to lead the industry with cutting-edge software security practices in just about as mature a form as we can find. Once again, Microsoft is, at the same time as we are, removing Waterfall SDLC artifacts from their SDLC.

We have reproduced our version of Adobe®'s Secure Product Lifecycle (SPLC) in Figure 1.2. The Adobe activity names have been placed into a circle similar to the way that Adobe describes their SPLC (equivalent to SDL).* Looking at Adobe's published SPLC, we believe that it might prove instructive to illustrate some of the problems that we deem essential to address if security is to be fully integrated fully into the many different variations of SDLC, including Agile and DevOps processes, and for architectures that span devices, cloud services, and backend cloud (or server) processing.

Although we have been told numerous times that much development at Adobe is Agile, you may note that the SDL is presented as a circle, with one activity flowing into the next, implying, of course, an orderly succession of SDL tasks. Training is first, although this isn't really true: Training is expected to be repeated and constantly available. Once trained, Requirements and Planning begins, which leads to Design. Threat modeling is subsumed into the Design bucket. The explanation, "builds defenses against potential threats directly into the initial design of new products and services"† is Adobe's description of threat modeling. Development and Testing then proceed based upon Requirements, Design, and the threat model that was implied as a part of Design.

The Adobe SPLC circle is meant to indicate that tasks feed each other continuously, that development isn't completed but rather a never-ending loop throughout the life of the product. A circle is a better paradigm than, perhaps, the older, linear ordering. Ordering and timing are necessarily implied by the Adobe model, nonetheless.

Iteration and parallelism have been collapsed out of Adobe's SPLC. There are other conceptual errors baked into the activities. For instance, privacy must be taken up both during requirements and planning and as a fundamental part of design activities, whereas privacy engineering will be addressed

---

* "Adobe® Secure Engineering Overview," p. 2. Retrieved from https://www.adobe.com/content/dam/cc/en /security/pdfs/adobe-secure-engineering-wp.pdf

† Ibid., p. 3.

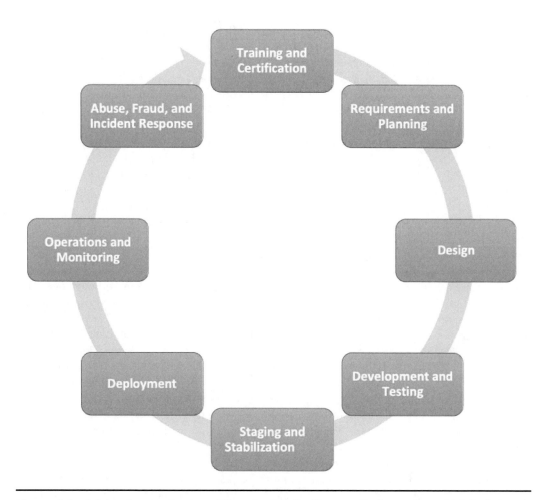

Figure 1.2 Adobe Secure Product Lifecycle (SPLC). (*Source:* Redrawn from "Adobe® Secure Engineering Overview," p. 2. Retrieved from https://www.adobe.com/content/dam/cc/en/security /pdfs/adobe-secure-engineering-wp.pdf)

both in the design and through implementation and validation. Threats to privacy will be a part of the threat model. Privacy requirements and behavioral attributes must be "engineered," that is, implemented and tested, like any other set of features. But privacy is only mentioned as a training item and in requirements in Adobe's "Secure Engineering Overview."

Likewise, although a threat model is an implied deliverable in design (and threat landscape is mentioned in the Requirements explanation), the analysis technique actually underpins much software security practice, and relevant to the SDL, threat modeling underpins all of secure design (as we shall see in Chapter 4). We cannot design security without imagining what attacks will most likely be promulgated against the software and then specifying those defenses that are believed to be necessary to prevent compromise. In essence, that's threat modeling, whatever SDL "task" one chooses to name it.

It has become apparent to the authors that threat modeling is an essential technique that must be applied repeatedly starting at idea conception, and then will underlie many design and specification decisions throughout development, including which validations may be necessary to either prove or correct the threat model. We will dive into threat modeling and secure design in subsequent chapters. Suffice it to note here that threat modeling mustn't take place at some particular "perfect moment."

Rather, it is an analysis technique that gets applied repeatedly as security needs are refined as structures (architecture), designs, implementation, and testing unfold.

We encourage the reader to analyze other published SDLs for their assumptions, their implications with respect to DevOps, and their continuous, Agile development practices. Those who understake a little light research will find any number of linear statements that appear to assume or couple to Waterfall development. Some organizations have moved beyond Waterfall to circles, and similar representations. We offer a model free of most, if not all, of these implications.

Of course, one could start with Microsoft's SDL. They continue to be among the leaders in software security, as is Adobe, which is why we chose to reproduce the high-level activities of each of them. However, the Microsoft SDL is tied to Microsoft's products (as it must be) and Adobe's to their product portfolio. Thus, either SDL (and any other company's published set) may not be as appropriate as an SDL designed, from the bottom up, to be generic. As you work through this book, you will find that our generic SDL activities match, perhaps not in precise name but certainly in intention, the vast majority of published SDLs. That is because the generic SDL found here is based upon a consensus SDL drawn from wide-ranging research across published SDLs and experienced and published development practices.

James and Brook (the authors) spent hours at a whiteboard early in 2014 mapping not just SDL tasks, but also how they relate to each other, their dependencies and preconditions. Although some SDL tasks are relatively independent, many rely on outputs from other tasks in order to begin or to complete properly. Capturing those relations is key to understanding how an SDL must flow.

Figure 1.3 was our early attempt at capturing the dependencies between SDL tasks. The diagram is heavily weighted to Waterfall SDLC and, thus, must not be regarded as representing our generic SDL. However, the diagram fairly accurately describes which SDL activities must receive the output of other activities. You may notice that the dependencies are not trivial and are also not particularly straightforward.[*] A few attempts at following arrows from tasks on the left through to tasks on the right should be enough to highlight the problems that originate from a failure to understand the relationships between SDL tasks. Most SDL tasks are not independent and discrete, although often, SDL tasks are conceptualized in this way.

For about 18 months (starting sometime in 2015), Bob Hale, Principal Engineer at Intel[†] (now retired); Catherine Blackadar Nelson, Senior Security Researcher at Intel (now at Google); and Brook (then a Principal Engineer at Intel Security) undertook a study of most of the published SDLs to look for commonalities and to identify differences. The team also had access to a prepublication draft of ISO's 27034 Application Security standard.[‡]

Unfortunately, the products of that study group belong to Intel and have never been published. We cannot provide the resulting SDL here. That Intel project produced what may have quite possibly been the world's first truly generic SDL based on a consensus analysis of a survey of extant SDLs. That SDL ensured that it did not favor any particular method of development and could readily be applied across various SDLCs. Once the team believed that they had an SDL, several development teams piloted the SDL and helped to refine it. The software in the pilot included differing runtime stacks and involved varying architectures, from firmware through operating systems, and included applications and cloud infrastructure code.

---

[*] Our diagram does not attempt to capture relationships at all, only dependencies. The question we were answering is, "Are there SDLC or SDL activity(ies)' outputs without which an SDL task cannot begin?" It must be noted that besides dependencies, the execution of some SDL activities affects others, as well as strict dependency upon outputs.

[†] Intel's Principal Engineer may be thought of as essentially equivalent to other organization's Distinguished Engineer. Promotion requires that the candidate meet technical, leadership, and strategic criteria, which are evaluated by a board of peers: other Principal Engineers. The title is not an honorific, but rather, a demonstration of technical excellence and depth, strategic delivery, and organizational leadership, as well as requiring continued leadership in each of these arenas.

[‡] Intel was a contributor and sponsor of the standard.

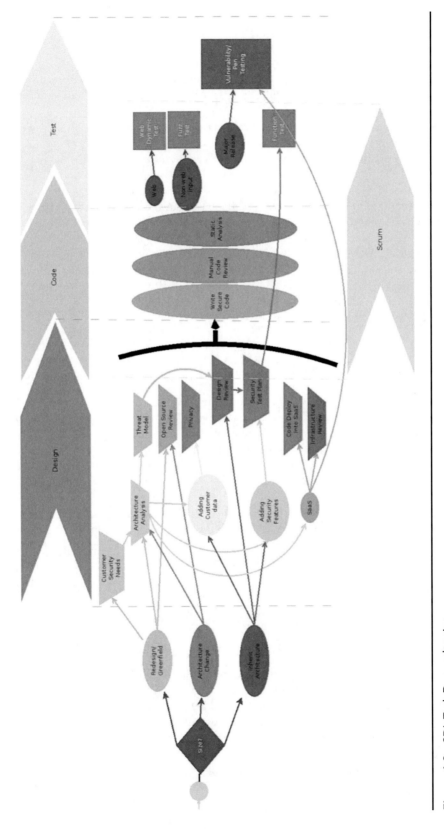

Figure 1.3 SDL Task Dependencies.

Although the resulting SDL cannot be reproduced, that work greatly influences what you will find in this book. Based upon what we learned building a truly generic SDL, such an SDL must:

- Be free from timing expectations based upon an assumed SDLC
- Express industry consensus on a comprehensive set of state-of-the-art software security practices
- State the necessary preconditions before any particular SDL task may be started, including any dependencies on other SDL task outputs
- Describe those conditions that must be met to consider the task complete
- Explain the output(s), if any, of each task
- Describe any conditions that may trigger a refinement or review of the task's outputs

When each task's preconditions, task dependencies, completion requirements, outputs, and triggers are fully described, the SDL is then freed from assumptions about and bindings to any particular SDLC.

What became obvious to us as we surveyed each SDL is that there exists a firm industry consensus on what high-level activities constitute a robust and complete SDL. Chapter 3 will dive into the details of the consensus SDL. At this point, it's important to note that although each SDL may name activities differently, and they most certainly do, the actual tasks are in fact the same, usually differing only in name, or how a particular security task is divided or set of tasks is combined. Based upon our 18 months of study, there is considerable industry consensus on how to best deliver software that exhibits security behaviors. (We explain "security behaviors" below.)

1.4 What Is Secure Software?

Given that there exists a consensus (even if not entirely formalized) on what constitutes a reasonable set of security activities—a consensus SDL—what is it that the SDL is trying to achieve? Unfortunately, ask 10 people what they believe constitutes "secure software" and you're likely to receive some apparently divergent answers, maybe even 10 different ones.

In *Secrets of a Cyber Security Architect*, Brook wrote the following in an attempt to define a set of criteria for describing "secure software":

What are the behaviors that secure systems must exhibit? How is a "secure system" defined? Over the years that I've been practicing, as I open a discussion about security with development teams, I've noticed that quite often (not every time, but regularly), team members will immediately jump to one of four aspects of software security:

- Protection of data (most often via encryption techniques)
- Implementations errors (most often, coding securely)
- Authentication and/or authorization of users of the system
- Network-level protection mechanisms

This set of responses has been remarkably stable for the last nearly 20 years, which is interesting to ponder all by itself. Despite the dramatic shift in attacker capabilities and techniques over the last 20 years—a huge shift in attacker objectives—developers seem to be thinking about one of the above aspects of the security picture. I don't know why development has not kept pace with the expansion of adversarial thinking, but apparently it hasn't (though, of course, my evidence here is completely anecdotal and not at all scientifically validated).

Lately in my threat modeling classes (and sometimes other presentations), I've been polling my audiences about what jumps first to mind when I say, "software security." Not surprisingly, members of my audiences typically find themselves considering one of the above categories unless a participant has broader security exposure. My informal polls underline a need to establish a baseline definition of just what software security must include, the field's breadth, its scope.

To address the challenge that development teams often lack a sufficiently complete picture of what software security entails, as well as to provide a set of secure design goals, I came up with the following secure software principles. "Secure" software must:

- Be free from implementation errors that can be maliciously manipulated: ergo, vulnerabilities
- Have the security features that stakeholders require for intended use cases
- Be self-protective; resist the types of attacks that will likely be attempted against the software
- In the event of a failure, must "fail well"—that is, fail in such a manner as to minimize consequences of successful attack
- Install with sensible, "closed" defaults

The foregoing are the attributes that "secure software" displays, to one extent or another, as it runs. These principles are aspirational, in that no running system will exhibit these behaviors perfectly; these cannot be implemented to perfection. Indeed, so far as exploitable conditions are concerned, whether from implementation, from a failure to identify the correct security requirements, or a failure to design what will be [implemented] correctly, software, at its current state of the art, will contain errors—bugs, if you will. Some of those errors are likely to have unintended security consequences—that is, vulnerabilities allowing adversaries leverage or access of one kind or another. This truism is simply a fact of building software, like it or not.

Then there is the matter of security context and desired security defensive state: a system or organization's security posture. Not every system is expected to resist every attack, every adversary, every level of adversary sophistication and level of effort that can be expended (given the universe of various threat agents).

Hence, presence and robustness of the above secure software behaviors must vary, system to system, implementation to implementation.

Still, I expect software to account for the above behaviors, even if by consciously accepting the risks generated by a considered absence or weakness of one or more of the principles given above. My software principles are meant to drive secure design decisions, to be goals to reach for. None of these principles is built as stated. These principles don't tell you how to protect a credential that must be held by a system. Rather, from these principles, design choices can be evaluated. These are guideposts, not design standards. (*Secrets*, pp. 29–30)

As Brook described in the quotation above, "secure" software (a meaningless statement by itself) exhibits a fairly distinct set of behaviors. The degree to which the software must or should behave in these "secure" manners is a matter of risk analysis and decision making: No software (nor any other human creation) is fully "self-protective."

Brook has noted from many a conference stage and in *Secrets of a Cyber Security Architect* that "whatever can be engineered by humans can be reverse engineered by humans." Given enough access and resources, pretty much any defense can be surmounted. In cryptography, strength is measured in the number of years of computation that are required to break it. That is, it is assumed that encryption can be broken; it's just a matter of time and resources. If the amount of time is beyond a human's typical working life span, the encryption is considered sufficient for a particular set of purposes.*

---

* Obviously, different encryption algorithms and key sizes have varying strengths. One must match the encryption's strength to needs. Usually, this is done via a risk analysis.

The amount of protection provided to an entity's (a system, a distinct piece of software, an organization) collection of security defenses is very much like cryptography: Effectiveness can only be measured in attacker cost; there is no bullet-proof defense. Furthermore, much of those defenses will be implemented through software, which we have already noted must be considered flawed (i.e., "has bugs"). We might restate our guiding assumption as, "Any defense created by humans can be circumvented by humans." There is no perfectly safe security. Besides, "safe" is a subjective quality.

And so it is with each of secure software's behavioral characteristics: What level of adherence to our software security principles is sufficient given the purposes to which the software will be put and for the level of attack and adversary sophistication that the software must resist in order to remain usable? In addition, what is sufficient to not impact the software's owners and users in ways from which they cannot readily recover.

The degree to which software adheres to these attributes is contextual and generally locally unique. It would be foolish for any author (pundit, expert) to declare that they know precisely what level of self-protection or failure resilience, as well as which security features every piece of software must adhere to. A tiny utility that I write for my own use and whose code and execution are confined to my presumably reasonably protected personal machine has a vastly different security posture from a public, commercial cloud offering. These two cases exist in entirely different orders of security posture magnitude and thus are not playing in even related leagues, other than both consisting of software.

How security principles are achieved is the purpose that an SDL is supposed to deliver. Of course, it's not quite that simple: Some parts of the SDL are intended to foster secure designs but are not, in and of themselves, secure designs. Likewise, activities in the SDL should reduce implementation errors but are not secure code. And so forth. The SDL is the blueprint for what sort of activities and skills will be required to achieve the correct levels of secure behavior. That is, the SDL is intended to tell us what we have to do to build software that will exhibit the correct amounts of each of the secure software principles given previously.

But an SDL is not the set of skills; it is our pointer to the correct skills. What to execute and how to achieve the goals of activities exist at a different level of implementation when building a secure software program.

For instance, secure coding requires an understanding of what types of coding errors attackers might leverage. The set of errors will be language dependent: Languages that allow programmatic manipulation of memory have classes of attacks that are far more difficult to make in languages where memory usage is opaque to the language. In the same vein, a failure to choose secure design patterns leads to weaker security postures, that is, may offer attackers leverage.

In short: An SDL sets out that set of processes, activities, and timings that, taken together, provide developers and system stakeholders a coordinated and holistic blueprint for achieving the security behaviors we have listed above—the set of activities that is most likely to achieve the desired security posture.

There are some intricacies that many extant SDLs fail to explain. For instance, some activities are dependent upon the initiation, completion, or availability of work products that occur during development. Some activities are dependent upon a work product having been started. Others require the completion of tasks. In contrast to SDL activities whose timing is dependent upon the initiation of the completion of development tasks, there are other SDL activities that start as soon as development produces code. These activities then proceed alongside of, in concert with, and perhaps are an integral part of the development process from the point at which code begins to be produced. An SDL activity's dependencies tend to be unique to it.

An obvious example would be verification. If no code has yet been generated, the code cannot be verified for correctness.[*] Likewise, if no major structures have been identified, then it will be difficult

---

[*] In test-driven SDLCs, however, the verification test is written before coding functionality. Even with this paradigm, the test isn't run until there's functionality on which the test can be run.

to understand at what system points attackers will begin their attacks: a key factor essential to threat modeling analysis. For manual penetration (pen) testing, typically, most of the development work and SDL activities should already have been completed. Skilled, manual penetration testing is usually most effective at the point at which nearly everything else in a cycle of change has been completed; penetration testing, thus, is highly dependent on the completion of most development.

Interestingly, pen testing can be independent of the remainder of the SDL. In our experience, that is not the most effective approach. (We will describe effective conditions for pen testing in a subsequent chapter.) We much prefer integrated pen testing that takes input from the preceding SDL activities and offers significant feedback to earlier SDL activities. However, pen testing does not require that any other SDL activities occurred previously.

Hence, an SDL must not only set out discreet activities and requirements, but it must also explain how the activities and requirements work in concert and how they fit together and support each other: their dependencies and relative timings.

We have not said "absolute timings" intentionally. An SDL that explicitly declares the timing of activities becomes tied to the processes through which software will be developed, that is, the specific Software Development Life Cycle (SDLC) that will be employed. A general-purpose SDL cannot be tied to any particular SDLC, as outlined previously in this chapter. As stated, timing assumptions restrict the application of the SDL to particular forms of SDLCs. Doing so then obviates the SDL's use for alternative SDLC.

We believe that, based upon work done for our previous employers (as described above), it is not only possible, but demonstrable to create and use an SDL that isn't coupled to a particular SDLC. To deliver such a general-purpose SDL, it must contain:

- A comprehensive set of security activities believed to express industry consensus on delivering software security
- An accompanying and integrated set of requirements that explains why and when to execute the activities
- Processes that explain how to execute the activities and requirements
- The set of prerequisite work-products that must be achieved before starting each activity and requirement
- The work-product(s) expected from execution and fulfillment of activities and requirements
- Any conditions that, when these exist, require the beginning of, and re-evaluation of, activities and their outputs
- A definition of done that explicitly states when an activity may be considered to have been completed and its security requirements fulfilled

The preceding bullet points describe, at a high level, a set of requirements that, if fulfilled, will meet the SDL needs of software development under any SDLC. Such an SDL will be fully independent of any particular SDLC and can be executed as an integral part of every SDLC.

As we have already noted, there exists a consensus among software security practitioners on that set of activities that, taken together, comprise the best opportunity to achieve software security objectives, given the current (as of this writing) state of our art.

There are differences in the names given to various activities. There are differences in granularity of activities: Some published SDLs tease apart activities that others lump together. This is particularly true for design-time activities wherein SDL framers attempt to provide linear order to work that, in reality, often doesn't require any particular or strict ordering.

We will dig into the nonlinearity of today's software development methods and the required, integral security work in fair detail in subsequent chapters. As we will see later, attempts to turn what must be an integral process into discrete (and individually named) activities is a common error that separates (and for some SDLCs makes nearly irrelevant) the SDL from software development with which SDL activities must integrate—the seeming need to carefully order SDL activities obviates that very integration that is necessary for achieving software security.

"Flattening" iterative SDLC activities, which often occur in parallel, draws a false demarcation between security and development, which is quite counterproductive. In our experience, when the SDL is no longer expressed as a highly defined progression of tasks, SDLC integration becomes easy, natural, and organic. Developers readily (and, importantly, eagerly) add security tasks as an integral part of the fabric of software development, which reduces to near zero opportunities for nonproductive process friction. In the chapters devoted to program building, we take up this subject in much greater detail. At this point, we set the context for the SDL that is offered in this book.

Establishing the set of activities that will deliver needed security postures through development isn't sufficient. An SDL must also contain explicit requirements about where and at what points during any change to execute each relevant SDL activity. A generic SDL needn't attempt to predict particular timings, nor do requirements need to tie themselves to assumptions about the SDLC.

It actually turns out that triggers for executing even the most craft-rich activities in the SDL are quite deterministic. We published several triggers throughout Chapter 9 in *Core Software Security*—in particular, Section 9.2.1 The Seven Determining Questions. We will reiterate those later; none of them has changed, though we are going to reshape the secure design activities around threat modeling—a subsequent understanding that we've gained since publishing *Core Software Security*. At this point in this work, it should be sufficient to understand that activity execution signposts can and have been defined without coupling those to any particular SDLC. It isn't necessary to definitively sequence the SDL in order to give developers security requirements.

Some SDL activities are stand-alone: These can be executed without reference to other activities. For instance, secure coding depends upon language-specific training on errors that must be avoided and those coding patterns, in that particular language and runtime environment that offer the least amount of (or better, no) adversary leverage. The only dependency, assuming training, is that there's code to generate. That's a coupling with SDLC activity, but it has no additional dependency on other SDL activities (other than the aforementioned training).

On the other hand, skilled penetration testing isn't particularly effective until a set of changes is pretty near completion—the software running as it will when released. Penetration testing doesn't necessarily depend upon completion of all other relevant SDL activities. Many organizations wrongly assume that skilled manual (penetration) testing is the most important activity, maybe the only one needed. That's a big mistake, frankly, since if so, one has used the most expensive, most unique and boutique tool to find issues that could have been identified much earlier and less expensively, or avoided entirely.

Hence, the ideal skilled, manual testing activity ought to (in our strong opinion) depend upon the successful completion of all previous relevant and applicable SDL activities. Penetration testing ought to be used as the proving (or not) of the previous SDL work. Penetration testing shouldn't be the catchall, single activity to achieve desired security objectives: Skilled penetration testing occurs much too late for that.

Likewise, it's usually a mistake to generate specific security designs before the right security structure is in place, ergo, levels of secure structuring (architecture) activity have been successfully completed before specific algorithms are tried (or chosen, depending upon SDLC methods). Design (security and other) depends upon relatively completed structural understanding. There's also an important feedback loop between these two: Design constraints may very well (should) influence structure (architecture) choices. These two activities are interdependent and, in some SDLC methods, conjoined tightly; there may be little need for division between them. Hence, the SDL must explicitly state how architecture and design interact or are joined or there will be misunderstanding, or worse, friction around execution.

Finally, every SDL activity must absolutely tell developers when they can consider the activity completed and what "success" looks like, how to measure effectiveness, what the activity is expected to achieve, and how to prove its objectives have been achieved. Those activities whose execution depends (sometimes heavily) on experience and human analysis, that is, "craft" as much as engineering, can appear to be an endless time sink. This problem can bedevil those whose role is to ensure that development completes—on time and under budget (often project management and similar roles).

We honor the many (hundreds) of people who tirelessly organize and drive what can seem from the outside to be a chaotic system: software development. Security must not add to that burden. The SDL we offer here has clear objectives for each activity. For activities such as threat modeling, we have previously published a fairly clear "Definition of Done," both as a blog post and in *Secrets of a Cyber Security Architect* (Appendix E, pp. 203–206), which we will reiterate here. Every SDL activity must contain conditions by which its completion can be established. There must be some way to measure at what level the activity has been effective or successful.

In summary, we believe, based upon our extensive experience, that an SDL can be achieved that is not tightly coupled to any particular SDLC and which does not express itself in a way that makes integration into software development difficult, even impossible. We've seen it. We've lived security as a part of the fabric of development; we have shifted development organizations from security avoidance to a culture of security, what Noopur Davis[*] calls, "culture hacking." We know in our bones that not only are these goals possible, they are readily achievable.

The journey isn't easy. Local variations and unique requirements always exist. Different business and organizational goals require different levels of security; there is no "one-size-fits-all" security posture. Ivory tower security pronouncements are exactly that: not real-world needs.

Still, by using a generic, consensus-based SDL, adapted to local needs, we have seen organizations achieve their security goals. We've measured the decline of preventable security leaks in the software for which we've been responsible. There is little in our career lives that is more satisfying. In this book, we hope to share our technical, process, and organizational methods so that you, too, can reap some of these rewards.

1.5 Developing an SDL Model That Can Work with Any Development Methodology

Ensuring that everyone touching the product development lifecycle has the knowledge they need to support an organization's software security process is a fundamental challenge for any organization committed to software security success. The goal is to remove the pain that organizations face in developing a custom program of their own resource constraints and knowledge vacuums. Developers are often under intense pressure to deliver more features on time and under budget. Few developers get the time to review their code for potential security vulnerabilities. When they do get the time, they often don't have secure-code training and lack the automated tools, embedded processes and procedures, and resources to prevent hackers from using hundreds of common exploit techniques to trigger malicious attacks.

Unfortunately, before DevOps and DevSecOps, many companies thought it made more business sense not to produce secure software products than it did to produce them. Any solution needs to address this as a fundamental market failure instead of simply wishing it were not true. If security is to be a business goal, then it needs to make business sense. In the end, security requirements are in fact the same as any business goals and should be addressed as equally important. Employers should expect their employees to take pride in and own a certain level of responsibility for their work. And employees should expect their employers to provide the tools and training they need to get the job done. With

---

[*] Noopur Davis, Executive Vice President, Chief Product and Information Security Officer, Comcast, Inc.

these expectations established and goals agreed on, perhaps the software industry can do a better job of strengthening the security of its products by reducing software vulnerabilities.

A new security model for DevSecOps is needed that requires new mindsets, processes, and tools to adhere to the collaborative, agile nature of DevOps. The primary focus is creating new solutions for complex software development processes within an agile and collaborative framework. To migrate to a new model, you must fully understand your current process and lifecycle so that you can bridge the traditional gaps between the software development, operations, and security teams. This should include focus on shared responsibility of security tasks during all phases of the delivery process. This will result in positive outcomes for the business as a consequence of combining development, security, and operations teams; shortening feedback loops; reducing incidents; and improving security.

Reinventing how you perform your SDL will be key to your success in optimizing security in an agile and DevOps environment. The goals of SDL are twofold: The first goal is to reduce the number of security vulnerabilities and privacy problems; the second goal is to reduce the severity of the vulnerabilities that remain (ergo, "security technical debt"). Although this SDL may look similar to other SDLs you have seen, our approach to implementing this SDL not only brings the tasks and organizational responsibilities back into the SDL but also keeps the centralized software security group and engineering software development teams empowered to own the security process for the products for which they are directly responsible.

Given the continued pressure to do more with less, we don't believe most organizations will have the luxury of having most of the elements that we include in "post-release support" as separate organizations. This has been typical in the past, but we believe that organizations will need to provide for innovative ways to include these elements as part of their overall software security program to leverage the use of available resources. Most important to the SDL are the organizational structure, people, and process required to deliver it, both effectively and efficiently, while maximizing the return on investment (ROI) for security in the post-release environment.

Inevitably, teams feel overwhelmed. It seems like even more has been placed on already heavily weighted shoulders. Immediately, the smart folks will ask, "What do I HAVE to do?" Since that depends, the next query will be, "Then what's the minimum?" We are getting away from all of that without sacrificing any security task.

Software developers know how to write software in a way that provides a high level of security and robustness. So why don't software developers practice these techniques? The model in this book will answer this question in two parts:

1. Software is determined to be secure as a result of an analysis of how the program is to be used, under what conditions, and the security requirements it must meet in the environment in which it is to be deployed. The SDL must also extend beyond the release of the product in that if the assumptions underlying the software in an unplanned operational environment and their previously implied requirements do not hold, the software may no longer be secure, and the SDL process may start over in part or as a whole, if a complete product redesign is required. In this sense, the authors establish the need for accurate and meaningful security requirements and the metrics to govern them, as well as examples of how to develop them. It also assumes that the security requirements are not all known prior to the development process and describes the process by which they are derived, analyzed, and validated.

2. Software executives, leaders, and managers must support the robust coding practices and required security enhancements as required by a business-relevant SDL as well as supporting the staffing requirements, scheduling, budgeting, and resource allocations required for this type of work. Part of this model covers the process, requirements, and management of metrics for people in these roles so they can accurately assess the impact and resources required for an SDL that is relevant to and works best in their organization and environment. The model is

approached and designed from real-life, on-the-ground challenges and experiences; the authors describe how to think about issues in order to develop effective approaches and manage them as a business process.

Because security is integrated tightly into every part of an Agile process, some of the engagement activities typically found in Waterfall SDLs are no longer required. Security is built into the process, from conception of a product and subsequently, throughout the process. In fact, early security requirements gathering must be accomplished for a completed Plan of Intent. This portion of the process equates to the engagement question, "[A]rchitecture is a complete redesign or is entirely new?" Similarly, once an architecture runway is initiated, the security architect should be included on the architecture team that shapes the architecture so that it fosters the appropriate security features that will be needed.

The security portion of an Agile process assumes an iterative architecture and design process. There is no tension between iteration and refinement on the one hand and security on the other within this process. Security does not attempt to "bound" the iterative process. Rather, since security expertise is integral to iteration and refinement, a secure design will be a natural result of the Agile process. In this way, security becomes Agile—that is, able to quickly account for changes. This approach produces flexible, nimble security architecture.

A high-level abstraction: Design, build, and verify remains relatively stable across methodologies, although, agile approaches shift some parts of these into an iterative, parallel set of ongoing and repeated tasks. Since the entire agile process emphasizes iteration, the usual SDL activities also must iterate or be left in the dust. Architecture before formal Sprints begin is not meant to be a completed process but rather a gateway that seeds, informs, and empowers the iterative design that will take place during Sprints. This alone is radically different from the way architecture has been perceived as a discrete and independent process. Rather, many formally discrete SDL tasks are taking place in parallel during any particular Sprint. Secure design, secure coding, manual code review, or any number of testing approaches that don't require a completed, more or less holistic piece of software are all taking place at the same time and by the same team. The foregoing implies that security can't jump in to interject pronouncements and then jump back out until some later governance step where judgment occurs about whether the security plan has been carried out correctly. The very nature of agile implies that plans will change based on newly acquired information. Our approach, then, is for security to benefit from that iterative process.

Previously, in *Core Software Security*, we provided a detailed overview of the Waterfall model we modified to create our first rendition of an agile development process. We also used it to move the security responsibilities into the development group before DevOps and DevSecOps became a model to do this. Before we move on to describe a model that can work with any development methodology, it is important to go back to where we started and the baseline upon which we built what we talk about in future chapters. A DevSecOps approach drives technical, operational, and social changes that help organizations address security threats more effectively, in real time. This provides security with a "seat at the table" with the development and operations teams and a value to speed of delivery rather than a hinderance. The next few sections describe the evolution of software development practices to include a previous Waterfall-type SDL model that we used in an Agile environment followed by a newer model fully optimized for the DevOps environment that can work with any development methodology.

1.5.1 Our Previous Secure Development Lifecycle Design and Methodology

We start this section by introducing the concept of overcoming the challenges of making software secure through the use of an SDL, as described in *Core Software Security*. Software security has evolved at a rapid pace since that book was published.

We will move quickly from a review of our previous design in this section to an approach better aligned with Agile methods and a design that is more appropriate for a DevOps environment throughout the remainder of the book.

Further discussions of the models, methodologies, tools, human talent, and metrics for managing and overcoming the challenges to make software secure can be found later in this book.

It should be noted that there is still a need for better static and dynamic testing tools and a formalized security methodology integrated into SDLCs that is within the reach of a majority of software development organizations. In the past decade or so, the predominant SDL models have been out of reach for all but the most resource-rich companies. Our goal in this book is similar to our previous book: to create an SDL based on leveraging resources and best practices rather than requiring resources that are out of reach for a majority of software security teams.

1.5.1.1 Overcoming Challenges in Making Software Secure

SDLs are the key step in the evolution of software security and have helped to bring attention to the need to build security into the SDLC. In the past, software product stakeholders did not view software security as a high priority. It was believed that a secure network infrastructure would provide the level of protection needed against malicious attacks. In recent history, network security alone has proved inadequate against such attacks. Users have been successful in penetrating valid authenticated channels through techniques such as cross-site scripting (XSS), Structured Query Language (SQL) injection, and buffer overflow exploitation. In such cases, system assets were compromised, and both data and organizational integrity were damaged. The security industry has tried to solve software security problems through stopgap measures. First came platform security (OS security), then network/perimeter security, and, now, application security. We need to defense-in-depth to protect our assets, but, fundamentally, it is a software security flaw and needs to be remediated through a software security approach (SDL) that tightly integrates and is organic to the SDLC developers' use.

We might call this integration software security's "SDLC approach," or something like "developer-centric security." Whatever we term it, the critical concept is that an easily implementable SDL must support the development methods (SDLC) in use by developers. Ours constitutes an about-face from software security approaches that force developers to also learn and accommodate security approaches that conflict with their SDLC.

The SDL has, as its base, components that all of the activities and security controls needed to develop industry and government compliant as well as best practices hardened software. A knowledgeable staff, along with secure software policies and controls, is required in order to truly prevent, identify, and mitigate exploitable vulnerabilities within developed systems.

Not meeting the least of these activities found within the secure SDLC provides an opportunity for the misuse of system assets from both insider and outsider threats. Security is not simply a network requirement, it is now an information technology (IT) requirement, which includes the development of all software for the intent to distribute, store, and manipulate information. Organizations must implement the highest standards of development in order to ensure the highest quality of products for its customers and the lives that they protect.

Implementation of an SDLC program ensures that security is inherent in good enterprise software design and development, not an afterthought later in production. Taking an SDLC approach yields tangible benefits such as ensuring that all software releases meet minimum security criteria, and that all stakeholders support and enforce security guidelines. The elimination of software risk early in the development cycle, when vulnerabilities are easier and less expensive to fix, provides a systematic approach for information security teams to collaborate with during the development process.

1.5.2 Mapping the Security Development Lifecycle (SDL) to the Software Development Life Cycle (SDLC)

Whatever form of SDL you use, whether it is one that already exists, one you developed yourself, or a combination of both, you must map it to your current SDLC to be effective. Figure 1.4 (formerly Figure 2.4) is an SDL activity and best practices model that the authors have developed and mapped to the typical SDLC phases. Each SDL activity and best practice is based on real-world experience, and examples from the authors show the reader that security can be built into each of the SDLC phases—a mapping of security to the SDLC, if you will. If security is built [as a core part of development tasks], then the software has a higher probability of being secure by default, and later software changes are less likely to compromise overall security. Another benefit of this mapping is that you will have presumably worked with the owner(s) and stakeholders of the SDL, which will serve to build buy-in, efficiency, and achievable security in both the operational and business processes of the SDLC and will include the developers, product and program managers, business managers, and executives. (As stated previously, the model in Figure 1.4 is based on the years of experience, research, and stakeholder/customer inter-action shared between the authors in the field of software and information security.)

Each phase of the SDL in Figure 1.4 was described in great detail in *Core Software Security* and was broken up as shown in Figures 1.5–1.10 below.

1.5.3 Software Development Methodologies

In *Core Software Security*, we discussed the various SDLC models and provided a visual overview of our mapping of our SDL model to a generic SDLC. It should be noted, however, that multiple software development methodologies are used within the various SDLC models. Every software development methodology approach acts as a basis for applying specific frameworks to develop and maintain soft-ware and is less concerned with the technical side than with the organizational aspects of the process of creating software. Principal among these development methodologies are the Waterfall model and Agile, together with their many variants and spin-offs. The Waterfall model is the oldest and most well-known software development methodology. The distinctive feature of the Waterfall model is its sequential step-by-step process of requirements. Agile methodologies are gaining popularity in indus-try, although they comprise a mix of traditional and new software development practices. You may see Agile or traditional Waterfall or maybe a hybrid of the two. We have chosen to give a high-level descrip-tion of the Waterfall and Agile development models and a variant or two of each as an introduction to software development methodologies.

1.5.3.1 Waterfall Development

Waterfall development (see Figure 1.11) is another name for the more traditional approach to soft-ware development. This approach is typically higher risk, more costly, and less efficient than the Agile approach, which is discussed later in this chapter. The Waterfall approach uses requirements that are already known, each stage is signed off before the next commences, and it requires extensive documen-tation because it is the primary communication mechanism throughout the process. Although most development organizations have already moved toward Agile methods, the Waterfall method may still be used when requirements are fully understood and not complex. Since the plan is not to revisit a phase using this methodology once it is completed, it is imperative that you do it right the first time: There is generally no second chance.

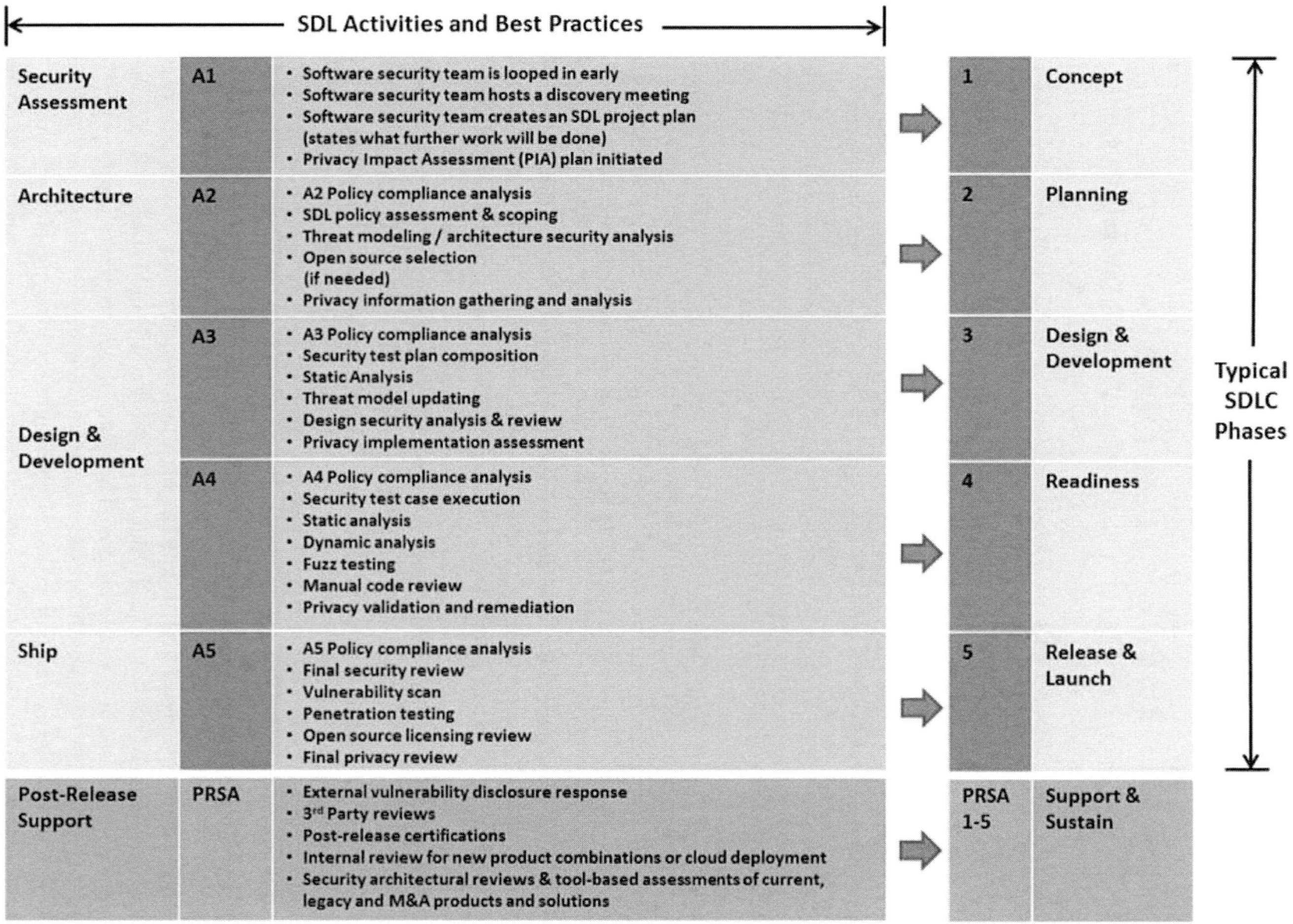

————— SDL Activities and Best Practices —————

		SDL Activities and Best Practices
Security Assessment	A1	• Software security team is looped in early • Software security team hosts a discovery meeting • Software security team creates an SDL project plan (states what further work will be done) • Privacy Impact Assessment (PIA) plan initiated
Architecture	A2	• A2 Policy compliance analysis • SDL policy assessment & scoping • Threat modeling / architecture security analysis • Open source selection (if needed) • Privacy information gathering and analysis
Design & Development	A3	• A3 Policy compliance analysis • Security test plan composition • Static Analysis • Threat model updating • Design security analysis & review • Privacy implementation assessment
Design & Development	A4	• A4 Policy compliance analysis • Security test case execution • Static analysis • Dynamic analysis • Fuzz testing • Manual code review • Privacy validation and remediation
Ship	A5	• A5 Policy compliance analysis • Final security review • Vulnerability scan • Penetration testing • Open source licensing review • Final privacy review
Post-Release Support	PRSA	• External vulnerability disclosure response • 3rd Party reviews • Post-release certifications • Internal review for new product combinations or cloud deployment • Security architectural reviews & tool-based assessments of current, legacy and M&A products and solutions

Typical SDLC Phases

1	Concept
2	Planning
3	Design & Development
4	Readiness
5	Release & Launch
PRSA 1-5	Support & Sustain

Figure 1.4 Mapping the Security Development Lifecycle (SDL) to the Software Development Life Cycle (SDLC). (*Source:* Reproduced from Ransome, J. and Misra, A. [2014]. *Core Software Security: Security at the Source.* Boca Raton [FL]: CRC Press/Taylor & Francis Group, p. 46, with permission.)

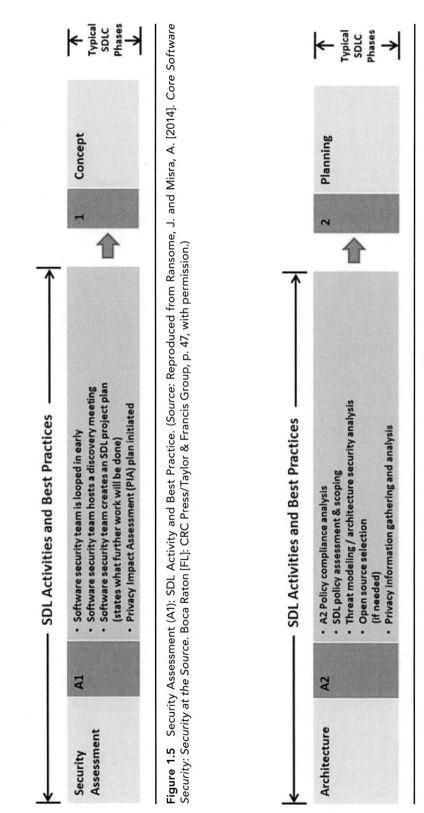

Figure 1.5 Security Assessment (A1): SDL Activity and Best Practice. (*Source:* Reproduced from Ransome, J. and Misra, A. [2014]. *Core Software Security: Security at the Source.* Boca Raton [FL]: CRC Press/Taylor & Francis Group, p. 47, with permission.)

Figure 1.6 Architecture (A2): SDL Activity and Best Practice. (*Source:* Reproduced from Ransome, J. and Misra, A. [2014]. *Core Software Security: Security at the Source.* Boca Raton [FL]: CRC Press/Taylor & Francis Group, p. 47, with permission.)

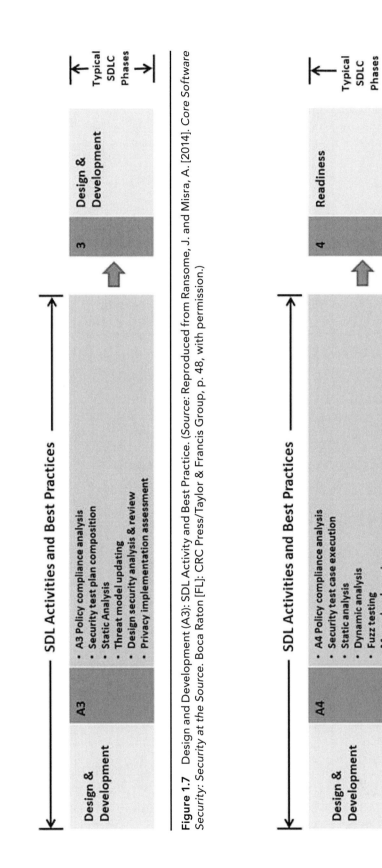

Figure 1.7 Design and Development (A3): SDL Activity and Best Practice. *(Source:* Reproduced from Ransome, J. and Misra, A. [2014]. *Core Software Security: Security at the Source.* Boca Raton [FL]: CRC Press/Taylor & Francis Group, p. 48, with permission.)

Figure 1.8 Design and Development (A4): SDL Activity and Best Practice. *(Source:* Reproduced from Ransome, J. and Misra, A. [2014]. *Core Software Security: Security at the Source.* Boca Raton [FL]: CRC Press/Taylor & Francis Group, p. 48, with permission.)

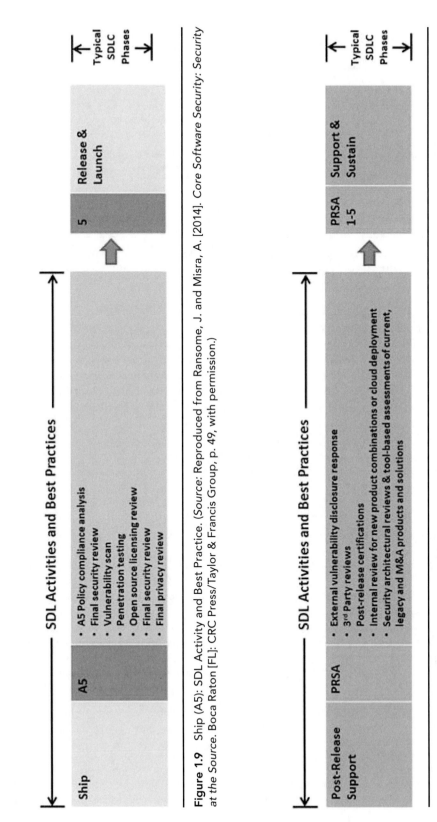

Figure 1.9 Ship (A5): SDL Activity and Best Practice. (*Source:* Reproduced from Ransome, J. and Misra, A. [2014]. *Core Software Security: Security at the Source.* Boca Raton [FL]: CRC Press/Taylor & Francis Group, p. 49, with permission.)

Figure 1.10 Post-Release Support (PRSA1-5): SDL Activity and Best Practice. (*Source:* Reproduced from Ransome, J. and Misra, A. [2014]. *Core Software Security: Security at the Source.* Boca Raton [FL]: CRC Press/Taylor & Francis Group, p. 49, with permission.)

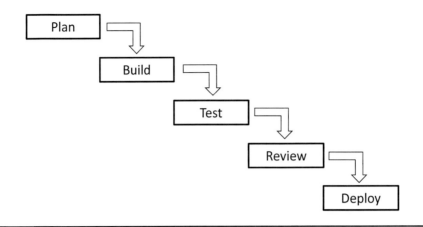

Figure 1.11 Waterfall Software Development Methodology. (*Source:* Reproduced from Ransome, J. and Misra, A. [2014]. *Core Software Security: Security at the Source.* Boca Raton [FL]: CRC Press/Taylor & Francis Group, p. 51, with permission.)

Although Waterfall development methodologies vary, they tend to be similar in that practitioners try to keep to the initial plan, do not have working software until very late in the cycle, assume they know everything upfront, minimize changes through a change control board (i.e., assume that change is bad and can be controlled), put most responsibility on the project manager (PM), optimize conformance to schedule and budget, generally use weak controls, and allow realization of value only upon completion. They are driven by a PM-centric approach under the belief that if the processes in the plan are followed, then everything will work as planned. In today's development environment, most of the aforementioned items are considered negative attributes of the Waterfall methodology and are just a few of the reasons that industry is moving toward Agile development methodologies. The Waterfall approach may be looked on as an assembly-line approach, which may be excellent when applied properly to hardware but which has shortcomings in comparison to Agile when it comes to software development.

1.5.3.2 Iterative Waterfall Development

The iterative Waterfall development model (see Figure 1.12) is an improvement on the standard Waterfall model. This approach carries less risk than a traditional Waterfall approach but is riskier and less efficient than the Agile approach. In the iterative Waterfall method, the overall project is divided into various phases, each executed using the traditional Waterfall method. Dividing larger projects into smaller identifiable phases results in a smaller scope of work for each phase, and the end deliverable of each phase can be reviewed and improved, if necessary, before moving to the next phase. Overall risk is thus reduced.

The iterative method has demonstrated a marked improvement over the traditional Waterfall method. You are more likely to face an Agile approach to software development rather than either a standard or an iterative Waterfall methodology in today's environment.

1.5.3.3 Agile Development

The Agile approach is based on both iterative and incremental development methods. Requirements and solutions evolve through collaboration among self-organizing, cross-functional teams, and a

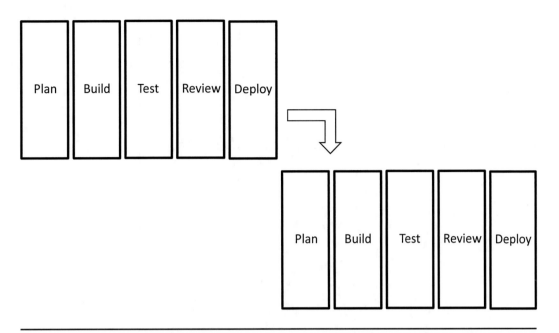

Figure 1.12 Iterative Waterfall Software Development Methodology. (*Source:* Reproduced from Ransome, J. and Misra, A. [2014]. *Core Software Security: Security at the Source.* Boca Raton [FL]: CRC Press/Taylor & Francis Group, p. 52, with permission.)

solution resulting from every iteration is reviewed and refined regularly throughout the process. The Agile method is a time-boxed iterative approach that facilitates a rapid and flexible response to change, which, in turn, encourages evolutionary development and delivery while promoting adaptive planning, development, teamwork, collaboration, and process adaptability throughout the lifecycle of the project. Tasks are broken into small increments that require minimal planning. These iterations have short time frames called "time boxes" that can last from one to four weeks. Multiple iterations may be required to release a product or new features. A cross-functional team is responsible for all software development functions in each iteration, including planning, requirements analysis, design, coding, unit testing, and acceptance testing. An Agile project is typically cross-functional, and self-organizing teams operate independently from any corporate hierarchy or other corporate roles of individual team members, who themselves decide how to meet each iteration's requirements. This allows the project to adapt to changes quickly and minimizes overall risk. The goal is to have an available release at the end of the iteration, and a working product is demonstrated to stakeholders at the end of each iteration.

1.5.3.4 Scrum

Scrum (see Figure 1.13) is an iterative and incremental Agile software development method for managing software projects and product or application development. Scrum adopts an empirical approach, accepting that the problem cannot be fully understood or defined and focusing instead on maximizing the team's ability to deliver quickly and to respond to emerging requirements. This is accomplished through the use of co-located, self-organizing teams in which all disciplines can be represented. In contrast to traditional planned or predictive methodologies, this concept facilitates the ability to handle churn resulting from customers that change the requirements during project development. The basic unit of development for Scrum is called a "Sprint," and a Sprint can last from one week to one month.

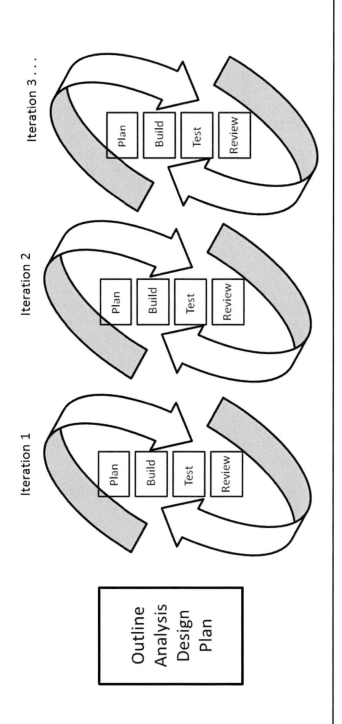

Figure 1.13 Scrum Software Development Methodology. (*Source:* Reproduced from Ransome, J. and Misra, A. [2014]. *Core Software Security: Security at the Source.* Boca Raton [FL]: CRC Press/Taylor & Francis Group, p. 54, with permission.)

Each Sprint is time-boxed so that finished portions of a product are completed on time. A prioritized list of requirements is derived from the product backlog, and if they are not completed during the Sprint, they are left out and returned to the product backlog. The team demonstrates the software after each Sprint is completed. Generally accepted value-added attributes of Scrum include its use of adaptive planning; that it requires feedback from working software early during the first Sprint (typically two weeks) and often; that it stresses the maximization of good change, such as focusing on maximizing learning throughout the project; that it puts most responsibility on small, dedicated, tight-thinking adaptive teams that plan and re-plan their own work; that it has strong and frequent controls; optimizes business value, time to market, and quality; and that it supports the realization of value earlier, potentially after every Sprint.

1.5.3.5 Lean Development

In our experience, for those of you who have recently moved from or are in the process of moving from a Waterfall methodology for software development, Scrum is the most likely variant of Agile that you will encounter. Lean (see Figure 1.14) is another methodology that is gaining popularity and is thus worth mentioning. Unfortunately, there are many definitions of Lean, which is a methodology that is evolving in many directions. Although Lean is similar to Scrum in that it focuses on features rather than groups of features, it takes this idea one step further in that, in its simplest form, you select, plan, develop, test, and deploy one feature before you select, plan, develop, test, and deploy the next feature. The objective is to further isolate risk to the level of an individual feature. This isolation has the advantage of focusing on eliminating "waste," when possible, and doing nothing unless it is absolutely necessary or relevant. Lean development can be summarized by seven principles based on Lean manufacturing principle concepts: (1) eliminate waste, (2) amplify learning, (3) decide as late as possible, (4) deliver as fast as possible, (5) empower the team, (6) build integrity in, and (7) see the whole. One of the key elements of Lean development is to provide a model in which you can see the whole, even when your developers are scattered across multiple locations and contractors. Although still considered related to Agile by many in the community, lean software development is a related discipline rather than a specific subset of Agile.

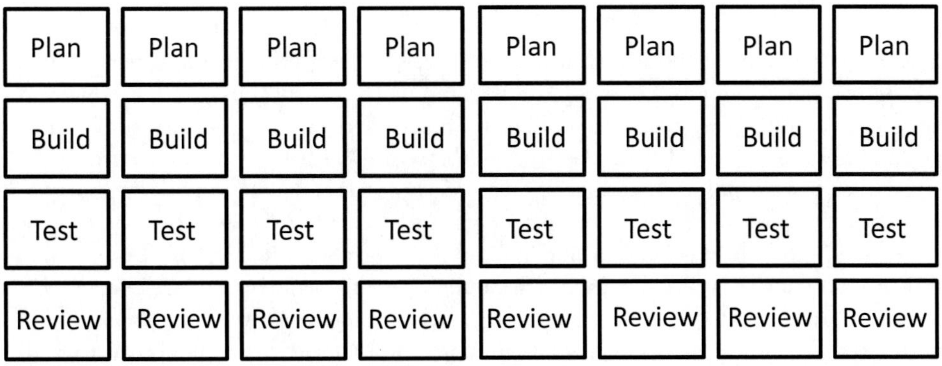

Plan	Plan	Plan	Plan	Plan	Plan	Plan	Plan
Build	Build	Build	Build	Build	Build	Build	Build
Test	Test	Test	Test	Test	Test	Test	Test
Review	Review	Review	Review	Review	Review	Review	Review

Figure 1.14 Lean Software Development Methodology. (*Source:* Reproduced from Ransome, J. and Misra, A. [2014]. *Core Software Security: Security at the Source.* Boca Raton [FL]: CRC Press/Taylor & Francis Group, p. 55, with permission.)

1.6 The Progression from Waterfall and Agile to Scrum: A Management Perspective

Up until just a few years ago, most software development projects were created using the Waterfall method, as described in *Core Software Security*. Typically, complex Gantt charts laying out every step, milestone, and delivery dates in great detail are used to manage the Waterfall process and convince management that there is complete control and predictability for a project. This type of process tries to restrict change and in-process creativity. It doesn't account for and adapt to the unknown or support short-term course corrections. Unfortunately, we still see teams using these charts and methodology to manage their projects in agile and just-in-time environments, which is a recipe for disaster. Compared to today's practices, this is a very slow process that can result in delays of months or even years, resulting in significant budget overruns.

Jeff Sutherland first created Scrum with Ken Schwaber, in 1993, as a faster, more reliable, and more effective way to create software in the tech industry.[*] Jeff states the following in his recent book:

> The term "Agile" dates back to a 2001 conclave where I and sixteen other leaders in software development wrote up what has become known as the "Agile Manifesto." It declared the following values: people over processes; products that actually work over documenting what that product is supposed to do; collaborating with customers over negotiating with them; and responding to change over following a plan. Scrum is the framework I built to put those values into practice. There is no methodology.[†]

Scrum provides a framework that enables teams to optimize their speed and quality through self-organization and realization of what and how they have created a product. The process underlying Scrum includes:

- The identification of incremental goals to be completed in a fixed length of time, a sequential part of the product build.
- A daily short sync meeting (typically 15 minutes or less) called a Daily Standup to ensure that you are headed in the right direction efficiently and effectively.
- Setting goals and systematically working out how to get there. And even more important, it identifies what is stopping the team from getting there.
- Teams that are cross-functional, autonomous, and empowered.
- The accommodation of necessary changes through the daily management of backlogs and use of short development cycles called "Sprints."

Sprints are short, typically two- to four-week cycles (although Sprint length varies considerably depending upon need and type of software to be built). Each cycle begins with a meeting to plan the Sprint, where the work to be completed is decided. This is also the meeting where security for the product and any adjacencies it may have are defined. In this regard, security is no different from other properties that the software must exhibit, that is, a level of performance or ease of use. The prioritized list of things to be accomplished are written on sticky notes and put on a wall or work board. Those working with the Agile SDLC are likely to also employ Lean to manage work items. Any items remaining that are still necessary to be completed as part of the product development are then put into a backlog to be completed in a later Sprint. To avoid distracting the team or interfering with accomplishing the goals set forth in the Sprint, the tasks are now locked in and nothing else can be added by anyone outside

---

[*]   Sutherland, J. (2014). *SCRUM: The Art of Doing Twice the Work in Half the Time*. New York (NY): The Crown Publishing Group, p. vii.
[†]   Ibid., pp. 12–13.

the team. Interrupting this process can significantly slow down the process and defeats the purpose of using Scrum.

The first thing you need to do when you're implementing Scrum is to create a Backlog. The Product Backlog is an ordered list of everything that is known to be needed for the product and the single source of requirements for any changes to be made to the product. Initially, it lays out the known and best-understood requirements. A Product Backlog remains dynamic and is never complete. It is constantly changing to identify what the product needs (including new items) and evolves as the product and the environment in which it will be used evolves. The Product Owner is responsible for the Product Backlog, including its content, availability, and ordering.

Establishing a work rhythm and consistency are also important, and Sprints are set for specific lengths of time throughout the development process. For example, if a decision is made for a two-week Sprint, then each Sprint will remain two weeks in length for the entire product-development process—not a one-week, followed by a three-week, and then a two-week Sprint, and so on.

As with anything in the development process, fix any mistakes or bugs you have identified immediately. Jeff Sutherland, the co-creator of Scrum, shares that in his experience, fixing it later can take you more than twenty times longer than if you fix it now:

It took twenty-four times longer. If a bug was addressed on the day it was created, it would take an hour to fix; three weeks later, it would take twenty-four hours. It didn't even matter if the bug was big or small, complicated or simple—it always took twenty-four times longer three weeks later. As you can imagine, every software developer in the company was soon required to test and fix their code on the same day.[*]

Kaizen is the Japanese word for *improvement* and is used commonly in Scrum to identify what is also called the "Sprint Retrospective," conducted at the end of each Sprint to identify what went right, what could have gone better, and what can be made better in the next Sprint. What can potentially be shipped to customers for feedback is also identified at this stage

Most importantly, rather than seeking someone to blame for their mistakes, this is where the team takes responsibility for their process and outcomes, seeking solutions as a team and their ability to act on them and make changes as needed.

In this sense, Kaizen is identifying what will actually change the process and make it better the next time. If you are familiar with Deming's PDCA (plan–do–check–act) cycle,[†] this is the "Check" part and why it is so important to make sure to set up the ability to get to the "Act" step. Each Sprint should identify and address at least one improvement or kaizen and make it the most important thing to accomplish in the next Sprint.

The Scrum team divides the work into functional increments called "user stories" that, when implemented, contribute to the overall product value. This is done in consultation with the customer or product owner. The elements of the user stories are captured through the use of the INVEST checklist. The acronym INVEST is used as a checklist for quickly evaluating user stories and originated in an article by Bill Wake, which also repurposed the acronym SMART (Specific, Measurable, Achievable, Relevant, Time-boxed) for tasks resulting from the technical decomposition of user stories.[‡] The successful completion of the criteria in the INVEST Checklist is used to tell if the story is ready, as shown below:

---

[*] Ibid., p. 100.

[†] The W. Edwards Deming Institute. (2020). "PDSA Cycle." Retrieved from https://deming.org/explore/p-d-s-a

[‡] Agile Alliance. (2020). "Glossary Definition of INVEST." Retrieved from https://www.agilealliance.org /glossary/invest/#q=~(infinite~false~filters~(postType~(~'page~'post~'aa_book~'aa_event_session~'aa_ experience_report~'aa_glossary~'aa_research_paper~'aa_video)~tags~(~'invest))~searchTerm~'~sort~false~sort Direction~'asc~page~1)

Independent. The story must be actionable and "completable" on its own. It shouldn't be inherently dependent on another story.

Negotiable. Until it's actually being done, it needs to be able to be rewritten. Allowance for change is built in.

Valuable. It actually delivers value to a customer or user or stakeholder.

Estimable. You have to be able to size it.

Small. The story needs to be small enough to be able to estimate and plan for easily. Preferably, this should be accomplished in a single Sprint. If it is too big, rewrite it or break it down into smaller stories.

Testable. The story must have at least one test it is supposed to pass in order to be complete. Write the test before you do the story.*

Each user story is written on an index card or sticky note as a brief descriptive sentence reminding the team of its value. This makes is easier for teams to collaborate in making collective decisions about scheduling by moving the sticky notes or cards around on a work board. A user story should not be confused with a Use Case. A Use Case is a description of all the ways an end user wants to "use" a system. Use Cases capture all the possible ways the user and system can interact that result in the user achieving the goal. In addition, the things that can go wrong along the way that prevent the user from achieving the goal are captured as Use Cases.

Traditional Waterfall teams could fail and wonder what went wrong by waiting too long to get actionable feedback from each other, the business, and the market. In contrast, when Scrum is managed correctly, things that could result in failure are visible and addressed quickly. Make work visible through the use of a work board with sticky notes that show all the work that needs to be done, what is being worked on, and what is actually done. It should be updated every day, and everyone should see it.

An "Epic" is a collection of related user stories that cannot be completed within a single iteration. Although the team decides how each task will be accomplished, the business value is what will be accomplished and is typically defined in the Epic.

The most important thing is for the Sprint to decide what you are going to do first. We believe Jeff Sutherland puts it best:

> *The key, though, is what you decide to do first. The questions you need to ask are: what are the items that have the biggest business impact, that are most important to the customer, that can make the most money, and are the easiest to do? You have to realize that there are a whole bunch of things on that list that you will never get to, but you want to get to the things that deliver the most value with the lowest risk first. With Scrum's incremental development and delivery, you want to begin with the things that will immediately create revenue, effectively "de-risking" the project. And you want to do that on the features level.*†

The Pareto Principle (also known as the 80/20 rule), when applied to software development, implies that 80 percent of the value is in 20 percent of the features. The 80 percent is considered wasted effort and a challenge for development teams to manage. In the days when the Waterfall development process was dominant, teams didn't know what that 20 percent was until product development was completed. One of the biggest challenges in Scrum is determining how you build that 20 percent first. However,

---

* Sutherland, J. (2014). *SCRUM: The Art of Doing Twice the Work in Half the Time.* p. 137.
† Ibid., p. 174.

it should be noted that security often doesn't fit the 80/20 rule; rather, 80% is likely to be exploited versus another 80% weight. We discuss this further, as well as how security gets into the "will do" list, later in the book. Unfortunately, there is often a misunderstanding that security is "nonfunctional." Later in this book, we explain how security fits into the critical 20% and how security must be viewed as bringing value to a product.

There are three roles in Scrum:

Team Member: Part of the team doing the work. Although it is management's responsibility to set the strategic goals, in Scrum it is the team members' responsibility to decide how they're going to do the work and how to reach those goals.

Scrum Master: The Scrum Master is responsible for the "how" to include how fast the team is going and how much faster they can get there, and is the team leader responsible for helping the team figure out how to do the work better. The Scrum Master is responsible to do the following:

- Act as a leader for the software development team
- Oversee design, implementation, QA, and validation of programming code and products
- Create project outlines and timelines and distribute responsibilities to team members
- Facilitate daily scrums, stand-ups, and meetings to monitor project progress and resolve any issues the team may be experiencing
- Shape team behavior through excellent management via the agile method
- Perform reviews on software development team members
- Remove project obstacles and develop solutions with the team
- Ensure milestones are reached and deadlines are met throughout the project lifecycle
- Build strong relationships with stakeholders, application users, and program owners
- Document progress and communicate to upper management and stakeholders
- Take responsibility for successful product delivery[*]

Product Owner: The Product Owner is responsible for the "how" defining what the work should be. They are the leader responsible for maximizing the value of the products created by a Scrum development team. This is a multifunctional role including being a business strategist, product designer, market analyst, customer liaison, and project manager. They are also the owner of Backlog, principally what is in and what order the items are in. It is important that the team has trust in the Product Owner to prioritize the Backlog correctly.

As the team's representative to the customer, it is ideal if the Product Owner has a stronger background in Product Marketing than engineering since they will be working with the customer a significant amount of the time. This will require time spent on obtaining input from the people who will use, perhaps purchase, or otherwise take ownership of the use of, the software. This includes customer's feedback to the team at every Sprint as to whether the product is delivering value and their feedback regarding what should be in the latest incremental release. This feedback will, of course, drive the content of the Backlog.

The Product Owner requires a different set of skills from the Scrum Master as they are accountable for translating the team's productivity into value. This requires that the Product Owner be not only a domain expert but also have enough knowledge of the market to know what will make a difference. A key requirement to their success is if they are empowered to make decisions. Without this

---

[*] Zip Recruiter. (2020). "Scrum Master Job Description Sample Template." Portions of this list have been reproduced from https://www.ziprecruiter.com/blog/scrum-master-job-description-sample-template/. This website uses data from GeoNames.org. The data is licensed under the Creative Commons Attribution 3.0 License.

empowerment, they will likely fail, regardless of how great a background they have for the role. They must balance this power in that, although they are responsible for the team's outcomes, they must let the team make their own decisions. This means that to be respected and accountable as the Backlog owner, they must be available to the team on a regular basis to communicate what needs to be done and why. This will typically require daily communication with the Scrum team. Discussing these working increments gives the Product Owner the ability to see how people react to it and how much value it does or does not create so that any needed change is implemented in the next Sprint. Innovation and adaptation are facilitated as a result of this constant feedback cycle. As a result, value can be measured.

One key value of Scrum is providing the team with the ability to manage change. This will depend on the team's ability to acknowledge uncertainty and that its current view of value task ranking is only relevant at that one particular moment due to the continuous change that is inherent to product development. The Product Owner acts as the gatekeeper, identifying and prioritizing constantly changing market needs and ranking these items per their value, thus avoiding the "everything is a top priority" syndrome and associated continuous scope creep, which is a death knell to the Scrum process.

If you limit the number of changes you will limit the cost associated with them. The increase in development costs resulting from unplanned and likely unnecessary disruptive pre- and post-release change requests has resulted in many companies in which software development exists to set up Change Control Boards. If managed correctly, Scrum will significantly reduce and possibly eliminate these types of change requests.

Later in the book, we describe how security is decided upon through the Scrum as well as how our fully integrated SDL works in in the process. The Product Owner and their relationship with customers includes understanding and then advocating for stakeholder security needs. We have, successfully, gotten this to take place, twice together, and it works!

1.6.1 DevOps and CI/CD

DevOps is more of an engineering cultural change than a process change as it prioritizes people over process and process over tooling. Building a culture of trust, collaboration, and continuous improvement enables the acceleration of the SDLC. As you may have seen, the Agile movement led a cultural shift from command and control to team empowerment. DevOps moves that shift forward and beyond coding to a holistic view of software development and operations.

DevOps also moves coding to Operations, breaking down the differences and silos between "creators" and "maintainers." There is a significant change in tech just as much, or alongside, the cultural shift. Ultimately, it causes development and security to work together to the benefit of all. This is accomplished by eliminating bottlenecks, increasing engineer empowerment and collaboration, reducing interpersonal communication issues, and resulting in increased team productivity. DevOps puts technology second to people and processes and focuses on engineers and how they can better work together to produce great software. A key element of DevOps success is gaining respect and shared understanding by unifying each department of the business and achieving a healthy working relationship and collaboration with your partners and stakeholders. This removes roadblocks and increases cooperation, resulting in improved speed of delivery for the development teams. Another positive result is that the business will see fewer customer complaints, faster delivery of new features, and improved reliability of existing services.

Emily Freeman provides an excellent and succinct overview of continuous integration, delivery, and deployment in her book "DevOps":

> **Continuous integration**: Teams that practice continuous integration (CI) merge code changes back into the master or development branch as often as possible. CI typically utilizes an

integration tool to validate the build and run automated tests against the new code. The process of CI allows developers on a team to work on the same area of the codebase while keeping changes minimal and avoiding massive merge conflicts.

Continuous delivery: Continuous delivery (CD) is a step up from CI in that developers treat every change to the code as deliverable. However, in contrast to continuous deployment, a release must be triggered by a human, and the change may not be immediately delivered to an end user. Instead, deployments are automated and developers can merge and deploy their code with a single button. By making small, frequently delivered iterations, the team ensures that they can easily troubleshoot changes.

Continuous deployment: Continuous deployment takes continuous delivery even one step further. Every change that passes the entire production release pipeline is deployed. That's right: The code is put directly into production. Continuous deployment eliminates human intervention from the deployment process and requires a thoroughly automated test suite.[*]

Continuous deployment also usually employs A/B, even A/B/C . . . testing so that changes which don't prove out, or for which there are multiple competing implementations, can be deployed, monitored, and then the results fed back to pivot to the very best implementation choice. As we shall see, security implementation can benefit greatly from an A/B/C testing strategy.

DevOps fills a gap that existed in Agile by addressing the conflict between the developer's technical skill sets and specialties and the skill sets represented by operations specialists. Eliminating the practice of developers handing off code to operations personnel to deploy and support helps in breaking down these pre-existing silos.

Some even suggest that automation should replace operations specialists. The term used for this is no operations (NoOps). Although some operational tasks can be done through automation, the operations specialists still have skill sets that typical developers do not have—for example, software infrastructure, which includes experience in system administration and hosting software. Ops specialists apply their specialized knowledge to the code that will operate software. Operations in DevOps apply these skills through code in the new pipeline tools. Rarely do Operations have to get into systems manually. Operations and core infrastructure knowledge is critical to the engineering teams success; therefore, we don't see the need for operations specialists going away; the rules of engagement, roles, and responsibilities just need to be modified and managed differently from in the past. It is important to note that operations people are coders, too: In DevOps, many roles, perhaps most, produce code of one kind or another.

NoOps focuses on automating everything related to operations to include the deployment processes, monitoring, and application management. Its goal is to eliminate the need for developers to ever have to interact with operations specialists, which is in direct opposition to DevOps, which promotes seamless interaction and working relationships between developers and operations. NoOps focuses on managing specific issues such as infrastructure and deployment pipelines through the use of automated software solutions, whereas DevOps provides a holistic approach that is focused on people, processes, and technology. Operations specialists are the most adept at automating daily required tasks as well as architecting systems with complex infrastructure components.

Another way to mitigate the divide between developers and operations specialists is for each side to provide high-level training to familiarize them with each other's disciplines. They won't be experts in each other's field but it will help the interaction between the two teams. For example, operations can teach the developers about infrastructure, and, conversely, the developers can teach the operations team

---

[*] Freeman, E. (2019). *DevOps for Dummies*. Hoboken (NJ): John Wiley & Sons, pp. 141–143.

source control and the critical aspects of specific languages that may affect elements of operations and associated architectures.

Software deployments are the most common action in software development that causes service disruptions and site outages. Before DevOps, the developers typically deployed new code to release new features in a siloed environment. This results from a disconnect between the development and operations team. In a non–DevOps environment, the developers will typically pass their code over to the operations team that does not understand the code's infrastructure requirements or how their code will run on the targeted infrastructure. There is an assumption that the operations team deploy the code and ensure that it runs perfectly. Since operations teams are rewarded by optimizing uptime, availability, and reliability, animosity between the two teams occurs when the code is poorly written because the operations team will be blamed for something they had no control over. James and Brook cannot count the number of times that siloed developers or security folk have made faulty assumptions about infrastructure that operations cannot ever meet. Readers can perhaps imagine the ensuing chaos that results as each side defends what they have built? Hence, the need for better communications and collaboration between the two teams, which is one of the key goals of DevOps.

1.6.2 Cloud Services

Some also believe that NoOps can be facilitated through cloud services. Cloud services can empower developers to take more ownership of their components by abstracting complex operations architecture in a way that makes that architecture easier for developers to work with, but it cannot completely replace all of the operations staff. It does, however, reduce the size of the operations staff needed and frees up the more experienced operations team members to work on more proactive solutions. When they are aligned and have common goals, the two teams will collaborate well together while functioning independently as the development and operations teams. As with many things in today's tech world, the biggest and hardest challenges are associated with human behavior, not technology. DevOps attempts to solve these problems.

1.6.3 Platform Services

Other than the hardware, cloud providers provide Platform as a Service (PaaS) environments that operations teams typically provide, such as development, quality assurance (QA), user-acceptance testing, staging, and production. The staging environment provides an area in which the developers can test their code without risking unintended effects from tests in a production environment and without worrying about the infrastructure it runs on before the final release of the product is ready. This, of course, accelerates the development, testing, and releasing of code. The infrastructure resources that the code will run on PaaS recreates infrastructure resources, such as servers, storage, databases, middleware, and network, as well as tools that enable the development team to operate as an operations function. The PaaS ability to automate, control, and tack and track code in a simulated and operational environment will ultimately and significantly change the structure and function of operations teams going forward. Operations specialists and their architect partners will still be needed. The question is whether they will be part of the PaaS or internal to the development team's company's organization. At a minimum, there should be operations specialists co-located with the team that runs the SDLC. Later in the book, we discuss how cloud providers take responsibility for the lower-stack security maintenance. We also describe the demarcation of the line of responsibility between what security the cloud provider provides and handles versus what the cloud consumer must handle.

Rather than involving operations after code release, in DevOps it is involved as part of the development process so that together developers and operations can properly plan and design infrastructure to support the code. This is reflected in the current DevOps literature when the phrase "moving left" is used for functions such as operations, security, and quality assurance. This refers to the standard graphic visualizing the DevOps cycle, as seen in Figure 1.20.*

1.6.4 Automation

For a team to be successful in automating any process, it must first understand the manual process for the issue they are trying to solve. If the manual process fails, you will only automate and possibly amplify this failure. You must also gauge whether automation is appropriate and the most cost-effective and efficient way to address the issue. Ensuring that the process is continuous and that the development process is not slowed down is more than trying to use tools just for the sake of using tools. Efficiency is imperative for successful software development and, in particular, when it comes to DevOps and CI/CD.

One critical element of DevOps and CI/CD that is distinctly different from the Waterfall approach for software development is the continuous use of an automated test suite throughout the entire development process. Continuous testing is more well known in CI/CD than it is in DevOps.† This is addressed in greater detail later in this chapter.

1.6.5 General Testing and Quality Assurance

Due to the complexity and continuous changes that DevOps and continuous integration face in current and future working environments, automating testing is mandatory, and manual testing will be rare. Humans and budgets just can't absorb the complexity and workloads required in current and future working environments. As with the operations teams, automation and cloud services will change how QA teams are used and where they are positioned in the organization. In traditional organizations, QA teams owned the testing environment and conducted code reviews after the development team had turned in their pre-release code to be tested in the QA testing environment. In today's DevOps environment, many QA teams no longer own the testing environment, and they are concerned that automation will replace their function. If the QA function wants to survive, they must transition from manual testing to becoming experts in automated testing and continuous integration. They must be more like software development engineers and write automated tests and serve as experts in testing practices, procedures, and approaches. These tests include performance and stability testing as well as tests for load and security. Load tests will simulate a large number of users or data that will stress the system, and security tests will eliminate vulnerabilities or, at least, reduce potential impact to survivable levels in each release.

Continuous testing starts in the development stage and continues throughout the development process, shorten your cycles, and enable the development teams to rapidly iterate. An organization just starting to develop their DevOps capabilities should not underestimate the amount of work required to build a robust testing program, associated security gates, and pipelines. They should consult with others who have been successful in similar environments before and, then, make a realistic plan to improve and adapt.

In DevOps, quality and security testing is everybody's job—most importantly, that of the developers. Developing good code includes the building in of quality and security.

---

* We address the implicit linearity of "shift left" thinking later as we discuss SDL activity triggers and timing.
† Many DevOps implementations, but not all, make use of CI/CD. Although not necessarily the same and certainly not equivalent, modern software development can pick and choose what will be most effective for the software that is to be built.

1.6.6 Security Testing

Security tests cover network security and system security as well as client-side and server-side application security. These tests include both those that occur in QA as well as the development teams as part of the SDL. Software patches (updates) are used to fix security issues discovered post-release. Minor changes typically contain new features, whereas major updates may not be backward compatible and include code that can break previous versions. Either way, it is imperative that these issues are discovered and mitigated to the maximum extent possible during the pre-release development process. If a software product is released and found to be untested and/or full of security issues, this can have a serious and likely permanent impact on your reputation as well as consequences for security or privacy noncompliance. If a product or application security team member is not in the "go/no go" product-release meeting and not empowered to contribute to a release decision, your organization has failed to take security seriously and is just a "paper tiger." A more detailed overview of security testing within the SDLC and SDL follows later in the book.

1.6.7 DevSecOps

DevSecOps is about everyone in the SDLC being responsible for security, with the goal of bringing operations and development functions together with security functions by embedding security in every part of the development process. This minimizes vulnerabilities and brings security closer to business objectives, and it includes the automation of core security tasks by embedding security controls and processes early in the DevOps workflow. Automation also reduces the need for security architects to manually configure security consoles.

Security's traditional reputation of bolting security in at the end of the process and being a road block to innovation and on-time delivery has become even more challenging to overcome with the advent of DevOps and CI/CD. Developers don't like that their code is insecure and needs to be fixed only after they've completed it. It's important to assess and respond to threats before they become security incidents. That is why there is a lot of talk about "shifting security left,"* which ensures that security is built into the DevOps development lifecycle early and not at the end. Security in DevOps should be part of the process—that is, DevSecOps—and arguably not a separate term, to signify that security is truly built-in.

Integrating security into DevOps to deliver DevSecOps requires new mindsets, processes, and tools. To make security truly everybody's responsibility will require that this be tied to your governance of risk security policies, by building those policies into your DevOps process. One of the goals of this book and the generic SDL is to assist in the success of DevSecOps by reducing or even eliminating friction between security tasks and development. Ultimately, the result of combining development, security, and operations teams will result in shortening feedback loops, reducing incidents, and improving security through shared responsibility. To discover and mitigate security threats at every point in the development life cycle, a member (or members) of the security team should be given a seat at the table at each stage of the DevOps process.

1.6.8 Education

Ongoing education is another key component of the process for teams that produce great software. This is particularly important for DevOps, where interdisciplinary knowledge about software, tools,

---

* We will comment on the use of "shift left" as a conceptual paradigm later in the book.

hardware, networks, and other technology and trends is key for success. In addition to developing code, your developers should be a knowledge resource that, if nurtured, can provide years of valuable advice and guidance to both your engineering team and the company they work for. Training can include outside reading, discussions with other developers, going to conferences, and taking courses.

However, a single break in focus can sideline a developer for hours. The challenge as an engineering manager is the balancing act of not unnecessarily taking away your team members' time needed for developing software, which requires intense focus work, while ensuring that they continue their education at the appropriate time. It is also important to support your developers and block off part of the budget for continuing education.

More about education and awareness follows later in this book.

1.6.9 Architects and Principal Engineers

It is important to give developers a path to promotion while retaining great talent. Unfortunately, there are only two paths for promotion for developers within an engineering organization—management or engineer. In many cases, this results in engineers who want a raise or a new title having no choice but to pursue a management position. There are exceptions to this, but this typically is a disaster for engineers without the people, communications, business, and other skills that are required to be a successful manager. Even worse, in many of these cases, they find themselves in a job they really don't want, which will ultimately create performance issues as well as diminish the morale of the team working for them.

The career path for development engineers should lead toward becoming an Architect or Principal Engineer, at the senior ranks of the organization, after they reach the highest grade available in the development team. Architects and Principle Engineers influence how the system is structured, which features are prioritized, and how to standardize code. They ensure reusability as well as how the engineering team will tackle the work ahead of them. These positions require knowledge in many areas, along with the experience to know what works and what doesn't work. Most important to development teams, they bring their critical, extensive experience to architectural and code reviews. In addition, they are able to interact with the operations specialists and others to assess issues before the code is integrated into the larger codebase as well as what may occur in the operational environments in which the software is to be deployed. All will benefit from this shared knowledge. We offer both roles—Architect and Principal Engineer—as distinct. Architects must have some aptitude for abstraction and structure and have a fairly high tolerance for interaction with others, sometimes involving conflict. But we also need a growth path for those who prefer to stick to technology, and who may have a lower tolerance for interaction. Those with a strong engineering focus must have a way to grow, and a promotion path, or they will either lose motivation or, worse, they will leave. Technical security leader roles may have "security" added to their title for clarification: "Lead Security Architect" and "Principle Security Engineer." We will detail these security leader roles in Chapter 2.

1.6.10 Pulling It All Together Using Visual Analogies

1.6.10.1 Tetris Analogy for Agile, Scrum, and CI/CD

The Agile SDLC model is a combination of iterative and incremental process models that focus on process adaptability and customer satisfaction by the rapid delivery of a working software product. Agile methods break the product into small incremental builds. These builds are provided in iterations. Each iteration typically lasts from about one to three weeks. Every iteration involves cross-functional teams working simultaneously on various areas, such as:

- Planning
- Requirements Analysis
- Design
- Coding
- Unit Testing
- Acceptance Testing
- Security

At the end of the iteration, a working product is displayed to the customer and important stakeholders.

The first analogy is the use of the timeless game of Tetris™ as a visual example of the operational interactions that take place when using Agile, Scrum, and CI/CD development practices. First, a description of the electronic Tetris board and how it is played:

> The game is played on a board that has 20 rows and 10 columns. The object of Tetris is to last as long as possible before the screen fills up with tetrominoes (Figure 1.18). To do this, you must assemble the tetrominoes to form one or more rows of blocks that span the entire playing field, called a line clear. **When you do so, the row will disappear, causing the ones above it to settle.**

First, each of the tetrominoes shown in Figure 1.15 are assigned a cross-functional team name, as depicted in Figure 1.16:

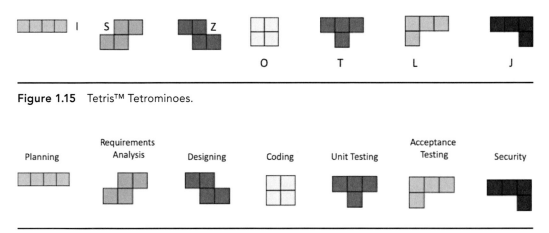

Figure 1.15   Tetris™ Tetrominoes.

Figure 1.16   Tetrominos Assigned Cross-Functional Team Names.

Next, the tetrominoes are used to show the iterations that occur in the Sprints within the Scrum development process (Figure 1.17).

Pulling it all together by looking through Figures 1.15–1.18, you should see the following:

- Most of the major decision making is made up front to include all components (analogous to Agile/Scrum planning and design sessions). It should be noted that some Scrum teams prefer to design as work items during Sprints. Not "all" or "most" design is necessarily done before a cycle of Sprints. It depends, and sometimes is up to the team.
- Implementing each component/requirement for each Sprint is maximized for speed and changed rapidly, when needed, to optimize the necessary fit to complete each/multiple lines (analogous to Agile SDLC/Scrum/Sprints and CI/CD).

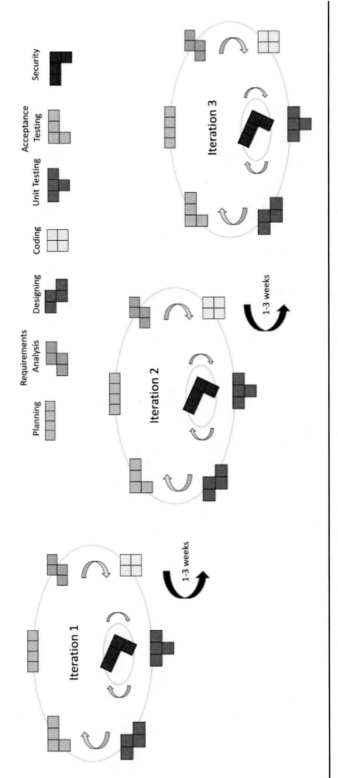

Figure 1.17 Tetrominoes in Sprint Iterations within the Scrum Development Process.

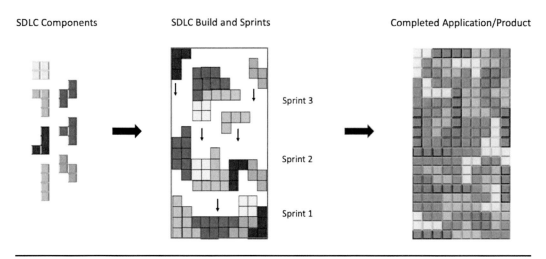

SDLC Components   SDLC Build and Sprints   Completed Application/Product

Sprint 3

Sprint 2

Sprint 1

Figure 1.18 Tetris™ as a Visual Analogy of the Complete Agile, Scrum, and CI/CD Development Process.

- Each completed row disappears and total focus is on remaining lines (analogous to Sprints and CI/CD).
- Note security (blue tetronimo) is cycled through each area/step of the development iteration which provides the ability to build security in at agile speeds.
- The overall Tetris analogy is analogous to CI/CD.

1.6.10.2 Nesting Doll Analogy for Solution Development

Solutions in software development usually comprise a system of products that interact with each other to solve a specific customer business problem. Products and product platforms are building blocks of the solution. This may also require a combination of hardware, software, and services. A suite of products designed to work together and are tested many times give the customers confidence that their business outcomes will be achieved. This will require a common understanding that an SDLC and SDL are to be used across all the products and platforms to be used as part of this solution. This will also

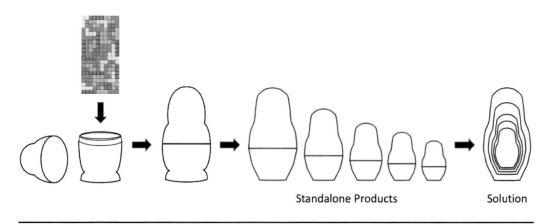

Standalone Products   Solution

Figure 1.19 Nesting Doll Analogy Visual for Product Solutions.

require seasoned architects and/or principal engineers with multidisciplinary experience in software, hardware, networks, and infrastructures to be properly assessed for all of the contingencies that exist in these environments.

In the nesting doll analogy (Figure 1.19), think of each nesting shell as a secured application or product that can be secured individually or as a collective nest of dolls forming a solution as part of an integrated approach to security. Each application or product will require a completed "full or partial SDLC" (Agile/Scrum/Sprints) that can be stand-alone or nested together as a solution.

1.6.10.3 DevOps Operations "Moving Down" Rather Than Moving Left Kettlebell Analogy

As mentioned earlier in this chapter, the phrase "moving left" is used in regard to teams such as operations, security, and QA. This idea simply refers to moving the work completed by these teams leftward in the development pipeline, or sooner in the process enhanced by automation, cloud, and, specifically, PaaS services. This means that the services shown in the typical figure eight graphic for the DevOps process shown on the left side of Figure 1.20 are to be moved to the left. Although not all components of these functions will move to the left, a significant amount will be provided by automation and cloud services. Essentially, the center of mass for the figure eight diagram will move to the left.

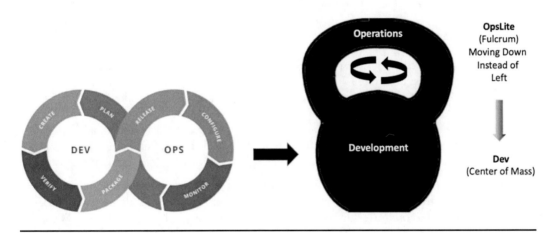

Figure 1.20   Traditional DevOps Graphic versus the Kettlebell.

Rather than using the figure eight diagram, we like to use the kettlebell analogy (Figures 1.20 and 1.21). "With a thick handle and off-set center of mass, the design of the kettlebell is unique and carries with it unique benefits and also some challenges. Traditional dumbbells and barbells tend to center the weight with your hand, but a kettlebell's center of mass is about six to eight inches from the handle, and that changes depending on what exercise you are performing."* Essentially, with the advent of DevOps, the center of mass or "heavy lifting" will occur on the development side of the house. Therefore, we like the analogy of a kettlebell rather than the figure eight diagram.

---

* Jones, B. (2020). "Understanding Center of Mass in Kettlebell Training." Retrieved from https://www.strong first.com/understanding-the-center-of-mass-in-kettlebell-training/

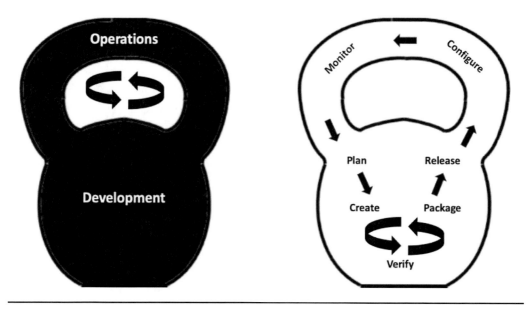

Figure 1.21   Kettlebell Visual Analogy for DevOps.

1.6.11 DevOps Best Practices

There are a lot of sources that list best practices for DevOps. We found the most succinct and most relevant to our discussion to be those that Cesar Abeid from LiquidPlanner® has identified in his online paper titled "8 Best Practices for Managing DevOps Projects," seven of which follow:

Minimum viable product: A minimum viable product focuses on high return and lost risk projects, and can be measured and improved upon with each iteration. Putting this into action is a way to create fast, small products that can be deployed quickly and measured for feedback

Use the right tools: Because DevOps is all about collaboration, communication, the removal of silos and unnecessary overhead, it's extremely important to use tools that will facilitate these principles. Success in DevOps is typically very much connected to the tools used. When considering tools for your DevOps project, look for solutions that will simplify aspects of configuration management, application deployment, monitoring, and version control.

Eliminate silos: DevOps has to do with flow and integration, which means development and operations move quickly and in a horizontal manner. Silos, on the other hand, are vertical and walled in.

Reduce handoffs: DevOps projects, on the other hand, see projects as a continuous flow from beginning to end. By minimizing handoffs, discrete steps tend to disappear, facilitating a DevOps culture.

Create real-time project visibility: In order to maximize flow and integration, everyone who's part of a DevOps system needs to know where the project stands. Creating real-time project visibility can be done by using the right tools and encouraging all involved to engage in a centralized way.

Reduce overhead: Work and resources saved from processing overhead can be redirected to increase productivity and collaboration.

Manage change collaboratively: Effective change management can be a struggle for any project. Having a systematic way to approach change management is critical.[*]

1.6.12 Optimizing Your Team Size

In 1975, Fred Brooks published a book titled *The Mythical Man-Month* in which he coined the phrase "adding manpower to a late software project makes it later," also known as "Brooks Law."[†] Being late is unacceptable and costly when it comes to software development.

Speed and predictable software delivery times are absolutely imperative to be competitive. This requires the right process to optimize the time and quality of delivery for a software product, discussed earlier in this chapter, as well as an optimized team size. Some key concepts to consider in optimizing your team size are below:

Groups made up of three to seven people required about 25 percent of the effort of groups of nine to twenty to get the same amount of work done. This result recurred over hundreds and hundreds of projects. That very large groups do less seems to be an ironclad rule of human nature.[‡]

In 2001, Nelson Cowan of the University of Missouri wondered whether that magic rule of seven was really true and conducted a wide survey of all the new research on the topic. It turns out that the number of items one can retain in short-term memory isn't seven. It's four.[§]

So, there's a hardwired limit to what our brain can hold at any one time. Which leads us back to Brooks. When he tried to figure out why adding more people to a project made it take longer, he discovered two reasons. The first is the time it takes to bring people up to speed. As you'd expect, bringing a new person up to speed slows down everyone else. The second reason has to do not only with how we think but, quite literally, with what our brains are capable of thinking. The number of communication channels increases dramatically with the number of people, and our brains just can't handle it. If you want to calculate the impact of group size, you take the number of people on a team, multiply by "that number minus one," and divide by two. Communication channels = n (n − 1) / 2. So, for example, if you have five people, you have ten channels. Six people, fifteen channels. Seven, twenty-one. Eight, twenty-eight. Nine, thirty-six. Ten, forty-five. Our brains simply can't keep up with that many people at once. We don't know what everyone is doing. And we slow down as we try to figure it out.[¶]

As you can see from the above, optimizing size matters, especially when it comes to the complex and dynamic nature of software development. Team size optimization has become even more important since the advent of Agile, Scrum, DevOps, and CI/CD and their influence on software development. Typically, seven team members are ideal, plus or minus two, depending on the complexity and any additional special skills needed for the project. The team must have every skill needed to complete a project as well as the freedom and autonomy to make decisions on how they take action and improvise.

---

[*] Abeid, C. (2020). "8 Best Practices for Managing DevOps Projects." Retrieved from https://www.liquidplanner.com/blog/8-best-practices-for-managing-devops-projects/

[†] Brooks, F. (1995 [1975]). *The Mythical Man-Month. Essays on Software Engineering.* New York (NY): Addison-Wesley Professional.

[‡] Sutherland, J. (2014). *SCRUM: The Art of Doing Twice the Work in Half the Time.* p. 59.

[§] Cowan, N. (2001). "The Magical Number 4 in Short-Term Memory: A Reconsideration of Mental Storage Capacity." *Behavioral and Brain Sciences,* vol. 24, pp. 87–185.

[¶] Sutherland, J. (2014). *SCRUM: The Art of Doing Twice the Work in Half the Time.* p. 60.

1.7 Chapter Summary

Hopefully, we have set the stage for a generic security development lifecycle (SDL). In this chapter, we've laid our foundation: Software development has shifted paradigms dramatically. Agile, CI/CD, DevOps, and cloud use have each contributed to the shift—changing culture, process, and technology. Security and, especially, software security practices haven't entirely kept pace with the changes, unfortunately.

We reviewed the current background of constant attack, with the repeated major compromises with which our digital lives exist. Software weaknesses are what attackers leverage; this will be obvious to most readers. One of our most important protective measures will be to reduce weaknesses to survivable levels—the main goal of an SDL. We presented five software security principles against which to measure the success of an SDL and which we have used to align and guide software security practices.

We've outlined the main goals of a generic SDL, and why there continue to be problems with SDLs that are tightly coupled to a software development life cycle (SDLC) and which assume SDLC linearity; a linear, waterfall SDLC has become the less-common case. Agile, continuous practices, and DevOps exacerbate the problems of a linear SDL. The way forward, as we discovered in our SDL research at Intel, is to eliminate SDLC dependencies in the SDL so that it will become workable for all SDLC timings and orderings. This becomes particularly true, we hope you'll agree, after our review of Agile/Scrum practices.

The authors, among other practitioners, have now implemented, led, lobbied, and stumped for a developer-centric view of software security—we might call it, "the SDLC security approach." We presented to you the Developer-centric Security Manifesto as a starting point. Empowering developers to own security tasks, while at the same time leveraging skilled security practitioners to guide and support that ownership, will be the most effective and scalable approach. We have tasted the sweet results from this approach in our programs; we have seen the reductions in released issues that such an approach delivers. A key tenet of an SDLC approach to software security is an SDL that enables developers to identify and build security as a natural, primary task of building software. To accomplish integral security, the SDL must also reduce friction against the execution of the SDL's tasks.

But the SDL is not the only ingredient for success. Ultimately, software security, as we have continued to note, is a people problem. Building and running a successful program will take investment, time, energy, and deft management and organization skills. Thus, the management of software security comprises a key element of this book.

Chapter 2

Software Development Security Management in an Agile World

2.1 Introduction

There's a widespread perception that introducing security will slow or derail the development process that, in some cases, is well deserved. Effective DevOps security demands cross-functional collaboration and buy-in to ensure that security considerations are integrated into the entire product development lifecycle (product design, development, delivery, operations, support, etc.). If you have aligned security with DevOps correctly, you will have enabled efficient product releases while avoiding costly recalls or fixes after code/products are released. For this to succeed, everyone needs to take ownership of adhering to security best practices within their roles.[*]

This chapter focuses on pragmatic approaches for software development security management in an Agile world that will enhance scalability, efficiencies, and cost savings for product security programs that are relevant for large, medium, or small size companies or organizations. This chapter's primary focus is on managing security within a DevOps environment; it will address Agile, Scrum, and Continuous Integration and Continuous Delivery (CI/CD), which are components that the DevOps philosophy and model cover, from a management perspective. This is an overview of how security should be managed in current and mature DevOps organizations. Later in the book, we will address the same areas covered in this chapter in relation to the new model that we are proposing.

Most importantly, and based on our experiences and those of our peers, the biggest challenge we face in DevOps, software development, and security are human, not technical, issues. Automated tools, libraries, and closed services can make things much faster and more efficient than previously, but the social dynamics and organization management of humans on engineering teams utilizing DevOps are a significant issue that needs to be addressed. One of the main goals of DevOps is to minimize the friction between humans so that everyone can focus on their work.

---

[*] Beyond Trust (2020). "DevOps Security Best Practices." Retrieved from https://www.beyondtrust.com/blog /entry/devops-security-best-practices

2.2 Building and Managing the DevOps Software Security Organization

2.2.1 Use of the Term DevSecOps

Agile[*] is a mindset encompassing values that promote a cultural shift in the organization and its departmental functions, project management practices, and product development. Both Agile and security within a DevOps environment share similar goals of eliminating silos, promoting collaboration and teamwork, and providing better, faster delivery. Security in an DevOps environment incorporates interdependent practices, such as CI/CD, which promote frequent code check-in, version control, test automation, and continuous low-risk releases and feedback, often with the aid of automated tools. Improving the efficiency of operations; reducing unnecessary revisions, product delivery, and cycle times; and quality improvements due to monitoring and automation result in business benefits that include cost savings and improved productivity.

The term "DevSecOps" is used to identify an organization's security team that is integrated into the traditional DevOps organization. When discussing DevSecOps, many authors assume that security isn't already built into the SDLC process; security review and testing is happening at the end of a development cycle bolted in at the end when the code is already written, compiled, and ready for production; and that static application security testing (SAST) and dynamic application security testing (DAST) or other automated security and management tools haven't been used. DevSecOps is a management approach that connects security and operations teams, similar to how DevOps unifies software developers and operations professionals. The goal behind DevSecOps is to ensure that security and operations teams share accountability, processes, tools, and information to make sure that the organization does not have to sacrifice security for higher uptime and better performance. Arguably, and based on our experience, many mature software development organizations have been doing this for years. Although some have not built security in as described in the book *Core Security: Security at the Source*[†] (in 2014), the real challenge in DevOps is both the speed of delivery required and the collaboration between traditionally separate teams' developers, production staff, and security professionals who are accustomed to working separately, with their own tools and information sources. This, of course, is what this book is about—that is, enhancing the ability for organizations to build security in at Agile and DevOps speed. Another advantage of DevOps, is that it helps to finally facilitate the concept of "everyone is responsible for security." This is something that leaders in security have been espousing for years, but, in reality, organizations have not bought into. Building the right holistic security organization, not necessarily a separate DevSecOps team that could become another silo counterintuitive to the DevOps approach, is critical to the DevOps methodology. Developing the right security organization also has the added business advantage of producing better collaboration between teams, faster time to market, improved overall productivity, and greater customer satisfaction.

2.2.2 Product Security Organizational Structure

2.2.2.1 The Right Organizational Location

Although there have been great advances in software security technology, processes, and methodologies over the last few years, we believe that people are still the most important element of a successful

---

[*]   Please see the description of Agile and its Manifesto in Chapter 1.

[†]   Ransome, J. and Misra, A. (2014). *Core Software Security: Security at the Source*. Boca Raton (FL): CRC Press/ Taylor & Francis Group.

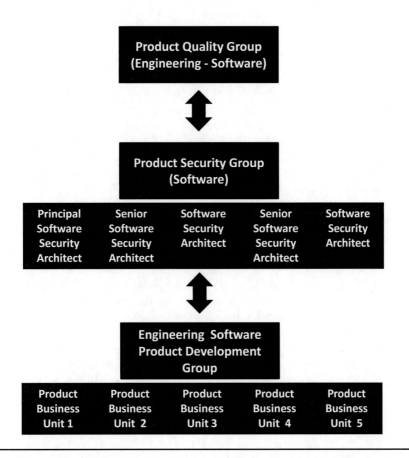

Figure 2.1   The Right Organizational Location. (*Source:* Reproduced from Ransome, J. and Misra, A. [2014]. *Core Software Security: Security at the Source.* Boca Raton [FL]: CRC Press/Taylor & Francis Group, p. 228, with permission.)

software security program that includes the implementation and management of the activities and best practices. In order to facilitate the best use of the people responsible for software security, they must be part of the right organization (see Figure 2.1). Having been in seven Chief Security Officer (CSO) and Chief Information Security Officer (CISO) roles, James Ransome, one of the coauthors of this book, has had software security reporting to him in several of his roles as CSO and CISO and has been in two solely focused product security executive roles over the last 23 years. Based on both his experience and communication with his peers in the industry, it is clear that the software security function ideally should fall within the engineering (software development) function and, in particular, within the quality function. The general consensus is that the application security role typically reports to the centralized information security role CSO/CISO position and should not be confused with the software security function. Typically, those who are in an application security role within an IT security organization are great at running tools but do not have the software development background necessary to fully interpret the results. To make this point clear, it is important to differentiate between software and application security. Perhaps the best way to clarify this distinction is with a quote from Gary McGraw:

> *Software security is about building secure software: designing software to be secure; making sure that software is secure; and educating software developers, architects, and users about how to build security in.*

> *On the other hand, application security is about protecting software and the systems that software runs in a post facto way, only after development is complete.*[*]

Another advantage of having the software security experts reporting to the engineering organization is that they are empowered by the fact that they are part of the same organization; are directly responsible for implementing the SDL policies and procedures and associated tools; and understand software development, its architecture, and the level of effort required to fix the same.

Our suggestion, of course, presumes that engineering (R&D) and IT are separate organizations, each at least fielding software, and probably each including software development as described in this book. Your organization may differ. For instance, where all software development takes place in IT (engineering does not exist or does not produce software), software security is best organized as a separate, empowered team within the IT software development function. Colocation is our intent. If all software is developed in an engineering department or group, then our suggestions may be taken, as described above.

As we've noted, software security must be approached holistically and should also be closely coupled to, organized with, and in tight collaboration with developers. Software security must not end up separated into some other function. Particularly and importantly, software security must not become (or start) isolated from development, as might occur if it is kept as a branch of a traditional security function. Doing so risks that developers will perceive software security as pretty much an irrelevant function that is out of touch with development realities and that they won't really understand how software and systems work, or the security efforts and solutions that development has already built. If this is your current situation, your software security team will have significant cultural work to do to dig itself out of this hole. We, the authors, have lived through this exact circumstance. It took a lot of work and quite a long time (time that we really couldn't afford, given the issues at play in that organization and its set of products) to gain development's trust and to prove our value to them so that we could establish the effective, close collaboration that is necessary. Which is why we don't recommend this, if it can be avoided.

The authors believe that software security should be a group of its own within engineering/software development and should work very closely with the central security group; it may even have a "dotted-line" relationship to the CSO/CISO.

2.2.2.2 The Right People

The right security team members are required to make any SDL model or DevOps organization a success—in particular, the one described in this book. They should include a minimum of one principal software security architect, a mix of senior and general software security architects, and, ideally, one software security architect representing each product business unit in the engineering software product development group. This relationship is represented in Figure 2.2. This talent pool provides the ability to scale, in that there will be one software security champion (SSC) per Tier 1 software product within each engineering software product development group. Another element of the talent is the software security evangelists (SSEs) for organizations that are large enough to have extra candidates for the SSC role, who can be candidates for SSEs until there is a slot for them as an SSC. SSEs have two roles—as an SSC in training and as an evangelist for the overall software product security program, promulgating and enforcing policy, and evangelizing the overall SDL process.

---

[*]   McGraw, G. (2006). *Software Security: Building Security In*. Boston (MA): Addison Wesley/Pearson Education, p. 20.

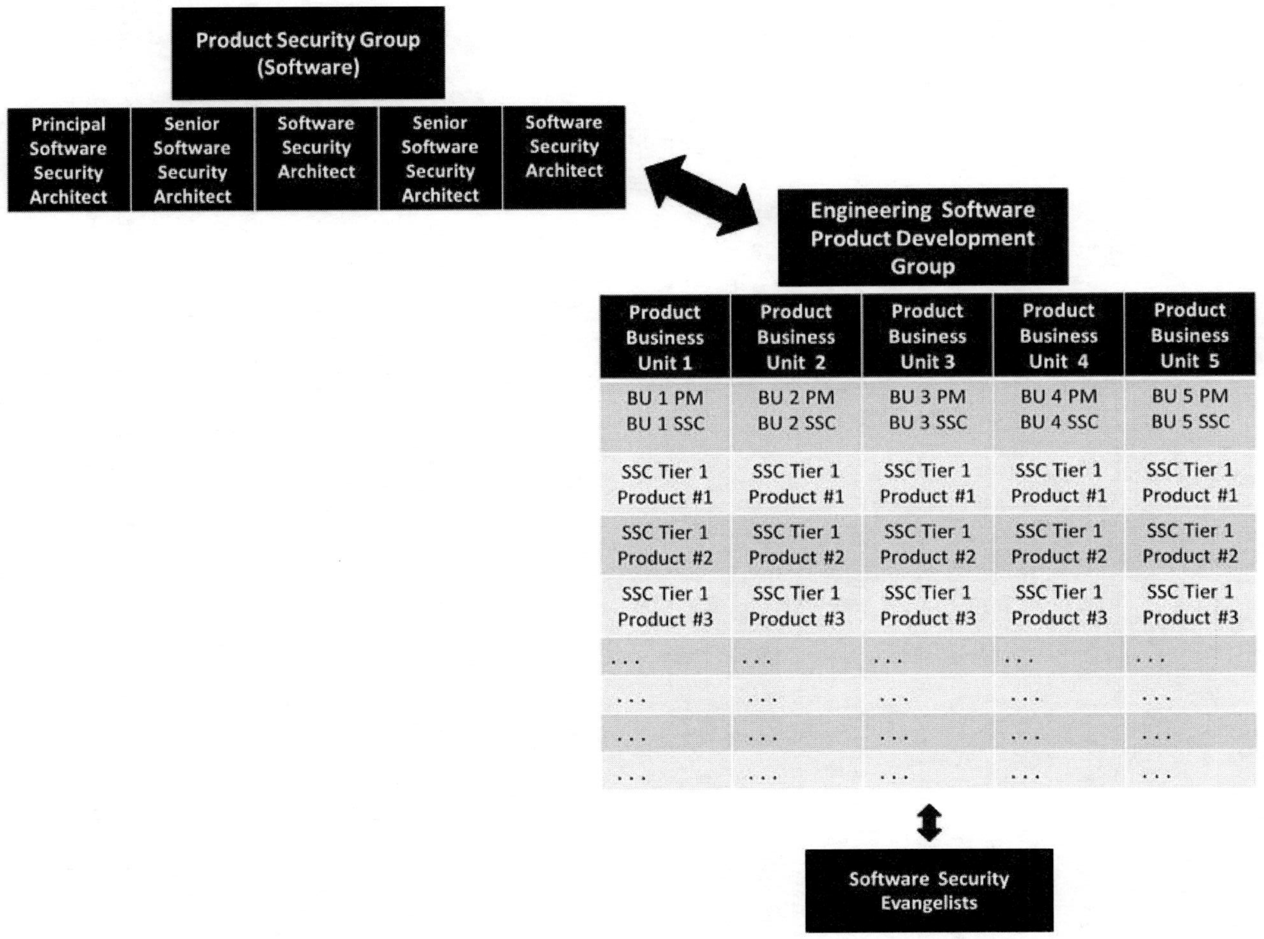

Product Security Group (Software)

Principal Software Security Architect	Senior Software Security Architect	Software Security Architect	Senior Software Security Architect	Software Security Architect

Engineering Software Product Development Group

Product Business Unit 1	Product Business Unit 2	Product Business Unit 3	Product Business Unit 4	Product Business Unit 5
BU 1 PM BU 1 SSC	BU 2 PM BU 2 SSC	BU 3 PM BU 3 SSC	BU 4 PM BU 4 SSC	BU 5 PM BU 5 SSC
SSC Tier 1 Product #1	SSC Tier 1 Product #1	SSC Tier 1 Product #1	SSC Tier 1 Product #1	SSC Tier 1 Product #1
SSC Tier 1 Product #2	SSC Tier 1 Product #2	SSC Tier 1 Product #2	SSC Tier 1 Product #2	SSC Tier 1 Product #2
SSC Tier 1 Product #3	SSC Tier 1 Product #3	SSC Tier 1 Product #3	SSC Tier 1 Product #3	SSC Tier 1 Product #3
...	...	...	...	...
...	...	...	...	...
...	...	...	...	...
...	...	...	...	...

Software Security Evangelists

Figure 2.2 The Right People. (*Source:* Reproduced from Ransome, J. and Misra, A. [2014]. *Core Software Security: Security at the Source.* Boca Raton [FL]: CRC Press/Taylor & Francis Group, p. 230, with permission.)

2.2.2.3 The Right Talent

Even though security practices are common to both software product and application security such as penetration testing, source code scanning, security-oriented testing, and security education, there is no substitute for integrating security into the software development lifecycle. The human element of the process is key to the success of any security development process and requires very seasoned software security architects and engineers to be successful. Threat modeling, applying principles such as *least privilege* and *defense in depth* are perhaps the least understood, important, and necessary elements of the software development lifecycle and require human expertise and not tools to be accomplished. One must also gather the real security requirements for a system and consider compliance, safety issues, contractual requirements, what data the application will process, and business risk. Training is another critical element of the SDL that requires the human element. Training helps to reduce the cost of security, and an effective training program will motivate your development team to produce more secure software with fewer problems with more efficiency and cost effectiveness. It should be emphasized that no point solutions will provide a single solution for software security; rather, a holistic defense-in-depth approach is required, including a blend of people, process, and technology with a heavy emphasis on people. Although tools can parse through large quantities of code rapidly, faster than a human could, they are no replacement for humans. For the foreseeable future, software security will still be considered an art, but the art can be augmented through process and technology, and, contrary to myths perpetrated by some practitioners, the art can be taught through proper mentorship by seasoned software security architects and engineers. These are the team members who have the experience and can think like an adversary throughout the development process, which is a key element for the success of any SDL. Some authors differentiate between secure-coding best practices and secure-design principles; we will address both in the software security best practices presented in this book and leverage the experience of the seasoned architects and engineers identified above to accomplish this. The two key positions to make your organization secure are the software security architect and software security champions.

2.2.2.3.1 Software Security Architects

Qualified senior software security architects will either make or break your software security program. On the people front, the most critical element of an effective software security program is a cadre of Senior Level 3 and 4 software security architects. These are individuals who have 5 to 10 years of development/coding experience before they enter the security field and who are also experienced in the areas of software, hardware, networking, and cloud/SaaS architectural design.

These are not the typical folks in IT security who run tools; they are experienced architects who understand development and system architecture as well as they understand security. In addition, they must also have great political and people skills. These are the folks who are going to touch every element of the SDLC and SDL; they should be part of the sign-off process at each stage of the SDLC process, and they must be involved from pre-commit to post-release. Your senior software/application security architects are critical to handle product security escalations, train development team members, provide internal/external customer responses, and solve complex software/applications issues in SaaS and cloud environments.

Distinguishing between architectural drivers and other requirements is not simple, as it requires a complete understanding of the solution objectives. Software security architecture is an interactive process that involves the assessment of the business value of system requirements and identifying the requirements that are most critical to the success of a system. These include the functional requirements, the constraints, and the behavioral properties of the solution, all of which must be classified and specified. These critical requirements are called *architectural drivers,* because they shape the design of the system.[*]

The security architect must figure out how, at the architectural level, necessary security technologies will be integrated into the overall system. In the cloud or SaaS environment, this includes network security requirements, such as firewalls, virtual private networks, etc. Architects explicitly document trust assumptions in each part of the system, usually by drawing trust boundaries (e.g., network traffic from outside the firewall is untrusted, but local traffic is trusted). Of course, these boundaries must be reflected in the business requirements. For instance, high-security applications should not be willing to trust any unencrypted, shared network media. Security requirements should come from the user. A typical job description for a seasoned software security architect might be as follows:

> *The Software Security Architect is responsible for providing architectural and technical guidance to product security across all of Company X. The Architect will design, plan, and implement secure coding practices and security testing methodology; ensure that practices meet software certification processes; drive the security testing of the products; test and evaluate security-related tools; and manage third-party vendors to meet these responsibilities.*

Specific roles and responsibilities of the software security architect should include the following:

- Drive overall software security architecture.
- Provide technical leadership in the comprehensive planning, development, and execution of Company X software security efforts.
- Work closely with product and engineering development teams to ensure that products meet or exceed customer security and certification requirements. This includes ensuring that the security architecture is well documented and communicated.
- Provide planning and input into the software engineering and product development process related to security while also being sensitive to the constraints and needs of the business.
- Monitor security technology trends and requirements, such as emerging standards, for new technology opportunities.
- Develop and execute security plans. This may include managing joint development with third-party vendors and providing guidance (with other departments) to the engineering and testing practices.
- Ensure and create, as needed, security policies, processes, practices, and operations to ensure reproducible development and high quality, while keeping costs under control.
- Engage in hands-on, in-depth analysis, review, and design of the software, including technical review and analysis of source code with a security perspective. This will include reviews of in-house developed code, as well as review of technologies provided by third-party vendors.
- Provide primary technical role in the security certifications process, including preparing extensive documentation and working with third-party evaluations.
- Provide training to staff, contractors, development, and quality assurance teams, as well as product/software security champions related to product security.
- Guide Company X software development teams through the Company X Security Development Lifecycle (SDL) for its SDLC by participating in design reviews, threat modeling, and in-depth security penetration testing of code and systems. These responsibilities extend to providing input on application design, secure coding practices, log forensics, log design, and application code security.

---

[*] Please see our Software Security Design Principles in Chapter 1 (Section 1.4) on the attributes and behaviors "secure" software must exhibit and against which the effectiveness of the SDL can be measured.

The cadre of software security architects will be critical in overseeing and training the efforts of software security champions who should be identified through a cross–business unit/software security education and awareness program. The architects will also spot and assess candidates for software security champions, as they are involved in various software products SDLs from concept commit to post-release.

2.2.2.3.2 Software Security Champions

Funding for corporate security departments—whether IT, physical, or software—is not likely to get any better in the foreseeable future, which means that you will have to be very judicious with your resources if you plan to be successful. As we implied earlier, seasoned software security architects are few and far between, and, at best, you will not likely be able to find and afford more than a handful in today's market. As you look at the SDL model used in this book or others referenced earlier in Chapter 1, you may be asking yourself how you can ever scale to this task given the resources that security software and the development teams working with them will have. The answer is that if you manage the software security team or have that function working for you, you will use the recruitment and leverage of software security champions (SSCs) to manage this daunting task. Candidates for this role should typically have a minimum of three to five years of software development experience; a passion for or background in software security; time to be trained in software security and on the centralized software security teams tools, plans, and processes; and, most important, must not only know how to develop (build) software but also how to deconstruct (take it apart) while "thinking like a hacker" regarding all possible paths or exploits (attack planes) that an adversary could take to exploit the software. Each product development organization should have at least one individual who has the technical capability to be trained as a software security champion and, eventually, as a software security architect to assist the centralized software security team in architecture security analysis/threat modeling. It is also important that SSCs be volunteers and not assignees who may lack the passion to succeed at this very challenging but rewarding role. Each business unit for software development within a company should have at least one SSC; for larger development organizations, it is preferable to have one for each tier product per business unit. A typical job description for an SSC is as follows:

- SSCs must have a minimum of three to five years of software development experience; a passion for or background in software security; time to be trained in software security and on the centralized and business unit–specific software security tools, plans, and processes; and, most important, must not only know how to develop (build) software but also how to deconstruct it (take it apart) while "thinking like a hacker" regarding all possible paths or exploits (attack planes) that an adversary could take to exploit the software.
- Each product development organization should have one individual that has the technical capability to be trained as a software security architect to assist the centralized software security group in architecture security analysis/threat modeling. Ideally, each team should have an additional software security champion whose role it is to assist as a change agent (a more project/program–oriented individual) in addition to the technically oriented software security champion, if deemed necessary.
- Specific roles and responsibilities include:
  ○ Enforce the SDL: Assist the centralized software security group in assuring that the security tenets of confidentiality, integrity, availability, and privacy are adhered to in the SDL as part of the Company X SDLC.
  ○ Review: Assist the centralized software security team software security architects in conducting architecture security analysis, reviews, and threat modeling.

- Tools Expert: Be the representative centralized software security team software security tool expert (e.g., static and dynamic, including fuzzing) within each development team, product group, and/or business unit.
- Collocate: Be the eyes, ears, and advocate of the centralized software security team within each development team, product group, and business unit.
- Attend Meetings: Participate in monthly phone meetings and, as budgets permit, twice-a-year face-to-face meetings, as members of a global Company X team of software security champions.

As noted in Brook's blog, there's a big difference between mandating that a development team member report about security issues and concerns to a central security team and empowering one or more members of the development team to become the team's security architect. When the approach is to appoint someone, the designated person quite possibly won't do the job. Importantly, the security role may quite likely place that person in conflict with the rest of their team. Furthermore, if the appointed security eye isn't given power, influence, or skills, they aren't being given much incentive to carry out the role. We might go so far as to suggest that someone whose job is to watch others might be considered a spy by those others. That role doesn't really sound very appealing to us, and, too often, it doesn't to the appointed "spy," either. At the other end of the spectrum, what we've done four times now is actually offer the necessary training and support for development team members to become security experts in various areas, one of which we hope will be a path to becoming a security architect for their team. We do everything possible to empower the developer who delivers the security function, essentially acting as a security architect. We empower them to enforce standards and policies. We empower them to escalate risks for decisions. But, because escalations might bring an on-team member into conflict with their own management, we don't hesitate to pick up tricky escalations and run with them for our satellite security architects. In this way, the people fulfilling this role are both empowered and protected; we never want to place one of our security architects in conflict with their own management. The "carrot" for people who pick up this role is that they can truthfully claim that they have fulfilled the role of security architect. Because for many organizations security is a premium skill, there is often a bump in pay somewhere in the near-to-medium future for these people. People who have fulfilled the satellite security architect role as we've outlined here actually have performed the work. A significant number of them continue on to become security architect leaders. Of course, not everyone who goes through the program and does the security architecture work chooses to continue in security as a career. That's okay. If they've gained nothing else, they will bring their security knowledge to whatever role they may fulfill in the future of their career. Generally, that will be a win in whatever roles they fill.[*]

2.2.3 Software Security Program Management

In many cases, development teams are still transitioning to DevOps, which requires an overall strategy that involves significant changes in culture, roles and responsibilities, team structure, tools, and processes. Program managers (PMs) are the primary change agents and drivers in DevOps in these efforts. They primarily provide for effective program management that pushes for greater agility by having all parties—from management to the development and operations teams—collaborate with each other and create increased customer satisfaction. Transitioning to and managing DevOps and an Agile environment requires more than simply adopting new tools and processes. It includes building a stable Continuous Integration infrastructure and an automated pipeline that moves deliverables

---

[*] Schoenfield, B. (2019). *Secrets of a Cyber Security Architect*. Boca Raton (FL): Auerbach Publications/Taylor & Francis Group, pp. 148–149.

from development to production. Roles and responsibilities should be redefined when moving to a Continuous Delivery methodology. In this case, in contrast to the product manager, who is accountable for the organization's roadmap and vision, responsible for release goals, and has the authority to make backlog decisions, the PM is accountable for release planning and responsible for release tracking, and has the authority to push for production. For the PM, the software development lifecycle doesn't end after the product has been released; it is also involved with getting customer feedback and determining how products are being used in the field. This continues through the next lifecycle and beyond. A security PM or lead should support the PM office and mirror or support their responsibilities in all areas of security within the DevOps environment. As mentioned previously in this chapter, silos have traditionally existed between the development and operations teams, with the link back to development being the production environment. The DevOps methodology gives operations a better opportunity to understand the product, bring valuable feedback to developers. and the ability for operations and product teams to work together on shared goals. The PM is a key catalyst for making this happen. Feedback loops between functions are key to DevOps. Each function or role, no matter how they are divvied up, must hear from and understand what other functions need and the experiences—good, bad, and ugly—of the other roles' outputs. The only way to achieve "continuous" is every role collaborating closely with and learning from the others: Feedback becomes the hub around which continuous spins. A PM can provide the necessary forums for interaction as well as ensure that feedback is forthcoming and being taken into account.

Developers like to move fast to develop new content, and product managers like to see new content. It is important that the PM educates and reminds developers and product managers of the importance of creating better release security and quality. Agile regression testing must be prioritized by the PM and be part of sprint development. Testing new content or fixing new defects or regressions in later stages in an Agile development process is unacceptable

A PM should ensure that features not be pushed to production unless they're developed with good security and quality as defined in the definition of done. Many startups and large companies push their software products to production almost daily, in contrast to some enterprises that still deal with releases in two-week or monthly cadences, based on their features' status. Only features that achieve the definition of done can be pushed to production.

Technical debt, in particular, security debt, still remains a critical issue in large companies and in smaller companies that have been around for a decade or longer. PMs should be responsible for ensuring that the software they are responsible for does not have any technical debt during content development. It is very important that they make sure their sprints end with the proper regression testing, security and performance testing, etc. This should include some time before the sprint ends to stop the development of content to allow for exploratory manual testing, regression fixes, and completion of missing automated tests. (We will expand on the need for interlocking and overlapping test tactics and what these are in the SDL (Chapter 3)

The PM and Product Owner will be the key team members managing Partner Engagement and Relationship Management in the DevOps environment and should be tightly coupled with the software security team or their representatives.

2.2.4 Software Security Organizational Realities and Leverage

Although an incremental headcount hire plan based on a progressive increase in workload is typically the norm for most organizations, incremental growth isn't the right model for what has been proposed in this book and certainly isn't a reality for those going through austerity realities within their organizations. Doing more with less is a reality we all face, regardless of the risks we are facing. To help solve this conundrum, we have proposed a model for a software security group that doesn't depend on continual growth, linear or otherwise. The virtual team grows against linear growth, allowing a fully staffed, centralized software security group to remain relatively stable. We believe that a centralized group composed of one seasoned software security architect per main software product group and one for each software product within that group in your software engineering development organization will be sufficient to scale quite nicely as long as the software security champion program is adhered to, as proposed in this book. In addition, by sharing the responsibility for a typical product security incident response team (PSIRT) among the key software security champions for each software product in a development organization, a single PSIRT manager should suffice, given the shared responsibilities of the task throughout the organization.

As described earlier in this book, excellence is not about increasing numbers; rather, it is about the quality of the staff you hire. Each of these seasoned software security architects can coordinate and support the implementation of the SDL within each business unit and software product line and will:

- Provide the SSC associated with the centralized software security group process and governance.
- Mentor the SSCs in security architecture and reviews.
- Support the associated business unit SSC in the mentorship of each software product line SSC.
- Coordinate with product management for early and timely security requirements.
- Help to calculate project security risk.
- Help to ensure that SSCs institute appropriate and full security testing.
- Ensure that appropriate security testing tools are available (static, dynamic, fuzzing) for use in the SDL, as appropriate.

Although these tasks benefit greatly from senior experience and discretion, there is a significant opportunity for cost savings in having these senior technical leaders mentor the SSCs and software security architects, as both a wonderful growth opportunity for the individuals involved and a cost savings to the company and the organization. Someone with the potential to grow into a leader through experience and mentorship is a perfect candidate for the SSCs in our model. We are the sum of everything we have ever done, which is constantly being revised and remembered. The same can be said of software security architects; it is a journey, not a point in time, and requires constant learning, mentoring, and collaboration with those who have been there before.

In our model, there are multiple paths to appropriate "coverage." Unlike a fully centralized function, a virtual team, handled with care, can be coalesced and led by a far smaller central team. The authors have made this model work, sometimes numerous times in a number of disparate organizations, and they consider this a proven track record for a model that will constantly evolve with the ever-changing realities we are faced with in software security. Each member of the centralized software security group must be able to inspire, encourage, and lead a virtual team such that the virtual members contribute key subject-matter expert (SME) tasks, but at the same time do not become overloaded with additional or operational tasks. "Just enough" such that the PSIRT function can reap huge benefits through having true SMEs contribute and enable, while at the same time making sure that no one person bears the entire brunt of a set of operational activities that can't be dodged. Since our model for a centralized software security group makes use of an extended virtual team, the need for a large central PSIRT staff, as may be found in other organizations, is not needed. Tasks that can be managed in a decentralized manner are done, such as technical investigations, release planning, and fix development. However, there is a coordination role that must be sophisticated enough to technically comprehend the implications and risks involved in various responses. Peer review is a powerful tool for avoiding missteps. Further, the central role within the engineering software development group itself provides coordination *across* teams, something that is lacking in most organizations. We must not respond individually to a vulnerability that affects many software products in unique and idiosyncratic ways. Further, it is essential to provide an interface between PR (and sometimes marketing) support and the technical teams who are involved in responding. You want your response to vulnerability reporters to be consistent and to avoid putting your company and your brand at risk, externally.

2.2.5 Software Security Organizational and People Management Tips

- Technical "rock stars" are great but only if they are team players as well as mentors. If not, they will be a boat anchor, a waste of a resource, and a distraction to meeting the goals of the team, and they will destroy your team's morale. Great teams always have a purpose that is greater than the individual. If you only need a critical, technical skill for a brief time, which doesn't currently exist on your team, it may be better to bring in a temporary hire or contractor to fill this need until they have completed the required work. Team performance isn't based on individual performance.
- We have always advocated the value of diverse teams, but you should always make sure they are the best qualified for your team or have the aptitude to be mentored to be equal contributors to the team. Quota systems without accounting for the right skill sets or potential to learn will always be a detriment to your team in today's world. There are plenty of diverse and qualified candidates to recruit as developers or product security specialists for your team. Recruiters that tell you otherwise are likely lazy or incompetent.
- Teams are like families, and once someone is part of the family any interpersonal or compatibility issues can be amplified. These issues can be detrimental to the dynamics of your team. Be careful who you bring on your team, and for Scrum teams, make sure all are involved in the interview process. Are their technical skills real? Are they committed to being part of the team for a couple of years, or are they just there to bide their time waiting for another role in the same company? Never settle.
- Experience, technical ability, and a relevant college degree is ideal, but technical ability and experience always trump a degree. In most cases, a college education is a good indication of the potential ability to write and communicate, but actual experience and proven success as a developer or security practitioner is superior to a degree only.
- Security certifications and experience are ideal, but as with college degrees, actual experience and proven success as a security practitioner is superior to a certification only. In most cases, certifications are a good sign for potential ability but are no substitute for actual experience.
- Always question why the person is available. You don't want somebody else's problem child. Check if they are on a plan and question why their current manager has no issues with their transfer or hire, if external. Some managers may actually be looking out for their employee's career growth, but our experience is that this is the exception rather than the norm. You owe this to your team because they may soon be part of your close-knit family.
- Loners and non-team players need not apply. This is a team effort; if they want to be individual contributors, these roles typically exist elsewhere in the organization. Be careful of managers who have employees on their team who they try to push onto your team because they are not performing in their current role. These employees can become a real detriment to your team dynamics.
- Understandably, much focus in the geek world is on technical chops when recruiting people, but collaboration and interpersonal/communication skills are arguably equally important.
- If at all possible, prevent cliques early in the development of your team. Successful development teams in today's world are typically small and, from a team dynamics standpoint, can't afford to have 2 to 3 cliques within their ranks.
- The buck stops and you must provide air cover for your teams. This means screening, when possible, any unnecessary senior management intrusions into the team, including tasks not directly related to the successful completion of any of your team's development projects. This also includes anything that may come in from stakeholders or partners.

- Pick team leads who will command respect for both their technical skills and their ability to deal with people both inside and outside your team. This not only enhances the productivity and morale of the team(s) that work for you but also the working relationship with your stakeholders and partners.
- Resist being pressured into hiring recommended hires from your team or higher management without running them through a thorough screening process and, when possible, before being interviewed by the entire team they will be working with.
- Continuing education and selected conference attendance are important to keep your teams up to speed on the latest technical aspects of their job and to be networked with those that can help them with future coding or security issues.
- Senior mentors play an indispensable role in development teams. But it's hard to find true, qualified senior developers with the experience to guide a team well. If you have multiple teams, it is possible to share these developers across your teams or bring in some from one of your peer's teams, if possible.
- Most importantly, make sure you lead by example and instill transparency, trust, and integrity into your team(s) and everything they do. This includes how you conduct rankings and evaluations in the team.
- Scrum allows for anyone to include stakeholders to go to any meeting, including observing the daily stand-up or review. As a manager, it is your job as well as your leads' to ensure there is zero tolerance for uncivil behavior, and never allow an employee to poison corporate culture through abuse or disrespect. This will include quick and direct feedback.
- Screen your people well and always check their references, and, if possible, check with folks you know who worked with them whom they didn't list as references. If you can't trust the people you're hiring to be on board with what you're doing, you're hiring the wrong people, and you've set up a system that has failure built in.
- Developing software takes intense focus. Where possible, avoid taking developers away from focused work. A single break in that focus can sideline a developer for hours. Don't scatter meetings throughout the week; ideally, limit them to two or less days a week. When providing educational opportunities to your developers, make sure that uninterrupted quiet time is available.
- You must make sure that your organization can handle any software issues that arise, quickly and effectively, 24×7×365. This will avoid burning out your team as well as missing service level agreements (SLAs). This will be managed through an on-call policy. To create an on-call rotation that is both fair and effective, consider best practices such as the following:
  - Structure your team and organization fairly
  - Be flexible and creative when designing rotations
  - Track metrics and monitor incidents
  - Adapt your policy to align with your company's situation[*]

2.3 Security Tools, Automation, and Vendor Management

Without automated security tools for code analysis, configuration management, patching and vulnerability management, and privileged credential/secrets management, you stand no chance of scaling security to DevOps processes. The closer you can match the speed of security to the DevOps process, the less likely you are to face culture resistance to embedding security practices.[†]

---

[*] New Relic. (2019). *DevOps Done Right Best Practices to Knock Down Barriers to Success*. San Francisco (CA): New Relic Inc., pp. 9–10.

[†] Beyond Trust. (2020). "DevOps Security Best Practices." Retrieved from https://www.beyondtrust.com/blog/entry/devops-security-best-practices

2.3.1 Security Tools and Automation

It is important to remember that DevOps is a philosophy and methodology. Although you can acquire or develop tools for processes such as the SDL, release management, and CI/CD tools, you still need teams, collaboration, responsibility, and ownership. You can't buy this; you must develop and manage the human aspects of DevOps correctly. This doesn't negate the need to assess, acquire, deploy, and manage automated tools to make the processes more cost effective and efficient. But this, of course, requires a human element as well.

In some environments, multiple versions of code can be pushed to production in a day. Automation of security is absolutely necessary to sync it with the speed at which code is delivered in a CI/CD environment. Given the speed required, choosing the wrong tool can be disastrous. Even with the right tool, proper vendor management will also be key to your success.

Automated tools assist in giving development teams more ownership in deploying and monitoring their applications while providing for faster ship times, quality, and better security. Security has to be part of the process and automated properly to not slow the development process down. In addition to helping to find security vulnerabilities and bugs, automated tools can help monitor security policies and standards without negatively slowing down the process.

Traditional tools used in the development process include static analysis, dynamic analysis, and fuzzing tools as well as vulnerability code analysis tools. Moving left (or down, in our analogy) in DevOps requires a few other families of tools for security teams to use. These include those that scan your configurations for security best practices in the cloud, automate security tests as you would unit tests or integration tests for things like provisioning new servers or deploying some Docker containers, and those tools used for runtime application security. An excellent list of tools that can be used in establishing a DevSecOps platform can be found at https://github.com/devsecops/awesome-devsecops#tools.

2.3.1.1 Security Tools for the SDL

In this section, we discuss the details of what functions and roles static analysis, dynamic analysis, and fuzz testing have in the overall SDLC/SDL process. One of the key changes that have occurred over the last few years regarding these tools is that they are now used throughout the development process, when using the DevOps methodology, rather than toward the end of the process, as in the past. The final goal of the security code review process is to improve the overall security of the product and to provide output that can be used by the development team to make changes and/or mitigations that will achieve improved software product security compared to what existed at concept commit for the start of the SDLC/SDL process. Before we begin, however, it is important to recognize that each approach has certain practical advantages and limitations.

Advantages of Static Code Analysis

1. Access to the actual instructions the software will be executing.
   - No need to guess or interpret behavior.
   - Full access to all of the software's possible behaviors.
2. Can find exact location of weaknesses in the code.
3. Can be conducted by trained software assurance developers who fully understand the code.
4. Allows quick turnaround for fixes.
5. Relatively fast, if automated tools are used.

6. Automated tools can scan the entire code base.
7. Automated tools can provide mitigation recommendations, reducing research time.
8. Permits weaknesses to be found earlier in the development lifecycle, thus reducing the cost to fix.[*,†]

Limitations of Static Code Analysis

1. Requires access to source code or at least binary code and typically needs access to enough software artifacts to execute a build.
2. Typically requires proficiency in running software builds.
3. Will not find issues related to operational deployment environments.
4. Time consuming, if conducted manually.
5. Automated tools do not support all programming languages.
6. Automated tools produce false positives and false negatives.
7. There are not enough trained personnel to thoroughly conduct static code analysis.
8. Automated tools can provide a false sense of security that everything is being addressed.
9. Automated tools are only as good as the rules they are using to scan with.
10. Does not find vulnerabilities introduced in the runtime environment.[‡,§]

Advantages of Dynamic Code Analysis

1. Limited scope of what can be found.
   - Application must be footprinted to find the test area.
   - That can cause areas to be missed.
   - You can only test what you have found.
2. No access to actual instructions being executed.
   - The tool is exercising the application.
   - Pattern matching on requests and responses.
3. Requires only a running system to perform a test.
4. No requirement to have access to source code or binary code.
5. No need to understand how to write software or execute builds.
   - Tools tend to be more "fire and forget."
6. Tests a specific operational deployment.
   - Can find infrastructure, configuration, and patch errors that static analysis tools will miss.
7. Identifies vulnerabilities in a runtime environment.
8. Automated tools provide flexibility on what to scan for.
9. Allows for analysis of applications without access to the actual code.
10. Identifies vulnerabilities that might have been false negatives in the static code analysis.

---

[*] Jackson, W. (2009, February). GCN—Technology, Tools and Tactics for Public Sector IT: "Static vs. Dynamic Code Analysis: Advantages and Disadvantages." Available at http://gcn.com/Articles/2009/02/09/Static-vs -dynamic-code-analysis.aspx?p=1

[†] Cornell, D. (2008, January). OWASP San Antonio Presentation: "Static Analysis Techniques for Testing Application Security." Available at http://www.denimgroup.com/media/pdfs/DenimGroup_StaticAnalysisTechniques ForTestingApplicationSecurity_OWASPSanAntonio_20080131.pdf

[‡] Jackson, W. (2009, February). GCN—Technology, Tools and Tactics for Public Sector IT: "Static vs. Dynamic Code Analysis: Advantages and Disadvantages."

[§] Cornell, D. (2008, January). OWASP San Antonio Presentation: "Static Analysis Techniques for Testing Application Security."

11. Permits validation of static code analysis findings.
12. Can be conducted on any application.[*,†]

Limitations of Dynamic Code Analysis

1. Automated tools provide a false sense of security that everything is being addressed.
2. Automated tools produce false positives and false negatives.
3. Automated tools are only as good as the rules they are using to scan with.
4. As for static analysis, there are not enough trained personnel to thoroughly conduct dynamic code analysis.
5. It is more difficult to trace the vulnerability back to the exact location in the code, taking longer to fix the problem.[‡,§]

If you have no access to source or binaries, you are not a software developer and don't understand software builds, or you are performing a "pen test" or other test of an operational environment, you will likely choose to use a dynamic tool. Otherwise, you will likely use a static analysis tool. Ideally, you should use both, when possible.

Advantages of Fuzz Testing

1. The great advantage of fuzz testing is that the test design is extremely simple and free of preconceptions about system behavior.
2. The systematical/random approach allows this method to find bugs that would often be missed by human eyes. Plus, when the tested system is totally closed (say, a SIP phone), fuzzing is one of the only means of reviewing its quality.
3. Bugs found using fuzz testing are frequently severe, exploitable bugs that could be used by a real attacker. This has become even truer as fuzz testing has become more widely known, because the same techniques and tools are now used by attackers to exploit deployed software. This is a major advantage over binary or source auditing, or even fuzzing's close cousin, fault injection, which often relies on artificial fault conditions that are difficult or impossible to exploit.

Limitations of Fuzz Testing

1. Fuzzers usually tend to find simple bugs; in addition, the more a fuzzer is protocol aware, the fewer weird errors it will find. This is why the exhaustive/random approach is still popular.
2. Another problem is that when you do some black box testing, you usually attack a closed system, which increases the difficulty of evaluating the danger/impact of the found vulnerability (no debugging possibilities).
3. The main problem with fuzzing to find program faults is that it generally finds only very simple faults. The problem itself is exponential, and every fuzzer takes shortcuts to find something interesting in a time frame that a human cares about. A primitive fuzzer may have poor code

---

[*] Jackson, W. (2009, February). GCN—Technology, Tools and Tactics for Public Sector IT: "Static vs. Dynamic Code Analysis: Advantages and Disadvantages."

[†] Cornell, D. (2008, January). OWASP San Antonio Presentation: "Static Analysis Techniques for Testing Application Security." Available at http://www.denimgroup.com/media/pdfs/DenimGroup_StaticAnalysisTechniques ForTestingApplicationSecurity_OWASPSanAntonio_20080131.pdf

[‡] Jackson, W. (2009, February). GCN—Technology, Tools and Tactics for Public Sector IT: "Static vs. Dynamic Code Analysis: Advantages and Disadvantages."

[§] Cornell, D. (2008, January). OWASP San Antonio Presentation: "Static Analysis Techniques for Testing Application Security."

coverage; for example, if the input includes a checksum that is not properly updated to match other random changes, only the checksum validation code will be verified. Code coverage tools are often used to estimate how "well" a fuzzer works, but these are only guidelines to fuzzer quality. Every fuzzer can be expected to find a different set of bugs.[*][†]

2.3.1.1.1 Static Analysis

Static program analysis is the analysis of computer software that is performed without actually executing programs. It is used predominantly to perform analysis on a version of the source code; it is also performed on object code. In contrast, dynamic analysis is performed by actually executing the software programs. Static analysis is performed by an automated software tool and should not be confused with human analysis or software security architectural reviews, which involve manual human code reviews, including program understanding and comprehension. When static analysis tools are used properly, they have a distinct advantage over human static analysis in that the analysis can be performed much more frequently and with security knowledge superior to that of many software developers. It thus allows for expert software security architects or engineers to be brought in only when absolutely necessary.

Static analysis (see Figure 2.3) is also known as static application security testing (SAST). It identifies vulnerabilities during the development or quality assurance (QA) phase of a project. SAST provides line-of-code-level detection that enables development teams to remediate vulnerabilities quickly.

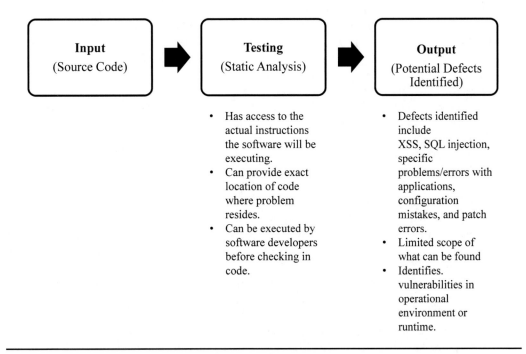

Figure 2.3   Static Analysis Flow Diagram. (*Source:* Reproduced from Ransome, J. and Misra, A. [2014]. *Core Software Security: Security at the Source.* Boca Raton [FL]: CRC Press/Taylor & Francis Group, p. 178, with permission.)

---

[*]   The Open Web Application Security Project (OWASP) (2012). "Fuzzing." Available at https://www.owasp.org/index.php/Fuzzing

[†]   R2Launch. (2012). "Fuzz." Available at http://www.r2launch.nl/index.php/software-testing/fuzz

The use of static analysis tools and your choice of an appropriate vendor for your environment is another technology factor that is key to success. Any technology that beneficially automates any portion of the software development process should be welcome, but this software has become "shelfware" in many organizations because the right people and/or the right process was not used in selecting the tool or tools. Not all tools are created equal in this space: Some are better at some languages than others, whereas others have great front-end governance, risk management, and compliance (GRC) and metric analysis capabilities. In some cases, you may have to use up to three different tools to be effective.

One of the challenges in using a static analysis tool is that false positives may be reported when analyzing an application that interacts with closed-source components or external systems, because without the source code, it is impossible to trace the flow of data in the external system and hence ensure the integrity and security of the data. The use of static code analysis tools can also result in false negative results, when vulnerabilities exist but the tool does not report them. This might occur if a new vulnerability is discovered in an external component or if the analysis tool has no knowledge of the runtime environment and whether it is configured securely. A static code analysis tool will often produce false positive results where the tool reports a possible vulnerability that in fact is not. This often occurs because the tool cannot be sure of the integrity and security of data as it flows through the application from input to output.[*]

Michael Howard, in his Security & Privacy 2006 IEEE article titled "A Process for Performing Security Code Reviews,"[†] proposes the following heuristic as an aid to determining code review priority. The heuristic can be used as a guide for prioritizing static, dynamic, fuzzing, and manual code reviews.

- **Old code:** Older code may have more vulnerabilities than new code because newer code often reflects a better understanding of security issues. All "legacy" code should be reviewed in depth.
- **Code that runs by default:** Attackers often go after installed code that runs by default. Such code should be reviewed earlier and more deeply than code that does not execute by default. Code running by default increases an application's attack surface.
- **Code that runs in elevated context:** Code that runs in elevated identities (e.g., root in *nix), for example, also requires earlier and deeper review because code identity is another component of the attack surface.
- **Anonymously accessible code:** Code that anonymous users can access should be reviewed in greater depth than code that only valid users and administrators can access.
- **Code listening on a globally accessible network interface:** Code that listens by default on a network, especially uncontrolled networks such as the Internet, is open to substantial risk and must be reviewed in depth for security vulnerabilities.
- **Code written in C/C++/assembly language:** Because these languages have direct access to memory, buffer-manipulation vulnerabilities within the code can lead to buffer overflows, which often lead to malicious code execution. Code written in these languages should be analyzed in depth for buffer overflow vulnerabilities.
- **Code with a history of vulnerabilities:** Code that has shown a number of security vulnerabilities in the past should be suspect, unless it can be demonstrated that those vulnerabilities have been effectively removed.
- **Code that handles sensitive data:** Code that handles sensitive data should be analyzed to ensure that weaknesses in the code do not disclose such data to untrusted users.

---

[*] The Open Web Application Security Project (OWASP). (2012). "Static Code Analysis." Available at https://www.owasp.org/index.php/Static_Code_Analysis

[†] Howard, M. (2006, July–August). "A Process for Performing Security Code Reviews." *IEEE Security & Privacy,* pp. 74–79.

- **Complex code:** Complex code has a higher bug probability, is more difficult to understand, and may be likely to have more security vulnerabilities.
- **Code that changes frequently:** Frequently changing code often results in new bugs being introduced. Not all of these bugs will be security vulnerabilities, but compared with a stable set of code that is updated only infrequently, code that is less stable will probably have more vulnerabilities.

In Michael Howard's 2004 Microsoft article titled "Mitigate Security Risks by Minimizing the Code You Expose to Untrusted Users,"* he also suggests a notional three-phase code analysis process that optimizes the use of static analysis tools:

Phase 1: Run all available code analysis tools

- Multiple tools should be used to offset tool biases and minimize false positives and false negatives.
- Analysts should pay attention to every warning or error.
- Warnings from multiple tools may indicate that the code needs closer scrutiny (e.g., manual analysis). Code should be evaluated early, preferably with each build, and re-evaluated at every milestone.

Phase 2: Look for common vulnerability patterns

- Analysts should make sure that code reviews cover the most common vulnerabilities and weaknesses, such as integer arithmetic issues, buffer overruns, SQL injection, and cross-site scripting (XSS).
- Sources for such common vulnerabilities and weaknesses include the Common Vulnerabilities and Exposures (CVE) and Common Weaknesses Enumeration (CWE) databases, maintained by the MITRE Corporation and accessible at http://cve.mitre.org/cve/ and http://cwe.mitre.org.
- MITRE, in cooperation with the SANS Institute, also maintain a list of the "Top 25 Most Dangerous Programming Errors" (http://cwe.mitre.org/top25/index.html) that can lead to serious vulnerabilities.
- Static code analysis tool and manual techniques should, at a minimum, address the "Top 25."

Phase 3: Dig deep into risky code

- Analysts should also use manual analysis (e.g., code inspection) to more thoroughly evaluate any risky code that has been identified based on the attack surface, or based on the heuristics, as discussed previously.
- Such code review should start at the entry point for each module under review and should trace data flow through the system, evaluating the data, how it is used, and whether security objectives might be compromised. Please see Chapter 3, which describes the elements of the SDL as well as a detailed discussion on how to get the most out of complex SAST tools while, at the same time, empowering developers to take charge of the analysis.
- Several commercial static analyzers (as of this writing) offer desktop or Integrated Development Environment (IDE) methods to perform static analysis on code as it is changing. This is the essence of "shift-left," that is, perform whatever analyses, checks, verifications that can be made as early as possible. We must stress the importance of the availability of these automation capabilities. As Brook wrote in *Secrets of a Cyber Security Architect*,

---

* Howard, M. (2004, November). "Mitigate Security Risks by Minimizing the Code You Expose to Untrusted Users." Available at http://msdn.microsoft.com/msdnmag/issues/04/11/AttackSurface

"Generally, diligent programmers expect errors in their code as they're working on it. Any tool that can find errors (without generating too many incorrect findings and not requiring too much configuration and tuning) will usually be appreciated and integrated.

But there's a mental shift that happens when a programmer believes that the code is stable and correct. Code that has been released to the next stage of the development process (which varies, depending upon the development methodology) can be a bit "out of sight, out of mind." Often, the programmer has moved on to other problems. There can be a bit of "prove to me that there's an error" once code has left the programmer's purview and moved on.

Hence, testing that occurs after a programmer commits code as "correct" may be a little too distant from the coding process, whereas tools that can integrate into the coding process and that find errors during coding generally receive greater programmer attention. Hence, we like to get at least some security checking onto the coders' desks and into their IDE early in the coding process. Even if the checks are less rigorous than those that can be placed within a later build process, early identification of security mistakes is more organic than massive sets of findings later on. Get secure coding analysis tools into the coding cycles. Then, perform a more thorough check during build. From experience, that seems to work the best."*

2.3.1.1.2 Dynamic Analysis

Dynamic program analysis is the analysis of computer software that is performed by executing programs on a real or virtual processor in real time. The objective is to find security errors in a program while it is running, rather than by repeatedly examining the code offline. By debugging a program under all the scenarios for which it is designed, dynamic analysis eliminates the need to artificially create situations likely to produce errors. It has the distinct advantages of having the ability to identify vulnerabilities that might have been false negatives and to validate findings in the static code analysis.

Dynamic analysis (see Figure 2.4) is also known as dynamic application security testing (DAST). It identifies vulnerabilities within a production application. DAST tools are used to quickly assess a system's overall security and are used within both the SDL and SDLC. The same advantages and cautions about using static analysis tools apply to dynamic analysis tools.

The following explanation of how dynamic analysis is used throughout the SDLC is taken from the Peng and Wallace (1993) NIST Special Publication 500-209, *Software Error Analysis.*†

- *Commonly used dynamic analysis techniques for the design phase include sizing and timing analysis, prototyping, and simulation. Sizing and timing analysis is useful in analyzing real-time programs with response-time and constrained-memory and execution-space requirements. This type of analysis is especially useful for determining that allocations for hardware and software are made appropriately for the design architecture; it would be quite costly to learn in system testing that the performance problems are caused by the basic system design. An automated simulation may be appropriate for larger designs. Prototyping can be used as an aid in examining the design architecture in general or a specific set of functions. For large, complicated systems, prototyping can prevent inappropriate designs from resulting in costly, wasted implementations.*
- *Dynamic analysis techniques help to determine the functional and computational correctness of the code. Regression analysis is used to re-evaluate requirements and design issues whenever any significant code change is made. This analysis ensures awareness of the original system requirements.*

---

* Schoenfield, B. (2019). *Secrets of a Cyber Security Architect.* p. 111.
† Peng, W. and Wallace, D. (1993, March). NIST Special Publication 500-209, *Software Error Analysis.* Available at http://hissa.nist.gov/SWERROR

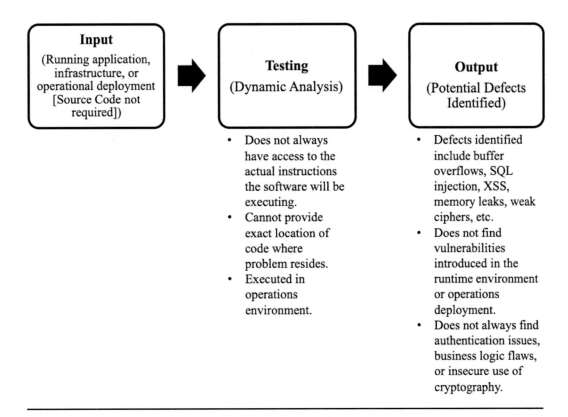

Figure 2.4   Dynamic Analysis Flow Diagram. (*Source:* Reproduced from Ransome, J. and Misra, A. [2014]. *Core Software Security: Security at the Source.* Boca Raton [FL]: CRC Press/Taylor & Francis Group, p. 183, with permission.)

Sizing and timing analysis is performed during incremental code development, and analysis results are compared against predicted values.

- *Dynamic analysis in the test phase involves different types of testing and test strategies. Traditionally there are four types of testing: unit, integration, system, and acceptance. Unit testing may be either structural or functional testing performed on software units, modules, or subroutines. Structural testing examines the logic of the units and may be used to support requirements for test coverage— that is, how much of the program has been executed. Functional testing evaluates how software requirements have been implemented. For functional testing, testers usually need no information about the design of the program, because test cases are based on the software requirements.*

- *The most commonly used dynamic analysis techniques for the final phase of the SDLC are regression analysis and test, simulation, and test certification. When any changes to the product are made during this phase, regression analysis is performed to verify that the basic requirements and design assumptions affecting other areas of the program have not been violated. Simulation is used to test operator procedures and to isolate installation problems. Test certification, particularly in critical software systems, is used to verify that the required tests have been executed and that the delivered software product is identical to the product subjected to software verification and validation.*

Static analysis finds issues by analyzing source code. Dynamic analysis tools do not need source code but can still identify the problem. During our discussion of static analysis, we reviewed an SQL injection attack example. For that example, the tool would identify that account_id is passed as a URL parameter and would try to tamper the value of the parameter and evaluate the response from the application.

2.3.1.1.3 Fuzz Testing

Fuzz testing (see Figure 2.5), or fuzzing, is a black-box software testing technique that can be automated or semiautomated and provides invalid, unexpected, or random data to the inputs of a computer software program. In other words, it finds implementation bugs or security flaws by using malformed/semi-malformed data injection in an automated fashion. Inputs to the software program are then monitored for exception returns such as crashes, failing built-in code assertions, and potential memory leaks. Fuzzing has become a key element in testing for software or computer system security problems. Fuzz testing has a distinct advantage over other tools in that the test design is extremely simple and free of preconceptions about system behavior.

Fuzzing is a key element of software security and must be embedded in the SDL. There are many vendors to choose from in this space, and some even develop their own tools. Fuzzing is used for both security and quality assurance testing. Fuzzing has recently been recognized as both a key element and a major deficiency in many software development programs, so much so that it is now a U.S. Department of Defense (DoD) Information Assurance Certification and Accreditation Process (DIACAP) requirement.

Fuzzing is a form of attack simulation in which unexpected data is fed to the system through an open interface, and the behavior of the system is then monitored. If the system fails, for example, by crashing or by failing built-in code assertions, then there is a flaw in the software. Although all of the issues found by fuzzing tools are critical and exploitable, unlike static analysis tools, fuzzing can only find bugs that can be accessed through an open interface. Fuzzing tools must also be able to interoperate with the tested software so that they can access the deeper protocol layers and test the system more thoroughly by testing multiple layers.*

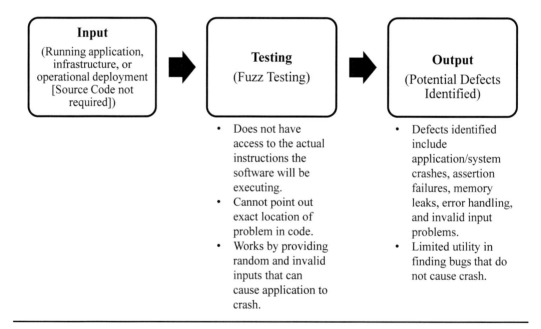

Figure 2.5 Fuzz Testing Flow Diagram. (*Source:* Reproduced from Ransome, J. and Misra, A. [2014]. *Core Software Security: Security at the Source.* Boca Raton [FL]: CRC Press/Taylor & Francis Group, p. 185, with permission.)

---

* Adversaries, especially well-resourced ones such as nation-state actors as well as security researchers, routinely fuzz test as a primary technique to find potential vulnerabilities in their targets. It behooves security-conscious organizations to fuzz their own code before an attacker exploits a zero-day vulnerability that they've found, or a researcher chooses to publish such an issue without reporting it first (zero-day).

Although static analysis has the benefit of full test coverage and is a good method for improving the general software quality level, it cannot easily provide test results that solve complex problems, and, as discussed previously, it also results in a large number of false positives, both of which require further analysis by a human and consume valuable and limited resources. There are no false positives in fuzz testing because every flaw discovered is a result of a simulated attack.[*]

Static analysis is performed on code that is not being executed, and it can only be performed offline. In contrast, fuzz testing must be executed against executable code, can be run against live software, and, therefore, can find vulnerabilities that may not be visible in the static code. Fuzz testing targets the problems attackers would also find and, therefore, is a good test for robustness while also streamlining the process by focusing only on the most critical interfaces that may be susceptible to attack. Because of its ability to test robustness, fuzz testing is typically used during the verification phase of the SDLC just before product release. As with static and dynamic analysis, fuzz testing can be used from the moment the first software components are ready and even after release—not just at some point in time during the SDLC process. This attribute, of course, can yield significant cost savings by finding and fixing vulnerabilities early in the SDLC.

Standard fuzz testing techniques are limited in their use of random mutations to create test cases, which will find only some of the software vulnerabilities. However, this testing still has value because these are the same vulnerabilities that attackers would find. It is important to remember that attackers use fuzzing tools as well, and it is a tell-tale sign of a weak software security development program if fuzzing tools by discoverers or attackers find flaws in products you have already released to your customers. More sophisticated fuzzing techniques are used to improve and optimize coverage by using protocol specifications to target protocol areas most susceptible to vulnerabilities and to reduce the number of test cases needed without compromising test coverage. Static code analysis is used to ensure that secure coding policies are being followed, but protocol fuzzing tools are used to gain an attacker's perspective on the threat and risk.

Another advantage of fuzz testing is that it can be used with black-box, gray-box, or white-box testing and does not require source code access. Similar to the dynamic analysis tools discussed in this chapter, this feature makes it a great tool for testing third-party software or software that has been outsourced for development. One drawback of fuzz testing, however, is that it is intrusive and may well crash the system, which will likely require initial testing to occur in a separate environment, such as a testing lab or virtualized environment.

There are two main types of fuzz testing—"smart" and "dumb."

- In "smart" (generational) fuzzing, the fuzzer pushes data to the program in a logical way, usually by waiting for responses and possibly altering the stack. This method requires in-depth knowledge of the target and specialized tools, but less crash analysis is required and also less duplication of findings than with dumb fuzzing.[†,‡]
- In "dumb" (mutational) fuzzing, the fuzzer systematically pushes data to the program without waiting for proper responses. This method is closely tied to denial-of-service attacks. This method requires no knowledge of the target and uses existing tools. However, more crash analysis is required, and there is more duplication of findings than with "smart" fuzzing.[§]

---

[*] In addition, every issue found through fuzzing indicates unintentional code behavior, that is, a bug. Whether exploitable or not, programs shouldn't misbehave when faced with unexpected input.

[†] Royal, M. and Pokorny, P. (2012, April). Cameron University IT 4444—Capstone: "Dumb Fuzzing in Practice." Available at http://www.cameron.edu/uploads/8d/e3/8de36a6c024c2be6dff3c34448711075/5.pdf

[‡] Manion, A. and Orlando, M. (2011, May). ICSJWG Presentation: "Fuzz Testing for Dummies." Available at http://www.us-cert.gov/control_systems/icsjwg/presentations/spring2011/ag_16b_ICSJWG_Spring_2011_Conf_Manion_Orlando.pdf

[§] Royal, M. and Pokorny, P. (2012, April). Cameron University IT 4444—Capstone: "Dumb Fuzzing in Practice." Available at http://www.cameron.edu/uploads/8d/e3/8de36a6c024c2be6dff3c34448711075/5.pdf

To carry out a fuzz test, the following steps are followed for each file or field that feeds into the application:

1. Enter random data or spaces to some part of the input file.
2. Execute the application with that input file.
3. Evaluate results. What broke? What ran as normal? What was expected to happen?
4. Number each test case and report findings to project management.[*]

2.3.2 DevOps Tools: Going Beyond the SDL

DevOps Security integrates and automates security processes and tooling into the entire DevOps workflow resulting in continuous rather than point-in-time delivery. Specific security tools for a DevOps environment that provide the capabilities listed below can be found at https://www.csoonline.com/article/3398485/28-devsecops-tools-for-baking-security-into-the-development-process.html:

- Provide developers with alerts and notifications about potential security anomalies and defects.
- Automatically scan for, discover, and remediate security defects.
- Include dashboard tools that allow the viewing and sharing of security information from the beginning of development through operations, in one graphical view.
- Identify, predict, and define threats across the complete attack surface, so that you can make proactive security decisions.
- Identify security flaws before they can be exploited.
- Manage security across an entire CI/CD pipeline and runtime environment for end-to-end security.
- Integrate security and compliance into the building, deployment, and running of public cloud applications. This provides automated testing and security enforcement.
- Build DevSecOps architecture into the CI/CD process.
- Built-in security for container-based applications.
- Discover and remediate security threats across resource configurations, network architecture, and user activities.
- Provide an automation platform designed to collect information about your software, identify threats and countermeasures, and highlight relevant security controls to help enterprises achieve their security and compliance objectives.
- Address open source vulnerabilities.

2.3.3 Vendor Management

Vendor risk management (VRM) and third-party risk management are important aspects of both your DevOps and your company's overall risk profile. You must protect yourself from business disruption and reputational damage. You must review workflows. This is particularly true for security commercial off-the-shelf (COTS) software products and services that typically deal with the most sensitive intellectual property and business information utilized and created as part of the development process. This must include authentication, audit, and control access by third-party vendors as well as any involvement they may have with workflows and user interfaces.

Multiple application reviews have concluded that somewhere between 65% and 85% of released code today is open source. That means that the majority of supposedly "invented here," "home grown"

---

[*] Grembi, J. (2008). *Secure Software Development: A Security Programmer's Guide*. Boston (MA): Course Technology.

code simply isn't. Open source communities are vendors from the perspective of development. To be blunt, as vendors, that is, suppliers of a key input to and portions of software releases, their security is your security. In Chapter 3, which covers the generic SDL, we dig deeper into software component management. Luckily, at least some open source management can be automated to reduce the burden, in line with a DevOps mindset.

Let us not forget that development tools are also supplied by vendors—commercial, open source, or supported open source commercial offerings. DevOps automation depends upon a rich, complex, and deep set of technologies, each of whose software security practices affects those of development, and, thus, the security posture of your organization and software. If appropriate security capabilities have not been built into a tool, then alternate mitigations will need to be put into place. Configuration of each tool will have to meet your security posture. In short, the supplier's security is part of your security, requiring VRM.

We will take up open source and included software components in the following section.

2.3.3.1 Managing COTS Security Products

DevOps and its focus on automation, where possible, substantially increase the use of the COTS solution, which increases the need for the acquisition and the use of third-party software to be part of a risk management framework. This should include a comprehensive plan for the identification and mitigation of business uncertainties, legal liabilities and reputational damage. The risks from third-party vendors providing gateways for cyber attacks and data breaches have been quite newsworthy over the last few years and highlight the need to identify and mitigate these risks. For some, mitigation may not be an option due to the potential exposure to operational, regulatory, financial, and reputational risk regulations, such as the Payment Card Industry Data Security Standard (PCI DSS), Sarbanes-Oxley Act (SOX), and the Health Information Portability and Accountability Act (HIPAA), which mandate that risk management policies extend to third-party vendors, outsourcers, contractors, and consultants.

Typically, procurement—legal, IT, and in some cases, engineering—will have a team to manage vendor lifecycle management that will collaborate with the DevOps security team in this effort, with strict rules of engagement. If you are a shop without this capability, it is highly recommended that you outsource for this function and guidance. This security team will define the needs, but experienced and reputable VRM specialists, to include procurement, will standardize assessments of all vendors, help in the bid, vendor, and selection process; define contract terms and time frames; ensure that vendor performance and relationship is monitored; and be fully engaged when the contract has ended or is being renewed. The key aspects of renewal are that pricing negotiation, past performance, and any vendor risks that may be identified will be reviewed. In some cases, if the vendor has proven to be high risk, early termination of contract may occur. High risk may not just be security, performance, or contract compliance related; some vendors may have financial or solvency issues during the life of the contract. In other cases, the vendor may have been acquired by a competitor, which can also be an issue. It is always good to have a backup vendor for these types of situations. Legal issues such as lawsuits, class actions, loss of work, or termination of relationship; potential compliance breaches, information security, and data security risks; and potential loss of intellectual property are all things that will be assessed as part of the vendor risk review. Even if you believe you have great internal security controls, if your third-party vendor handles confidential, sensitive, proprietary, or classified information on your behalf, this is very risky and requires legal, the risk team, compliance, and others responsible for accepting the business risk to review and sign off on.

In addition to selecting and using the COTS security product to be used, it will be important for the security team to work closely with their vendor risk partners, identified above, to see how the products can enhance DevOps methodologies and goals, where possible. For example, can the product deliver on clearly defined and measurable business metrics to meet customer and business outcomes?

Can it assist in the DevOps cultural changes required—in particular, those of security? And can the product help facilitate or enhance the continuous improvement cycle?

2.3.3.2 Managing Open Source Security Products

Sonatype and research partners from IT Revolution and Galois produced a paper titled "2019 State of the Software Supply Chain Report."[*] From 2017 to 2019, their analysis found that the rate of open source component releases has picked up by 75% and that download requests from teams using these components have risen 68% year over year. They also found that 85% of the average code base in modern software applications is composed of open source componentry libraries and depends heavily on them. Some other quotes from the report state "The practice of assembling open source component releases into the form of an application screams of efficiency. Developers no longer need to code every line from scratch" and "[d]evelopers can download component releases in seconds that deliver new capabilities, built by experts outside of their organizations who make their code freely available to others." The report highlighted that open source components that developers download and integrate into their code are full of dangerous vulnerabilities. An example is given that just over half of all JavaScript package downloads contain known vulnerabilities, with 1 in 3 rated as high vulnerabilities. One in 10 of those flaws were rated as critical.[†]

The move to use open source components by commercial software development has increased substantially over the last few years and so have the risks. As the DevOps security teams move quickly to mitigate these risks, the successful teams will leverage the high-quality open source projects and avoid the riskier open source dependencies, where possible.

Our focus in the previous section was on COTS, but in reality, open source software is a dominant part of today's code base. For the most part, open source equivalents, if not all of which is available in COTS security software, are available. See the open source security products that are available by function at https://www.notsosecure.com/achieving-devsecops-with-open-source-tools/. Managing open source security software will require the same methodology and risk mitigation that is used for the general open source risk management described in the following paragraphs.

As DevOps moves things "left" for more automation, there is a tendency to lean toward open source software to reduce costs. Open source not only has the reputation for cost efficiency but also facilitates productivity and innovation. Open source is predominant in today's world as software stacks are loaded with open source code. Even more daunting, as of 2019, there has been a "75% growth in supply of open source component releases over the past two years."[‡]

The downside is that there has been a "71% increase in confirmed or suspected open source related breaches since 2014,"[§] "many open source components come with liabilities in their license agreements, and one out of every 16 open source download requests is for a component with a known vulnerability."[¶] Given that a significant amount of the software products being released contain open source content, this also means that this code can be analyzed by potential attackers. Attackers also have the advantage of knowing any publicly reported vulnerability, as they can find these through sources such as the National Vulnerability Database (NVD), software development project home pages, GitHub issue lists, and mailing lists. This provides attackers with a target-rich environment.

---

[*] Sonatype. (2019). *2019 State of the Software Supply Chain: The 5th Annual Report on Global Open Source Software Development.* Fulton (MD): Sonatype Inc., pp. 3, 28, 29, 37.

[†] Ibid.

[‡] Ibid.

[§] Ibid.

[¶] Rahn, C. (2017). "Open Source Vulnerabilities in Application Software." Retrieved from https://softwaretesting .news/open-source-vulnerabilities-application-software/

Unfortunately, many companies are not aware of the risks that open source has or are accepting the risk in spite of the consequences. Those that know the risk are tracking and effectively managing its use. Commercial software pushes its updates to users whereas open source requires that you pull the fixes and updates as well as tracking the vulnerabilities yourself. Without an open source tracking system in place for open source entering their code base, development organizations cannot mitigate and defend against vulnerabilities added through these open source components. A recent 2019 Synopsys Open Source and Security Analysis report found that "[s]ixty percent of the codebases audited in 2018 contained at least one vulnerability—still significant, but much better than the figure of 78% from 2017."[*] Open source software and components can have significant benefits to organizations that use it, but not if it isn't being tracked while also identifying any related security and legal compliance issues. Unpatched open source components in software add to the security risk.

Earlier in this chapter, we mentioned the use of SAST and DAST tools and described their use in software development programs and, specifically, as part of the SDL. These tools are very useful at identifying common coding errors and known vulnerabilities in your code, but they are not effective at identifying vulnerabilities introduced through open source components. Most open source projects have access to at least one commercial SAST vendor's product for free. There is little reason for open source projects to fail to run SAST and then fix those findings, which present any attacker leverage (vulnerabilities).

Organizations are increasingly using software composition analysis (SCA) tools to analyze—both to build an inventory of open source components and to identify vulnerabilities. Analyzing open source component vulnerabilities in an DevOps environment will require an increased frequency of testing and feedback loops than what has been found in the traditional SDL environment.

In short, open source communities must be required to implement activities from the generic SDL. Failure to do at least the minimum is usually an indication that the resulting software component has not been built with adequate security and, therefore, should be avoided. We will pick this topic up more fully in a succeeding chapter.

It shouldn't be misconstrued that open source is any less secure than COTS or that the open source community doesn't generally do an excellent job at issuing patches; but manually tracking components, their versions, and their vulnerabilities, and manually downloading patches are tasks that greatly exceed most organizations' capabilities. You cannot maintain adequate software asset management procedures without a complete inventory of the code you are using. Most importantly, you can't patch something if you don't know that you are using it. A staff report by the U.S. Senate Permanent Subcommittee on Investigations (PSI) stated that Equifax's lack of a complete software inventory was a contributing factor to its massive 2017 data breach.[†] As stated previously, open source software isn't any riskier than COTS, but the unmanaged use of open source software most assuredly is.

To defend against open source security and compliance risks, Synopsys, one of the leaders in open source security software management tools and services, recommends that organizations take these steps to manage the security of open source in their environments:

- Create and enforce open source risk policies and processes
- Perform a full inventory of their open source software
- Map open source to know vulnerabilities
- Continually monitor for new security threats

[*] Synopsys. (2019). "2019 Open Source Security and Risk Analysis (OSSRA)." Report. San Francisco (CA): Synopsys, Inc., p. 9.

[†] U.S. Senate Committee Permanent Subcommittee on Investigations/U.S. Senate Committee on Homeland Security and Governmental Affairs. (2020). "How Equifax Neglected Cybersecurity and Suffered a Devastating Data Breach." Retrieved in 2020 from https://www.hsgac.senate.gov/imo/media/doc/FINAL%20Equifax%20 Report.pdf

- Identify licensing risks
- Make sure open source is part of Mergers and Acquisitions (M&A) due diligence[*]

As we shall see when we dive deeper into the SDL activities necessary for secure open source management, some of the required work can be automated. As always, taking the DevOps view, as much as can be automated, must be.

2.3.3.2.1 Open Source Licenses

Open source software is free to use, but it comes with a license. Open source components are, by law, commercial items. A majority of these licenses are either permissive or copyleft. Permissive open source licenses have minimal requirements as to how they can be redistributed. Copyleft licenses are like copyrights in that they are laws that restrict the right to use creative works without the permission of the author. When an author releases a program under a copyleft license, he makes a claim on the copyright of the work and issues a statement that other people have the right to use it as long as the reciprocity obligation is maintained. This means that software that is written based on a component that is copyleft licensed and must be released as open source. The result is that such software is required to release its full source code and all of the rights to modify and distribute the entire code. This results in severe implications on your ability to protect your intellectual property. It may also substantially reduce your company's or product's value, if either are acquiring your company as part of a mergers and acquisitions.[†]

Although open source software is free and it increases innovation, efficiency, and competitiveness for software product development, it must also be managed as an asset, the license obligations observed, and it must be as secure as internally developed software standards and requirements require. These sometimes unique and complex license and business risks can delay, and potentially prevent, software deployment or shipment if not properly managed. It is essential to be in compliance with applicable open source requirements to avoid costly and time-consuming litigation. The two primary areas that need to be of concern for those managing an SDL in which open source software is used as part of the product or solution are license compliance and security.

1. **Open source software license compliance.** Noncompliance with open source software licensing requirements can result in costly and time-consuming litigation, court time, copyright infringement, public press exposure, bad publicity, and negative risk to the noncompliant organization's reputation and business relationships. Mismanagement and noncompliance with open source licenses may also result in the difficulty or inability to provide software product support, delay of current release and ship dates, or the stoppage of orders currently scheduled to ship.
2. **Open source software security.** SDL and development teams, as well as their executive sponsors, need to be aware of and understand vulnerabilities associated with open source software code to be used in their own software product. As with the software being developed in-house, all vulnerabilities known to the open source and software security community must be identified, assessed, and mitigated throughout the SDL process and include the same threat modeling, architectural security and privacy review, and risk assessment rigor as the code being developed in-house.

---

[*] Synopsys. (2019). "2019 Open Source Security and Risk Analysis (OSSRA)." Report. p. 16.

[†] White Source. (2020). "On the Verge of an M&A? Don't Ignore Open Source Due Diligence." Retrieved from https://resources.whitesourcesoftware.com/blog-whitesource/on-the-verge-of-an-m-a-don-t-ignore-open-source-due-diligence

If possible (as we shall see from those SDL activities devoted to third-party components), it is more efficient to have the open source component's community enact some or, better, most SDL activities, rather than making up for an inattentive or incompetent community. Importantly, under many open source licenses, any changes to the open source must be contributed back to the project—that is, your development team must become part of the component's community. Being an active part of many open source communities requires much more than the odd few lines of code. Doing so often entails ongoing discussions about what will be built and what not, the monitoring of change requests and suggestions, and even might include assessing designs and reviewing code. Community participation requires resource investments that some organizations may not be able to spare.

For some organizations, such investment and sharing code may not present too great a barrier. For others, those who must hold as much of their software proprietary as possible (there are many reasons to do so), contributing any in-house development to open source may not be feasible or desirable. In these cases, it is better to choose components that are well-supported and demonstrate a reasonable level of software security practice, rather than internally performing any SDL activities, which will result in changes to the open source software.

Using manual methods to find, select, monitor, and validate open source code is time consuming, inefficient, and an unnecessary drain on scarce development team resources. Automation through tools such as Black Duck Software (www.blackducksoftware.com), FlexNet Code Insight (https://www .flexerasoftware.com/protect/products/flexnet-code-insight.html), or WhiteSource (https://www.white sourcesoftware.com) are essential to effectively and efficiently incorporate open source software into SDLC development efforts to drive down development costs and manage the software and its security throughout the SDL. We will return to further automation opportunities in a subsequent chapter.

2.3.3.2.2 Open Source Due Diligence

Open source due diligence will require that you create an open source inventory list to include all dependencies. If you don't know what components you are using, you will not know what open source licenses you need to be in compliance with. Your organization can either do this manually or through the use of an automated tool. The automated method is recommended because it will significantly reduce the time, resources, errors, and inconsistencies that can occur doing it manually. Using the automated method will reveal all your open source components within minutes by integrating with your build tools. After your open source components have been identified, you can then identify all the licenses that your components have. The licensing analysis must be comprehensive: Compliance must account for sublicenses and licensing implied by subcomponents.

The next step will be to identify all open source licenses and check compliance. Part of this stage of due diligence is to check what each license requires you to do if your company is in compliance. After you have completed the open source inventory list and verified that you are in compliance with your open source licenses, you can then check to see if any of your open source components have any known security vulnerabilities due to your open source components.

The final step is to identify vulnerable and outdated open source components. There is a NIST database that maintains a record of all the reported open source security vulnerabilities. It would be nearly impossible to track all the CVEs related to the open source software being used in your products since thousands of vulnerabilities are published every month. There are several automated tools that can do this for you. If a security vulnerability affects your product you should consider updating your libraries with newly released versions of the open source component because it will likely have a fix.

The "2019 State of the Software Supply Chain Report," mentioned previously, found that several software supply chain practices contributed to reduction of risk, with the following five standing out as the most impactful:

- Develop a governance program with standards policies
- Have a process for evaluating and adding new components to include how these components are evaluated, approved, and standardized
- Proactively remove problematic components—by taking the initiative to look for and eliminate potential sources of open source vulnerabilities in existing code
- Aim to always use the latest versions of components since they will likely have the least vulnerabilities
- Use automated enforcement tools to track, manage and/or ensure policy compliance of open source dependencies[*]

2.4 DevOps Security Incident Response

The U.S. Department of Homeland Security (DHS) states that 90% of security incidents result from exploits against defects in software.[†] It is critical to prevent your products from being part of this statistic. Without an effective incident response plan to include effective communication rules of engagement—both internal to the company and external to the customer—a company puts both its products and reputation at risk. This may result in regulatory fines, lawsuits, and loss of market share.

The organizational structure for incident response is also important, as it must optimize collaboration while also controlling the process. Organizations without proper process and communications operate in an *ad hoc* or firefighting mode with everybody scrambling to try to address the issue. This has negative consequences for the company that goes beyond the development team to include other organizations and upper management all the way up to the CEO and possibly the Board of Directors. Correctly building and managing the incident response capability will minimize disruption and give the development engineers the support they need to respond efficiently and effectively.

Due to the sensitivity of incident response and liability issues, organization, relationships, and preparedness are all key to survival. Although every organization may have differences, executives, public relations, legal, customer support, sales, as well as relevant developers, the product managers, project managers, Scrum leaders and security—both management and technical—are likely to be involved, especially for those issues that pose the greatest risk to owners, users, clients, and customers of the software, and may be the most technically complex and challenging.

The authors have survived a number of very serious incidents; we can assure readers of the efficacy and effectiveness of taking an inclusive, holistic approach. Failure to include the right skills and have a clear and standard set of responsibilities and accountability, and not establishing a clear process and chain of command, results in chaos. Management and technical leaders will all waste time trying to "do the right thing"—few of whom have much that they can actually contribute beyond urging someone, somewhere, to "do something now." Lack of a plan, and failure to thoroughly exercise it, can readily result in the apocryphal Abbott and Costello comedy routine, "Who's on First?" Confusion reigns as many well-meaning people scream, but few hold sufficient information to act, and act decisively.

Unprepared incident response quickly devolves to a circus of the many all screaming at who knows whom to react. Managing such a three-ring circus will easily and rapidly eat up more time and resources than the incident actually requires. Woe to those who remain unprepared. Due to the current state of software development art, every organization that makes software or integrates it will at some point

---

[*] Chickowski, E. (2019). "5 Ways DevSecOps Can Manage Software Supply Chains." Retrieved from https://devops.com/5-ways-devsecops-can-manage-software-supply-chains/. (Data is derived from the 2019 State of Software Supply Chain Report.)

[†] Morgan, S. (2019). "Is Poor Software Development the Biggest Cyber Threat?" Retrieved from https://www.csoonline.com/article/2978858/is-poor-software-development-the-biggest-cyber-threat.html

have to face an incident. We've been through this; we pray that no organization buys into, "It can't happen here." It will and does.

Incidents that require response may not originate from your organization's development efforts. Consider the Edward Snowden disclosure (2013[*]) that the United States' National Security Agency (NSA) had planted a master skeleton key within a widely accepted encryption standard. Any organization owning software that made use of the algorithm and whose objectives included not disclosing encrypted data to the NSA was put into a tailspin four days before Christmas, when many workers were already on holiday with their families. Such an announcement will put one's incident response plans to the test.

Or, take the Spectre/Meltdown announcement in January 2018.[†] Every organization using any of the standard central processing units (CPUs) and operating systems (OSs) was touched by these issues. In other words, just about every computer user was potentially vulnerable. Failure to respond was not an option, as two weeks past the announcement, exploitation code from Javascript™ running in a standard browser became publicly available.

Certainly, if you make software, incident response must be part of your organization. Some issues affect organizations far beyond the makers of the software. Be prepared.

Doing more with less is a reality we all face, regardless of the risks we are facing. To help solve this conundrum, we have developed a model for a software security group that doesn't depend on continual growth, linear or otherwise. The virtual team grows against linear growth, allowing a fully staffed, centralized software security group to remain relatively stable. We believe that a centralized group comprising one seasoned software security architect per main software product group and one SSC fulfilling the role as a software security architect for each software product within that group in your software engineering development organization will be sufficient to scale quite nicely. Another element of the talent is the SSEs who can be candidates for SSCs, when there is a slot for them. Most importantly for this section, by sharing the responsibility for a typical product security incident among the key SSCs for each software product in a development organization, a single PSIRT manager with a very minimal-sized staff should suffice, given that the responsibilities of the task are distributed throughout the organization.

2.4.1 Internal Response to Defects and Security Vulnerabilities in Your Source Code

Software development organizations have large teams of people dedicated to search for, document, store, track, and manage defects as well as security flaws and vulnerabilities prior to product release. In the past, security engineers and the quality assurance (QA) teams did much of their work towards the end of the development cycle, and security wasn't really built in—it was bolted on at the end, if at all. It was common for some defects and security vulnerabilities to be released into production rather than be fixed. In DevOps, testing is the responsibility of everybody involved in software development, and it occurs throughout the entire software development process.

In mature DevOps organizations, continuous integration results in code being checked on more frequently, resulting in more frequent code changes rather than large changes less frequently. Through

---

[*] "The NSA secretly paid the computer security firm RSA $10 million to implement a 'back door' into its encryption." Szoldra, P. (September 16, 2016, 6:00 AM). "This Is Everything Edward Snowden Revealed in One Year of Unprecedented Top-Secret Leaks." December 20, 2013. Retrieved from https://www.businessinsider.com/snowden-leaks-timeline-2016-9

[†] Gibbs, S. (Thursday, 4 January 2018 19.52 EST). "Meltdown and Spectre: 'Worst Ever' CPU Bugs Affect Virtually All Computers." The Guardian. Retrieved from https://www.theguardian.com/technology/2018/jan/04/meltdown-spectre-worst-cpu-bugs-ever-found-affect-computers-intel-processors-security-flaw

the use of continuous testing, the focus is on ensuring that all code passes the tests as defect free and free of known vulnerabilities. The problems are then either fixed so that they pass the test, or the changes are rolled back from the build and the problem is fixed in the development environment. Code is also treated as infrastructure (moving left) to ensure that the change is updated throughout the delivery environment. This results in the increased delivery time, quality, and security of the product as well as delivering better business value. When the cycle time between creation of issues and discovery is short-ened, the developer can quickly fix, rebuild, and retest, substantially deceasing the time to produce a product that is ready to release. The team will prioritize production defect and security fixes based on impact to end users, and after these are rectified, the root causes will be identified. The outcome of the root case determination should include how new tests, improved automation, better collaboration, or other changes can prevent issues such as those discovered to happen.

SLAs that require specific reporting requirements for internally discovered vulnerabilities are usu-ally differentiated by severity levels such as the Common Vulnerability Scoring System (CVSS). It is important for a product security incident response team member to be involved with procurement and legal to prevent contract language that doesn't meet your incident response process and procedures or that promises something you cannot deliver.

2.4.2 External Response to Security Vulnerabilities Discovered in Your Product Source Code

One of the key elements of our post-release methodology is that the typical PSIRT function can be a shared responsibility within our proposed leveraged organizational structure for software security and privacy that covers responses to both post-release security vulnerability and privacy issue discoveries. No matter how good your software security program and associated SDL is, the fact is that something will be missed at some point, and you need a plan to respond to this. Most important, if discovery of software security vulnerabilities and privacy issues in post-release software products is a common occurrence, that is a clear sign that building security into the organization's SDLC through an SDL-like process is weak or nonexistent. Such weakness can result in negative visibility due to publicly disclosed exploitation of vulnerabilities or security flaws inherent to the post-release software, subsequent loss of market share due to brand defamation, and lawsuits or breach of contracts, as well as create a major target for further exploitation by adversarial opportunists.

Based on our experiences, we cannot emphasize enough how important it is to have a single group that acts a focal point of all communications with customers about security vulnerabilities. Often, we have seen at least three different groups communicating with customers: customer support, sales, and an information security group. PSIRT may or may not be part of the information security organization in a particular company, though this is certainly desirable. To summarize, a clearly defined chain of communications with customers is of critical importance to prevent disclosure of unintended informa-tion and to avoid panic and putting entire accounts at stake.

2.4.3 Post-Release PSIRT Response

In relation to software security, a PSIRT is responsible for responding to software product security incidents involving external discoveries of post-release software product security vulnerabilities. As part of this role, the team manages the investigation of publicly discovered security vulnerabilities of their company's software products and the systems they interact with. The external discoverers might be independent security researchers, consultants, industry organizations, other vendors, or benevolent or possibly even nefarious hackers who identify possible security issues with software products for which the PSIRT is responsible. Issues identified are prioritized based on the potential severity of the vulnerability, typically using the CVSS scoring system described earlier in the book as well as other environmental factors. The resolution of a reported incident may require upgrades to products that are under active support from the PSIRT's parent company.

Shortly after its identification and during the investigation of a claim of vulnerability, the PSIRT should work collaboratively with the discoverer to confirm the nature of the vulnerability, gather required technical information, and ascertain appropriate remedial action.

When the initial investigation is complete, the results are delivered to the discoverer along with a plan for resolution and public disclosure. If the incident reporter disagrees with the conclusion, the PSIRT should attempt to address those concerns.

The discoverer(s) will be asked to maintain strict confidentiality until complete resolutions are available for customers and have been published by the PSIRT on the company's website through the appropriate coordinated public disclosure, typically called a security bulletin (SB). During the investigation and pre-reporting process, the PSIRT coordinates communications with the discoverer, including status and documentation updates on the investigation of the incident. Further information may also be required from the discoverer to validate the claim and the methods used to exploit the vulnerability. Discoverers will also be notified that if they disclose the vulnerability before publication by the PSIRT, then the discoverers will not be given credit in the public disclosure by the company and the case will be treated as a "zero day," no-notice discovery that has been reported publicly by an external source. In the case of a zero-day discovery, the PSIRT and development teams work together to remediate the vulnerability as soon as possible, according to the severity of the CVSS (http://nvd.nist .gov/cvss.cfm) scoring for the particular vulnerability. In the case of a zero-day, highly scored vulnerability, the company's PR team will work closely with the PSIRT to manage potential negative press and customer reaction.

During the investigation of a reported vulnerability, the PSIRT coordinates and manages all sensitive information on a highly confidential basis. Internal distribution is limited to those individuals who have a legitimate need to know and can actively assist in resolution of the vulnerability.

The PSIRT will also work with third-party coordination centers such as the CERT Coordination Center (CERT/CC) (http://www.cert.org/certcc.html) and others to manage a coordinated industry disclosure for reported vulnerabilities affecting the software products they are responsible for. In some cases, multiple vendors will be affected and will be involved in the coordinated response with centers such as CERT. If a coordination center is involved, then, depending on the circumstances, the PSIRT may contact the center on the behalf of the discoverers, or assist them in doing it themselves.

If a third-party component of the product is affected, this will complicate the remediation process because the PSIRT will be dependent on a third party for remediation. A further complication is that the PSIRT will have to coordinate and, in many cases, notify the vendor directly to ensure coordination with the third-party coordination center and likely direct involvement with the discoverer. Even though a third-party component has been used, the assumption is that the owner of the primary software product is ultimately responsible for all components of the software, whether they own them or not.

As mentioned above, PSIRTs generally use the CVSS to assess the severity of a vulnerability as part of their standard process for evaluating reported potential vulnerabilities in their products and determining which vulnerabilities warrant external and internal reporting.

The CVSS model uses three distinct measurements or scores that include base, temporal, and environmental calculations, and the sum of all three scores should be considered the final CVSS score. This score represents a single moment in time; it is tailored to a specific environment and is used to prioritize responses to a particular externally discovered vulnerability. In addition, most PSIRTs will consider modifying the final score to account for factors that are not properly captured in the CVSS score. PSIRTs typically use the following CVSS guidelines when determining the severity of a particular vulnerability and the need to report it:

- High (H)—Critical—CVSS base score of 7.0–10.0
- Medium (M)—CVSS base score of 4.0–6.9
- Low (L)—CVSS base score of 0.1–3.9[*]

If there is a security issue involving a third-party software component in the product the PSIRT is responsible for, then, depending on the situation, and whether the third party has a CVSS score, the PSIRT may use the CVSS score provided by the component creator and/or may adjust the score to reflect the impact on the overall software product.

Public disclosure, including the relevant base and temporal CVSS scores and a CVE ID[†] report, is typically made for an external post-release discovery event when one or more of the following have occurred:

- The incident response process has been completed and has determined that enough software patches or other remediations exist to address the vulnerability. Public disclosure of code fixes can be issued to address high-severity vulnerabilities.
- Active exploitation of a vulnerability that could lead to increased risk for the PSIRT company's customers has been observed that requires a published security vulnerability announcement. The announcement may or may not include a complete set of patches or other remediation steps. When possible, compensating controls are included in the public announcement to provide interim protection that will limit exposure until the permanent fix is announced.
- A zero-day announcement or other potential for increased public awareness of a vulnerability affecting the PSIRT company's product is probable that could lead to increased risk for customers. In these cases, the PSIRT has worked closely with the company's PR team to help assess public indicators and warnings such as Twitter feeds and blogs that this exposure is imminent and will have prepared for a statement ahead of time. Again, this accelerated public vulnerability announcement will not include a complete set of patches or other remediation steps, but, ideally, interim compensating controls to limit exposure can be identified.
- There have been a series of documented checks and balances through the process to verify the integrity of the information collected and assessed to include the efficacy and fairness in CVSS scoring.

A typical step-by-step PSIRT case-handling process will include the following steps:

1. Notification of vulnerability as assessed by an individual discoverer or organization is received.
2. The responsible software product development group is identified, together with resources required for assessment of the discoverers' vulnerability claim.
3. If the claim is credible, an impact assessment is made and a timeline for a fix is determined. The level of effort needed and priority to develop a fix is balanced against the likelihood of public disclosure of the severity and risk of the vulnerability. In some cases, external resources may be required due to other critical tasks the development team is carrying out. If the claim is not credible, additional information is requested from the discoverer to ensure that the threat was properly re-created in the testing environment. If it is not credible after the testing environment has been confirmed, then the discoverer is notified of the company's findings. If the discoverer goes public claiming the vulnerability is credible even though the company has determined it is

---

[*] FIRST.org. (2020). "Common Vulnerability Scoring System v3.1: Specification Document." Retrieved from https://www.first.org/cvss/v3.1/specification-document

[†] MITRE. (2013). "CVE—Common Vulnerabilities and Exposures—The Standard for Information Security Vulnerability Names." Retrieved from http://cve.mitre.org/ index.html

not, then the PSIRT typically works with the company's PR team to publish the results of the company's finding as a counter to the discoverer.

4. The time frame for remediation, the resources needed to fix a confirmed vulnerability, and the reporting format (e.g., security bulletin, knowledge base article, or other form of public notification) are committed to.

5. After patch or other remediation methods have been identified, all customers are notified simultaneously on the date of the availability of the fix through the reporting format determined in Step 4. (*Core Software Security*, pp. 232–236)

2.4.4 Optimizing Post-Release Third-Party Response

Collaboration between different teams and stakeholders provides the best possible chance of success in post-release response. The collective of SSCs, SSEs, and an ongoing formal software security programmatic relationship with the software development product managers and quality team to support and collaborate with the centralized software security team as proposed in this book provides several distinct advantages over solely dedicated teams to handle post-release PSIRT and privacy support:

- Direct PSIRT and privacy response ownership is achieved by imbedding these functions into the engineering and development groups directly responsible for fixing the product directly affected by the discovered vulnerability or privacy issue.
- Direct knowledge of the code, architecture, and overall software product design and functionality with a direct influence on the remediation process will result in increased efficiency, control, and response over an external organizational entity without direct knowledge of the product. Essentially, this removes the middleman and streamlines the process.
- This process provides for better return on investment (ROI) for both the PSIRT and the privacy response function through the leverage of resources, and direct knowledge of the software product at the source through the direct involvement and ownership by the development teams.
- Direct empowerment of the development teams and project managers, their more direct ownership of the remediation process, and a centralized software security group embedded in the engineering/software development group provide single organizational responsibility for the response.
- SSCs and SSEs operate locally with the software product manager and appropriate product development resources to directly drive the assessment and remediation (if needed) of the claimed vulnerability by an external discoverer.
- All the above result in faster time to execution and response and, most important, help speed up the mitigation of negative press exposure and customer risk. We believe there is an advantage to our proposed organizational infrastructure in providing a cost-effective, minimal resource and an efficient way to respond to this type of incident while reducing the burden on resources dedicated to the development of the software itself.

2.4.4.1 ISO 29147 and ISO 30111

Two International Organization for Standardization (ISO®) standards relate to the proper functioning of a vendor PSIRT:

1. **ISO/IEC 29147:2018** [ISO/IEC 29147:2018]—Information technology—Security techniques—Vulnerability disclosure

This standard provides requirements and recommendations to vendors on the disclosure of vulnerabilities in products and services and is applicable to vendors who choose to practice vulnerability disclosure to reduce risk to users of vendors' products and services.

Vulnerability disclosure enables users to perform technical vulnerability management as specified in ISO/IEC 27002:2013, 12.6.1. Vulnerability disclosure helps users protect their systems and data, prioritize defensive investments, and better assess risk. The goal of vulnerability disclosure is to reduce the risk associated with exploiting vulnerabilities. Coordinated vulnerability disclosure is especially important when multiple vendors are affected. This standard provides:

- Guidelines on receiving reports about potential vulnerabilities
- Guidelines on disclosing vulnerability remediation information
- Terms and definitions that are specific to vulnerability disclosure
- An overview of vulnerability disclosure concepts
- Techniques and policy considerations for vulnerability disclosure
- Examples of techniques, policies (Annex A), and communications (Annex B)*

2. **ISO/IEC 30111:2019** [ISO/IEC 30111:2019]—Information technology—Security techniques—Vulnerability handling processes

This standard provides requirements and recommendations for how to process and remediate reported potential vulnerabilities in a product or service and is applicable to vendors involved in handling vulnerabilities. Other related activities that take place between receiving and disclosing vulnerability reports are described in ISO/IEC 30111.†

2.4.5 Key Success Factors

2.4.5.1 External Vulnerability Disclosure Response Process

In this post-release phase of the SDL cycle, it is critical to have a well-defined and documented external vulnerability disclosure response process. Stakeholders should be clearly identified, and a responsibility assignment or RACI matrix should be created. Most important, only one team should have responsibility to interface with customers to discuss vulnerabilities and remediation. All other teams and stakeholders should work with that team and assure them that there are no other channels of communication or any information leaked selectively to customers. It is often the case that large accounts or enterprise customers are given preferential treatment and are privy to information that small- and medium-size businesses are not. This is not a good security practice. Vulnerability information should be disclosed to everyone or no one. Selective disclosure is not a good idea, plays favorites with customers, and, in some cases, may be illegal and/or counter what constitutes fair and equitable treatment of all customers.

It is also important to define and formalize the internal vulnerability-handling process as part of overall vulnerability management and remediation programs. In addition to security teams and external researchers, employees or internal customers of the products/services will often identify security problems and communicate them to the product or operations team. There needs to be a well-defined process to make sure all relevant security vulnerabilities are captured and put through the remediation queue.

2.4.5.2 Post-Release Certifications

Relevant certifications needed after the product is released (or deployed in the cloud) should have been identified in one of the earlier phases of the SDL cycle. Requirements for certifications should have

---

* ISO®. (2018). ISO/IEC 29147:2018 [ISO/IEC 29147:2018]—Information technology—Security techniques—Vulnerability disclosure. Retrieved from https://www.iso.org/standard/72311.html
† ISO®. (2019). ISO/IEC 30111:2019 [ISO/IEC 30111:2019]—Information technology—Security techniques—Vulnerability handling processes. Retrieved from https://www.iso.org/standard/53231.html

been included in security and privacy requirements. This will prevent any retrofitting or findings during compliance audits for certifications. Certifications often do require annual audits or surveillance audits. The security team should work with the security compliance team to ensure that all relevant controls requirements are met.

2.4.5.3 Third-Party Security Reviews

Third-party reviews are often critical to demonstrate "security" to end users and customers. A preferred list of vendors should be created by the software team, and these vendors should be vetted for their skills as well as ability to handle sensitive information. Since these vendors will be handling sensitive security information, it is important to note if they use full disk encryption, communicate securely, dispose of any customer data as soon as testing ends, and so on. Any time there is a need for security testing, one of these vendors should be selected for the testing. Security testing of the entire software stack and product portfolio should be performed at least annually.

2.4.5.4 SDL Cycle for Any Architectural Changes or Code Reuses

Any architectural or code changes or code/component reuses should trigger SDL activities (though not all may be needed, depending on the significance of the changes).

2.4.5.5 Security Strategy and Process for Legacy Code, M&A, and EOL Products

Legacy code most likely will never be updated or modified. In addition, a legacy software stack will also never be patched or upgraded. Software running on old Apache® Web Server will have severe dependencies on it as well as the operating system and thus will not be upgraded without the application itself being changed. Any security issues identified in legacy code will take a long time to remediate (if at all). The best way to deal with legacy code is to move away from it as soon as you can. Alternatives include defining a security process for managing security vulnerabilities in legacy code, monitoring legacy code closely (at least annually), and quarantining products running legacy code so that they pose minimal risk to the environment.

M&A security assessment strategy is one of the key success factors in the post-release phase. As mentioned earlier, you may not have access to source code, so assessment strategies need to take this into account—that is, you may need to use binaries rather than source code. In the end, M&A security assessment should provide input into the overall quality of the software being acquired. If this assessment is not thought through carefully or done correctly, the software security group or the information security group may end up dealing with repercussions for a long time to come. A weakness in acquired software may weaken the software posture of other products deployed in the same environment.

In addition to a strategy for treating legacy code and products and M&A, it is important to define end-of-line plans for the current version of the product/release. An end-of-line road map can guide security strategy from this point on.

2.5 Security Training Management

As we are being asked to do more with less, the rate of vulnerabilities in our systems are accelerating. In a DevOps world, product security managers struggle with what aspects of training need to be added to their existing training programs. Rather than just technical training, this will require courses that can result in real organizational change, such as roles and capabilities beyond security and understanding of and adherence to change management:

Roles: In addition to the traditional training courses for product security specialists in software development, such as SDL best practices, security tools, and threat modeling, this will require areas that enhance their existed product security role so that they can be specialists in a number of areas. A broader perspective such as systems thinking is essential to drive the necessary change in behavior required for a DevOps environment. Rather than traditional training, much of this will be taken care of through mentoring by the Senior Security Architects and Principal Engineers.

Capabilities: Outside the typical product security skills, an in-depth understanding of testing and automation within the DevOps CI/CD environment is critical. It is also important for the security team members to be mentored with an expert beside them to practice in real-world situations.

Change management: Change management, in particular, from "production" and "release" will make or break you in the traditional software development world, and in DevOps this is only intensified. The adherence to a change control process, in particular, for code changes required for security are critical for the success of CI/CD within an DevOps environment.

DevOps by its nature will constantly be changing, as well as the training needed, as it continues to evolve. The standard type of training methods available, such as formal courses, mentoring, online courses, and self-study and research, will remain the same, but the training will need to continue to evolve. You should consider the following when managing your education and training programs:

- Given the limited time that coders and security practitioners have, as well as a low tolerance for multi-hour training courses, they tend to do better with shorter "TED-like" training of 15 to 20 minutes or less.
- In general, people integrate skills quicker and more completely when they learn something and then use it enough for the new skill to become fully incorporated. When using shorter, focused "TED"-like trainings, ensure that learners have sufficient practice time between sessions. We have found that for coders, securely implementing an algorithm involving patterns in the lesson, or reviewing code for issues just learned, positively reinforces new material.
- Formal in-house training courses provided through outside vendors as well as those provided internally through a learning management system (LMS) require a significant investment of time, money, and resources. You may want to try a third-party vendor that provides Web-based training that won't be tied to your systems but that can be customized by your program with grading and proof of completions. Some of the more popular offerings have different levels of training, such as the black belt programs, as well as different training paths and course for developers, security specialists, and managers
- Certification training provided by various professional organizations will certify you in certain security and development specialties requiring successful passing of an exam, work experience, and continued education. If your organization requires or values certain product and security certifications, then you will be obligated to have a training budget and allocate time for these individuals to participate in continuing education to maintain these certifications.
- There are numerous established security conferences that offer application or product security tracks. DevSecOps-focused conferences now exist, and tracks for DevSecOps are becoming available that will provide more focused and relevant training for your teams.
- Mentors such as senior security architects, principal engineers, and experts in solving a particular coding challenge can be useful by creating short videos that will be beneficial for to a particular

team, select individual, or the organization as whole. These videos can be used in a focused meeting on the topic being covered or linked to an internal Web page for individual use, when needed. This can be very successful when used to describe how to overcome a sensitive technical or security issue specific to your organization. This is much more relevant than a third-party providing specialized training and limits the amount of sensitive IP being exposed outside your organization. It can also be useful when a team solves a problem that can be used by multiple teams in the engineering group. It will be relevant to the environment you are working in, up to date and nearly in real time, and unique to your working environment and infrastructure.

- As soon as those on a leadership development track have something to teach, they must be encouraged to do so. Teaching solidifies what we have learned, as we must figure out some way to explain it. Make the expectation to teach be a part of your career development strategy. Over time, there will be less pressure on the senior team members while also building leadership capabilities. The authors have seen this go viral within our teams. Teaching, sharing, and mentoring become a way of life.

- Negotiate training packages with your security products so that you can train a small cadre of employees such as your SSCs and then have them do hands-on training with the development teams on an "as-available" and "as-needed" basis, to not only save money but to leverage time. If you have a global team, you can also save travel costs needed for vendor on-site training by having an employee who is already trained to do in-house training. Of course, internal webinars are less expensive, but sometimes there is other organizational value to providing in-house face-to-face training. Your SSCs are your next generation leadership.

- Unless team members absolutely need to go to a conference to speak, learn a new skill, or gain some knowledge and network with those that have been successful in implementing or using a tool or process you are rolling out or struggling with, try to limit conferences to one or two a year for training purposes. This will not only save your budget but also the morale for those on the ground doing work who may believe there is inequity when others are attending five or more conferences a year.

- Websites, blogs, VoDs, and online documents are useful for staying up on latest trends in DevSecOps Product and Application security.

- Don't forget the old school way of learning through hard copy books and industry white papers. Although hard copy books tend to be expensive, you can save a lot of money by leveraging the use of digital tech book vendors that many larger companies have contracted out to. Professional development e-book subscription services typically have large libraries of tech books in digital format that are at a significant cost savings for the reader. This will save your development and security organization a significant amount of money when multiplied over larger development groups.

- If you have a large IT shop, they will likely have budgets for mandatory InfoSec training. You may be able to share costs with IT for internal training courses, since application security courses are typically offered as part of their vendors' available curriculum. They can typically add this training course to their curriculum to be shared by the engineering team, thus resulting in significantly reduced cost for the development and security teams.

- Don't discount education courses that are available at local colleges, distance learning, or through professional organizations.

- For security training that is often considered passive, "Capture the Flag" (CTF) contests offer a new approach to cybersecurity training and simulation by gamifying training in a way that keeps contestants engaged while imparting real skills. This can be used within an organization, or your teams can participate in CTFs and other similar contests offered by a number of vendors and numerous conferences.

2.6 Security Budget Management

Software security is no longer an afterthought within a company that develops software but a board-level issue that can cost people their jobs when security vulnerabilities in the code are discovered and exploited in a post-release product. Simply investing larger amounts of money for security, however, is not a solution and does not ensure higher security for the organization. Spending wisely, efficiently, and appropriately is the true solution and will maximize the ROI. This, of course, includes security technologies and the people who run them as well as the identification of the strengths and weaknesses of the current secure development practices and infrastructure and where security needs improvement. Managing your security budget correctly will determine the most cost-effective way to do so. Some of the line items in your budget will include security software, hardware, education and training, personnel, external audits required in customer contracts or regulatory requirements, third-party services, and consultants.

There can be a budget-allocation struggle due to historical friction that has developed between security and the DevOps teams. The security teams typically believed developers introduce risk to organizations by releasing code that might not be secure, and the DevOps teams believed the security practices and engagements were a drag on innovation. As discussed previously, one of the goals of DevSecOps is to build alignment through better synergy and collaboration to alleviate this misunderstanding and the friction that can follow. Unless you are in a very mature DevOps organization where security has been truly been built in, be cognizant that these perceptions may still exist and will need to be addressed as you are negotiating your security budget. There are also cases in which an executive or other senior leader is hired from another company that had a less mature DevOps/DevSecOps organization and relationship. If that person is involved in the budget negotiations, some education may be in order by yourself or someone senior to you.

2.6.1 Preparing and Delivering the Budget Message

Negotiating with security practitioners and developers is typically very different from with the CFO and their finance team as well as other non-engineering business executives. This requires establishing business drivers as part of your budget proposal. To optimize your ability to succinctly articulate your message, a model for articulating security benefits into business value messages will help you identify your business drivers. Gartner's 4I Model describes four dimensions against which the business value of investing in strategic information security activities can be captured, summarized, and communicated in a concise format:

Investment, which captures the expected returns—The value can be typically articulated as expected financial returns, brand enhancement, competitive differentiation, future agility, organizational adaptability, and so on.

Integrity, which emphasizes the impact of the reliability and availability of daily business operations— The benefits are manifested as continuous improvement in the confidentiality, availability, and accuracy of business information and processes.

Insurance and assurance, which address the risk management benefits—These result from an increased insight into the information risk factors facing the organization, resulting in more-effective and appropriate risk management activities. Risk management options include accepting, avoiding, transferring, mitigating, or ignoring assessed risks.

Indemnity, which highlights the compliance benefits of limiting regulatory and stakeholder exposure—This results from improved awareness, increased accountability, stakeholder support and, improved compliance.[*]

---

[*] Scholtz, T. (2016). *Articulating the Business Value of Information Security.* Resource Report—ID Number: G00141091. Stamford (CT): Gartner Inc.

The security strategy, plans, and continued and record of improved execution must support the business value expectations and strategy. If not, the security budget approval will be at risk.

2.6.2 Other Things to Consider When Preparing Your Budget

DevSecOps, by definition, gives security teams a seat at the table with development and operations teams to ensure that security is built into DevOps initiatives. DevSecOps must consider more than just choosing the right security tools. It's about building a culture in which security is both a priority and a shared responsibility right from the start of development initiatives. Anything that helps provide this needs to be considered in the security budget. Some key things to consider during the budget process include the following:

- Some legacy systems can't properly help your development teams discover, help provide solutions to guard against today's advanced and sophisticated threats, or adjust to the fast and continuous pace of DevOps, CI/CD, and Agile working environments. In short, they are no longer relevant to the new development methodologies or best practices.
- Having too many security tools in your environment can result in unnecessary work and costs, duplicate data, questions from your development team as to your credibility, and, in some cases, a total disaster. Before putting additional solutions in your budget, due diligence must be done to look at the security tools you already have in place. Legacy security tools need to be modified or removed and then assessed to determine whether these have overlapping capabilities with existing tools or that a gap or gaps need to be filled with a new tool or tools. Before replacing or consolidating your tools, you must know how many and what security tools are already in place and being used as well as the capabilities they provide. Once you understand their effectiveness, you can consolidate wherever possible, freeing up your budget for other needs. In the generic SDL (Chapter 3), we will cite a DevSecOps reference architecture from Sonatype™ that places many security tools into the context and ordering of a hypothetical DevOps chain.
- As with security tolls, minimize the number of vendors you are using. This includes those vendors for both tools and professional services. More is not better. The most important thing is the ability to manage (resources and budget), the quality of the vendors tools, and the competence of those providing professional services.
- When assessing and defending your security budget in an DevOps world, it is important to show how the tools, people, and services being proposed will help drive social and cultural changes with regard to security in the DevOps environment. This will help sell your ROI to others during the negotiation process.
- In the Agile environment, there is a very close tie with the customer. The customers are able to see the value they need because they are able to evaluate and have an impact on the working software. The ability to show how things in your security budget will have a positive effect on customer satisfaction can be a big budget selling point.
- I highlighted a few things that you can do to reduce training and education costs in the previous section. Keep these in mind when assessing the need for training services and defending your budget for education and training.
- Security features built into products help to enhance and sell the product just as other features do. Where applicable, keep this in mind when you are doing your ROI.
- As security moved left in DevOps, DevSecOps has resulted in the combination of development and security to mitigate risk. Although developers still seem reluctant to take on the cost of incorporating security into their processes, security budgets should move left, so that development can invest in security.

- Nontechnical executives may not understand your environment, but they will likely understand regulatory and compliance requirements. Use this as leverage in your budget request when these requirements exist in your environment and your team is part of the compliance process.
- Hosting costs must be accounted for if you have a product or new feature that will be or is being hosted in the cloud.

2.7 Security Governance, Risk, and Compliance (GRC) Management

Governance, risk, and compliance (GRC) management must always be involved in the software development process; otherwise, the released products provide liabilities that will be passed on to the company, its customers, and its shareholders. GRC refers to all the capabilities that integrate the governance, management, and assurance of performance, risk, and compliance activities. A common blind spot in GRC deployment in DevOps is the SDLC. Although standard GRC approaches have a way to go to complement DevSecOps and DevOps concepts, automated tools and appropriate processes and procedures are moving in that direction. It is crucial that GRC requirements (that include security requirements) are incorporated effectively into all DevOps automated and manual processes, which, of course, will include the entire SDLC, ideally built into the SDL. This will result in the ability to successfully pass audits and avoid regulatory fines.

In order for GRC to be a DevOps enabler rather than an obstacle, it must be able to adapt to the fast pace and highly Agile nature of the DevOps team. Conversely, the DevOps team must support governance, where regulations are constantly changing and evolving and new versions are either in the pipeline or will be introduced in the near future along with new compliance standards. This will require that the legal and compliance teams work closely with the developers to design and implement changes that satisfy risk and control points. This will require awareness and training provided or coordinated by the legal and compliance teams so that the developers can learn the rules and laws specifically governing their particular industry and collaboratively figure out how to implement their associated control points and software elements that will ensure compliance. This will typically require breaking down the same organizational communications silos that existed for security. If the DevOps teams are properly trained in GRC and empowered with the right technology, they will be a true asset with regard to technical vulnerability and threat management. Effectively incorporating security and other GRC measures, and automating them where possible into the development and operations processes, allows your organization to truly reap the maximum benefits of security and GRC.

In our programs, James and Brook have made use of a lightweight governance technique that fosters individual responsibility, while also providing reasonable governance to ensure that teams are, in fact, enacting the SDL. Rather than manual, in-person boards of experts, we have governance of the SDL that can be successfully accomplished through peer+senior review of task results. This has been particularly effective in governing the parts of the SDL that require significant experience to execute well, for instance, threat models. We present our current approach in Chapter 4, which is devoted to threat modeling and secure design. (The peer review and escalation model has already been discussed in *Securing Systems* (2015)[*] and *Secrets of a Cyber Security Architect* (2019).[†]

Another area that is critical for both GRC and security is what we call "consequence management." There must be consequences for both willful and mistaken violation of requirements that have been mandated by both organizations as well as course corrections identified to make sure this doesn't occur

---

[*] Schoenfeld, B. (2015). "12.2 Some Thoughts on Governance," Chapter 12. *Securing Systems*. Boca Raton (FL): CRC Press/Taylor & Francis Group, pp. 348–350.

[†] Schoenfeld, B. (2019). "4.3.1 Nimble Governance," Chapter 4. *Secrets of a Cyber Security Architect*. Boca Raton (FL): Auerbach Publications/Taylor & Francis Group, pp. 90–92.

again. The severity of these consequences will be predicated on the potential or real damage to the company and whether the violation was willful.

In addition to the role of audits to conduct internal audits or bring in a third party to audit, to ensure compliance with regulatory requirements and standards, as well requirements to meet customer contracts, you can also use audits to help drive cultural changes. This is done with security when organizations encounter resistance to change the product to meet regulatory or customer security requirements or resistance to organizational changes required to support GRC and security. Given that the audit organization typically reports to the board, this usually fixes the problem.

Keep in mind that you can inherit your customers' security requirements. This is particularly true with financial and government customers. This needs to be considered from a business and resource perspective when marketing and sales start pitching your products to these types of customers. For example, if your company decides to take on a customer that requires you become FedRAMP* certified, this may result in a significant amount of overhead to make sure you can meet things such as infrastructure; the ability to eliminate shared environments; meet personnel, citizenship, and clearance requirements; specific software and physical security requirements; and SLA requirements. FedRAMP stands for Federal Risk and Authorization Management Program and is mandatory for Federal Agency cloud deployments and service models at the low-, moderate-, and high-risk impact levels.

SDL and other related tools have supported GRC compliance checks for the last few years, but it has been a small market that has started to expand rapidly with the advent of DevOps. GRC collection, compliance, training, and management hooks are now embedded in the most popular SDLC frameworks tools.

Automated tools can help you achieve and maintain compliance with regulatory standards. These tools deliver a proactive and collaborative platform to effectively integrate tools, processes, and technology for compliance reporting; set thresholds for compliance like HITRUST, HIPAA, and PCI frameworks; and strengthen and improve regulatory compliance responsiveness to new change or risks.†

One area of particular interest for automation is the Application Security Risk Threat Management (ASTRM). which is essentially GRC for DevOps. ASRTM complements but does not replace SAST, DAST, and interactive application security testing (IAST). Coupled with a solid foundation of security awareness training, ASRTM enables teams to systematically build and maintain secure software. ASRTM solutions have four major capabilities: threat modeling, requirements generation, Application Lifecycle Management (ALM) integration, and testing integration and aggregation.‡ ASRTM vendors are still maturing, and it is important that GRC and security practitioners in a DevOps environment should keep a close eye on how they are managing applicable frameworks such as GDPR and NIST.

Another area of interest for automation is configuration management. Configuration management systems enable you to configure, update, and patch systems more efficiently and effectively. Their ability to address GRC challenges are often overlooked. Organizations have a set of policies by which they must abide, which include how the organization is to comply with legal requirements and relevant regulations or standards. Information is created and read by applications that run on servers accessing the data across networks and can be used to identify the connections between each of these components so that they can better understand the overall environment and use this information to address GRC challenges such as meeting specific compliance standards, for example, the Payment Card Industry (PCI) and Data Security Standard (DSS) for financial control systems. The resulting asset discovery information in the configuration management database (CMDB) has enough data on all elements of

---

* U.S. Government. (2020). FedRAMP Website. Retrieved from https://www.fedramp.gov

† Tauruseer. (2020). "Audit—Automate Compliance to Regulatory Standards." Retrieved from https://www.tauruseer.com/why-tauruseer/unite-devsecops-teams

‡ Security Compass. (2020). "Introducing Application Security Requirements and Threat Management (ASRTM)." Retrieved from https://resources.securitycompass.com/blog/introducing-application-security-requirements-and-threat-management-asrtm-2

the hardware and software to enable admins to search for patterns and usage, which is also useful in combating GRC challenges. This is another area for GRC and security practitioners to keep an eye on.

The GRC, legal, and security teams will work closely to ensure the creation, updates, and compliance with the DevOps security policies. The purpose of a software security policy is to define what needs to be protected and how it will be protected, including reviewing and incorporating policies from outside the SDL that may impact the development process. These might include policies governing software or applications developed or applied anywhere in the organization. During this phase, any policy that exists outside the domain of the SDL policy is reviewed. Corporate security and privacy policies will likely instruct designers and developers on what the security and privacy features need to be and how they must be implemented. Other policies may include those that govern the use of third-party and open source software or the protections and control of source code and other intellectual property within and outside the organization. Assuming the software security group is separate from the centralized information security group, it is important that both groups collaborate on all policies and guidelines related to the development and post-release security support and response of software from that organization. It is also important to collaborate with the privacy function of the company, whether it is a centralized group or outside legal counsel.

The SDL also provides an invaluable guide for software developers setting a security standard for their organization and should offer a roadmap for implementation without disrupting the core business of producing quality software applications. This is another key area that the GRC and security team will collaborate on. Unless the senior leadership of the development organization and the management team support this model, the SDL will likely fail. It must be driven by a policy that is signed off, promulgated, and provides support by the software development management team and ideally by the CEO. An organization should have a documented and repeatable SDL policy and guideline that supports the SDLC, including its business needs and as a complement to the engineering and development culture that it supports. The culture and maturity of the organization are very important to consider in the development of the SDL policy, so that you ensure it will be both feasible and practical to implement. The management style, complexity of people, process, and technology needs, including the overall architecture of the product, will help determine how granular or objective in focus the guidelines will be. The amount of outsourced development, if any, will need to be assessed as part of this process as well. An internal development team will require more detailed procedures, whereas an outsourced function will require more contractual objects, service levels, and detailed deliverables.

2.7.1 SDL Coverage of Relevant Regulations, Certifications, and Compliance Frameworks

One key criterion for success early in the SDL is whether all key regulations, compliance frameworks, and certifications for the product (or libraries) have been identified. This success factor depends on understanding product objectives and customer uses. One can easily make the mistake of thinking that certain regulations will not be applicable because their use cases are not considered valid. Customers, however, often have a different take on this. A cloud product that a customer uses to interact with other customers might not need to be compliant with HIPAA from one viewpoint. However, for a customer, it is crucial that this product, if not compliant with HIPAA, at least does not create issues that may result in noncompliance.

For nearly 30 years, Brook has regularly reminded us that any piece of software that its users find even moderately useful will be employed for tasks that the makers of the software never imagined. It's very important when thinking through use cases, that one does not preclude those imaginative uses such that one also excludes potential customers.

Compliance frameworks are another thing to watch out for. Depending on how the product is used (in-house or in the cloud), different permutations are expected by customers. If customers are going for an ISO 27001 certification and are using your product in a cloud environment, they will expect a demonstrable and verifiable operational and product security posture. If customers are paying for your service using credit cards, not only they but your environment may fall under the regulations of PCI standards. Though we are focusing on product security here, operational security is equally important.

Finally, many times, while covering regulations, compliance frameworks, and certifications, security and development teams fail to look closely at dependencies. For example, if the product needs to comply with the Federal Information Processing Standards (FIPS), how will using an open source library affect compliance? If the product needs to obtain Certification A, will dependent software make or break this certification? These questions need to be carefully considered to prevent future firefighting.

2.7.2 Third-Party Reviews

Over the last few years, customers of software vendors have increasingly requested independent audits to verify the security and quality of software applications that they have either purchased or are evaluating for purchase. Software vulnerabilities have increasingly been tied to high-profile data breaches over the last few years and have resulted in more customers requiring independent and visible proof that the software they purchase is secure. This, of course, has helped put pressure on companies that develop software to ensure that the secure software development processes are built into the SDLC to avoid the very costly discovery of vulnerabilities that are caught post-release—often a sign of an immature, ineffective, or nonexistent software security program. Because of the preponderance of post-release code having security vulnerabilities and privacy issues that should have been caught during development, third-party assessment of post-release or near-release code has become the norm in the industry, whether the company producing the software has a reputation for producing secure code or not. In some cases, it is demanded by the prospective or current customer, and, in other cases, it is conducted proactively by the company producing the code.

Even for companies that have outstanding software security programs, software applications can alternate in and out of compliance with policies or regulatory requirements over long periods of time for a variety of reasons. For example, a new functionality or use case in a new version of the application may introduce new vulnerabilities or planes of attack, causing the application to drop out of compliance. Additionally, these requirements may change over time. Many companies use third-party code reviews to help identify these situations rather than spend the limited resources of their internal teams.

Third-party testing should include testing the entire stack, not just your product. That means performing testing as outlined in earlier chapters as well as continuous post-release testing. At a minimum, post-release testing should include annual penetration (pen) testing (application and software stack). Any new code released after initial release should follow the SDL requirements outlined in previous chapters.

The biggest challenge is to do this in a timely and cost-effective manner while also protecting the source code and other intellectual property during the process. Some of the choices for third-party testing include the following.

1. *Hand over source code to a third party for inspection.* This is not a real option for those who want to protect the most precious intellectual property that a software development organization possesses—their source code.
2. *Contract manual penetration testing services that can also do deep-dive code and software architectural design reviews for each new release.* To avoid the risk of source code leaving the control of the company that is developing it, contractors must be required to work onsite in a controlled environment, under special nondisclosure agreements and under specific guidelines. These typically include a source-code protection policy and IP-protection guidelines. An alternative to this

approach is to employ a company that only uses tools that require the exposure of binary code only. In this case, the contractor inspects the application at the same level as it is attacked—the binaries—and can ensure that all threats are detected. This type of testing can be done onsite or remotely, as a service.

3. *Purchase, install, and train development teams to use on-premise tools and function as lower-level software security architects as an extension of the software security group to conduct the "people side" of the software security architectural review.* Then invite auditors into your organization to document your processes. Many mature software security organizations have done this. A mature software security program such as that described in this book will help scale and reduce the need for additional headcounts to do this work. Building this into your SDL/SDLC process is a cost-effective, efficient, and manageable way to do this.

4. *Require third-party suppliers of code in your application to do the same.* In today's software development environments, a majority of software development organizations make use of code developed elsewhere, either commercial off-the-shelf (COTS) or open source software. Just as with internally developed software, a third party should prepare an attestation report per the software application owner's requirements, which may include an attack-surface review; review of cryptography; architecture-risk analysis; technology-specific security testing; binary analysis, if source code is unavailable; source code analysis, if it is; and fuzz testing, in addition to a general pen testing routine.

Third-party reviews are often critical to demonstrate "security" to end users and customers. A preferred list of vendors should be created by the software team, and these vendors should be vetted for their skills as well as ability to handle sensitive information. Since these vendors will be handling sensitive security information, it is important to note if they use full disk encryption, communicate securely, dispose of any customer data as soon as testing ends, and so on. Any time there is a need for security testing, one of these vendors should be selected for the testing. Security testing of the entire software stack and product portfolio should be performed at least annually.

2.7.3 Post-Release Certifications

Relevant certifications needed after the product is released (or deployed in the cloud) should have been identified in one of the earlier phases of the SDL cycle. Requirements for certifications should have been included in security and privacy requirements. This will prevent any retrofitting or findings during compliance audits for certifications. Certifications often do require annual audits or surveillance audits. The security team should work with the security compliance team to ensure that all relevant controls requirements are met.

There are numerous security-focused certifications that a software development team may face after the release of the product that are added on as a requirement rather than during the development process, for a variety of reasons. These reasons may include use of the software in industry or government sectors that were not planned for during design and development; new uses for the software; and new government, country, regional, business or industry sector, or regulatory requirements that did not exist prior to the release of the product. Post-release certification requirements that did not exist prior to the release of the product are a forgivable offense, but missing any that are currently required and were missed early in the SDL are not. Avoiding noncompliance with certifications required for the use of the software that is being developed requires either an internal resource in the company dedicated to following software use certifications and other requirements, including privacy requirements, or an individual or organization that specializes in this area of experience. This becomes particularly challenging as the number of these types of certifications and requirements increases rapidly around the globe.

2.7.4 Privacy

Stricter regulations, increased liabilities, and heightened public awareness mean that protecting personally identifiable information (PII) is no longer a luxury but rather a requirement and priority. If your software lacks the security necessary to protect PII, your organization risks steep fines, costly litigation, and a violation of public trust, from which you might never recover. Regulations can also vary significantly from one region to the next, adding to the complexity of ensuring compliance throughout the data's lifetime. And some of those regulations can have far-reaching implications.[*] For example, the General Data Protection Regulation (GDPR) went into effect in the European Union (EU) in May 2018, and over the last two years, the industry is only now starting to feel its full impact. Since 2018, there have been a significant number of reported data breaches. Organizations that fail to comply with the GDPR can face stiff penalties. There are two levels of fines based on the GDPR. The first is up to €10 million or 2% of the company's global annual turnover of the previous financial year, whichever is higher. The second is up to €20 million or 4% of the company's global annual turnover of the previous financial year, whichever is higher.[†] The potential fines are substantial and are a wake-up call for companies to ensure compliance with the GDPR. Google[®], for example, was fined €50 million in January 2019 for GDPR violations, representing the majority of fines collected in the first year of GDPR enactment.[‡] GDPR requires organizations to report breaches within 72 hours of being discovered. The regulation more clearly defines what constitutes protected data, provides individual users with greater control over their data, and regulates how organizations can use that data. The GDPR can also impact organizations outside the EU that do business either directly or indirectly with the EU, affecting their operations, workloads, and data protection strategies, wherever that data resides.[§]

The enforced consequences of GDPR resulted in numerous other privacy-related regulatory requirements and regional laws to pop up around the world defining user protections and corporate responsibilities. For example, The California Consumer Privacy Act (CCPA) is the first comprehensive privacy law in the United States. The CCPA also provides a private right of action, which is limited to data breaches. Under the private right of action, damages can come in between $100 and $750 per incident per consumer. The CCPA went into effect on January 1, 2020. However, enforcement by the California Attorney General (AG) started on July 1, 2020.[¶]

As with security, privacy must be built into the development process ensuring that data is protected during all phases of the DevOps process. The best way to do that is to build privacy into the application delivery pipeline right from the start. In many cases, the controls required for privacy will also be security controls.

Since building privacy into software requires planning, structure, and design, privacy must be seen as a parallel assessment to SDL design activities. The threat model will highlight both attacks that breach security and hurt assets, and that break privacy requirements. Hence, privacy requirements are one of the outputs of threat modeling. In Chapter 4, we expand our discussion on secure design and threat modeling, including the use of the threat model attack scenarios to drive privacy requirements, as these relate to security. (There are other privacy requirements that aren't security related. Privacy must not be constrained to just its security elements.)

[*] Sheldon, R. (2019). "Redgate Hub: Introduction to DevOps: Security, Privacy, and Compliance." Retrieved from https://www.red-gate.com/simple-talk/sysadmin/devops/introduction-to-devops-security-privacy-and-compliance/

[†] GDPR Associates. (2020). "GDPR Fines." Retrieved from https://www.gdpr.associates/data-breach-penalties/

[‡] msbiinfo.com. (2019). "Introduction to DevOps: Security, Privacy, and Compliance." Retrieved from http://www.msbiinfo.com/2019/09/introduction-to-devops-security-privacy.html

[§] Sheldon, R. (2019). "Redgate Hub: Introduction to DevOps: Security, Privacy, and Compliance."

[¶] Microsoft. (2020). "California Consumer Privacy Act (CCPA)." Retrieved from https://docs.microsoft.com/en-us/microsoft-365/compliance/offering-ccpa

Protecting users' privacy is another important component of the SDL process and should be considered a system design principle of significant importance in all phases of the SDLC. Just as with a failure in security, a failure to protect the customer's privacy will lead to an erosion of trust. As more and more cases of unauthorized access to customers' personal information are disclosed in the press, the trust in software and systems to protect customers' data is deteriorating. In addition, many recent privacy laws and regulations such as GDPR and the California Consumer Privacy Act (CCPA) have placed an increased importance on including privacy in the design and development of both software and systems. As with security, software that has already progressed through the development life cycle can be very expensive to change; it is much less expensive to integrate privacy preservation methodologies and techniques into the appropriate phases of the SDLC to preserve the privacy of individuals and to protect PII data. Some key privacy design principles contained in Microsoft's SDL include the ability to provide appropriate notice about data that is collected, stored, or shared so that users can make informed decisions about their personal information, enable user policy and control, minimize data collection and sensitivity, and the protection of the storage and transfer of data.[*]

It is imperative that privacy protections be built into the SDLC through best practices implemented through the SDL. Ignoring the privacy concerns of users can invite blocked deployments, litigation, negative media coverage, and mistrust.

2.7.4.1 Privacy Impact Assessment (PIA) Plan Initiated

There are a number of methods that can be used for privacy protection and management. In the past, however, privacy tools have generally been applied in an *ad hoc* way, or in a piecemeal fashion to address immediate issues. As with security, these issues are typically addressed post-release. Just as with security, treating privacy as a secondary consideration or as an issue for future exploration during system design does not provide an effective level of privacy protection. Addressing the components of privacy issues— not through a holistic design and implementation—leads to further potential privacy issues. Privacy must be a fundamental design consideration that is integrated into every phase of SDLC.

There are a growing number of privacy regulatory requirements on a variety of levels—state, federal, and international—resulting in a patchwork of compliance requirements that have serious penalties for noncompliance. Rather than devote an entire chapter to recent and upcoming privacy requirements and the potential ramifications of each, we will discuss the best practices needed to adequately cover a majority of what you will face in terms of privacy, regulatory, and policy compliance. Software programs are designed to integrate with the user's computer and, therefore, may be able to access and store personal information. Software developers must adhere to the guidelines and privacy policies that relate to the operating systems and platforms for which their software is designed. The bottom line is that when customers entrust your company with sensitive information, every employee is obligated to protect that information. As with security, privacy violations have significant implications for the trust customers have in you, which, in turn, will affect your company's reputation and the potential revenue from the software you develop.

Before you can begin developing a Privacy Impact Assessment (PIA), you will need to evaluate what regulatory legislation or policies are applicable to the software you are developing. In some models, this is called the data sensitivity assessment. Since most developers do not have a background in law, and regulators generally do not have a background in software development, understanding the issues surrounding regulatory compliance can be difficult and frustrating. It is often very difficult for developers to fully understand the language and requirements described by legislation, and it is often not easy to pin down explicit software requirements. To successfully translate regulations into requirements, it will

---

[*] Microsoft SDL details can be found at https://www.microsoft.com/en-us/securityengineering/sdl/practices #practice7

be necessary to engage with your corporate legal counsel and any external legal privacy experts who may be on retainer. If you happen to have a Chief Privacy Officer (CPO), this person can be an ideal partner who can offer you the resources and training you will need to meet the challenge of building privacy into the SDL and ultimately the SDLC.

The PIA created at this phase is only a preliminary version for initial system specifications and requirements and is designed to guide developers in assessing privacy through the early stages of development. For simplicity, we have included only the privacy design principles requirements analysis and part of the initial PIA analysis. At its core, this stage of the PIA is the planning, documentation, and assessment of preliminary requirements for PII and personal information used by the software and includes or accesses the following:

- **Education of stakeholders.** All stakeholders should be educated on the "four C's" of privacy design (comprehension, consciousness, control, and consent) at the Security Assessment (A1) discovery and kick-off meeting. The architects and developers should be asking whether they need to collect the data, have a valid business need to do so, and whether the customer will support the software's business purpose for collecting their PII.
- **Additional software interaction.** External system processes, other systems interacting with the new software and their use of PII, personal information, and system users.
- **Collection of PII.** The purposes and requirements for the collection of PII.
- **PII storage retention.** Proposed personal information retention periods and reasons for the lengths of those periods.
- **Access.** Determine what entities will have access to the PII and personal information and the preliminary design for separation of duty/tasks/roles/data in the software.*
- **Privacy management tools.** Identification of privacy management tools and system processes that may be needed to manage personal information in the software and the solution it may be part of. This is particularly important if the software is going to be a component of an SaaS- or cloud-based solution.
- **Security safeguards.** The setting of requirements for security safeguards that will be used to protect PII and personal information. These defenses will be a natural result of threat modeling who will attack, through what interfaces, and by what means—that is, threat models must include privacy protection requirements.
- **Integrity of the data.** Determine that PII and personal information are kept up to date and accurate.
- **Assess whether there are any conflicts between security and privacy requirements.** If so, they need to be addressed and resolved at this stage of the development process. This step includes the categorization of the level of privacy and security protection that the software will require.
- **Apply the principle of least privilege.** Essentially, this entails limiting access to "need to know." Access to user data should be limited to those who have a legitimate business purpose for accessing the data. In addition, nonusers such as administrators or database managers should only be given access to the smallest amount of user data needed to achieve the specific business purpose. This must include third parties that have access to the data or to which it is transferred: They should only be given the specific data they need to fulfill their business purpose. Data protection provisions, including retention and destruction requirements, are typically required of third parties through contract agreements.
- **Websites and Web services.** All externally facing websites must have a link to a privacy statement on every page. This includes pop-ups that collect PII. Whenever possible, the same privacy statement should be used for all sites within a domain.

---

* The comprehensive list of required access points toward the defenses that will be needed to keep everyone else out.

- **The use of cookies.** PII and identifiers that facilitate tracking may be stored in cookies as small files that are stored on a user's computer. They are designed to hold a modest amount of data specific to a particular client and website, and can be accessed either by the Web server or the client computer. Privacy guidelines for cookie usage apply to locally stored text files that allow a server-side connection to store and retrieve information, including HTTP cookies (e.g., Web cookies) and Flash cookies (e.g., Flash Shared Objects). Persistent cookies must not be used where a session cookie would satisfy the purpose. Persistent cookies should expire within the shortest time frame that achieves the business purpose. PII stored in a persistent cookie must be encrypted.

- **IP addresses.** The customer's IP address is always sent with the data as part of the communication protocol when it is transferred over the network. As of the date of this writing, there is still a lot of debate and discussion as to whether an IP address is PII. Privacy regulations such as the GDPR define an IP address as PII since it is a data point that can be used to identify a person. The fact that privacy regulators are even discussing this is a warning sign that we may need to consider the possibility that this information will fall into the category of PII in the foreseeable future. Storing an IP address with PII should be avoided if anonymity is required in order to avoid correlation between the two. If possible, the IP address should be stripped from the payload to reduce its sensitivity by limiting the number of digits. The IP address can also be discarded after translating it to a less precise location.

- **Customer privacy notification.** Software that collects user data and transfers it must provide and give notice to the customer. These are also called disclosure notices and must inform users of the type of information that software will collect and how it will be used. GDPR requires an opt-out clause to allow users the ability to withhold certain types of personal information if they so choose. The type of notice and consent required depends on the type of user data being collected and how it will be used. Customers must also be presented with a choice about whether they want to share this information. All notices must be written in clear, easy-to-read language. There are two types of notification—prominent and discoverable. A "Prominent Notice" is one that is designed to catch the customer's attention and invites customers to inspect the current privacy settings, learn more about their options, and make choices. GDPR requires a Prominent Notice. A "Discoverable Notice" is one the customer has to find. This can be done by selecting a privacy statement link from a Help menu in a software product or by locating and reading a privacy statement on a website. This notification typically includes the type of data that will be stored, how it will be used, with whom it will be shared; how it is protected; available user controls, including the update process if the PII is stored and reusable; and company contact information. If you are developing a product to be used by another company or as an original equipment manufacturer (OEM), the customer company typically has specific privacy statements that third-party software developers are required to include. Other companies may require that software that is designed to work with their products contain a privacy statement that informs users that their information will not be sold to other companies or displayed publicly. Software developers must inform users of the software's method of safeguarding users' personal information in the privacy policy and notification. As we discuss later in the book, this can be done via a valid SSL certificate or by using other security and encryption methods. As with other privacy-related areas, regulatory and other requirements are dynamic, and you should consult your privacy expert or legal counsel for the latest guidance for your software.

- **Children's privacy.** Care must be taken to consider children's privacy, since they may lack the discretion to understand when disclosing their PII that doing so may put them at risk. This has become particularly important with the advent of collaboration and sharing features found in social software. Parental controls are typically added to products, websites, and Web services to help protect the privacy of children. Special efforts must be made to ensure that parents retain control over whether their children can reveal PII. There are numerous privacy requirements for those offering websites and Web Services that target children and/or collect the age of their customers. There are numerous existing and forthcoming state, local, and international requirements for this area. Make sure you consult your privacy expert and/or corporate counsel (or equivalent) if you have software that will fall into this area.

- **Third parties.** Two types of third parties must be considered when assessing your privacy requirements. One type of third party is authorized to act on the company's behalf and uses data in accordance with the company's privacy practices. An independent third party follows its own privacy practices and uses customer information for its own purposes, which require a contract specifying data protection requirements. This requires a software provision for the customer to provide opt-in consent. The customer must provide opt-in consent before PII is shared with an independent third party. Only a Discoverable Notice is required if PII is transferred via a third party authorized to act on the company's behalf.

- **User controls.** User controls give users the ability to manage and control the privacy of their data and change their settings. These controls should be intuitive and easy to find. The data may reside on a computer, within a Web service, or on a mobile device. A Web page is used as the privacy site for Web services. Privacy controls for mobile devices can be on the device itself or via a computer-based user interface or a website that links to the device.

- **Privacy controls required for software used on shared computers.** It is common for software used in home or small office/home office (SOHO) environments to be shared by multiple users. Software designed for use in these environments that also collects or stores PII must provide controls over which users have access to the data. These controls may include strict computer/file/document access control and file permissions or encryption. Controls must also be a default setting and not opt-in. Shared folders must be clearly marked or highlighted.

- **Collaboration, sharing, and social software privacy features.** This is an area with very complex challenges in that content can be shared among a community, and, in some cases, linked community members and shared friends or contacts. Software that supports these types of applications should provide controls and notifications to help prevent the inadvertent sharing of PII with unintended audiences.

- **Security.** Security, of course, is the topic of this book, and a critical element of both privacy and quality. The security requirements will depend on the type of user data collected and whether it will be stored locally, transferred, and/or stored remotely. The end goal for security controls and measures is to protect PII from loss, misuse, unauthorized access, disclosure, alteration, and destruction. The controls and measures include not only software controls such as access controls and encryption in transfer and storage but also physical security, disaster recovery, and auditing. Compensating controls may be needed when standard protection is not possible due to business needs, such as the use of PII as a unique identifier or an IP address or e-mail address used for routing.

- **Privacy Impact Ratings.** The Privacy Impact Rating (P1, P2, or P3) is a practice used in the Microsoft SDL. It measures the sensitivity of the data your software will process from a privacy point of view. Early awareness of all the required steps for deploying a project with high privacy risk may help you decide whether the costs are worth the business value gained. General definitions of privacy impact are as follows:
  - **P1 High Privacy Risk.** The feature, product, or services that store or transfer PII or error reports, monitors the user with an ongoing transfer of anonymous data, changes settings or file-type associations, or installs software.
  - **P2 Moderate Privacy Risk.** The sole behavior that affects privacy in the feature, product, or service is a one-time, user-initiated, anonymous data transfer (e.g., the user clicks a link and goes out to a website).

○ **P3 Low Privacy Risk.** No behaviors exist within the feature, product, or service that affect privacy. No anonymous or personal data is transferred, no PII is stored on the machine, no settings are changed on the user's behalf, and no software is installed.[*]

The risk assessment questionnaire and risk ranking system developed by Microsoft can be a great tool in assessing the risk and prioritizing the work to remediate those risks in the SDL.

In summary, the purpose of the PIA is to provide details on where and to what degree privacy information is collected, stored, or created within the software that you are developing. The PIA should continue to be reviewed and updated as major decisions occur or the proposed use of the software and scope change significantly.

The PIA can occur before threat modeling begins. This is less efficient for developers since they will have to analyze their architecture twice, in some of the same ways. It is better if the PIA and the threat model start as a single activity. Architecture understanding, attack surfaces, attack scenario development, and harms affect the security of all assets, including PII. PIA protection needs are an important input to the threat model. The threat model returns the security controls required to protect PII. Although these two analyses must not be confused, they work in close tandem. Communication between privacy subject matter experts (SMEs) and threat modelers is compulsory for success.

2.7.4.2 Privacy Implementation Assessment

It is imperative that your estimate of work required in adhering to privacy policies and practices, both within the company and outside it, is as accurate as possible. This will enable significant cost savings down the road. For example, if privacy practices require that PII data be encrypted across the board, it is critical that this need is identified during the design phase. Once the software is in the execution and release stages, it is often cost prohibitive to do this. We have seen Fortune 500 companies in which such decisions are taken during service pack release. By then, however, it is extremely difficult to fix the problem accurately. It is also very expensive. Another example of the problem is network segmentation. In a cloud/SaaS-based environment, this is an important decision to make. Often, there will be multiple products hosted out from this shared environment. How to best protect one product from another is an important question for the design phase.

Security controls that help to protect PII data must consider all aspects of data protection, including, but not limited to, access controls, data encryption in transfer and storage, physical security, disaster recovery, and auditing. In many cases, the same security controls that are essential to protecting critical business data, including confidential and proprietary information, from compromise and loss are the same that will be used to protect personal information of customers and employees and should be leveraged whenever possible. This can only be determined after identifying, understanding, and classifying the PII data that the organization collects, stores, or transfers.

2.7.4.3 Final Privacy Review

Typically, privacy requirements must be satisfied before the software can be released. Although the final security review must be completed before release, security exceptions, as discussed previously, highlight that not all security issues have to be satisfied before release. Privacy requirement verification is typically verified concurrently with the final security review and, in many cases, is now considered part of the same process. This requires that significant changes that occurred after the completion of the general

---

[*] Microsoft. (2020). "SDL Phase 1: Requirements." Retrieved from https://docs.microsoft.com/en-us/previous-versions/windows/desktop/cc307412(v%3Dmsdn.10)

privacy questionnaire, such as collecting different data types, substantively changing the language of a notice or the style of consent, or identification of new software behavior that negatively affects the protection of privacy, are addressed. This entails reviewing the software for any relevant changes or open issues that were identified during previous privacy reviews or as part of the final security review. Specific privacy requirements for the final review should include the following:

- If the project has been determined to be a P1 project, then the SDL team and privacy lead must review the Microsoft SDL Privacy Questionnaire (Appendix C)* or its equivalent to determine whether a privacy disclosure is required. If the privacy lead determines that a privacy disclosure is waived or covered, then there is no need to meet this requirement. The privacy lead will give final approval for release of the privacy disclosure statement.
- If the project has been determined to be a P2 project, then the privacy lead will determine if a privacy design review is being requested, provide a confirmation that the software architectural design is com- pliant with privacy standards applicable to this software product, or determine if an exception request is needed. The privacy lead typically works with the SDL and developer lead and legal advisor, as appropriate, to complete the privacy disclosure before public release of the product and ensure that the privacy disclosure is posted appropriately for Web-centric products.
- If the project is a P3 project, then no changes affecting privacy requirements compliance have been identified, no additional reviews or approvals are needed, and the final privacy review is complete. If not, then the SDL team and privacy lead will provide a list of required changes.

In addition to the responsibilities, process, and procedures required for a response to software product security vulnerabilities discovered after release and shipment, a similar function to the PSIRT is created for responses to privacy issues discovered after release and shipment.

2.7.4.4 Post-Release Privacy Response

In addition to post-release security issues that may be discovered and disclosed, potential privacy issues may also be discovered. In our experience, privacy-related issues do not get as much attention as security vulnerabilities, nor is a group charted specifically to deal with such issues. A software development company may have a CPO or the equivalent, such as a specialized counsel on retainer, but most do not have a staff and are likely limited to one privacy support expert, at best. This necessitates a close alignment and working relationship between the PSIRT function and the centralized software security group and the privacy function of the company, whether the latter is in-house or outsourced. Post-release privacy response should be built into the PSIRT process just as security should be built into the SDLC. Given the potential legal nature of privacy issues or privacy control vulnerability exploitations, the privacy advisor should script basic talking points, response procedures, and legal escalation requirements for the response team to use to respond to any potential privacy issues discovered post-release. Some basic guidelines follow:

- Privacy experts should be directly involved in all incidents that fall into the P1 and P2 categories described earlier in this book.
- Additional development, quality assurance, and security resources appropriate for potential post-release privacy discovery issues should be identified during the SDL process.
- Privacy experts should participate in the remediation of any post-release privacy incident response issues.

---

* Microsoft Corporation. (2012). "Appendix C: SDL Privacy Questionnaire." Available at http://msdn.microsoft .com/en-us/library/windows/desktop/cc307393.aspx

- Software development organizations should develop their own privacy response plan. This should include risk assessment, a detailed diagnosis, short- and long-term action planning, and implementation of action plans. As with the PSIRT responses outlined above, the response might include creating a patch or other risk-remediation procedures, replying to media inquiries, and reaching out to the external discoverer.

2.8 Security Metrics Management

2.8.1 The Importance of Metrics

In the words of Lord Kelvin, "If you cannot measure it, you cannot improve it."[*] This maxim holds true today, as it applies to product security and the need to measure a software development organization's security posture accurately. Meaningful security metrics are critical, as corporations grapple with regulatory and risk management requirements, tightening security budgets require shrewd security investments, and customers demand proof that security and privacy is being built into their products rather than through the historical post-release fixes.

Metrics tracking is like an insurance policy for your software projects and also assists in managing protection against vulnerabilities. As we have noted repeatedly, the cost of detecting a defect in successive stages of the SDLC is very high compared with detecting the same defect at the stage of the SDLC where the defect originated. Metrics can track these costs and provide significant help in various ROI calculations throughout the SDL/SDLC process. It costs little to avoid potential security defects early in development, especially compared to costing 10, 20, 50, or even 100 times that amount much later in development. A visual representation of the cost of fixing defects at different stages of the SDLC as part of the SDL process is given in Figure 2.6. It can be argued that the cost of preventing just one or two defects from going live is worth the cost of tracking metrics. The ability to foresee defects and remediate them is a good indicator of a healthy software security program, but quality metrics throughout the SDL/SDLC process can help in managing and often avoiding excessive remediation costs.

One goal of the SDL is to catch defects throughout the process as a multistaged filtering process rather than through a single activity or point in time, thus minimizing the remaining defects that lead to vulnerabilities. Each defect removal activity can be thought of as a filter that removes some percentage of defects that can lead to vulnerabilities in the software product.[†] The more defect removal filters there are in the software development lifecycle, the fewer defects that can lead to vulnerabilities will remain in the software product when it is released. More important, early measurement of defects enables the organization to take corrective action early in the SDLC. Each time defects are removed, they are measured. Every defect removal point becomes a measurement point. Defect measurement leads to something even more important than defect removal and prevention: It tells teams where they stand versus their goals, helps them decide whether to move to the next step or to stop and take corrective action, and indicates where to fix their process to meet their goals.[‡] The SDL model that we presented in *Core Software Security* focuses on filtering out defects throughout the SDLC, with a particular emphasis on phases S1–S3 of our model (see Figure 2.7).

Security metrics can be an invaluable resource for assessing the effectiveness of an organization's software security program. Meaningful metrics can be used to continually improve the product security

---

[*] Quotationsbook.com. (2012). "Lord Kelvin Quote." Retrieved from http://quotationsbook.com/quote/46180/

[†] U.S. Department of Homeland Security. (2012). Build Security in "*Secure Software Development Life Cycle Processes*" online document. Retrieved from https://buildsecurityin.us-cert.gov/bsi/articles/knowledge/sdlc/326 -BSI.html

[‡] Ibid.

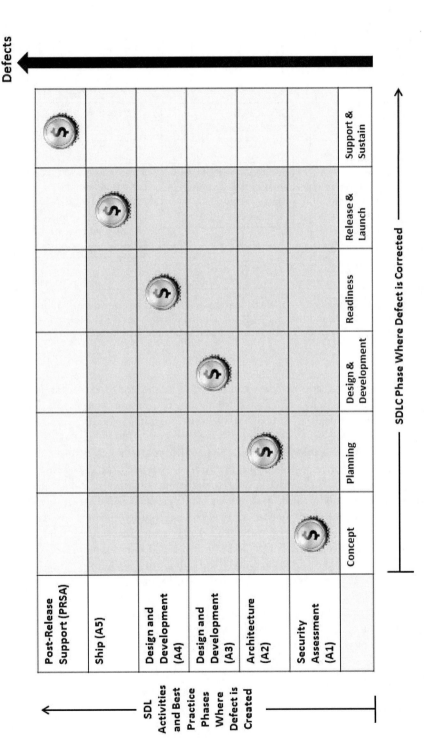

Figure 2.6 Visual Representation of the Cost of Fixing Defects at Different Stages of the SDLC as Part of the SDL Process. (*Source*: Reproduced from Ransome, J. and Misra, A. [2014]. *Core Software Security: Security at the Source*. Boca Raton [FL]: CRC Press/Taylor & Francis Group, p. 43, with permission.)

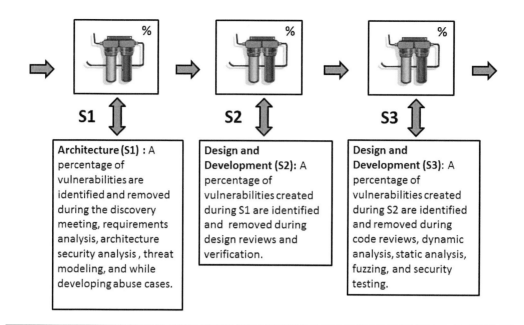

Figure 2.7   SDL Phases S1–S3: Defect Identification and Remediation Filtering Process. (*Source:* Reproduced from Ransome, J. and Misra, A. [2014]. *Core Software Security: Security at the Source.* Boca Raton [FL]: CRC Press/Taylor & Francis Group, p. 44, with permission.)

program's performance, substantiate regulatory compliance, raise the level of security awareness among management and stakeholders, and assist decision makers with funding requests. Without metrics, organizations are reduced to operating their product security programs under FUD: fear, uncertainty, and doubt.

Meaningful security metrics allow an organization to determine the effectiveness of its security controls. To measure the security posture of an organization effectively, product security must first ensure that the proper framework is in place in order to derive meaningful metric data. This includes a product security governance model suited to the entity's strategic and operational requirements. Such a model should support the implementation of practical product security policies and procedures, consistent deployment of best practices and measures, and require strong executive management support across the organization. Best practices dictate a model under which security is managed as an enterprise issue—horizontally, vertically, and cross-functionally throughout the organization. This model is better suited to enable consistent monitoring, measurement, and reporting of an organization's product security posture.

For security to be measured effectively, it must be managed effectively. As companies struggle to protect valuable information assets and justify risk-based decision making, a centralized metrics reporting mechanism is crucial for producing meaningful metrics and providing an ongoing assessment of the state of product security within a software development organization.

2.8.2 SDL Specific Metrics

The following list comprises a compilation of useful metrics from our experience applying SDL in the real world:

- Maturity of security coding program
- Percent of vetted APIs used in the code
- Percent of software code manually reviewed at time of check-in
- Number of lines of code manually reviewed at time of check-in
- Percent of findings missed by manual review but found during expert review
- Percent of findings missed by static analysis but found during manual review
- Number of teams auditing software needed to be tweaked significantly during the SDL
- Percent of developers using integrated static scanning software from their integrated development environment (IDE)
- Number of defects found during manual review, static analysis, and expert review
- Percent of SDL phases "built in" to the SDLC
- Number of "upcoming" architects in the organization
- Percent of software systems assessed to systems produced (Are you reaching every project and every system?)
- Percent of security reviews completed for designs produced
- Maturity of security design review process
- Number of exceptions granted based on recommendations from design review
- Percent of Web servers covered by Web dynamic analysis
- Number of defects found by input fuzzing
- Number of major releases receiving independent Attack and Penetration (A&P) testing
- Number of externally reported security vulnerabilities
- Number of requirements identified through design activities that are part of releases

Even though the waterfall methodology has been replaced by Agile and Scrum methodologies, for the most part, the metrics from that process are still relevant and can be extrapolated and used as appropriate in supporting the business and security needs required for an Agile environment and DevOps security requirements. As a point of reference, see Table 2.1 (formerly Table A.3), which outlines suggested security metrics to use per each stage of a traditional waterfall SDL

2.8.3 Additional Security Metrics Focused on Optimizing Your DevOps Environment

One of the key components of DevOps is to help the organization achieve its business goals. Team-level metrics are still required to effectively manage the process, but this also requires metrics at the organizational level to show you are meeting the needs of the business. This also requires that you are measuring outcomes not just outputs. You must show whether the hours and tests performed are reducing vulnerabilities.

DevOps focuses on continuous delivery and shipping code as fast as possible while optimizing quality and application performance. The speed at which you will be able to do this will be dependent on your team's ability, type of product, and risk tolerance. A key challenge is how you can develop code fast while ensuring its performance and security. Some key metrics to consider in addition to those listed in the previous section are:

- **Automated tests pass %:** DevOps requires a heavy reliance on automation which not only includes unit and functional testing, but security testing as well. This tracks how well your automated tests are working. Identifying if code changes are causing your security tools to fail is also of value, since failure can point at improper configuration, lack of tuning to the code base and architecture, or worse, poor tool placement (wrong tool for the intended task).

- **Customer tickets:** Monitoring for customer support tickets for feedback is important. This can be a good indicator of security issues that you may have not identified yet before they become PSIRT issues. In some cases, what they identify as application quality and performance problems, may be due to security issues in the product.
- **Defect escape rate:** This will track how often defects make it to production. In DevOps, you must be able to ship your code fast. This will tell the business and your team how well you are finding security defects in your software before it goes into production.
- **Deployment size and frequency:** In DevOps, the goal is to have smaller sized deployments as often as possible. Smaller size makes it easier test for and fix security bugs or vulnerabilities.
- **Deployment of QA:** In a DevOps environment, the role of QA is no longer just to detect bugs, but rather to prevent bugs from occurring. The challenge will be to deploy QA early and often to ensure time for testing for any security bugs that will keep your defect escape rate down.

Table 2.1 Metrics for Each Phase of the SDL

Phase	Metric
Security Assessment (A1): SDL Activities and Best Practices	Time in weeks when software security team was looped in
	Percent of stakeholders participating in SDL
	Percent of SDL activities mapped to development activities
	Percent of security objectives met
Architecture (A2): SDL Activities and Best Practices	List of business threats, technical threats (mapped to business threats), and threat actors
	Number of security objectives unmet after this phase
	Percent of compliance with company policies (existing)
	Number of entry points for software (using Data Flow Diagrams [DFDs])
	Percent of risk (and threats) accepted, mitigated, and tolerated
	Percent of initial software requirements redefined
	Number of planned software architectural changes (major and minor) in a product
	Number of software architectural changes needed based on security requirements
Design and Development (A3): SDL Activities and Best Practices	Threats, probability, and severity
	Percent of compliance with company policies (updated)
	Percent of compliance in Phase 2 vs. Phase 3
	Entry points for software (using DFDs)
	Percent of risk accepted vs. mitigated
	Percent of initial software requirements redefined
	Percent of software architecture changes
	Percent of SDLC phases without corresponding software security testing
	Percent of software components with implementations related to privacy controls
	Number of lines of code
	Number of security defects found using static analysis tools
	Number of high-risk defects found using static analysis tools
	Defect density (security issues per 1000 lines of code)

(Continued on following page)

Table 2.1 Metrics for Each Phase of the SDL (*Continued*)

Phase	Metric
Design and Development (A4): SDL Activities and Best Practices	Percent of compliance with company policies (updated) – Percent of compliance in Phase 3 vs. Phase 4
	Number of lines of code tested effectively with static analysis tools
	Number of security defects found through static analysis tools
	Number of high-risk defects found through static analysis tools
	Defect density (security issues per 1000 lines of code)
	Number and types of security issues found through static analysis, dynamic analysis, manual code review, penetration testing, and fuzzing – Overlap of security issues found through different types of testing – Comparison of severity of findings from different types of testing – Mapping of findings to threats/risks identified earlier
	Number of security findings remediated – Severity of findings – Time spent (approximate) in hours to remediate findings
	Number, types, and severity of findings outstanding
	Percentage compliance with security test plan
	Number of security test cases executed – Number of findings from security test case execution – Number of re-tests executed
Ship (A5): SDL Activities and Best Practices	Percent of compliance with company policies (updated) – Percent of compliance in Phase 5 vs. Phase 4
	Number, type, and severity of security issues found through vulnerability scanning and penetration testing – Overlap of security issues found through different types of testing – Comparison of severity of findings from different types of testing – Mapping of findings to threats/risks identified earlier
	Number of security findings remediated (updated) – Severity of findings – Time spent (approximate) in hours to remediate findings
	Number, types, and severity of findings outstanding (updated)
	Percentage compliance with security and privacy requirements
Post-Release Support (PRSA1–5)	Time in hours to respond to externally disclosed security vulnerabilities
	Monthly FTE (full-time employee) hours required for external disclosure process
	Number of security findings (ranked by severity) after product has been released
	Number of customer-reported security issues per month
	Number of customer-reported security issues not identified during any SDL activities

Source: Reproduced from Ransome, J. and Misra, A. (2014). *Core Software Security: Security at the Source.* Boca Raton (FL): CRC Press/Taylor & Francis Group, pp. 356–358, with permission.

- **Error rates:** This is an indicator of quality and security problems as well as ongoing performance and uptime related issues. Error rates can be voluminous but it is important to keep an eye on them and look for spikes. Well-understood and adhered to exception handling best practices are critical to reducing error rates.
- **Lead time for security commitments:** This metric measures the capacity of the organization to respond to change and deliver business value as the time it takes to design and deliver requested

security features. This will also require service level agreement (SLA) monitoring. It is important for the security teams to know what they are being committed to by sales, marketing, legal, and others. Typically, security teams will have a standard language for what they will and will not agree to that legal has agreed to, and exceptions will always be negotiated. Potential resource requirements must be considered when committing teams to additional work or compliance requirements not currently committed to. Some commitments can result in significant delays in delivery and performance.

- **Mean time to detection (MTTD):** This shows how fast you identify issues when they do happen. In an Agile environment, these issues must be fixed quickly. Robust automated application monitoring and good coverage will optimize your ability to detect these issues quickly.
- **Mean time to recovery (MTTR):** This will track how long it takes you to recover from failures. The business will want this measured in business hours rather than clock hours. MTTR in business hours measures actual business impact, as well as evaluating efforts to recover. Robust automated application monitoring in place will optimize your ability for discovery and time to fix. In addition, employing A/B testing groups* helps to identify and then remove releases with issues quickly before the issues foster serious impacts.
- **Mean time to failure (MTTF):** This has been a popular metric for security teams over the years. One of the tenets of Scrum is that failure is inevitable but must be learned from. Be careful about prioritizing or using this metric at all in a DevOps environment. This may take attention away from the metrics that actually help remediate threats.

2.9 Mergers and Acquisitions (M&A) Management

To be competitive, most companies want to develop new products and access new markets and will seek alternatives such as a mergers and acquisitions (M&A) when they cannot do this with their current resources. M&As occur for many reasons but are typically driven by the desire to improve competitiveness, profitability, or other value to the company and its products. In the software world, this is typically a function that you need in your solution set or in the product itself. The talent that may come with acquisition will be a bonus if the primary focus of the M&A is the software of the target company. The activities of an M&A start when the initial discussions for the M&A begin and continue through the due diligence phase and on to the integration of the target company and/or the acquired technology into the parent company. The level of effort and scope of work in the process will depend on the size and complexity of the effort. It should be noted that M&As do not always include all of the resources of the target company. They may include the code for one software product, or multiple technologies or products that are attractive and of value to the acquiring company.

The due diligence phase of an M&A is critical, and security plays a vital role in helping make it successful. If software is included as part of the M&A, a security architectural review and use of automated tools will be required. This may be done either through the use of the potential acquirer's software security staff or through a third party, depending on the restrictions that are imposed as part of the assessment and whether source code can be reviewed. Due to the proprietary nature of source

---

* A/B testing is a strategy where several competing versions of software are run in production at the same time. Although "A/B" might imply two versions, there is no practical limit, especially with today's cloud expansion capabilities: multiple versions of the software. A/B tests are typically implemented via DevOps deployment chain code. These are run in heavily monitored subsets of the horizontally scaled virtual environment, again through DevOps code techniques. Any failures, user confusion, or other abnormalities will cause one of the subset tests to fail, with users automatically being transferred to more successful or stable versions of the software. Hence, in typical Cloud A/B tests, user impact is kept to an absolute minimum, whereas software experiments can be heavily exploited to determine which changes should survive and which abandoned.

code, most target companies with not allow a review of their source code during the M&A assessment process. Thus, an automated tool will be needed that can conduct comprehensive code review via static binary analysis. This is done by scanning compiled or "byte" code at the binary level rather than reviewing source code and typically includes static, dynamic, and manual techniques.

Perhaps the best checklist for conducting an M&A software security assessment can be found in Table 1, "Software Assurance (SwA) Concern Categories," and Table 2, "Questions for GOTS (Proprietary & Open Source) and Custom Software," in the Carnegie Mellon *US CERT Software Supply Chain Risk Management & Due-Diligence, Software Assurance Pocket Guide Series: Acquisition & Outsourcing, Volume II, Version 1.2,** which can be accessed at https://buildsecurityin.us-cert.gov/ sites/default/files/ DueDiligenceMWV12_01AM090909.pdf. Another similar and useful resource is the Carnegie Mellon Software Engineering Institute Working Paper, "Adapting the SQUARE Method for Security Requirements Engineering to Acquisition,"† which can be accessed at https://resources. sei.cmu.edu/library/asset-view.cfm?assetid=51609. SQUARE stands for Systems Quality Requirements Engineering. This particular paper describes the SQUARE for acquisition (A-SQUARE) process for security requirements engineering and is adapted for different acquisition situations.

Some key items that a software security assessor should keep in mind during an M&A software security review include the following:

1. The intent of the M&A software security review is not to focus on getting rid of elements of the target software but rather to assess any business risk that could result from any security risks identified.
2. Highlight anything that may shift the nature of the deal or negatively affect the integration.
3. Look for anything that may be a possible deal breaker.

2.9.1 Open Source M&A Considerations

As part of a due diligence process when software is involved, you will want to purchase it without any legal implications. As the acquiring team, you should check your company's compliance with each one of the licenses for any open source components they may have in their software. This will include whether they have an inventory of all open source components within any software that will be acquired as part of the M&A process as well as license compliance verification and vulnerability management with fix updates in place. You do not want to inherit known open source issues, such as losing their proprietary rights, breaking licensing terms, security risks, and other patent implications. You do not want to proceed with the deal until you are fully aware of the licenses used and the existence of security and quality issues.

2.10 Legacy Code Management

Although they may have once been viewed as an unnecessary cost burden, the best activities and best practices we have outlined in our model are a consequence of the discovery that security was not always

---

* United States Government—US CERT. (2009). *Software Supply Chain Risk Management & Due-Diligence, Software Assurance Pocket Guide Series: Acquisition & Outsourcing, Volume II Version 1.2,* June 16, 2009. Retrieved from https://buildsecurityin.us-cert.gov/swa/downloads/Due DiligenceMWV12_01AM090909.pdf

† Mead, N. (2010). "Carnegie Mellon Software Engineering Institute Working Paper: Adapting the SQUARE Method for Security Requirements Engineering to Acquisition." Retrieved from https://resources.sei.cmu.edu/ library/asset-view.cfm?assetid=51609

a key element of the software development process and sometimes led to security vulnerabilities and risk mitigation costs that rivaled the initial cost of the software to be developed. The acceptance of legacy code is based on an assumption of what is expected to happen, in that the software must be proven to be functionally correct and operationally viable. However, when it comes to software security, the unexpected is what typically causes the vulnerabilities. Not only are these security vulnerabilities financially unacceptable, they are also unacceptable from an operational, functional, and overall risk perspective. This is particularly true when the software supports embedded critical systems and applications, such as those found in national and regional infrastructures, transportation, defense, medicine, and finance. In these applications, the liabilities, costs, mission, and business impacts associated with unexpected security software and system vulnerabilities are considered unacceptable. Unless the architecture of legacy software is correctly assessed and analyzed from a security perspective, the impact of changes cannot be predicted, nor can changes be applied effectively. This is why the same testing and review rigor that is followed during the SDL must be followed during legacy code reviews: as a means of mitigating the unexpected. If done with the proper process and rigor, this will go far in ensuring secure code implementation that is consistent between legacy and new code.

A legacy software application is one that continues to be used because of the cost of replacing or redesigning it and often despite its poor competitiveness and incompatibility with newer equivalents. The most significant issue in this regard is that the organization has likely been depending on this legacy software application for some time, and it pre-dates software development security activities such as those described in our SDL and the mandates that currently drive these practices. Further, a considerable amount of money and resources may be required to eliminate this security "technical debt." Technical debt is the difference between what was delivered and what should have been delivered. The importance of working with legacy code and technical debt is critical for most companies because the product should have been put in "end-of-life" status, and one or more customers do not or cannot upgrade to a newer version of the software. Even if the code was written to an SDL, the SDL has changed over time, along with the threat landscape, which has more exploit types and a vastly better tool set for finding issues compared with the landscape for which the legacy was designed.

Legacy code with technical debt can also exist because even though the product should have been put in "end-of-life" status, one or more customers do not or cannot upgrade to a newer version of the software, and that customer happens to be a critical customer who considers this product essential to its business. This "critical-customer" status often leads to legacy code and products staying in service so that the relationship with the customer(s) still using the product is not jeopardized.

It is not always necessary to pay your technical debt, as it is your financial debt. There may be parts of the code that should be fixed, but the software product still works as advertised; optimizing the code and removing known technical debt may not yield a worthwhile ROI. You may also decide to just take the code out of the program because it no longer serves a purpose. In cases like these, you may never need to pay off that technical debt.

Most important to this discussion is that the technical debt in legacy software may contain security vulnerabilities. Over the course of a project, it is tempting for an organization to become lax regarding software quality and security. Most commonly, this results when teams are expected to complete too much functionality in a given time frame, or quality and security are simply not considered high-priority characteristics for the software.[*] Technical debt may not be from laxity; it can also result because there are new threat types against which the software wasn't prepared because they didn't exist when the software was developed, and no one could have foreseen them. In these situations, there may be security vulnerabilities in the legacy code that exist as a result of the technical debt. From a

---

[*]   Mar, K. and James, M. (2010). "CollabNet Whitepaper: Technical Debt and Design Death." Retrieved from http://www.danube.com/system/files/CollabNet_WP_Technical_Debt_041910.pdf

software product security perspective, the key task when looking at legacy code is to balance the ROI of addressing the security technical debt against the risk of leaving it in. Two primary decisions must be considered:

1. How much new code presumably scrubbed by the SDL are you writing to replace the existing old code? At what rate will the volume of old code be replaced, and what security risk is there for whatever remains?
2. Reviewing old code is a slow and tedious process. Serious ROI decisions must be made. You must reserve resources for this work to reduce the technical security debt for current resources. The level of effort for this work will depend on whether the SDL existed at the time the code was developed. If there was no SDL at the time the legacy code was being developed, the level of effort will be high.

The following points outline the basic process for assessing the security of legacy software applications:

- Assess the business criticality of the application. The software application has likely been successfully relied on for years, and this may be the first time it has been looked at from a security perspective. In fact, it is highly probable that this is the first time it has been examined with this level of scrutiny. If any security vulnerabilities or flaws are discovered, even though there may be only one or two, they will likely require a large-scale effort and significant resources to mitigate. It is important to identify business criticality in order to balance the business risk versus the security risk and ROI in these cases.
- Identify someone who is very familiar with the code. Since the legacy code is "old" code, it most likely has not been updated recently, and there may be few if any people in the organization who understand the software anymore. Further, it may have been developed on top of an old language base, and/or poorly documented or commented on. If this is the case, then the next step will be to conduct a software security assessment very similar to what is done during the SDL process. If the original developers, documentation, and history exist for the legacy software, and some security was built into the software, then the security assessment process can be shortened to focus just on assessing the gaps in current knowledge.
- Other basic questions should also be asked, such as:
  - Has this application previously been exploited because of a known security vulnerability or flaw?
  - Has it been fixed? If not, what can be done about it now?
  - Have there been any changes in the software architecture, function, or use that may have added new security vulnerabilities or new planes of attack?
- Assess the security of the software using the key software security assessment techniques of the SDL.
- Create a proposal that will tell the business how to remediate the security vulnerabilities or flaws in the software (cost + time) or how quickly they should think about replacing it (cost). If it is determined that the software is to be replaced, there will be risks in the interim, so you need to make sure you know where the security vulnerabilities and flaws are and develop a plan to mitigate and limit any damage that may result from an adversarial attack or exploitation of the software until the legacy code is replaced.
- If the cost of remediation is considered unacceptable by the business and there are no customer, industry, or regulatory requirements that require that security vulnerability or flaws be fixed, then the senior management for the business unit developing the software, and possibly the head of the software engineering development organization and legal counsel, will be required to sign off on accepting the risk for the continued use of the legacy software.

2.11 Chapter Summary

In this chapter, we have introduced the length and breadth of software security. The basics of each consensus-based, generic SDL activity have been explained. In addition, the management and programmatic elements of building and then maintaining an effective software security program have been presented.

We've taken up quite a fairly lengthy amount of space to describe how software is built today—Agile Scrum, Dev Ops, Continuous Integration/Continuous Delivery/Continuous Deployment, Cloud—taking these methods not only in isolation but also attempting to explain how they integrate and interact. We've also tried to describe how security and, in particular, software security have been profoundly impacted by these changes in the way that software is conceived, built, and run. These changes were afoot when we wrote *Core Software Security: Security at the Source.** As of this writing, this is the way a majority, or nearly all, of the current software is built.

But software security practices haven't kept pace with the changes in the way software is developed, creating too much confusion and, unfortunately, sometimes leading to ineffective software security programs. Our sincere hope is that this book can help point us toward effectiveness.

Each technical activity's basic details have been explained. We've covered, soup to nuts, secure design activities, those security activities that are a core part of generating software, and the interlocking and overlapping set of verification tactics without which vulnerability and compromise statistics demonstrate all too well that issues will leak into production software, and they will be misused by malefactors.

This summary won't reiterate each activity, since in subsequent chapters we dig deeply into these disciplines. We've used this chapter to set the groundwork for the book. Still, we hope that through the explanations presented in this chapter, you feel fairly familiar with what we believe and have experienced as effective SDL activities that, when taken together, build a comprehensive, robust, and rigorous approach to software security.

Alongside the technical SDL, we've gone to fairly great lengths to introduce the complexities of building software security programs and then managing them. Again, in this chapter, our intention was to introduce, head to toe, all that need be considered. Still, we covered not just standard management aspects, like hiring the right skills, but we went much further, taking in, among other topics, how to build a culture of security and how to integrate code originating from third parties, whether open source, commercial, or acquired. We have tried to be as thorough as humanly possible in this introductory chapter. As with the technical aspects, in subsequent chapters, we dive deeper into the subtleties of what we believe is, at its essence, a people problem that takes grit, collaboration, and careful cohesion of activity to solve—that is, building and running software that meets its security objectives.

"Meeting security objectives" implies that practitioners can identify these and turn the objectives into actionable and achievable tasks. That is precisely what a complete software security program encompasses, including a generic Security Development Lifecycle (SDL) that can be used across any and a multiplicity of Software Development Life Cycles (SDLCs). But an SDL is only as good as the people who enact it, who perform the technical tasks, and who understand how to manage the program and its people.

---

* Ransome, J. and Misra, A. (2014). *Core Software Security: Security at the Source.*

Chapter 3

A Generic Security Development Lifecycle (SDL)*

3.1 Introduction

Much of our generic security development lifecycle (SDL) was published in *Core Software Security: Security at the Source*, Chapter 9: Applying the SDL Framework to the Real World.† There are subtle differences for Agile development to account for DevOps and high cloud adoption. Some method and tool approaches have matured in the intervening years. And our experiences since drafting Chapter 9 have shown that security architecture is better served by acknowledging the primacy of threat modeling as a foundation for achieving resilient secure designs.

Despite these developments and the migration to Agile development, the extensive use of public clouds, the transition to DevOps, and continuous integration and delivery techniques (CI/CD), as we discussed in Chapter 1, many of the SDL activities and requirements remain relatively stable in their essence. Software has to be designed for security and with appropriate security features. Coders must learn what comprises "secure code" in the languages and runtime environments in which they will work. Coding errors still occur, despite the best efforts of developers to write securely. Hence, the SDL must account for the appearance of implementation errors in code that the programmer considers complete. A comprehensive SDL must check and test for issues in a variety of ways because each approach is better at finding certain types of errors and is worse at, or misses, other types. There continues to be a need for a combination of testing and verification methods such that the code and types of errors are covered as much as is humanly possible. No one test approach will catch everything that needs to be found.

There is another fairly dramatic change that we've purposely left out of our list: machine learning (ML). In 2014, machine learning techniques had just completed a revolution that greatly improved effectiveness and applicability to many distinct problem areas. These improvements were redefining areas such as image classification and natural language recognition and translation. The successes in

---

* This chapter is an update to Chapter 9 from *Core Software Security*. We have retained the heads from all of the text taken from this chapter.

† Ransome, J. and Misra, A. (2014). *Core Software Security: Security at the Source*. Boca Raton (FL): CRC Press/ Taylor & Francis Group.

these fields have led to the application of ML to hundreds of computing problems. ML has become nearly as widespread and usual as cloud use.

At the same time, ML does not present a radically different software security problem that forces changes to an SDL. Security issues specific to ML most certainly exist; please see the Berryville Institute of Machine Learning's (BIML) comprehensive Taxonomy of ML Attacks[*] for a set of ML-focused security issues. Like other algorithm and technology choices, ML will require unique security requirements along with requirements that are typical across software types and architectures. As we shall see in this chapter's Architecture and Design section, and in Chapter 4, one of the SDL's functions is to identify security requirements, usually through threat model analysis. From an SDL perspective, ML is not unique, even though it does have particular security aspects that must be attended to. Hence, we have left ML out of our list of changes that affect an SDL, despite the importance of ML security needs and its growing use.

At the SDL's most basic, there are activities that help to construct appropriately secure designs. There are activities to help program secure code and, then, to help identify errors in that code. And there are several testing strategies that, when employed together, remove many, but never all, errors and misses. Design, code, verify, operate. These software development fundamentals haven't changed, though the timing of SDL tasks, the resonances among them, and interactions between various SDL activities have greatly shifted (as we have explained in preceding chapters).

Tools for security testing have matured. But the two fundamental technological differences in tool approach currently remain:

- Tools that examine source code (static application security testing—SAST)
- Tools that expose potential security issues in running software (dynamic application security testing—DAST)

Newer tools integrate source code examination and runtime misbehavior, which is called Interactive Application Security Testing (IAST). Some tools even combine IAST with Software Composition Analysis (SCA). The generic SDL given here will divide the testing world into SAST and DAST, with a subtype: fuzzing (a form of DAST). Use of an IAST may then be thought of as meeting the SDL requirements for both SAST and DAST, though usually such tools do not also perform fuzzing. This is why we continue to call out fuzzing separately, since this technique and associated tooling are a discrete test methodology.

As was mentioned in Chapter 1, Brook, Bob Hale, and Catherine Blackadar Nelson undertook a study of every published SDL at the time (~2015 to 2016). One of their primary discoveries was that though naming of activities varies (often significantly), the underlying requirements of most published SDLs are remarkably similar if not precisely the same. There exists a consensus set of SDL activities, name these what you will. The SDL described in *Core Software Security* (Chapter 9) sits squarely within that industry consensus, containing that set of activities believed by software practitioners to deliver appropriately secure software that is as error free as humanly possible using today's software security state-of-the-art.

For our generic SDL, we start with Chapter 9 in *Core Software Security* (published in 2014) and amend to the needs dictated by current methods employed to develop software. Chapter 4 will dive deeply into secure design and threat modeling. We will only set out the required design-related SDL activities in this chapter. Wherever Chapter 9's SDL requires updating or amendment to achieve the generic SDL's requirements (set out in Chapter 1 in this book and repeated just below for reference), we provide the appropriate corrections and updates just before or just after particular Chapter 9

---

[*] Shepardson, V., McGraw, G., Figueroa, H., and Bonett, R. (2019, May). "Taxonomy of ML Attacks." BIML. Retrieved from https://berryvilleiml.com/taxonomy/

explanations. Those portions of *Core Software Security*'s Chapter 9 that have entirely changed have been removed and rewritten here.

- Be free from timing expectations based upon an assumed SDLC
- Express the industry consensus on a comprehensive set of state-of-the-art software security practices
- State the necessary preconditions before any particular SDL task may be started, including any dependencies on other SDL task outputs
- Describe those conditions that must be met to consider the task complete
- Explain the output(s), if any, of each task
- Describe any conditions that may trigger a refinement or review of the task's outputs

Note to reader: Quoted text from Chapter 9 will appear indented and in italics for clarity. Amendments and updates will appear in standard body text.

> *Software security depends on a series of properly executed tasks. There is no "silver bullet" task whose execution will deliver "good enough" software security. Security must be designed in from very early in the development lifecycle. And each activity for finding defects is complementary to the others. Leave out one of the activities and the others compensate only so much for what's been missed. The differences between software projects dictate which tasks will deliver the most security return for investment; some activities will be irrelevant for some systems. While the application of some SDL security tasks depends on each project's particular attributes, there are other SDL tasks that lie at the heart of secure development. These tasks are core to developing software that can be relied on and that is also self-protective. This set of core activities applies to every software project that must maintain a security posture, whatever that posture may be. These tasks are applied to every project.*
>
> *Regardless of the development methodology employed, there will be high-level system architecture tasks, software architecture considerations, and software design issues. . . . After there is code to test, there is the test plan to execute, which must include the functional tests as well as testing from the attacker's point of view. In between these process markers, that is, design time and testing, code will be written. Code production is the heart of software development. In some methodologies, there may be some design work that occurs just before writing, or even as code is developed. Whatever the approach, there are table-stake tasks that lie at the very heart of secure development: correctness for security, peer review, and static analysis (if available).* (*Core Software Security*, pp. 256–257)

In 2014, it was still generally believed that there were distinct software phases: design, coding, and testing even though, for Agile development practices, this hadn't been strictly true for quite a while. At that time, many representations of development, including ours, continued to portray development as distinct phases.

Strict phasing is no longer true in Agile SDLC coupled especially to DevOps. Design and testing often occur in parallel with coding. In fact, attempts to code a particular design may cause the design to change, both of which have profound implications for what will get tested and how the testing will best be approached. It may better be thought of as a set of interacting activities with strong feedback loops for rapid adjustment during progress. A statement such as, "These constitute those tasks that must be done before much production code has been written . . ." is now obsolete. Some design usually must take place in order to build intentionally. But the design need not be complete, and may in fact, offer coders no more than a skeleton upon which to build. Likewise, "In between these process markers, that is, design time and testing" is equally inappropriate. There is no "in between"; there is just "proceed and communicate results."

We offer the diagram in Figure 3.1 as an alternative view of DevOps parallelism.

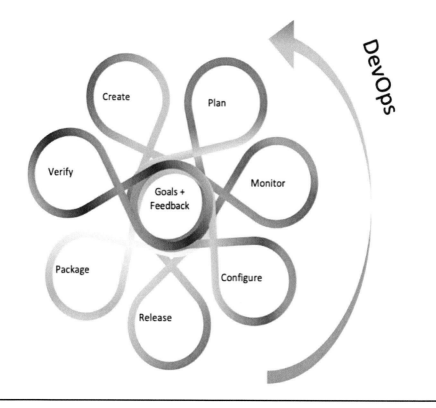

Figure 3.1 Continuous DevOps.

Each development task is continuously executing (or nearly so such that we represent the activities as continuous infinite loops). Each infinite activity loop revolves around the central communications and feedback hub. Each activity, though shown as distinct, in fact depends upon and interacts with all other activities. Further, the goals for the software and the process tightly glue different task loops together. No loop is independent or solo. Software cannot be produced and run without every activity contributing both its results and its learnings to the whole. Taken together, we visualize an ideal DevOps process, as follows:

- Plan
- Create
- Verify
- Package
- Release
- Configure
- Monitor

It should be noted that dividing tasks up as we have done is more or less a matter of taste and aesthetics. Other DevOps representations use alternate task divisions and/or names. Some of these distinctions may be artificial, depending upon the skills of the people building and running the software and how they may choose to divide up the work into tasks. There is nothing special or canonical about our task list. We offer these for example only.

None of these tasks, by itself, constitutes a silver bullet activity that will deliver secure software. Each task complements the others. Creating a secure and securable architecture, with flows that can be understood and with controllable trust boundaries, enables the software's features to be written into an environment that supports security. A thoughtful security architecture should require those features that will foster secure deployment and usage. Once the architecture supports the required security features, these can be designed from the start rather than attempting to bolt security on after the fact.

Since secure coding is still very much an art, with local language and runtime variations adding to complexity, a strong, real-world SDL operates by "trust but verify." Trust your developers to write secure code. But check that code with multiple, independent, and complementary assurance methods: peer review, static analysis, functional testing, and dynamic analysis of the input paths.

In short, prepare for security, think about how to implement required features, build these, then test the code to make sure that the security features work as intended and that no vulnerabilities have been introduced while coding. (Core Software Security, p. 257)

In the intervening years, we have abandoned "trust <u>but</u> verify" in favor of "trust <u>and</u> verify." We found through experience and by listening carefully to the concerns of the engineers with whom we have worked that the word "but" implies a lack of trust and is disempowering for developers who must take responsibility for the security of the software that they are creating. We trust developers to do their best in executing the SDL. We offer our help, support, and expertise in the service of our shared goals with respect to the security and delivery of useful software (whatever that means, in each context). In that spirit, we say that we trust developers and ourselves. At the same time, we all make mistakes; each of us can miss important security items, as well as mis-execute security tasks. Therefore, each one of us individually and all of us working together must do all that we can to "verify" our work, no matter the SDL context or development task. It's just too easy to make errors. We have shifted to the collaborative, "trust and verify."

We believe that, ultimately, software security is a problem that people must solve; technology is merely an extension of the human mind. Relationships, as we will see, are the key to a successful SDL. Obviously, humans design, write, and test code. Humans must do each of these things with security in mind in order for the finished product to have all the attributes that comprise "secure software." Since execution of each of the SDL tasks requires intelligent, highly skilled, creative people, it is the people who execute the SDL who are the most important ingredient. As we explore each portion of the security development lifecycle, we will take note of the approaches that strengthen relationships and provide people with motivation to produce secure software.

Figure 3.2 [formerly Figure 9.1] illustrates the flow of activities through the SDL:

Architect => Design => Code => Test

Ultimately, the SDL flow in Figure 3.2 [Figure 9.1] reduces to a simple SDL paradigm: Architecture feeds design, which is then built, that is, "coded." The coded design must be put through a series of validations, "test." This chapter [Chapter 9 of Core Software Security] details exactly which activities fit into each of the high-level buckets illustrated by Figure 3.2 [Figure 9.1], and how those activities are used within either Waterfall or Agile development. As we examine the SDL from the implementation view, we will ask key questions to determine precisely which activities must be engaged to what type of software project. In order to apply the security development lifecycle activities appropriately, it's important to understand that not every activity is required for every project. Applying every security task to every project, from entirely new concepts ("greenfield") and/or complete redesign to a minimal set of user interface changes, is wasteful and expensive. Requiring that

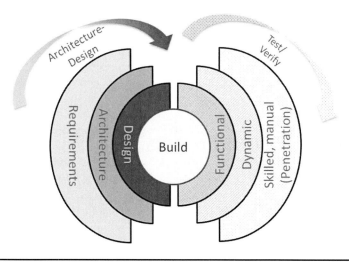

Figure 3.2   Gross SDL Activity Relations. (*Source:* Reproduced from Ransome, J. and Misra, A. [2014]. *Core Software Security: Security at the Source.* Boca Raton [FL]: CRC Press/Taylor & Francis Group, p. 258, with permission.)

every project go through Web vulnerability scanning, even those that have no Web server, is just plain silly. Not only will effort be expended with little security reward, but development teams are likely to resist the SDL as meaningless "administrivia," ergo, work with no benefit, empty bureaucracy. (Core Software Security, pp. 257–258)

We abandon the linearity implied in Figure 3.2 and its explanation. A bit of architecture usually precedes coding, since architecture is the playground for the expression of what might be built and establishes fundamental structures and functions. The phrase, "architecture feeds design" is not incorrect, by itself, but may imply that all structuring and planning must be completed before there is more specificity, such as designs typically detail. But an architecture only *seeds*, rather than *feeds*, design and code. All of these, plus testing, proceed together such that the architecture reflects the realities of implementation and testing needs. Please consider the connected loops in Figure 3.1. Architecture is improved by reaching for specificity in design. These are not separate but rather a part of the same effort: to understand what to code, both in relationship to the system and its functions as a whole, as well as to attempt to find the correct algorithms and structures. Designs detail the intentions of architecture as it can be expressed in code. Code is not acceptable until it can be tested and has been verified. Each of these learns from and feeds back information to the whole, as shown in Figure 3.1.

Just as design specificity refines structure, so too implementation refines design and architecture. Indeed, verification removes issues from code, as expected. In addition, verification must provide useful review and refinement for design and architecture, as well. Likewise, packaging, release, deployment, and post-release monitoring are also part of a continuing "learn-and-refine" loop as new changes are planned and architected. In DevOps, these are not distinct "phases" so much as aspects or views of a whole: delivering value through software.

We use the term "design" in two ways: as a specification for how to implement a function or algorithm in source code and (as also used elsewhere) as the over-arching term for planning, structuring, and specifying what will be implemented, as in "design-time." We will try to disambiguate as required.

In some types of development, designs may be minimal or entirely expressed by the source code and its comments. The architecture(s) may be the sole document(s) representing the "design" as understood, needing no documentation dedicated to specific designs. Because some system types are well known, with ample public documentation of the structures and specifics to build, a specific design artifact may be unnecessary and, thus, not produced.

However the architecture and design tasks are distributed within development, analysis of attack resistance and resilience takes place as security's contribution to the structuring and specification of software (that is, "security architecture" and "secure design"). The analysis commonly known as "threat modeling" sits underneath much software security thinking.

Building a threat model will not comprise the entire security architecture. Other aspects include:

- Joining together of individual security controls into a structure that works together, known as a "security architecture," to build a defense in depth
- Fitting security controls, mitigations, and other defensive actions into the structures and implementation of the target software: solution and software architecture for security
- Expressing the security needs of system stakeholders into security features and controls
- Building security architectures that contribute to an organization's goals: security business acumen

Still, when it comes to finding the relevant and appropriate set of security requirements, practitioners will be threat modeling, even if informally and, perhaps, mentally. The threat model pulls attack considerations into the other analyses listed above in order to divine the "right stuff" versus hoping that a particular security implementation will be sufficient. The threat model provides discrimination and focus. Without the attacker's view, defenses are built "in the dark."

In the past, choosing the appropriate set of tasks out of the complete SDL menu has been performed by skilled security professionals, often the security architects or security engineers. As the security architect came to understand the system, she or he was able to prescribe the correct activities to deliver secure software. Knowing that there is a Web server that will be deployed only within a segregated network and that will be used only by a few trusted administrative staff, the architect might choose to forego a detailed Web vulnerability scan in favor of network and application access restrictions. The required security posture defense in depth can be achieved through applying multiple controls, each complementing the other. Like a painter with a palette of technical controls, the architect builds the security posture out of his or her palette.

Some organizations don't have much flexibility in the security controls that can be deployed: They can only deploy a few; a complete "palette" of solutions isn't possible. Or the organization may not have the project analysis skills that are required to appropriately assign SDL tasks to projects. Or there may be too few analysts to scale to a large or diverse software development portfolio. In these and similar situations, one tendency has been to employ a "one-size-fits-all" approach. This approach applies every SDL task to every project, regardless of project size, the amount of intended software change, or change of the included components. In our experience, this approach is fraught with pitfalls: resistance, misapplication, missed schedules, or teams simply ignoring security tasks altogether. Integrating security into software projects is not a "one-size-fits-all" problem. Not only will there be wasted, even useless effort, but the engineers tasked with carrying out the tasks will lose faith in the SDL. This can lead to apathy, even gaming the system to get around what appears to developers to be a valueless bureaucracy.

Instead, we propose a straightforward approach that builds on years of successful security analysis of hundreds of software projects at many diverse organizations. This extensive experience has been distilled into a set of key questions and the task flows that follow from the answers. Successful application of the SDL activities can be accomplished by asking these few important questions, either at project initiation or before each high-level phase of development. Each defining question must be answered before the SDL phase in which its associated tasks are to be completed. (Core Software Security, pp. 258–259)

Although we have eliminated an artificial set of design-time activities, it is still useful for security architecture to understand at what level of specificity threat modeling will be required as development unfolds. The questions that we used in our programs at the point of *Core Software Security* have changed to reflect the foundational nature of threat model analysis. We now understand that threat modeling is used to derive various artifacts, requirements, and details for achieving the security objectives necessitated by each particular software development effort. There are still determining questions, which we set out below. The names have changed to reflect what threat modeling is aimed at and what must be produced by the analysis. We have jettisoned confusing architecture assessment names in favor of simplification.

This is not to suggest that executing these tasks is trivial. As has been pointed out by Microsoft threat modelers, threat modeling can be performed by anyone with an inquisitive mind. Still, in current practice, it usually takes an experienced architect who understands the project's architecture, the intended deployment model, the development languages, and runtime. The architect must also have a strong grasp of the sort of threat agents who are active against this sort of software. Indeed, she or he must understand the relevant attack methods in order to build a realistic threat model. Static analysis tools require considerable expertise, as do most forms of dynamic testing, from Web vulnerability scanning to input fuzzing. The existing tools are nontrivial to learn and run effectively. Code review requires an understanding of general security correctness, the flow and structure of the particular code under review, as well as how the intended function should be implemented. Your most junior engineer is probably not the best resource to apply to any of these tasks—at least, not without significant support from experienced practitioners. (*Core Software Security*, pp. 259–260)

By now, we have also seen the valuable effects derived from training and then supporting developers to perform most, if not all, threat modeling. The experienced security architect we called for in 2014 must now be a teacher, a mentor, the most experienced review escalation point, rather than performing all threat models. That centralized model does not scale well to thousands of developers. Besides, with sufficient training and support, developers can and will take responsibility (and accountability) for identifying security requirements. Security practitioners must empower developers, as well as provide whatever support is necessary to make developers become effective threat modelers. We've seen the results: Threat modeling becomes part of the fabric of development. Brook's *Secrets of a Cyber Security Architect* goes into some depth about how to build such programs, as well as the other benefits that ensue from empowering developers to threat model as an integral part of designing and building software.

If one can build the right set of questions into the SDL, choosing the correct set of high-level tasks turns out to be fairly straightforward. This is true even if executing those tasks is nontrivial. There are dependencies, process flows of tasks that follow logically out of the answers. Once the task flow is engaged, the appropriate activities will take place in a more or less linear fashion. (*Core Software Security*, p. 260)

As of this writing, much development activity no longer occurs in a "more or less linear fashion." As we discuss each, we will note dependencies and interactions among the SDL activities. Thus, in whatever order teams decide to take their development tasks, they can readily identify those SDL tasks that are relevant to the work at hand and those SDL tasks that will have to have been completed previously and whose output the current tasks depend on. Ergo, security activities are SDLC ordering independent.

Making the SDL relevant and obviously appropriate opens the door for meaningful interactions among the different stakeholders of the SDL. As has been noted, asking intelligent, busy people to do things about which they cannot perceive value does not enhance confidence in the security team. Conversely, a transparent process that is inherently obvious has the opposite effect. Empowering

SDL participants to answer basic questions about which activities are appropriate for their current project is inherently trust-building. It remains true that execution of many of these tasks requires deep technical (and often interpersonal) expertise. (Core Software Security, p. 260)

It may be instructive to note that in 2014 we were still fairly dependent upon a central security team. Naturally, our description from that time reflects that bias. Chapter 5 will dig deep into how our programs have successfully scaled to large development organizations with hundreds of teams and thousands of developers through enlisting, training, mentoring, and supporting developers to acquire and practice the "deep technical and interpersonal expertise" mentioned in the last paragraph. We continue to advocate for a small, central software security team to provide strategy, guidance, training, and support. Nevertheless, we've seen dramatic results from empowering developers to "own" security. It is the central team's obligation to make that empowerment happen.

The current state of the art does not simplify many SDL tasks enough to allow these to be executed by "just anyone," even when every member of the development team holds a modicum of technical skill. For most organizations in which we have participated, architecture assessment or vulnerability scanning remain expert domains. Because of this state of affairs, relationships become even more important. Achieving secure software requires many people to pull together toward shared goals— which, obviously, means that non-security participants must understand that security is a "shared goal." Hence, we advocate as much transparency as possible coupled to an SDL implementation that stresses people and relationships as much as technology. The key determining questions are one step toward achieving a "people" focus of the SDL in the real world.

The key determining questions will be presented later in the chapter [Chapter 9 of Core Software Security, as reproduced in this chapter], in context. First, we will examine the heart of every SDL; those activities that are not dependent on the amount of change or type of interface. Without these core tasks, the SDL lacks its most essential ingredients to produce code that is written correctly for security and that contains as few defects as possible: writing secure code, reviewing the code, and then running the code through static analysis.

As we examine the SDL tasks as they are applied to real-world projects, this chapter [Chapter 9 of Core Software Security, as reproduced in this chapter] will detail the supporting parts of a software security program that will foster and grow the required skills to execute the tasks well. (Core Software Security, pp. 260–261)

It remains absolutely true that it is not humanly possible to deliver bug-free and, thus, vulnerability-free code. Everyone makes mistakes, some more than others, and untrained coders more than secure coding–trained developers. For rapid, nimble development and especially for CI/CD shops, training coupled to rapid and accurate error identification is key. Older paradigms of reserving automated analysis for system builds isn't fast enough and doesn't provide the right kind of "just-in-time" coding-error feedback. In addition to the statements about the "heart of the SDL" given in this section, desktop code security analysis typically using SAST must be employed. As Brook wrote in *Secrets of a Cyber Security Architect*:

"[Give] programmers as much security checking, as early in their coding process as possible. Nearly all the commercial static analysis tools as of this writing have a desktop version or option that allows coders to check their work as they code. This is very powerful because of a typical cultural expectation.

Generally, diligent programmers expect errors in their code as they're working on it. Any tool that can find errors (without generating too many incorrect findings and not requiring too much configuration and tuning) will usually be appreciated and integrated.

But there's a mental shift that happens when a programmer believes that the code is stable and correct. Code that has been released to the next stage of the development process (which varies depending upon the development methodology) can be a bit "out of sight, out of mind." Often, the programmer has moved on to other problems. There can be a bit of "prove to me that there's an error" once code has left the programmer's purview and moved on.

Hence, testing that occurs after a programmer commits code as "correct" may be a little too distant from the coding process, whereas tools that can integrate into the coding process, that find errors during coding, generally receive greater programmer attention. Hence, I like to get at least some security checking onto the coders' desks, into their integrated development environment (IDE), early in the coding process. Even if the checks are less rigorous than those that can be placed within a later build process, still, early identification of security mistakes is more organic than massive sets of findings later on.

Get secure coding analysis tools into the coding cycles. Then, perform a more thorough check during build. From experience, that seems to work the best." (*Secrets*, p. 111)

3.2 Build Software Securely

At the heart of secure software development, there are three core activities. . . . Every programmer must attempt to write safe, defensive, self-protective code. There is no secure path around the need for coders to understand what must be done in the language in which they are working. Different languages and different execution environments demand different emphases. In fact, issues in one language may not be worth considering in another; one only has to look at the differences between C/C++ and Java to understand this fact. The C/C++ language allows the mishandling of memory; in fact, it's very easy to do something insecure. In contrast, the Java programming language takes care of all memory handling; programmers need not worry about the allocation and the de-allocation of memory at all.

Even experts at writing correct, secure code make mistakes. And the current reality is that there are very few coders who are experts in security, much less the security issues of a particular language and runtime. In addition, it should be remembered that writing software code is as much an art as it is engineering. While there are correct implementations and incorrect implementations (engineering), a great deal of creativity is involved in expressing that correctness. There may be several algorithmic approaches to a particular problem. There will be many possible expressions of whatever algorithm has been chosen. And this does not take into account innovation: The programmer may encounter computer problems that have not yet been attempted; she or he will have to create an entirely new algorithm or significantly modify a standard. And, even with naming conventions and other coding standards, programming languages are, in essence, expressive. That may be one of the motivators for becoming a programmer: creativity at one's job. But with creativity and innovation come mistakes. Mistakes are the price we pay for innovation. Not every idea works; perhaps most fail? One very successful approach is to learn about a problem by trying to solve it. Such an iterative approach is often used when building software, but iterative discovery guarantees a certain level of failure and error. We would posit that defects and vulnerabilities are a direct result of innovation (although, of course, innovation and creativity are not the only causes of vulnerabilities).

The software security practitioner is faced with a trade-off between curtailing innovation and perhaps job satisfaction and delivering code whose security can be assured. This is where the assurance steps provide appropriate help. We recommend that at the heart of whatever development process is used, include manual code review and static analysis. That is, give the creative coder considerable help to deliver correct code.

Figure 3.3 [formerly Figure 9.3] visually reinforces the central coding flow: Produce secure code which is then statically analyzed and manually code-reviewed. This is the essential "secure" version of "build" in software construction terms, that is, the "heart" of a security development lifecycle. These core tasks lie at the center of secure software, regardless of the development process being used. (Core Software Security, pp. 261–263)

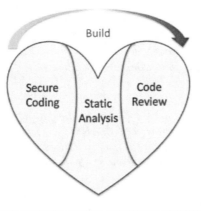

Figure 3.3   Promote Secure Coding. (Source: Reprinted from Ransome, J. and Misra, A. [2014]. *Core Software Security: Security at the Source.* Boca Raton [FL]: CRC Press/Taylor & Francis Group, p. 263, with permission.)

3.2.1 Produce Secure Code

Every program has (at least) two purposes: the one for which it was written and another for which it wasn't.[*]

If software engineers, those who write software, could produce correct, error-free code, there would be far less of a software security problem.[†] *And with only correct software there is no need for all the non–design-related tasks of the SDL. At the risk of stating the obvious, writing correct code has always been difficult, even without security considerations. Since the dawn of the software industry, when software engineers adopted the term "bug," meaning "software error," engineers have struggled to produce code that is correct, both logically and without runtime error. Inferring from the vast experience of all the software that has been written, we can conclude that writing error-free code is very, very difficult. It's not impossible, but it remains an expensive ideal rather than a norm.*

Realizing the error-prone nature of producing code, software engineers have attempted to find a metric that shows how dependable and error-free any particular piece of code might be. One measure is the number of defects, "bugs," per line of code written. It is generally accepted that production software contains approximately 1 error per 1000 lines of code. This is a very general statistic. It is possible to produce software that has far fewer errors; one need look only at critical space mission or military software, which often must adhere to much stricter defect limits. And, of course, poorly written software may have orders of magnitude more errors than 1 in 1000. Generally, however, there are errors in any moderately complex piece of code. As far as we can tell today, there is no way for us to ensure that 100 percent of the software or security errors will be eliminated before software is released. The best approach is to go through the required SDL activities . . . to ensure that most of the errors can be caught and fixed before a product is deployed or sold. If errors are found after software release, one should essentially follow a foreshortened SDL cycle to get the errors remediated, tested, and released.

---

[*] Perlis, A. (1982). *Epigrams on Programming.* ACM SIGPLAN Notices 17 (9), September, p. 7. Retrieved from http://www.cs.yale.edu/quotes.html

[†] There would still be logical errors, errors of architecture and design omission and commission. Logical errors are not dependent upon correct code. It is quite possible to insecurely specify, and then code that mistake correctly to the specification. That is, it is possible to correctly follow the incorrect specification and introduce a logical vulnerability.

Testing shows the presence, not the absence of bugs.[*]

Out of the population of extant errors, some proportion will have effects that can be manipulated to the advantage of an attacker; that is, these errors will be security "vulnerabilities." We focus here on vulnerabilities.

There is reasonable certainty that developers will produce incorrect code at least some of the time, and some of those errors will be subject to malicious manipulation; ergo, there will be vulnerabilities in the code. This is not a reason to abandon efforts to write correct code. The advantages of correctness at the outset far outweigh the expenditure; it is an established fact that achieving correctness as early as possible in the development cycle is by far cheaper and easier. The earliest point will be when the code is written.

There are several complementary activities that, when put together, will contribute to fewer security defects as code is being written: developer training, safe libraries, and proven implementations generalized for reuse.

Obviously, developers must know what is expected of them, where to pay attention to security, and what the correct behavior is that must be programmed. Any and all training approaches have benefit, although some approaches have less effectiveness than may be obvious. (Core Software Security, pp. 264–265)

In his book, *Secrets of a Cyber Security Architect*, Brook grappled with the problems inherent in coding, secure code training, and a few ideas for greater effectiveness. We reprint that portion here in order to underline that the training must match the problem and what is to be learned, and in the case of coding, *practiced,* oftentimes, over and over again so that the learning becomes integrated and ingrained.

"Coding Is Fraught with Error

One of the challenges that I've seen over and over again is the demand that people 'code securely.' Training programs are instituted. Coders take the courses, but mistakes keep occurring. Secure code analysis tools are purchased and integrated into build systems, but preventable vulnerabilities still leak out into releases. Why?

My first realization, thinking back to my own coding, is that coding mistakes happen. Period. The truism that coding mistakes will occur must be the ground upon which every part of solutions must stand.

There are two situations that increase the likelihood of coding errors, security and otherwise:

1. When coding something new, innovative, or creative
2. When coding really boring, rote, run-of-the-mill aspects

Obviously, whenever we try something new, we are bound to make errors. This is expected when learning to play a musical instrument. Why do we expect a different result when coding innovative algorithms?

Sometimes, when I'm in front of developers, I ask them if they've ever finished a piece of code that they felt was implemented very well. Then, when a bug has appeared in the field, perhaps six months after release, have they taken a look at the code, only to realize that it's very wrong? I get a lot of chuckles and knowing nods from my question. It's certainly happened to me. Many programmers have experienced something similar, because it's easy to miss some detail of logic or side effect. It's possible to pass even rigorous testing regimes and still have coded a nasty bug. Many of us who've written significant

---

[*] NATO Science Committee. (1969). "Software Engineering Techniques." Report on a conference sponsored by the NATO Science Committee, p. 16, quote from Edsger Dijksta, Rome, Italy, 27th to 31st October 1969. Retrieved from http://homepages.cs.ncl.ac.uk/brian.randell/NATO/nato1969.PDF

amounts of code have dealt with these issues and many more: The library our code depends upon doesn't behave the way that we thought it did, or the way that the documentation claims.

Many years ago, I had to write an infra-red (IR) driver for one of the consumer versions of Windows® (before Windows migrated to the NT device driver model). IR is incredibly time sensitive. I chased inconsistent behavior for months before I realized that the time function in that version of Windows was unreliable. Sometimes my code got called in the correct periodicity, but a lot of the time, it did not. When I changed the code to rely on a hardware clock, it finally worked as expected.

The story offered above is but a single example of code that's been written correctly as per its specification(s), but still misbehaves. That's because our code often runs on complex systems that depend upon huge volumes of code, all of which is prone to error. Software bugs are legion. I think that it's fairly safe to assume that any reasonably complex piece of code will have a few errors in it. Some of the unintended behavior will likely have security implications. Furthermore, the newer the code, the more likely it is that the code will have mistakes in it, some of which will be vulnerabilities.

The other situation that can foster errors is boredom. When coding commercially, there are generally standards about how the code is to be written, where the comments go, etc. One very typical task will be to "cover" a library (say open source software [OSS]) that implements needed functionality. *Cover* in this context means to build functions calling the library to implement the needed functionality. There are a host of code structure reasons for doing it this way, rather than calling the code directly. For one thing, if the library needs to be swapped for another, only the covering routines need changing, not all the places in the code where the functionality will be used.

However, setting up a bunch of covering routines to an organization's standards is not the most interesting task. It's a job that needs doing, and it needs to be done well. However, it doesn't take a computer scientist to write a bunch of cover routines. Hence, this task can be quite boring: setting up the standard class or method or function headers multiple times. It's mostly boilerplate. Boring work leads to mistakes, just as innovative work can.

Effective Secure Coding Training

Whatever the reasons, software mistakes happen, and happen regularly and repeatedly. What can be done about it?

Obviously, we can train people to generate more secure code in the first place. But do those five-day, secure coding classes really improve things? Maybe. Chris Romeo, CEO of Security Journey, and I have talked quite a bit about what might constitute highly effective training. There are two problem areas:

1. People need to practice what they learn in order to integrate the knowledge into their coding.
2. Different programming languages and systems have fairly different security requirements.

It's more cost effective for trainers to deliver several days of training in a block rather than on demand. So, instructor-led trainings have tended to be multi-day affairs. But that makes it hard for coders to integrate each technique into the code that they write. Class exercises are all well and good, but they might not match closely enough to what participants are actually writing.

Plus, each training has to be general enough to cover a range of situations and programming languages. That means that some of the work for some attendees will very likely be irrelevant.

Chris and I have discussed very short webinars, 15–30 minutes, focusing on a single area of secure coding, in a particular language, for a particular set of coding problems. Then, let the learners go off and apply what they've learned to their code, try to recognize the approach or lack thereof when reviewing others' code. The focus should be on practical application until the learners have integrated the knowledge into their skills. That is how most people learn: Do a single new thing until it's understood and integrated. Apply what has been learned until it becomes a part of what one does.

I've spoken to a few training companies about such an approach. We'll see if this works better than the five-day cram.

Still, people will forget, will mis-apply, just plain make errors. As I wrote, above, that's a given." (*Secrets*, pp. 108–110)

Developers should understand, at a very high level, that some defects have profound effects within the software they write. Functional specifications describe how the software will be used. Among these specifications will be those security attributes and features that users and the owners of the software require. Generally, that which has been specified gets built. That is not to say that errors don't creep in; they do. But since the properties are a part of the requirements, developers have an organic exposure to systems such as authentication and authorization, and to the API functions and classes that implement communications protections, such as TLS/SSL. If specified, the developer will generally attempt to build the functionality.

The security industry has primarily been interested in vulnerability (something that can be exploited), that is, in security weakness. Vulnerabilities are defects that when manipulated cause side effects that can be used to advantage; vulnerabilities are bugs. Since security practitioners ultimately must assess risk, a part of which is vulnerability, it is a natural focus of the occupation. Unfortunately, developers do not focus on vulnerability. They must focus on correctness. Is the algorithm written correctly? Does this code implement the specification exactly? Will this logical series produce the correct paths? Is this code clear enough to be maintained by someone who has never seen it before? Will this code reject invalid input? Can this code fail and the program recover after that failure? These are the sorts of questions that dominate developer thinking. Vulnerability is generally a side effect of error, often not an error by itself.

Tracking back from vulnerability to defect or code error is one of the big misses in information security as of this writing. Security people talk about vulnerability. Developers want to know where the bug is and how to fix it: Developers typically ask, "What is the correct behavior that must be implemented?"

It's useful for coders to understand that bugs can make a program vulnerable. However, training should focus on what is correct, self-defensive behavior. US-CERT's Key Practices for Mitigating the Most Egregious Exploitable Software Weaknesses[*] are a refreshing start, focusing on correct, secure programming. The focus of this publication is not vulnerability side effects or attack patterns, but rather, on the system properties and algorithms that will prevent issues. For instance, for cross-site scripting (XSS, also represented as XXS) errors, which are endemic to today's Web applications, Key Practices recommends complementary programming solutions that together will prevent XSS. The following quote recommends a specific algorithm which would then be "correct" and also prevents one variation of the vulnerability, XSS.[†]

When the set of acceptable objects, such as filenames or URLs, is limited or known, create a mapping from a set of fixed input values (such as numeric IDs) to the actual filenames or URLs, and reject all other inputs.[‡]

Training that focuses on correct behavior is a key to fewer security vulnerabilities. A secure coding training program might begin with the necessary high-level attributes of a secured system. There

---

[*] U.S. Department of Homeland Security. (2013). Software & Supply Chain Assurance: Community Resources and Information Clearinghouse (CRIC). "Mitigating the Most Egregious Exploitable Software Weaknesses: Top 25 CWE Programming Errors." Retrieved from https://buildsecurityin.us-cert.gov/swa/cwe

[†] The algorithm quoted is not intended to be an XSS "fix-all"; it is chosen for specificity, not for its completeness.

[‡] The MITRE Corporation. (2013). "Common Weakness Enumeration (CWE)." *CWE-434: Unrestricted Upload of File with Dangerous Type. Phase: Architecture and Design*. Retrieved from http://cwe.mitre.org/data /definitions/434.html

are any number of security design principle collections. The Open Web Application Security Project (OWASP) provides a distillation of several of the most well-known sets of principles:

- *Apply defense in depth (complete mediation).*
- *Use a positive security model (fail-safe defaults, minimize attack surface).*
- *Fail securely.*
- *Run with least privilege.*
- *Avoid security by obscurity (open design).*
- *Keep security simple (verifiable, economy of mechanism).*
- *Detect intrusions (compromise recording).*
- *Don't trust infrastructure.*
- *Don't trust services.*
- *Establish secure defaults.*[*]

Even if developers thoroughly understand these principles without further training, as they design and implement, security correctness will be one of the key attributes that will emerge as programs take shape.

Training must be readily available and easily consumable. Generally, week-long courses are very difficult to schedule broadly due to lost productivity and lost opportunity costs. While an immersive approach certainly has benefits, any material that is not quickly applicable to tasks at hand may be rapidly lost. Instead, shorter segments that can be taken in small doses and then practiced on the job will likely deliver better results. One pattern that we've found very effective is to establish a baseline understanding and skill level with:

- *High-level application vulnerability introduction*
- *Secure design and coding principles*
- *Three to five required, easily understandable short courses (30 minutes maximum), demonstrating correct fixes for common vulnerabilities applicable to the developer's platform and language.*

Once the baseline training has been established, provide additional training on common fixes. Training in these commonly encountered patterns must be easily consumable. Developers tend to be very jealous of their time. Alongside highly focused, shorter pieces, also provide more in-depth training on software security. In this manner, developers may follow their own interests. If they have to fix a particular error, they may choose to take the short, focused training. Or, if they catch the "security fire," they may want to pursue such deeper topics as encryption implementations or access control systems. Any training program should remind engineering staff that security skills are marketable and a premium skill.

Training by itself is less effective without opportunities to use the learned skills. Practice definitely makes perfect. This is a strong reason to give developers time between training sessions to apply the new skills. A natural rhythm of training, then practice, should be established:

- *30–60 minutes of secure coding training*
- *Several weeks of practical application*

Those who become experts can assist those with less skill. Further, these experts become senior code reviewers, capable not only of finding defects during manual code review, but also disseminating the correct approaches and algorithms.

---

[*] Open Web Application Security Project (OWASP). (2013). "Some Proven Application Security Principles." Retrieved from https://www.owasp.org/index.php/Category:Principle

Alongside a robust secure coding training program, thoroughly debugged implementations can be created. These libraries should be designed to generalize solutions across many implementations. They should provide easily implementable Application Programming Interfaces (APIs) to the correct implementations contained within the library. These correct libraries may then be included in each software project with the knowledge that security has been well implemented. And, if an error is found in the library, it can be fixed in only one place rather than in many disparate implementations.

The OWASP Enterprise Security API* is an example of a vetted implementation that solves various security problems within a Web application. For instance, to prevent XSS, there are functions that will validate all input against a whitelist before passing on the input for use within the application:

All input must be validated against a strict whitelist pattern using the Validator.* methods before used.† (Core Software Security, pp. 265–268)

One of the most effective anti-XSS mitigations for input data insertions into the HTML body is "escaping." That is, changing dangerous input characters into their named HTML characters, as in, "&" in the input is substituted with "&amp." For more information, please see OWASP's "Cross Site Scripting Prevention Cheat Sheet."‡

Whether correct APIs are built internally or acquired, these should be a key technology to ensure that code is correctly secure. Creating and using vetted libraries ensures that correct implementations are used and reused. This will also avoid the problem of implementation errors creeping into each coder's individual realization.

Another solution that may be of help is pairs programming. Kent Beck defines pairs programming as follows:

Pairs of programmers program together. Pairs don't just make test cases run. They also evolve the design of the system. Changes aren't restricted to any particular area. Pairs add value to the analysis, design, implementation, and testing of the system. They add that value wherever the system needs it.§

In this manner, both design and implementation are improved by the collective skill of the pair of programmers.

Writing secure, correct code is a product of several approaches taken together. Training complements practice. Practice creates expertise that can be applied to vetted implementations, which can be reused to minimize implementation errors. Collaborative approaches build team expertise while catching errors during the writing process. However, secure writing is not enough; correctness must be verified.

3.2.2 Manual Code Review

Due to the expressive nature of computer languages and the infinite variety of logical problems tackled in programs, it is important to employ independent, skilled reviewers who can provide a safety net for

---

*   Open Web Application Security Project (OWASP). (2013). "OWASP Enterprise Security API." Retrieved from https://www.owasp.org/index.php/Category:OWASP_Enterprise_Security_API

†   Ibid.

‡   OWASP. "Cross Site Scripting Prevention Cheat Sheet." Available from https://cheatsheetseries.owasp.org/cheat sheets/Cross_Site_Scripting_Prevention_Cheat_Sheet.html#rule-1-html-escape-before-inserting-untrusted -data-into-html-element-content

§   Beck, K. (1999). *Extreme Programming Explained: Embrace Change*. Reading (MA): Addison-Wesley Professional, p. 18.

the coder, and a check on correctness. Manual code review is particularly good at finding errors in the logic of the code. If the reviewer understands what the code will be doing but has not been involved in writing the code, he or she can often spot errors, especially logical errors. The reviewer can certainly check to see that coding standards have been adhered to. If the reviewer has security expertise, she or he may also spot security defects as well. Since there is a dearth of secure coding experts, it may be necessary to focus on logical and stylistic elements. However, if every developer is trained in basic defensive programming, particularly with respect to inputs, manual code review can at least find the egregious input validation errors that plague so much of the code produced today. In any event, code review is not a panacea. While it is possible to get expert manual code reviewers who can literally rewrite your code to be not only secure but also be efficient, elegant, and maintainable, these are very expensive. And there are very few such "code gurus" from which to draw. Making use of these experts may be very valuable for critical code, but it is infeasible for most projects in most organizations. What is feasible is to complement several different approaches, some targeted assurance, some broad, both manual and automated. A methodology that maximizes the complementary nature of approaches has proven to find the broadest level of defects while also being scalable.

To maximize manual code review, for the large amount of grunt, well-understood, typical code that must surround the critical pieces and the proprietary business logic modules, it's probably sufficient for most organizations to use peer review. Manual peer code review is when one or more of the coder's peers reviews code before commit for build. Members of the same development team will likely be familiar with what was intended by the code, the environment in which the code will run, and the general architecture of the project. It should therefore not be too difficult for them to understand and comment constructively. For code that is not too complex, such as routines that call a broadly understood API, a single reviewer may be sufficient. For more complex code, multiple reviewers may be employed. In fact, one of the soft benefits from a strong peer review program is the trust that members of the team develop in each other. Further, reviewers will become backups to the coder so that no single person becomes indispensable. On one team, the coders came to trust each other so much that they would often ask for three or four reviewers on their code; the resulting code was much more correct and efficient than it had been previous to this team code review. If the team is sufficiently skilled by themselves, peer review may be adequate for even critical or highly sensitive algorithms. (Core Software Security, pp. 269–270)

At the time of *Core Software Security*, we'd seen just a single team exhibit this behavior: coders seeking multiple reviewers for their code. After years of code review as an expected norm, seeking multiple reviews, more than required, became quite common, if not typical, for some development groups. It remains that writing correct code is difficult; responsible coders will seek review when the review is experienced as adding value to the coder's process. We have learned to never underestimate developers' (and other engineers') sense of responsibility and pride in work well accomplished. These are powerful motivators, not just for creating software but also, and especially, for security.

Typically, however, especially at fast-moving organizations where there may be movement between teams or even periods of turnover, peer review will be insufficient for critical code. The worst situation is where a junior programmer shows her or his code to another junior programmer who looks at it and replies, "Your code looks just like mine. Pass." Inexperienced coders are not going to find many sophisticated errors. Still, one of the more interesting code review processes we've seen involved a junior reviewer explaining code to a very senior developer.* While this may be a more time-consuming approach, the training and development benefits are obvious. A code review becomes an opportunity to mentor and instruct.

---

*   Instituted by Joe Hildebrand, CTO of Jabber, Inc.

We recommend that critical algorithms, complex functions, security modules, and cryptography implementations be manually reviewed by someone who has the skill to assess correctness and who understands the types of vulnerabilities that can be introduced. This will typically be someone very senior on the team or who can be made available to the team. It should be someone who is familiar with the intended functionality; usually, it's someone who has implemented the same or similar functions successfully in the past.

3.2.3 Static Analysis

*Static code analysis is the process of running an automated tool that reads either the source or the compiled object code after it has been written. The tool has preprogrammed patterns and errors for which it searches in the body of the code. Since, as has already been noted, computer languages are expressive, this is what's known in computer world science as a "nontrivial" problem. That is, static analysis must understand not only the legality and semantics of a language (duplicating what the compiler does), but must also understand typical constructs and those constructs' mistakes and misuses. Further, the static analysis must create a graph of all the possible interactions, "calls" within the code, in order to arrive at vulnerable interactions. One limited and simplified way to describe modern static analysis is that the compiler finds what is illegal or disallowed in the language. A static analyzer builds on legality by finding that which is "ill-advised." Again, this is a gross oversimplification of the capabilities bundled within an industrial-strength static analyzer. (*Core Software Security*, pp. 270–271)*

We must note that since 2014, a number of static analysis tools (i.e., SAST) have added machine learning and even artificial intelligence algorithms to their products. We wrote in 2014 that our description was a "gross oversimplification." That is even more true today.

Further, new entrants have experimented with combining static analysis with dynamic analysis techniques—IAST (as described, above). Our problem with replacing SAST with IAST is timing: As Brook wrote in his book *Secrets of a Cyber Security Architect*, quoted earlier in this chapter, for today's rapid and continuous development methods, at least some code analysis must occur early in the coding cycle. IAST requires running code. IAST has proven quite effective at both identifying issues and offering some runtime protection. A few IAST tools even point into the source code to where the error occurs. But IAST is late in the development game, long past that critical time during which the programmer is expecting to commit errors, that part of the process during which rapid error identification is so very useful. Hence, we continue to underscore the need for desktop static analysis during coding cycles. As we wrote above, even if the checks are less rigorous and thorough than full-build SAST or some form of IAST, finding errors early keeps them from releases and has the side effect of secure coding training reinforcement.

With respect to the SDL, how a static analysis takes place is not particularly important. More important is the sorts of errors that static analysis finds, and the sorts of errors that will be overlooked. For languages where direct memory manipulation, allocation, and de-allocation are required, static analysis has proven excellent at identifying code where memory is susceptible to misuse. For instance, common stack-based overflows in C/C++ occur when the size of data to be copied into a stack-based buffer is not checked before the copy or the length of the copy is not limited to the size of the buffer. This is considered a classic security vulnerability. If that buffer can be accessed from a point outside the program (that is, through an input path), the overflow can be used to execute code of the attacker's choosing.

Most static analysis tools will readily identify failure to check size of the copy as a memory-handling error. Some tools may even be able to establish seriousness by identifying an input path that leads to the copy. This is particularly true for static analysis which builds an execution graph of the software before error analysis.* Or, conversely, the analyzer may find that there is no such input path, thus downgrading the seriousness of the issue. In the latter case, dynamic analysis will never find the issue, as there is no input leading to the buffer copy. In the former case, dynamic analysis may or may not find the issue, depending on the inputs attempted.

Because static analyzers can view all the code, not just the code that can be reached through inputs, we place static analysis at the point where the code is still close to the developer. Several of the industrial-strength static analyzers build a code graph of every path through the code. Building such a graph gives the analyzer a holistic view not only of paths through the code but of relations between modules, use of APIs, data exposure and hiding, and other subtle programming patterns. With the true graph, the analyzer can assign seriousness to issues with far more information about relations between pieces of the code when it finds an error. And, of course, since the static analyzer has the source code, it can point precisely in the code where a potential error lies. This saves significant amounts of time for developers fixing defects.

The downside of the holistic but not executing view is that errors that may have less potential to get exercised may be reported alongside and equivalent to those that absolutely are exposed. These unexposed errors, in fact, may not be particularly significant even when they are exposed, due to runtime considerations. That is, not all potential buffer overflows have equal impact. The classic example is a buffer overflow that requires very high privileges in order to exploit. Attackers who have escalated privilege to the required level have no need to exercise an additional attack that executes the attacker's arbitrary code. On most modern operating systems, at that privilege level, an attacker can execute whatever he or she wants without a further exploit. In other words, such a buffer overflow has no potential attack value. Such an overflow is entirely theoretical. Still, because the static analyzer is not executing the program and has no notion of user privileges, the analyzer cannot distinguish between a high-privilege arbitrary code execution and a low-privilege one. It will take developer analysis to qualify such a reported defect.

The Embarrassment of Riches problem means that a modern commercial static analysis tool generally finds more bugs than the user has resources, or willingness, to fix.[†]

One practical solution to the "embarrassment of riches" problem is to start with a well-understood, high-confidence analysis. "High confidence" means: "Report only those defects for which there is very high confidence that there is in fact an exploitable defect that must be fixed." This means turning down the "aggressiveness" or similar configuration to a low setting. Configure only those checks that the manufacturer of the static analyzer believes will deliver 90 percent or better confidence in the results—that is, 10 percent or less false positives. Obviously, this means that some defects will flow through. We offer the adage that any reduction in attack surface is a significant win for security. It is extremely hard to achieve 100 percent; even 80 percent may be difficult in the first few releases of a program. A reduction in attack surface or vulnerability of even 20 percent in the early stages of a program to build secure software (an SDL program) is quite significant.

---

* The advantage of the call graph is that every possible path through the code can be examined. The disadvantage of a call graph is that many of the possible paths enumerated in the graph may never be executed. There are limited approaches for static analysis to determine which paths are critical and actually exposed to an attack surface. The analyzer takes a "best guess" approach.

† Sheridan, F. (2012, June 13). "Deploying Static Analysis I—Dr. Dobbs." Retrieved from http://article.yeeyan .org/bilingual/334758

Political resistance to static analysis bugs is sometimes warranted, sometimes mere laziness, but sometimes deeper and cultural: Avoiding the kinds of bugs that static analysis finds is largely a matter of discipline, which is sometimes unpopular among programmers. Fixing these bugs, and verifying that your organization has done so, will require adaptability and judgment. Attempts to design simple rules and metrics for this are, in my opinion, at best premature, and perhaps impossible.[*]

Starting with lower targets that will deliver high-confidence results will be accepted much faster, as engineering teams quickly gain confidence in the tools' results. We suggest a soft target of engineers trusting the static analyzer similarly to the way they trust their compilation tools. Starting small and focusing on high confidence is likely to gain that sort of trust. And once that trust is gained, teams can begin experimenting with more checks, broader defect analysis, and more aggressive scans. Still, in our experience, engineering team confidence and trust is critical to the success of the static analysis program.

In other words, it is typically a mistake to simply turn on the default or "everything but the kitchen sink" analysis when first getting a start. Teams will be bombarded with unmanageable defect totals (sometimes in the tens of thousands from a single analysis). Defect tracking systems will be overwhelmed. Such numbers are likely to generate "political resistance" to adoption. Engineers will lose confidence that the tool can deliver usable and reliable results. (Core Software Security, pp. 271–274)

Addressing the issue of how to gain programmer confidence in static analysis tools, and what can go wrong with "find all" approaches, Brook wrote the following in *Secrets of a Cyber Security Architect*:

"Just like a compiler checks to see if the code is syntactically correct, so static analysis can check to see if there are potential security errors in the code. That should be a big help. Where does this go wrong?

One of the problems is that many (most) static analysis tools, and especially the commercial ones, are sold through broad coverage of types and variations of possible errors. But, lots of the checks aren't all that reliable. Although some types of errors might be found with very high confidence (say, 80% or 90%), many of the checks have a much lower confidence level. The tools then rely on a human to figure out whether or not there really is an error.

Plus, these tools benefit from a lot of configuration and tuning. They often need to be told about some of the details of the code and its standard libraries. Mostly, one cannot just add the tool to the build chain and expect reasonable results.

When I got to one organization, one team had a backlog of 72,000 static analysis findings. Another team there had 46,000. I'll bet astute readers can guess what those teams did with all those errors? Absolutely nothing. There were too many findings to begin to deal with any of the results; it would take years of work to winnow through that many findings, at the expense of actually generating any code.

The tool had not been tuned to the code base. It was not configured correctly. The two teams I mention simply turned on "all checks" and then, when there were too many findings with which to deal, they perceived the static analysis tool as useless. Security demanded that they add the tool. But its results were too noisy to be useful.

There is a solution to this problem, and this is precisely what we did at that organization. We configured that rather complex commercial tool to render only high confidence results. Most of these tools can be configured to deliver everything. But they can also be configured to analyze only for findings of high confidence. Once the two teams began to get valuable results, they became our model for all the other teams. Within a year, all the teams were finding great value in their static analysis because

---

[*] Ibid.

they focused on high confidence results first. Teams were free to experiment with confidence settings beyond the basics. Each team reached its own tolerance for tool noise. Security issues decreased significantly." (*Secrets*, pp. 110–111)

> *Instead, we advise starting small, clean, and manageable. Build on successes. Template successful builds, configurations, and test suites that teams can adopt easily and quickly. Have successful teams assist those that may be struggling. Let the teams that have reduced their defect counts evangelize to those that are just getting started or are new to analysis. We have successfully used precisely this approach several times in different organizations.*
>
> *One key is to place static analysis in the correct development "spot." Like the compiler, through which the code must pass successfully in order to generate object code, the code must pass through static analysis and likewise be free from incorrect uses and identified vulnerabilities before it can be built (that is, linked into a library, executable, or other fully linked and executable object). Static analysis can be thought of as a part of the check-in and build process; static analysis is the mandatory step for qualifying code as buildable.*
>
> *If the analysis tool supports developer use during development, let engineers have this additional check for the code they produce. Programmers will learn and trust the tool. They will also learn about security and secure coding; security mistakes will be pointed out during code creation. Still, we believe that while this use delivers obvious benefits, the code should still be analyzed again when committed for build into the product or release. Give coders every advantage. Give them every possibility for delivering correct code. And verify correctness at some formal gate through which the code must pass. If the code is clean, there is little lost from putting it through static analysis—commercial analyzers are generally quite fast once they are properly configured and tuned. However, if there are vulnerabilities, this is the bottom line. These "must not pass" into executable objects that then have the potential for getting into production uses. "Trust, but verify." We recommend empowering coders to verify their work while also verifying implementations before these can be fully committed for potential release. (Core Software Security, pp. 274–275)*

At the time of *Core Software Security*, the established commercial SAST vendors were experimenting with desktop and coding workflow analyzers. A couple of startups (by now these are also established) bet their success on desktop analysis. Still, the concept was fairly new and less well-tried. At this point, there is no doubt in our minds that desktop analysis is a critical piece of the "successful secure coding" puzzle. Experience demonstrates clearly that given useful analysis as coding unfolds (as long as the analysis is fast enough and reasonably accurate) will be heartily embraced. Finding and removing bugs while coding is absolutely the most effective way to use static analysis. That is true even if the analysis is less thorough and covers significantly less of the final software. The goal for desktop SAST will be to remove a set of issues from code as it's being written and remove these issues consistently. The side benefit is reinforcement of secure coding training leading to increased secure coding skill.

> *At the heart of every development lifecycle, there are three processes that interlock and complement each other to deliver secure code. Developers need to be trained and have the discipline to try and write correct, error-free, vulnerability-free code. This practice and discipline will require training, practice, and a space in which developers can make mistakes, try new things, learn, and be relatively free during the learning process. It takes astute management to work with high-functioning, creative people who are learning their craft while practicing it at the same time. After the code is written, the next core step of the secure build process is manual code review. Like secure programming, manual code review is also a discipline and a practice. Code review is also an opportunity for learning and mastery; manual code review is the other side of writing correct code. Great code reviewers become great coders. Great coders become great code reviewers. The two processes work hand in hand to deliver cleaner code*

and more sophisticated programmers. Finally, at the heart of the development process, checking and complementing the code review, is static analysis. Complementing the human element, static analysis is an automated procedure that looks holistically across multiple dimensions at the same time. Whether Waterfall or Agile, secure coding, code review, and static analysis should lie at the heart of any security development lifecycle. (Core Software Security, p. 275)

3.2.4 Third-Party Code Assessment

Today, a large proportion, often the majority of code in released software (depending upon the software), will be from third parties, most often, open source software (OSS). There is no doubt that using OSS saves an enormous amount of code-generation effort; for many systems, a great deal of what must be coded is repetitive across all similar systems. Why write an entirely new Web client menu system when there exist several richly featured and well-supported options? Open source has been a programmer's dream come true by supplying repeating functions and services seemingly virtually for free and easily available.*

Open source isn't the only third-party code that may become included or used. Critical functions or services may be purchased. For instance, cryptographic functions may need to comply with various regulations. Purchasing such a library might make business sense for compliance reasons, or for the vendor's support, and to ensure that tricky and difficult to implement and maintain code is correct: Cryptographic algorithms are notoriously difficult to get right.

There's a common misunderstanding about the trade-offs involved in the use of third-party code, especially open source. The development effort during coding is traded for maintenance for the life of the released software. We will address that problem below, in the section devoted to vulnerability patching.

And there is a more subtle problem that must be addressed *before* including third-party code: Has it been built with software security practices that meet the standards of the including organizations? For OSS, there are vendors who claim to offer ratings of software security "risk." If one of these vendor's rating system is used, we suggest that organizations measure the rating system against their own software security standards or this Generic SDL's practices. We have found significant differences between the things that the vendor assesses and an organization's SDL (software security practices).

Another method is to perform assessments, when needed. One could measure against the practices set out in this book. Alternatively, The Open Web Application Security Project (OWASP) offers a rich set of Web software security advice and standards. There are other standards that might be used for a third-party software security assessment. The point is to find out what the OSS community or software vendor actually does, if anything. And then, after the information has been collected, assess whether what they do is sufficient to avoid degrading the including/consuming software's security posture.

The essential problem is that inclusion of software built without security practices is nearly guaranteed to contain issues. And without the active involvement of the open source community or the vendor, no one will know until discovered. One can hope that the discovery will be by reputable security researchers rather than attackers who exploit conditions before these are announced. In any event, inclusion of issues means that some portion of those issues may be available in the including software. (This is not always true. It often requires vulnerability analysis to determine if an issue can be exploited and has negative effects for the including software.) Whatever issues the third-party software has can

---

* Make no mistake: Fortunes have been made through "giving away" open source software. The open source version might lead users to paid versions as the user's system and needs grow. Alternatively, open source vendors sell support for their software. Even established software makers will open source portions of the inventions to fuel adoption and interchange. There are numerous interesting ways that open source has been used to generate revenue.

easily become the issues of the including software. It's imperative that the makers of the software care enough about security to at least notify about issues, if not try to fix them.

There is one other dimension of open source assessment that's also important: community. In the open source world, software is supported by a community, not a vendor. Community participants usually donate their time to the upkeep and improvement of the software. For software to be well-maintained, it needs an active community to support it. Along with assessing OSS security practices, we also recommend assessing the activity of the community. Imagine that a choice was between two similar libraries, and one of them had been written by a single person who hadn't contributed anything or made a fix to the library for several years. Consider that the other library has an active community. It may be obvious to readers which library is more likely to be updated in the case of an issue being found. We take a look at the records (usually public) of community discussions, trouble tickets, issue dispensation, and the like to ensure that someone, hopefully, more than one, is actively and consistently engaged in the support of the software. OSS maintained by an active community will more likely receive timely fixes.

A word of caution: Open source communities rarely perform every task exactly as termed in this SDL. Or, if they do, the tasks aren't necessarily named the same way as described herein. It's critical in an open source assessment to find out how issues are tracked, how design discussions unfold, etc., to determine if the spirit of the SDL is being met, even if rather informally. The authors aren't particular about SDL naming conventions. OSS communities in which requirements are identified (probably through threat modeling, even if informal or *ad hoc*), and in which coders try for secure code and then verify code through manual and automated checks meet the essential spirit of a consensus SDL, no matter the names given to the activities.

In any event, there are few barriers to OSS projects and communities running static analysis (SAST). A number of major SAST vendors make their product available and free to use to open source projects. Failure to run SAST (and fix the errors) is a failure of software security and must be taken into account when choosing among essentially equal OSS alternatives.

In a choice between software options in which the other SDL assessment dimensions are relatively similar, the failure to use static analysis in one option would cause us to avoid it in favor of the alternative that does.

3.2.5 Patch (Upgrade or Fix) Issues Identified in Third-Party Code

Vulnerabilities in OSS arrive in what can seem to be a nearly constant stream. The constant announcement of new issues may seem more like a firehose than a manageable flow for large organizations building and fielding a complex portfolio of software. As we noted in the section on OSS, for some types of software, the majority of the code may very well be OSS, which might be spread across many platforms, many execution stacks, and many different types of functionality. It can be a lot to contend with. But contend we must.

On the other hand, raw totals of issues are rarely meaningful. "GitHub: Our dependency scan has found four million security flaws in public repos."[*] The headline we've quoted may sound scary (which might be the intention?), but we don't know how much code is in the "public repos," what it does, which code has been adopted for use (many Github projects have little or no adoption), how wide the code that is used is spread, whether particular vulnerabilities are exposed or not (exposure tends to be quite contextual), and, importantly, which of the 4 million vulnerabilities attackers find useful. Is that 4 million different issues, or a count of instances? (Most probably, the latter.)

---

[*] Tung, L. ZDNet, March 22, 2018—12:10 GMT (05:10 PDT). Retrieved from https://www.zdnet.com/article/github-our-dependency-scan-has-found-four-million-security-bugs-in-public-repos/

The problem with a raw count such as Github announced is that it makes salacious headlines but doesn't tell us what we need to know. We need to know the following:

- Do attackers believe that an issue offers leverage? If so, what sort?*
- Are attackers currently exploiting the condition, or has it been exploited in the past?
- Has a preprogrammed exploit been added to an Exploit Kit (EK—i.e., "weaponized")?
- Generally, what level of impact can compromise entail (severity: Common Vulnerability Scoring System [CVSS])?
- In the technical and usage context of a particular system or software, what are the impacts from compromise? (The contextual impact of compromise often varies significantly from the general case.)
- How difficult or easy is it to deliver an exploit to the issue to each particular system that includes the issue? What are the mechanisms of delivery?
- What are the preconditions to exploitation? Are these typical? Edge cases? Artificial, requiring unreal access or privileges?

Some of the above questions must be answered in the context of a particular system or piece of software, often with an understanding of how the software is used, by whom, under what circumstances, and how it is configured. In other words, a generalized analysis only points a finger at potential problems. Further analysis is often necessary to determine the contextual risk rating.

These types of analyses aren't generally automated and also require technical understanding of the exploitation mechanisms of the issue and some fairly deep knowledge about the software in which it resides.

We've had a lot of success pairing experienced security analysts with developers to perform these analyses. Doing so can save a lot of effort by avoiding fixing issues that present little attacker usefulness or leverage, or not chasing issues whose exploitation involves uses or configurations that lie outside those found in real-world usage.

The caveat to our above statement is situations where customers perceive an issue as dangerous even if provably not so. In these situations, it may behoove software makers to provide a fix to retain customer good will. We've found that technical explanations about the relative insignificance of an issue can too often fall on the deaf ears of a panicked customer.

In a highly automated DevOps world, analyses as we've described above may be too costly and may derail or block continuous delivery of software. There is an alternative that maximizes automation: patch and test with monitored A/B tests. (We explained A/B testing strategy in Chapter 2.)

The concept is to patch everything that is identified. Having information about issues as soon as announcements are made may require investment in a commercial OSS monitoring service. Alternatively, an organization could monitor every OSS project that has been included. That might prove expensive where a great deal of OSS has been used (many projects). Given some means to monitor all relevant issue announcements, downloading the patch and queuing it for build can be accomplished automatically.

Whenever a new patch has been updated into the releases or deployed software, the software would automatically be run in a separated environment against an environment running the same software except that it has been built without the latest patches applied. If any issues are encountered, the patched build is removed from service for analysis. Customers can be moved to the stable version until all problems have been understood and fixed.

Many patches install without issue. Considering that many patches may not actually be used or accessible within a program or application, some portion, perhaps the majority, sometimes the vast majority of patches will run without issue, since the patched code isn't executing.

---

* Please see MITRE®'s ATT&CK® Navigator for an attacker's view of leverage and how such leverage is actually used to proceed towards attacker goals in well-known campaigns.

In this scenario, operators are interested only in issues that cause the software to behave in unexpected ways. All issues that have no effects are passed into releases with no human interaction.

Our scenario requires the ability to build A/B(/C/D . . .) test environments and the ability to move users from one version of software to another seamlessly. For many cloud environments, such A/B testing and user movement is trivial and can be automated with DevOps code. The firehose of issues can thus be reduced to issues that affect the behavior of the software. These will require human analysis in any case, so nothing is lost in terms of resources. Such a tactic replaces human analysis to reduce the flow to issues that present some risk to the stakeholders of the software with human analysis around patches that don't behave correctly. Either approach will require some human analysis. Either approach can turn the firehose back to a manageable stream. We offer both as potential solutions to the SDL requirement to patch issues that pose significant harm to the stakeholders of the software.

3.3 Determining the Right Activities for Each Project

3.3.1 The SDL Determining Questions

Recurring often, continually, and across every organization with which we've worked, is a sense from developers and engineering teams that adding security will be yet another impediment to delivery. It's important to note that many if not most software organizations reward at least in part upon the delivery of features on time, and under budget. Typically, the focus on timely delivery is well embedded at the point when a software security practice is started or improved. It is only natural that teams will want to know how, in their already busy schedules, they will manage to accomplish a series of what appear to be additional tasks.

Obviously, one can argue that developers should have been integrating security into development practices already. Interestingly, many times, teams have responded that they are, in fact, doing just that: producing "secure" software. "Secure" here is an operative term; "security" has no precise meaning and is highly overloaded. (Core Software Security, pp. 275–276)

We reprise from Chapter 1 the following software security principles to remind the reader of the complete set of software behaviors that should be expected to result from enactment of an holistic SDL.

- Be free from implementation errors that can be maliciously manipulated: ergo, vulnerabilities
- Have the security features that stakeholders require for intended use cases
- Be self-protective; resist the types of attacks that will likely be attempted against the software
- In the event of a failure, must "fail well"—that is, fail in such a manner as to minimize consequences of successful attack
- Install with sensible, "closed" defaults

A widespread amount of confusion over what, precisely, "secure software" is persists as of this writing, as we noted in Chapter 9 of *Core Software Security*, quoted above. We ask the reader to bear in mind the aspirational set of software behaviors given here and in Chapter 1 of this book as we discuss aspects of the SDL. Each SDL activity is intended to build software that embodies these principles to whatever degree is needed by the stakeholders and users of the software in order to get the intended benefits from the software.

Digging a little deeper, we will be told that the authentication mechanism for the software has been well thought through and is built and tested. Or, perhaps, all communications going over the network can be placed within an encrypted tunnel (usually, TLS). Rarely, previous to the instantiation of a strong SDL program, do teams respond in a holistic manner, acknowledging the range of tasks that must receive attention, from design through testing. And that is precisely the problem that working with the SDL is supposed to address: holistic, built-in security, soup to nuts, end to end.

Because security is often presented as a matrix of tasks, teams may see the large number of tasks and become overwhelmed as a result. Time and again, we have heard team leads and development managers ask, "What do I have to do?" Since the answer to that question really should depend on the type of project at hand, the security architect may answer, "Well, that depends." This answer is not very satisfying to people who have made a practice out of timely and orderly software delivery: product managers, project managers, technical leads, and development managers.

Then, the security person will be asked, "What is the minimum set of activities that my project will have?" Requesting a minimum task set is certainly a relevant and worthy question. The answer, "Well, that depends," is once again not at all satisfying. We realized that having the security architect as the sole arbiter of what must be done too often makes a mystery of the entire process. Planning becomes more difficult. Yet again, security is seen as a hindrance and an obstacle, not as one of the required deliverables that must be a part of production software.

After much trial and error over many years, on divergent development groups operating within multiple enterprise organizations, we have crystallized a set of questions that can be easily answered by project managers, architects, technical and engineering leads, and/or product managers. These people typically have the understanding to assess the amount of planned architecture and design change, whether there will be additions of sensitive data and third-party code, the types of interfaces to be added or changed, and the expected deployment models. Each of these dimensions influences which security activities must be executed in order to generate the correct set of security features and requirements. Some of these dimensions determine what types of security testing will be required. Together, the answers to these questions will map the required SDL security task flows to individual project circumstances.

We do not recommend a "do it all" approach. Threat modeling additions that make no substantive change to a previously and thoroughly analyzed security architecture delivers no additional security value. Plus, requiring this step when it has no value will not engender trust of security's process judgment. Engineers often spot valueless activities (they tend to be smart, creative people!). Nobody likes to waste time on useless bureaucracy. Most engineers will quickly realize that requiring dynamic Web testing when there is no Web server has no value. Rather, let teams exercise their skills by allowing them to answer fundamental questions that sensibly add activities only when these are applicable.

These questions can be asked up front, at the beginning of the development lifecycle, or at appropriate stages along the way. Timing is critical. Answering each question after the appropriate time for the associated activities in the SDL has past will cause delays; required security tasks will be missed. As long as each question is asked before its results are needed, your security results will be similar. Architecture questions can be asked before any architecture is started, design before designing, testing answers need to be gathered for the testing plan, and so on throughout the lifecycle. However, asking these seven determining questions at the very beginning allows those responsible for budgeting and resource allocation to gather critical information about what will need to be accomplished during development. (Core Software Security, pp. 276–277)

Readers may note once again, the implied linearity of development in the statement, "Answering each question after the appropriate time for the associated activities in the SDL has past will cause delays." Timing is, indeed, critical. Certain SDL (and SDLC) activity cannot be started without the outputs of other activities. There are task dependencies. Our development questions attempt to capture those dependencies, both intra-SDL and between the SDL and associated (if any) SDLC activities. Still, as we shall see, we have revised those questions (taken up front before a cycle of changes, or as needed) to reflect continuous development.

Take as an example, threat modeling. Completed software does not benefit at all from threat modeling, although the software's stakeholders may wish to understand what under/unmitigated risks remain in the software. Threat modeling, often accompanying and in partnership with penetration testing, provides risk information. However, if the software is not going to be changed any further, risk ratings of the issues is all that one gets from the exercise. Hence, we hope that you see that the threat model offers valuable security insight to the architecture, to designs, sometimes for secure coding, and, certainly, important avenues of verification. Therefore, the threat model is best started alongside the architecture, if not before, as a part of the first conceptualizations. The threat model generally continues to be refined as more and more is known about what will be built and how it will be realized. Chapter 4 will go into greater detail about secure design and threat modeling's important contributions to that end.

1. *What changes are proposed? (The following answers are mutually exclusive; choose only one.*
   a. *The architecture will be entirely new or is a major redesign.*
   b. *The architecture is expected to change.*
   c. *Security features or functions will be added.*
   d. *Neither changing the architecture nor adding security features to the design will be necessary (i.e., none of the above).*
2. *Will any third-party software be added? Yes/no*
3. *Will any customer data (personally identifying information [PII]) be added? Yes/no*
4. *Will this organization or any of its partners host any of the systems? Yes/no*
5. *Is a Web server included? Yes/no*
6. *Will there be any other inputs to the program? (i.e., non-Web input, configuration file, network listeners, command line interfaces, etc.) Yes/no*
7. *Is this a major release?*

Very early in the process, even as the concept begins to take shape, it's important to ask, "What's new?" That is, find out how much change is intended by this project, through this effort. The question is meant to be asked at the architecture level; there are four possible answers:

1. *Everything is new. This is a "greenfield" project or a major redesign.*
2. *The architecture will change significantly.*
3. *Security features will be added.*
4. *None of the above.*

What Changes Are Proposed?

When everything will be new, there are certain pre-architectural activities that can help determine the set of requirements and features that will meet the security challenges for the intended use and deployment of the software. . . . Having a complete set of requirements has proven to deliver more inclusive and effective architectures, by far. Among the complete set of requirements must be security. The goal is to "build security in," not to bolt it on later. If the required features are not included in the architecture requirements, they most likely will not get built. This forces deployment teams to make up for missing security features by building the required protections into the encompassing runtime or infrastructure, often as a "one-off," nonstandard implementation.

When everything or almost everything will be new and there is no existing legacy architecture or design for which architects must account, there is an opportunity to thoroughly consider not only current threats and their attacks, but the likely attacks of the future against which the software must protect itself. This kind of early, strategic thinking is rare in the world of software re-use. It's a great advantage to take the time and think about what the security system will need holistically. Software security strategy is best done before making decisions that cause the secure design course to be ruled out entirely or made much more difficult to implement. (Core Software Security, pp. 277–279)

The preceding paragraph is critically important: Start analyzing for security needs as soon as possible. The first standard we've found requiring early security requirement analysis is NIST 800-14 from 1996! This is not a new idea. For years, both the authors have written, lobbied, presented, called out, and embodied early analysis for security in their programs. Organizations continue to struggle with starting security analysis as they start analyzing for other software properties and requirements: The single most consistent problem that we hear from software security programs, and especially from security architects, is late security engagement. Engagement after the architecture is complete is too late because architects have failed to build security into the architecture in order to consider security needs that then lead to architecture changes. Alongside any needed architecture change or additions, those security needs that cannot be accommodated in the architecture, or worse, have been made impossible through architectural assumptions or decisions will have to be cobbled together to work with structures and functions not designed to include security—that is, "bolted on" not "built in." The more complete the software when security analysis begins, the bigger the negative effects from late engagement. Identifying security requirements the day before release is essentially a useless, pro forma security engagement. And yet, this is a common complaint.

Nearly universally, developers hate receiving security requirements after much of the software has been built.

Why do we keep this disfunction going? Part of the answer to that question is misconception about threat modeling—that it cannot be done alongside and as a part of other design work. It can. We've proven the efficacy of iterative, collaborative threat modeling not once, but multiple times at multiple organizations. When Brook teaches or speaks, he often challenges developers to contact security as early as possible. At the same time, security people shouldn't sit around waiting for developers to "phone home." Security people can be proactive, asking about new projects, new development, proposed changes, cycles of Sprints, and the next Epic. Executives cannot legislate closer collaboration. We believe that everyone involved must take responsibility to start early and then proceed. Please see Chapter 4 for more detail about how threat modeling underlies secure design.

Figure 3.4 describes an ideal secure design process that begins as new software is conceived and continues to be refined as the software is developed.

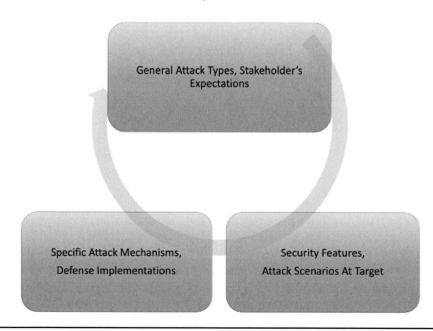

Figure 3.4 Early, Iterative Threat Modeling.

If the architecture is changing, then. refine the existing threat model. The changes must be examined in light of the existing architecture so that any additional security requirements can be smoked out. The assumption is that the existing architecture has been assessed and threat-modeled to ensure that appropriate security requirements have been built into the design. In cases where there never has been an architecture assessment and threat model, the architecture should be treated the same as a greenfield project.

Even if there are no additions or changes to the existing architecture, adding any feature with security implications indicates the necessity for design work. The design makes the architecture buildable. Programmers work from the design. So, it's important that any security requirement or feature be designed correctly and completely. Security expertise is critical; the purpose of the design review is to ensure that the appropriate security expertise is applied to the design. (Core Software Security, p. 279)

Figure 3.5 shows that refining and reviewing the threat model in light of proposed and in process changes is a continuing process. Assuming that a threat model began alongside the concept or idea, as development proceeds, so does the threat model as a part of normal development. It serves as a key security input into what should be built and how it should be implemented in order to deliver on the security behaviors listed at the start of this section and introduced in Chapter 1.

Figure 3.5   Iterative Threat Modeling.

Figure 3.6 visually demonstrates the iterative refinement of the threat model as DevOps infinite task loops execute. Threat modeling cannot be a one-time interjection, or the threat model cannot keep pace as software changes and, just as importantly, keep pace with learnings and improvements due to stakeholder interaction and team reflection on the ongoing work (a key attribute of Agile Scrum SDLC). Performing exactly one threat model will ensure that at least parts of the model's output will become irrelevant as DevOps cycles evolve the software. Therefore, threat modeling must become part and parcel of development, just like considerations for usability, or performance, or scalability, and the other aspects of the software. Security is not different in this respect: Appropriate security behaviors are a result of continuing and iterative analysis in light of current and new information.

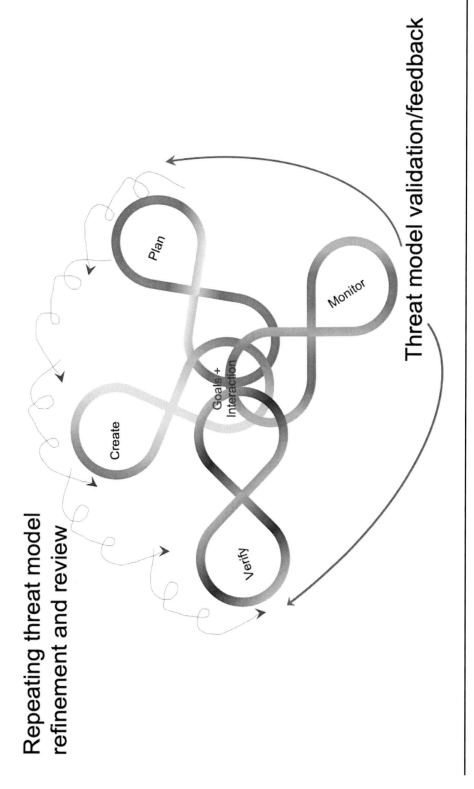

Repeating threat model
refinement and review

Plan

Monitor

Goals +
Interaction

Create

Verify

Threat model validation/feedback

Figure 3.6 Iterative Threat Modeling In DevOps.

Like any other feature or function, every security function must be thoroughly tested for correctness in the test plan. Creating the test plan is part of the design work. The test plan is an artifact of the design.

The answers to the question, "What's new?" are a pick-list choice. There should be one and only one choice. The answers are not mutually exclusive. Rather, the second choice, "architecture changes," is a subset of the first; "greenfield" implies that the architecture will change. The answer, "security features," is independent of the first two. "Security features" is meant to catch changes for which the project's design must be considered. If the architecture is changing, it can be presumed that the design will change as well.

The answers to the remainder of the questions are "yes/no" or binary.

Will Any Third-Party Software Be Added?

Adding third-party software presents two challenges.

1. *The additional software may have security vulnerabilities that then become incorporated into the finished product. Typically, for commercially created software, the development team does not have the source code to the software. An organization will be entirely dependent on the third party to fix vulnerabilities. Or, if the software is open source, there may be legal and monetary considerations if the development team chooses to fix security defects. According to many licenses, that fix must be contributed back to the open-source community for everyone to use. That may not be commercially viable.*

2. *Added to the conundrum surrounding whether to fix a third party's defects are the licensing issues attached to the software that will be added. Different open-source and freely available licenses vary widely in restricting what a commercial organization can or cannot do with software that incorporates this functionality. Your ability to sell your product might be constrained. Or proprietary intellectual property may have to be exposed. Because of these considerations, we believe it is essential that decisions to use third-party software include consultation with an expert familiar with software licensing (usually someone in the legal department). The software licensing expert will review the licensing details thoroughly.*

Answering "yes" to this question adds a legal licensing review to the required tasks. It may also require the need to monitor for security patches of the third-party software for as long as it's included. (Core Software Security, pp. 279–281)

The third-party SDL tasks and their linear flow are illustrated in Figure 3.7.

In 2014 we wrote, "It may also require the need to monitor for security patches." Experience since writing *Core Software Security* convinces us that there's no "may," no uncertainty, about this SDL activity: Inclusion of third-party software always requires monitoring for issues throughout the life of the software.

Figure 3.7   Third-Party Software Tasks.

If third-party software is included, one is making a contract with the future security of the software to regularly, perhaps continually, watch for new issues in that software. As new issues arise, one must analyze for potential applicability to the use case(s) for which the software has been employed: Not every issue can be exploited or returns the same effects in every technical context. We will take this analysis up, as well as other potential remedies to the problem of keeping third-party components up to date, later in this chapter. The important point to bear in mind with reference to the SDL activity determining questions is that inclusion of third-party software requires continued vigilance. We have already explained that nearly all, if not all software will eventually have issues, and that some of these will allow attacker leverage, that is, be "vulnerabilities."

We find when interacting with developers that there is a widely held misconception that open source software is "free." There is no "free" about the implicit contract with the software's emerging issues. Use of open source software trades development time today for security vigilance continuing into the future for as long as that software will be used. When issues that affect the security posture of the software arise, the analysis is essentially a single-issue, single-attack scenario threat model:

- Who can misuse the issue?
- How will the attacker gain access to misuse?
- What are the preconditions to misuse (if any)?
- What does the attacker gain (if anything) through misuse?
- What are the impacts should the attacker be successful?
- Have similar misuses been observed against other systems and similar software? If so, how frequent are successful compromises?

Answers to these questions help to rate the urgency, or not, for updating the software ("patching") or identifying other mitigations, if deemed necessary. With an analysis based upon the answers to the above questions in hand, one can then build a risk rating from the frequency of similar issues' successful use and from the potential impacts in this context. The frequency of use will often require research through threat intelligence reports and/or new reports. Published lists* of vulnerability use may also provide frequency information.

Will Data About Human Entities (Personally Identifying Information) Be Added?

If your software will face privacy challenges and regulations, it's imperative to find out if personally identifying information (PII) will be handled by the application under development. Depending on the organization, security may be tasked with protecting customers' information and meeting each legal jurisdiction's privacy regulations. Privacy duties may also reside in a dedicated team, or as part of legal, or some other part of the organization. Whatever team is responsible, these will need to be brought in for a data protection review. Hence the question, "Are you adding customer data?" This is a much easier question to answer without specialized privacy knowledge.

We phrased this question as "customer data" because, depending on the jurisdiction, the definition of PII varies widely. And those organizations that will be subject to regulations in multiple jurisdictions must ascertain how they will meet regulations that may in fact conflict. Generally, legal privacy expertise is required for these determinations. Most development teams will not have the expertise to understand the various regulations and laws that define PII and to which an application may be subject. However, we have found that it's very easy for teams to understand whether the application is handling customer data or not. Depending on your development team expertise, you may want to let

---

* There are several yearly "Top 10" lists of exploits that are getting regular use. Inclusion of a vulnerability type on one or more of these lists should be taken as a firm validation that attackers are currently exploiting the issue.

determination about whether or not there are privacy issues be answered by the appropriate personnel with privacy expertise. Simply flagging customer data ensures that, at the very least, the right team will be engaged for privacy issues.

Well-designed and well-implemented security protects data; that is one purpose of information security. However, it should be noted that security of customer data is not the only dimension of appropriate (and legally compliant) privacy. Privacy also may encompass policies, presentations, consent, limitations to geographic transportation and storage of data, and other dimensions that have little to do with the security design and implementation. Thus, security does not equal privacy. On the other hand, the ability to comply with some privacy laws and expectations certainly demands sufficient security. And, of course, many dimensions of digital security are independent of the privacy domain. (Core Software Security, pp. 281–282)

In the intervening years since addressing privacy needs in *Core Software Security*'s SDL, new regulations have refined what privacy means. At the same time, Privacy Engineering has coalesced into a discipline and set of practices. Privacy Engineering is beyond the scope of this book. But helping to achieve privacy goals is very much a security problem: Adequate security protection is essential to prevent a breach of privacy. Privacy, as a domain, is much broader than adequate security protections.

Not every situation requiring privacy involves "customer" data. In retrospect, perhaps it would have been better to use a more inclusive data term. Unfortunately, "Personally Identifying Information" (PII) is defined by the regulations in force in each jurisdiction, and thus, has no precise, universal meaning. At the time of *Core Software Security*, the authors were working primarily with product software, so "customer data" was easy for product developers to grasp. A generic SDL must not assume to what purposes software will be put.

"User data" would perhaps be better, but still does not cover all the subjects of data that may require privacy analysis. For lack of a better term than "PII," we now ask the question, "Will data about human entities (personally identifying information) be added?" which seems to cover the vast majority of situations, while still not forcing developers to have full knowledge of what constitutes PII in every jurisdiction in which their software will be used.

Will This Organization or Any of Its Partners Host Any of the Systems?

The deployment model and execution environment of a system influence not only what security features and controls will be required, but, at a higher level of abstraction, the security lens through which these controls and features will be filtered. Not every control is required in every system. How to choose?

Software that is intended to be deployed by others outside the organization, for instance, by customers, must have sufficient capabilities to fulfill the customer's security posture from within the customer's environment. The security goal is to empower the customer while at the same time not reducing the customer environment's security posture.

On the other hand, software that will be hosted from within the perceived borders of an organization has fundamentally different security responsibilities. We use the term "perceived borders" because customers, media, and public influencers often don't make a fine discrimination between a "partner" and the organization. In the face of a successful attack, the largest or most well-known entity or brand will get tagged with responsibility for the failure, regardless of any tangle of arms-length relationships. In light of this aspect of perception, we suggest taking a broad view of responsibility. Of course, each organization will have to define its acceptable boundaries for incident responsibility.

A system to be hosted by a known and controlled infrastructure inherits the security posture of that infrastructure. Thus, systems that will be deployed by the organization can make assumptions that are not possible with systems that will be deployed by those outside the organization, beyond

Figure 3.8   Hosted Infrastructure Activities. (*Source:* Reproduced from Ransome, J. and Misra, A. [2014]. *Core Software Security: Security at the Source.* Boca Raton [FL]: CRC Press/Taylor & Francis Group, p. 283, with permission.)

organizational boundaries, on third-party premises. Assumptions can be made about which security functions are built into the infrastructure on which the system will be deployed. Indeed, the other side of that coin is that a locally deployed system also can be prepared for weaknesses within a known infrastructure. That is, an organizationally hosted system inherits the security posture of the infrastructure on which it is deployed. Figure 3.8 [formerly Figure 9.8] represents the set of tasks associated with deployment to a hosted infrastructure.

A hosted system also must meet all local policies and standards. This makes configuration, hardening, and tuning much more specific. For software to be deployed by others, it's important to design for unknown security requirements. In the case of hosted software, the requirements are typically apparent; these requirements can be anticipated, planned into the design, and pre-built.

In order to understand what security will need to be prepared and what weaknesses will need to be mitigated, it is important to ask "Organizationally hosted?" during requirements gathering and architecture. If those responsible for security requirements (typically, the security architects) are not familiar with the infrastructure into which the system will be deployed, an assessment of the infrastructure must take place. Likewise, policies and standards must be thoroughly understood in order to apply them to the system being built.

Typically, for a running security architecture practice, there will be experts in the existing infrastructure and policy experts. For hosted systems, these subject-matter experts can be engaged to help refine the analysis so the requirements precisely fit the infrastructure into which the system is to be deployed. In this way, the hosted systems will meet organizational policies. On the other hand, if it is a new infrastructure, there is a due diligence responsibility to examine every security factor that is applicable. Insist that the new infrastructure be studied as a part of the systems under analysis.

*Failure to look at the infrastructure, instead focusing solely on the systems being built, opens the possibility that an attacker could walk right through that infrastructure despite a designer's best efforts to build a sound defense in depth. Security architecture must, by dint of its due diligence responsibilities, always be front to back, side to side, bottom to top, thoroughly analyzing all components that support or interact. Every system that connects opens the distinct possibility that the interconnected system's security posture will in some way affect the security posture of the system to which it connects. This is a fundamental law of doing architectural analysis for security. Failure to be thorough is a failure in the security analysis. That analysis must include the infrastructure into which systems will be deployed if that infrastructure is under the control of the organization's policies. Thus, always ask, "Will any part of this system be hosted by this organization or its partners?" (*Core Software Security*, pp. 282–284)*

Everything we stated about internally hosted, third-party hosting, and customer hosting remains absolutely valid. However, in 2014, we missed an important dimension: cloud, especially, public, commercial cloud hosting. As of this writing, commercial cloud use is ordinary and usual. Although the wise software security person will always perform some due diligence research on the security practices of any new cloud vendor, most practitioners have dealt with the well-known vendors multiple times, perhaps several repeatedly. Cloud use changes the responses to this question in that the well-known, long-term cloud vendors handle many security practices for the cloud consumer.

At one of Brook's roles, he spent considerable time researching Amazon Web Services™ (AWS™) security practices, including time spent talking to AWS security architects, etc., in order to fulfill the requirements of the "hosting" SDL activity for his employer. The conclusion derived from that research is that major cloud vendors' business depends upon their executing security maintenance well, well enough that most cloud consumers will satisfy their security posture needs. Our statement is not meant as an endorsement of AWS versus Google® versus Azure® versus any other cloud vendor. The vendor in use at that particular time just happened to be AWS. Subsequent evaluations of other major vendors lead to the same conclusion: Much of what the cloud consumer requires for infrastructure and platform security is provided by the cloud service.

The foregoing in no way should be taken to imply that cloud consumers have no security responsibilities, that all security necessities are provided through cloud use. That is far from true. When using a cloud, everything provided to the cloud, to be run on the cloud is the security responsibility of the cloud user, not the cloud provider. There is hard line of responsibility demarcation between cloud provider and cloud consumer. That line exists between those services provided by the cloud, those services consumed by the user, and what the user supplies that will be run with and supported by the cloud provider's offerings.

A cloud vendor takes no responsibility whatsoever for security issues in code that consumes their services, nor in the configurations and deployment chains used by that consumer. The security of the configuration, deployment, packaging, coding not provided by the cloud vendor is the unconditional responsibility of the user of cloud services, not of the supplier.

Misconfigure cloud storage so that it is publicly available? That's the consumer's mistake; all resulting impacts must be borne by the cloud consumer. Steal the cloud administrative password? All resulting impacts must be borne by the cloud consumer. Release an issue that allows misuse of the consumer's code, or even allows misuse of one or more cloud services? All resulting impacts must be borne by the cloud consumer.

Hence, we add an additional dimension to "Review Infrastructure" SDL activity. For commercial cloud use (especially of one of the major vendors), review the services consumed. Establish the line of security responsibility between cloud provider and cloud consumer. Everything above that line belongs as a part of the SDL infrastructure review. Everything below (i.e., belonging to the cloud vendor) can be assumed to be executed as correctly as humanly possible.

Are There Any Web Protocol Inputs?

As of the writing of this book, security testing of Web servers utilizes a specialized set of tools and skills. For this reason, we have found it useful to identify the need for Web server testing so that the appropriate testing is engaged. Generally, every input into the software must be thoroughly tested. Specialized tools are run against custom Web application code. These tools take expertise not only in understanding Web attacks and their variations, but also each particular tool, what it does well, and its limitations. So, we include a separate path within the overall testing plan that identifies the presence of the Web server so that the Web inputs get the needed specialized attention. This kind of testing is called dynamic testing. While there is certainly overlap among most of the various dynamic testing tools, we recommend that tools specific to Web applications be applied. Importantly, many attackers specialize in Web vulnerabilities. And, of course, if the system will be exposed to the public Internet, it will be attacked constantly and must prepare itself to defend against these common variations. However, even if the system will normally be deployed on a more trusted network, we believe that strong Web server dynamic testing is important. Sophisticated attackers sometimes manage to breach their way onto these trusted networks. A weak Web server can be a target in and of itself, or a server can present a hop-off point to more valuable targets. Therefore, it is good practice to identify all Web servers in order to benefit from this specialized testing. (Core Software Security, pp. 284–285)

We wish that we had been more inclusive with this determining question in 2014. There were then, and remain now, many types of Web/network attack exposure possibilities:

- Web Servers
- Web Application Programming Interfaces (API)
- Web services
- Web applications
- Numerous, competing, Web integration protocols and methods
- Etc.

The above collection of types of Web interfaces all require a specialized set of tools, some of which only handle one of the above cases, others of which may handle multiple. The tester must understand the testing target and know their toolset in order to apply as thorough a collection of security verifications as needed to attain the required security posture. Web testing is complex and multifaceted. It is too large a subject for this book. Still, we were wrong to focus on Web servers to the exclusion of the other possibilities, all requiring specialized Web-centric testing. Today's appropriate determining question reads, "Are there any Web protocol inputs?"

Are There Non-Web Inputs to the Program?

Beyond Web server inputs, there are myriad other inputs that may be built into a system: command-line interfaces, configuration files, network inputs, native forms, scripting engines, and so forth. Each of these is an attack surface. Each input has the potential for a logic mistake that goes around access controls such as authentication and authorization. Logic mistakes may allow the misuse of the program to do unintended things, such as sell a product for a reduced or nonexistent price. Additionally, in programming languages where the programmer manipulates computer memory directly, poor input handling may allow serious abuse of the program or even the operating system. Memory-related errors often allow privilege escalation on the system or permit code of the attacker's choice to run. Inputs are an important attack point in any program, often the prime attack surface.

Before the test plan is written, all the inputs to the system should be enumerated. Each of the enumerated inputs should be tested to determine that the correct input values are handled properly. Further, tests must be run to prove that variations of incorrect input do not cause the system to fail or, worse, act as a vector of attack beyond the boundaries of the software (as in a buffer overflow allowing privilege escalation and code of the attacker's choice). A common tool as of this writing is a fuzz tester. These tools simulate the many variations that attackers may run against the software. Once a fuzzer is prepared for a particular input, it will automatically run through a set of variations that attempt improper inputs. The fuzzer will stop when the program begins to misbehave or crashes. In this way, unsafe input handling, even improper memory handling, can be smoked out. We recommend that every input that has been changed during this development cycle be fuzzed.

There is some overlap between what fuzzers cover and Web vulnerability analysis tools. If testing time is short, we recommend that Web vulnerability tools be run against the Web server [any input via a Web protocol], and all other inputs be fuzzed. However, it's not a bad idea to overlap the vulnerability scan by fuzzing the Web server's inputs as well. Since Web scanning tools look for known

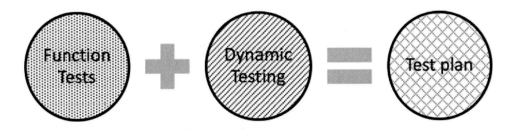

Figure 3.9   Functional Testing Overview. (*Source: Reproduced from Ransome, J. and Misra, A. [2014]. Core Software Security: Security at the Source.* Boca Raton [FL]: CRC Press/Taylor & Francis Group, p. 286, with permission.)

exploit patterns and fuzzers check generally bad input, employing both types of dynamic analysis provides better coverage than using either alone.

The test plan will likely include both testing of intended security functions and dynamic tests to ensure that no vulnerabilities have crept through manual review and static analysis, as indicated in Figure 3.9 [formerly Figure 9.9]. (Core Software Security, pp. 285–286)

In order to appropriately revise the preceding section describing SDL requirements for non–Web-related inputs, please replace "Web server inputs" with "inputs through Web protocols."

Is This a Major Release?

The seventh and last question is about the importance of this project or release in relationship to the software as a whole. Are the additions to the software in this development cycle going to be considered a major addition and/or revision? If there are going to be significant architectural changes, possibly accompanied by major feature additions or maintenance revisions of currently running code, there is a likelihood of introducing subtle logical changes, perhaps even errors, into the code base. Some of the most subtle bugs occur due to unintended side effects affecting other pieces of the code. Indeed, it is very hard to test thoroughly for interactions; this is particularly true when adding new features whose side effects interact with legacy code in unanticipated ways.

In addition, consumers of software tend to expect more from larger revisions. A major release will tend to get more scrutiny and perhaps wider distribution than a minor update.

For these reasons, it may be worthwhile considering a more thorough and holistic look at the security properties and vulnerabilities of a major release when the release is considered "code complete." This can be accomplished through an independent attack and penetration. "Independent" in this context means independent from building the software and testing it. Since penetration testing requires significant skill, experts should be employed. It should also be remembered that no two testers deliver the same results; each penetration test is more or less unique to the tester and to the software under examination. Therefore, it is good practice to have a major release penetration test performed by someone with significant skills in the deployment model, execution stack, and even language in which the software is written. Failure to match tester to software type will likely deliver suboptimal results. You want a tester who understands how to attack the kind of software you're producing.

Through the application of a highly skilled attacker against your software, you can discover the sorts of vulnerabilities that sophisticated attackers will likely find and exploit. Subtle and sophisticated errors can be uncovered and fixed before the software goes live. Plus, you will have a much clearer picture of any residual risks in this release.

In this way, you can deliver both to your organization and to the consumers of the software assurance that the software is indeed self-protective as well as correct. We have found that for highly competitive markets and/or widely distributed software, a provable penetration test can provide a competitive advantage, demonstrating not only the security of the software but also the commitment of the software maker to customers' safety. (Core Software Security, pp. 286–287)

Nothing has changed: Penetration testing remains a strong addition to the SDL. At the present state-of-the-art, penetration testing continues to be one of the best methods for proving (or not) the security features and protections built into and around software. We make that statement, however, with a proviso: The skill and knowledge of the tester must be well matched to the architecture of the software and the technologies that have been employed. Failure to carefully match a penetration tester skill set to architecture and technology can result in poor findings, which may offer assurances that do not actually exist or, alternatively, cause developers to chase insignificant issues.

Below, in a dedicated subsection, we will take up some of the issues that surround penetration testing. Still, we believe that major inflection points in the change cycles of a system, body of, or piece of software offer stakeholders an opportunity for dealing with problems that may have been ignored previously. Especially important, a major cycle of change (perhaps a significant change or update to the underlying design or design assumptions) is a time when security backlog items and legacy issues should be considered or reconsidered. This is why we have development teams answer this determining question: "Is this a major release?" Major releases can oftentimes allow for investment in deeper or broader tests, manual testing (as described above), validating threat model analyses, researching the current state of threat actor activity and capabilities (threat landscape), and the like.

Astute readers may ask, "Why wait until a major release?" which is a fair enough question. In a development world of limited resources arranged across competing business and technical drivers, some planned change will typically get put off and, perhaps, put off for multiple releases. This is as true of security items as others. In our experience, few organizations execute their SDL perfectly, though the ones we've worked with do their best, given current circumstances and skill.

We've found that assessment in light of major changes provides a golden moment for reflection and realignment. This can be particularly true for software that will be used for an extended time period. Stakeholder expectations may run high for a major set of changes to such long-life software. A spotlight may focus during a major release, which will afford an opportune time to pick up security items that may have been dropped or given short shrift due to competing concerns. Identifying major change cycles is, then, the seventh determining question.

Answering these seven determining questions can control security task flow for both Waterfall and Agile processes. Placement of the appropriate activities into each flow of development differs. These differences will be described below.

The answer to each of the seven questions supplies, "What is the minimum set of activities my project must perform?" However, it should never be suggested to teams that they can't supplement the minimum set with other activities if these might provide additional security value. For instance, if there's time, even threat modeling an existing architecture and design may uncover something useful. Attack patterns change over time; yesterday's popular attack may be superseded by another, easier or more successful approach.

Ask "What's new?" to assess the scope of proposed change. There are additional activities that flow from each answer. And these earlier, more architectural activities will lead to the later design, build, and test tasks. Table 3.1: Architecture, Design, and Hosting Activities Indicated by SDL Determining Questions [derived from Table 9.1] and Table 3.2: Coding Imperatives and Testing Activities from SDL Determining Questions [derived from Table 9.2] describe the selection of activities.

Table 3.1 lists the activities that apply regardless of whether you are using a Waterfall or an Agile methodology. These have been previously described in the respective sections.

**Table 3.1 Architecture, Design, and Hosting Activities
Indicated by SDL Determining Questions**

Question	Step 1	Step 2
Greenfield or redesign?	Begin threat model to determine the required security posture and the intended security strategy with the stakeholders. Generate the high-level security requirements.	Revisit the threat model as structure is defined and technologies chosen. Revise, refine, and review threat model. Analyze for greater specificity and thoroughness.
Architecture change?	Revise, refine, and review threat model. Analyze for greater specificity and thoroughness. Review the architecture for security and create a threat model for architecture. Produce architecture requirements.	Update the threat model as security-impacting changes are made. Revise, refine, and review threat model. Analyze for greater specificity and thoroughness.
Will any security features be added?	Security designs must be reviewed by an experienced practitioner to ensure correctness and eliminate logical vulnerabilities.	Add functional tests for each security feature to the test plan.
Adding data about human entities (Personally Identifiable Information [PII])?	Conduct a privacy review. Update the threat model and security requirements to meet privacy needs.	
Will this organization or any of its partners host any of the systems?	Review infrastructure security of unassessed environments. For vetted cloud vendors, enumerate the services to be used. Identify the security requirements to be fulfilled when using the collection of cloud services.	Should do third-party vulnerability test on the software in the infrastructure before release or receive all current security certifications and assessments for the infrastructure.

Source: Derived from Ransome, J. and Misra, A. (2014). *Core Software Security: Security at the Source.* Boca Raton (FL): CRC Press/Taylor & Francis Group, p. 288, with permission.

Table 3.2 Coding Imperatives and Testing Activities from SDL Determining Questions

Question	Step 1	Step 2
Are you adding any third-party software?	Assess whether sufficient software security practices were used. Assure that the software will continue to be supported. Perform a legal licensing review.	Post-release, monitor for vulnerabilities that are discovered in the third-party software. Fix or patch every impacting issue.
Is this a waterfall build cycle or a cycle of Sprints in Scrum/Agile?	Code Securely. Perform manual code review. Run static analysis.	Fix defects as discovered.
Are there any Web protocol inputs?	Perform Web dynamic vulnerability testing.	Fix defects.
Are there non-Web inputs to the program?	Fuzz all non-Web inputs.	Fix defects.
Is this a major release?	Consider an independent vulnerability assessment and pen test.	

Source: Derived from Ransome, J. and Misra, A. (2014). *Core Software Security: Security at the Source.* Boca Raton (FL): CRC Press/Taylor & Francis Group, p. 289, with permission.

For a Waterfall development methodology, the following tasks will flow in a linear fashion: design, then build, then test. For an Agile methodology, the following tasks will be iterated through in each development cycle ("Sprint" in Scrum). Rather than a single period of design which must be completed before development may begin, each short cycle will design for the increments that have been selected for build. The cycle will complete when those features have been tested and are ready for release, that is, "code complete." Hence, in Agile development, there are short, focused design periods, followed by coding, and then testing. However, it is not uncommon to redesign as more is known about any particular increment. And testing may begin whenever there is code to test. For this reason, the table contains the security tasks for each development cycle, to be executed as needed by the Agile team during Sprints. All three activities may be occurring in parallel during a Sprint. Table 3.2: Coding Imperatives and Testing Activities from SDL Determining Questions" shows those activities that fall within the "build" portion of either a Waterfall or Agile process and their associated determining questions. (Core Software Security, pp. 287–290)

Our 2014 Agile Scrum description is more "mini-Waterfall" surrounding a constrained Scrum Sprint than fully Agile Scrum (or other Agile SDLC). As we noted in our explanation of Scrum in Chapters 1 and 2, design may occur while coding and in parallel to testing. Design, coding, and testing may intertwine into a seamless whole. Generally, one needs to have some ideas about how a function will be coded before starting (design), but the design needn't be complete. There are numerous different approaches, including "code it to design it." Brook is not a particular fan of "coding to find out," but there are adherents. A generic SDL mustn't prescribe order or specific timing, but rather what each SDL activity requires in order to start, and what conditions constitute completion. We weren't wrong in 2014 so much as describing only a single possibility out of the universe of Scrum work styles. Please bear in mind that how the work (including the SDL) is taken up is up to each Sprint team and therefore, mustn't be dictated from outside.

It's important to assess the security impact of legacy code and projects that have not been through a formal SDL. When a mature SDL hasn't been in place for previous development (that is, before the current round of changes), a due diligence responsibility will be to decide whether there is a need to assess previous work. In the case of a brand-new SDL, it may be presumed that no review has taken place; but it's always a good practice to ask rather than assume. The determining questions are phrased, "Are you adding. . . ?" because this process assumes that in prior development cycles security has been attended to as per the SDL. Therefore, the seven questions focus on what is being changed rather than any inherited legacy. When implementing or changing your SDL, one of the tasks will be to assess how much change will be required to your legacy code and projects as you apply your new SDL to your current development. What is your security technology debt? How many design misses exist, and how much vulnerable code are you carrying forward in the current development cycle?

One approach to SDL legacy technology debt is to ask, "How fast are my applications changing?" In periods of rapid change, it may make sense to carry the debt until it is replaced.

Concomitantly, in situations where legacy code will be carried forward for the foreseeable future, it may make sense to whittle away at vulnerabilities and exposures. One successful approach devotes a day each month to "bug bashes." Developers take a day off from producing new code and instead fix older defects. Such a "bash" can be done as a party, a relief from the rigors of code production. In this way, "tech debt" is whittled away and removed from production code bit by bit.

Bug bashes usually don't treat design issues. Architecture and design features to bolster an existing product's security will have to be considered against other feature requests. If sales are being missed due to the lack of security features, then the value of these features should be obvious. Often, however, the customer's security people interact with the software producer's security people in a separate dialog. Security people understand each other. Also, the customer's security folks want to gain some assurance that the vendor's security people are involved in the software's security as it's designed and built. Product management must be included in these customer security conversations. Product managers need to understand that the customer's security team often has a "no" vote, or may be expending extra resources on exceptions in order to deploy the software. When product managers and security architects align, security features can be taken in their rightful place as customer-enhancing rather than as a "nonfunctional" set of requirements.

Any security requirements that come out of an assessment of legacy software need to be added to the backlog of feature requests. These should be prioritized through risk rating. The risk rating can then be taken into consideration alongside customer needs. Likely, a security subject-matter expert should be included in this dialog.

Ultimately, treatment of technological debt is a risk decision. If the treatment is more expensive than the loss, it may not make sense to treat the risk. Various factors will have to be weighed, including the opportunity cost lost when not building new technology. We have seen situations where as many as 75,000 defects have been listed for large code bases. The known set of automated tools as of this writing is not sophisticated enough to provide absolute assurance that every discovered finding is in fact a defect. Simply determining which of 75,000 findings are actually defects is a significant chore. The execution of this chore, not to mention fixing the defects that are qualified, should be carefully considered. It's important to remember that, as Brad Arkin, CSO for Adobe, told one of the authors, "Vulnerabilities are not exploits." Indeed, defects are not necessarily vulnerable. A risk-based approach will focus on exploitable vulnerabilities when the vulnerabilities are exposed by the intended deployment model. Raw defect numbers, by themselves, are meaningless. (Core Software Security, pp. 290–292)

We note that as this book was being written, Brad Arkin became the SVP, Chief Security and Trust Office for Cisco Systems, Inc.

3.4 Architecture and Design

Systems Architecture is a generic discipline to handle objects (existing or to be created) called "systems," in a way that supports reasoning about the structural properties of these objects. . . . Systems Architecture is a response to the conceptual and practical difficulties of the description and the design of complex systems. Systems Architecture helps to describe consistently and design efficiently complex systems.[*]

"[S]ecurity architecture is the modeling of complex systems in order to divine their security properties and structures and then to specify these security properties and structures so that they may be implemented."[†]

"This broader definition leaves the security architect free to be an architect, to model things in the abstract that will eventually become digital systems and software. Indeed, if architecture is a practice concerned with modeling complex things, then security architecture is the modeling of digital security.

---

[*] Golden, B. (2013). "What Is Systems Architecture?" Retrieved from http://www.lix.polytechnique.fr/~golden/systems_architecture.html#principles

[†] Schoenfield, B. S. E. (2019). *Secrets of a Cyber Security Architect.* Boca Raton (FL): Auerbach Publications/Taylor & Francis Group, p. 37.

The scope of 'digital security' for our definition must include systems intended to deliver digital security as well as the digital security of any computer system or set of systems. We must further refine our working definition because we don't know what digital security consists of. Digital security is meant to encompass any possible exploitable weaknesses of a computer system and the potential defenses for those exploitable conditions. If you prefer, digital security will be the preservation of the classic security triad, Confidentiality, Integrity, and Availability (CIA).

Digital (or computer, if you will) weaknesses and their defenses are the basic language of information security. Security architecture deals with these in a structural manner rather than delving into each particular weakness's technical details." (*Secrets*, pp. 37–38)

Why include architecture in the SDL at all? There is a dictum in information security: "Build security in, don't bolt it on." Architecture is the structure, flow, and data of a system. Decisions made about the architecture can radically influence the security posture of the system. Failure to add an authentication mechanism may at best mean adding it after the architecture is set. The worst case is that there is a requirement for authentication, but no authentication mechanism can be added to the architecture: Authentication has been designed out.

Over and over, we have seen systems that assumed they were running on a highly restricted network. Assuming the network will provide appropriate restriction, the application is then designed to pass sensitive information between components without any protections in the architecture. Flows may not be protected because it is assumed that only the components in the target system would be deployed to that protected network. In a world of heterogeneous networks, advanced persistent threat attacks, and huge cloud-based server farm environments, the likelihood that any application will get its own highly restricted network is exceedingly small. The vast majority of networks are shared; there are very few highly trusted networks deployed. The assumption that the network will protect all the components of the system and all the intercomponent flows is a major architectural error. And yet, we see it repeatedly. The result will be a choice between exposing components and flows on the shared network or attempting to manage complex firewall rules in the shared environment. Also, the firewall capabilities may not provide the deep application protections that are required.

Security architecture has particular characteristics:

- *Security architecture has its own methods. These methods might be the basis for a discrete security methodology.*
- *Security architecture has its own discrete view and viewpoints.*
- *Security architecture addresses non-normative flows through systems and among applications.*
- *Security architecture introduces its own normative flows through systems and among applications.*
- *Security architecture introduces unique, single-purpose components into the design.*
- *Security architecture calls for its own unique set of skill requirements in the IT architect.[*]*

The vast majority of architectural design choices will have at least some security implications. Some of those choices will have profound security effects that suggest very particular patterns of security control. Hence, the security dictum, "Build it in."

Generally, the architecture flow starts with requirements gathering. From those requirements, an architecture that meets the requirements is proposed and then refined iteratively. This is true for an entirely new system as well as for changing an existing system. Other influencing factors, of course, are what can be built currently, what currently exists, and general architectural goals and strategies

---

[*] The Open Group. (2005, November). *Guide to Security Architecture in TOGAF ADM*, p. 5. Retrieved from http://pubs.opengroup.org/onlinepubs/7699949499/toc.pdf

into the future. Current capabilities have a profound influence on proposed solutions. This is true for security capabilities just as much as database, network, server types, and the people and processes that support these. In fact, maximizing current capabilities might be one of the requirements. Using an existing authentication mechanism might be one of the security requirements of the system.

We strongly suggest that security be included during the requirements-gathering phase. As we have noted, part of a holistic security picture for a system will be the security features that get built into it. A Web system that gives access to financial information will likely have requirements for authentication to make sure that the information is given only to the holder of the information. Such a system is likely to have an authorization mechanism as well, so that the right access is given to the appropriate user. Indeed, such a Web system will also have other, less obvious security requirements: hardening of the systems so they can resist the omnipresent level of attack on untrusted networks, careful layering such that compromise of front-end systems or even middle systems does not provide access to the data, authentication from business logic to the data store such that inappropriate access from untrusted or inappropriate applications is not granted. Some of these requirements are obvious. However, we have seen many systems that ignored the necessity of gathering specific security requirements, to the peril of project success. We have even seen a security requirement stated as: "The system will be secure." Obviously, this sort of nonspecific, generalized requirement is useless. (Core Software Security, pp. 292–294)

As we have noted repeatedly in our commentary on the text in *Core Software Security*, the wording "requirements-gathering phase" is misleading when applied to today's software development methods. There may very well be no "requirements" or any other "phase." Please see the connected infinite loops depicted in Figure 3.1 All development activity might be occurring in parallel, connected by shared goals and constant communication and feedback. It is more accurate to say, "We strongly suggest that security be included while identifying requirements." Beyond a timing-perspective shift, our introduction to architecture still applies, just as it did in 2014.

Enterprise security architecture is the component of the overall enterprise architecture designed specifically to fulfill . . . the overall objective . . . to preserve the availability, integrity, and confidentiality of an organization's information.[*]

In the case of a completely new architecture (or a complete redesign), security should be engaged early to strategize how the proposed system can meet future as well as present expectations, change, and growth. The security architect must have a strong grounding in the current types of threat agents and their attack methods whose targets are similar to the system under consideration. In these strategy sessions, the security architect should also have a good feel for emerging trends in threats and attack methods. What new threat agents are just beginning to become active? Of these new threats, what will be their likely attack methods? As the threat agents' organization and sophistication grow, how might they expand attack patterns? With these sorts of questions, the architecture can be designed not only for the intended use cases of the present, but also for the foreseeable future. Typically, enterprise-level architects consider similar questions regarding the growth of the organization, growth in user populations, growth in data, and expansion of capabilities. The same sort of consideration should be given to security needs of the future just as much as for the present.

Out of any architecture assessment will come requirements that the architecture must meet. Typically, early requirements are of a more general nature: Users will be authenticated, systems will

---

need to be hardened, Payment Card Industry (PCI) certification (at the appropriate level) will need to be met, and so forth. The details will then be baked into the emerging architecture.

As architecting the system proceeds in earnest, the security requirements will begin to take on specificity. A particular authentication system will be chosen: For a major server farm, for instance, a system may be chosen which can handle millions of authentications per minute, can handle millions of user identities, can interface with the appropriate runtime and execution environments, and so forth. Or, if the authentication system will be very modest, perhaps there is an integral library, or another module which will suffice. Using the former implies tremendous growth and heavy user traffic, perhaps even heterogeneous systems. When using the latter authentication system, the smaller library may preclude major server farm growth. In considering the intended use (say, an authentication system for a customer-deployable appliance), a relatively constrained mechanism may be warranted. In any event, a particular choice will be made based on the requirements of the system in the intended deployment and with respect to the expected growth. The architecture will grow more specific and particular. The output of the security architecture process is specific components providing particular services and communicating using known protocols. (Core Software Security, pp. 294–295)

Please see Chapter 4 for greater detail on attack and defense analysis, that is, threat modeling.

For systems within an existing architecture, any change to that architecture may have security implications, so the security of each architectural change should be considered. For instance, the addition of a third-party partner to whom finance data may flow will engender the addition of mechanisms to protect that finance data in transit. Further, protections will need to be put into place such that only the intended partner will be able to interact. In other words, the security needs of an existing architecture will change in the face of new components, or new communication flows, or new data types. Changes to any part of the architecture must be considered in light of the whole architecture, of all the existing security services. This work is very similar if not identical to the design work when building an entirely new architecture. Hence, we specify architectural assessment of the security of the system after the security strategy for the system has been considered or when any architectural changes are being made to an existing system. This set of SDL task flows presumes that the existing architecture has been through a holistic, thorough security assessment as required for an entirely new system. If there has been no previous security assessment, then the existing architecture should be treated as entirely new. (Core Software Security, pp. 295–296)

The preceding paragraph uses the phrase, "security assessment." We prefer to think of the various levels of analysis and assessment as levels of threat modeling, since at no matter what level of specificity, attack scenarios will generate requirements, architecture elements, security tasks, etc., that is, defenses. Chapter 4 digs into threat modeling as a key foundational technique for secure design. Chapter 4 will explain how a threat model begins as a part of requirements gathering, and then is repeatedly (sometimes continuously) refined and reviewed as a part of the practice of security architecture and secure design. Threat modeling is a fairly big topic, about which Brook has written a book titled *Securing Systems: Applied Security Architecture and Threat Models** and which also takes up a considerable amount of space in *Secrets of a Cyber Security Architect*. Please see Chapter 4 and other works for more information on secure design in the generic SDL.

It is always true that any requirements output from the threat model will create new test plan items. These new test cases ensure that the security requirements have been built correctly. Thus, if the threat

---

* Schoenfield, B. S. E. (2015). *Securing Systems: Applied Security Architecture and Threat Models*. Boca Raton (FL): CRC Press/Taylor & Francis Group.

model produces requirements, the test plan will receive new test cases. Security test cases are dependent on architecture analysis and threat modeling.

Generally speaking, if there is no architectural change, then architectural analysis and threat modeling can be bypassed. (This assumes that the existing architecture went through security assessment and threat modeling.)

The design of the system must implement all the requirements given from the architecture. If an architecture is the structure, flow, and data, then the design is the expected implementation of that structure. The design must have enough specificity that it can actually be coded. (Core Software Security, p. 298)

Please bear in mind as you read this chapter that architecture, design, and implementation may have no discreet perceptual or process boundaries: These activities are intimately linked in any case. It was perhaps artificial in the past to separate them out as absolutely distinct. Through security's active participation and iterative threat modeling, security takes part in and has input into the cycle of changes that require architectural thinking, design specificity, and the generation of code.

Given adequate, clear, and detailed enough requirements or user stories (Scrum), skilled software designers generally have no trouble translating architecture and its requirements into a software design. This can be done before coding in a Waterfall process, or for each incremental build cycle in an Agile process. In either process case, it's important to pay particular attention to the security features and requirements. These must be absolutely correct or the implementation may open up vulnerabilities or, worse, create a new, unprotected attack surface. The logic has got to be watertight for critical security functions such as encryption routines or authorization schemes. Users of the system will be depending on these features to protect their resources.

We place a security design review at a point when designers believe that the design is very nearly completed. A security design review should be performed by a security assessor who understands the architecture and functionality well; usually, the review is best done by someone who has experience designing and even implementing security features. We further suggest that the reviewer be independent of the design team. Peer review is a powerful tool for validating design correctness and completeness. Another set of eyes can often spot errors which those closer to the design may have missed. If any security features or requirements are to be built in the current cycle, perform a security review. (Core Software Security, pp. 298–299)

Before completing the code for security functionality and other items that have security implications, we have seen that reviewing how the target functionality will be/is being/has been implemented provides another important bulwark against security weakness, and particularly, poor or insecure design. Our experience and thinking have not changed. But, like other timing aspects of the generic SDL, the assumption that "security design review" must occur before any code is written is mistaken, and for many development teams, will be plain wrong. If timing assumptions are off, they then create barriers to and unneeded friction with today's development practices.

In 2014, we failed to mention that design review needn't be a formal SDL step. Reviews can be very short and discreet. The reviewer must have a working knowledge of the architecture and requirements that are being implemented. As we noted in 2014, the reviewer should have some experience building functionality similar to that under review. Still, at the daily stand-up meeting, a quick conversation about the design of the item may be more than sufficient. If there are problems, then finding a solution can become another work item that can then be managed as a part of this or a subsequent Sprint (change cycle). Design review becomes part of the normal warp and weft of building software, not some formal, explicitly managed process, perhaps imposed from outside. Responsible developers want to implement correctly. Plus, they prefer not to waste precious time coding something that will be flawed.

Spending time with developers and listening to their concerns should convince even the most hardened security person that correctness is a developer virtue.[*]

Review, security and otherwise, is natural, and thus, can be organic, if allowed to be. Some organizations may prefer to perform or have compliance needs that require formal design reviews. If this is not the case, then design review can become another avenue for pride in work. We call design review out as an SDL step but do not prescribe how reviews should be accomplished.

As has been noted, every portion of the intended design must engender a thorough functional test plan. This is true of security just as well as any other part of the design. If Transport Layer Security (TLS) is to be added as an option to the network protocol stack, the test plan must include a test with and without TLS, each case having a pass condition. Security in the design always means security in the test plan.

How does an organization train people so that they can perform these difficult, architectural tasks? Software security expert Gary McGraw says:

For many years I have struggled with how to teach people . . . security design. The only technique that really works is apprenticeship. Short of that, a deep understanding of security design principles can help.[†]

McGraw's statement implies that, in order to build a qualified team, each organization will either have to invest in sufficiently capable and experienced practitioners who can also mentor and teach what they do, or hire consultants who can provide appropriate mentorship. Neither of these is likely to be cheap. As of this writing, there is a dearth of skilled security architects, much less the subset of those who can and want to impart what they know to others. The architecture and design skills necessary to an SDL program are probably going to require time to find key leaders, and then time for those leaders to build a skilled practice from among the available and interested people at hand. In one such long-running mentorship, even highly motivated junior people have taken as long as two or three years before they could work entirely independently and start to lead in their own right. This is a significant time investment.[‡] *(Core Software Security, p. 299)*

Please see *Secrets of a Cyber Security Architect* and, especially, Chapter 5: Learning the Trade for a deep dive into the skills security architects require and how the authors have sought to train, coach, mentor, empower, and amplify security architecture tasks and capabilities.

In the same blog entry quoted above, McGraw cites Salzer and Schroeder's seminal 1975 paper, "The Protection of Information in Computer Systems,"[§] *as a starting point for a set of principles from which to architect. These may also be used as a training and mentorship basis. McGraw's principles are*

1. *Secure the weakest link.*
2. *Defend in depth.*
3. *Fail securely.*

---

[*] Which is why some developers have difficulties thinking through so-called "abuse" cases: the misuse of systems. Quite often, they will exclaim, "But that's not how the system is used." Misuse is the province of threat modeling; correctness belongs to design review, so review becomes a natural and expected activity.

[†] McGraw, G. (2013, January 18). "Securing Software Design Is Hard." Cigital Justice League Blog. Retrieved from http://www.cigital.com/justice-league-blog/2013/01/18/securing-software-design-is-hard

[‡] Please note that not every person who begins training will have the aptitude and motivation to finish. Our experience is that between one-third and one-half of those starting will not become security architects.

[§] Saltzer, J. H. and Schroeder, M. D. (1975). "The Protection of Information in Computer Systems." Retrieved from http://www.acsac.org/secshelf/papers/protection_information.pdf

4. *Grant least privilege.*
5. *Separate privileges.*
6. *Economize mechanisms.*
7. *Do not share mechanisms.*
8. *Be reluctant to trust.*
9. *Assume your secrets are not safe.*
10. *Mediate completely.*
11. *Make security usable.*
12. *Promote privacy.*
13. *Use your resources.*[*]

An in-depth discussion of these principles is beyond the scope of this work. Security practitioners will likely already be familiar with most if not all of them. We cite them as an example of how to seed an architecture practice. From whatever principles you choose to adopt, architecture patterns will emerge. For instance, hold in your mind "Be reluctant to trust" and "Assume your secrets are not safe" while we consider a classic problem. When an assessor encounters configuration files on permanent storage the first time, it may be surprising to consider these an attack vector, that the routines to read and parse the files are an attack surface. One is tempted to ask, "Aren't these private to the program?" Not necessarily. One must consider what protections are applied to keep attackers from using the files as a vector to deliver an exploit and payload. There are two security controls at a minimum:

1. *Carefully set permissions on configuration files such that only the intended application may read and write the files.*
2. *Rigorously validate all inputted data read from a configuration file before using the input data for any purpose in a program. This, of course, suggests fuzz testing these inputs to assure the input validation.*

Once encountered, or perhaps after a few encounters, these two patterns become a standard that assessors will begin to catch every time as they threat model. These patterns start to seem "cut and dried."[†] If configuration files are used consistently across a portfolio, a standard can be written from the pattern. Principles lead to patterns, which then can be standardized.

Each of these dicta engenders certain patterns and suggests certain types of controls that will apply to those patterns. These patterns can then be applied across relevant systems. As architects gain experience, they will likely write standards whose patterns apply to all systems of a particular class.

In order to catch subtle variations, the best tool we have used is peer review. If there is any doubt or uncertainty on the part of the assessor, institute a system of peer review of the assessment or threat model. (Core Software Security, pp. 299–301)

"Nimble Governance

Some readers may find themselves disturbed by the idea of allowing beginners to perform threat models. After all, the whole purpose of a threat model is to identify those defenses that more obvious approaches such as using the various vulnerability and code security scan tools cannot find.

---

[*] McGraw, G. (2013, January 18). "Securing Software Design Is Hard." Cigital Justice League Blog. Retrieved from http://www.cigital.com/justice-league-blog/2013/01/18/securing-software-design-is-hard

[†] Overly standardizing has its own danger: Assessors can begin to miss subtleties that lie outside the standards. For the foreseeable future, assessment and threat modeling will continue to be an art that requires human intelligence to do thoroughly. Beware the temptation to attempt to standardize everything, and thus, attempt to take the expert out of the process. While this may be a seductive vision, it will likely lead to misses which lead to vulnerabilities.

I've already made the point that there are special skills that security architects bring to the work—often significant skills that take years to develop. And now I am asserting that even rank beginners ought to be allowed into the process.

Suggesting that beginners threat model may seem inconsistent on my part, but it's not, really.

First, one of the subject matter experts who should be included in a threat model process is an experienced security architect who is familiar with the types of technologies that will be used in the system under analysis. The security architect should also have a working knowledge of the sorts of attacks that have been successful against these technologies and what defenses are typically used to thwart or slow these attacks. That is the best programmatic approach I know of.

Unfortunately, there aren't enough skilled security architects available for every threat model, which is one reason I've written this book (and *Securing Systems* before it). Those of us with some skill have to learn how to share it and to teach others. Still, as of this writing, there is a severe shortage of people with sufficient skill, call them what you will.

In many organizations with which I've worked, or about which I know, the strategy then is to throw the skilled folk at so-called "critical" systems. *Critical* in this regard has no definitive industry meaning and is usually locally determined based on budget, revenue generation, data sensitivity, and a host of other factors. The point is, the skilled folk can't be everywhere, especially in really large engineering organizations in which there are many different development teams and many different project threads. Some criteria or other are used to find a line above which the project will get security architecture engagement and below which it will not.

Another strategy will be to highly over-resource the few skilled architects such that they drop into a project and make some security requirement pronouncements which, supposedly, must be adhered to, no matter what else changes during development. Unyielding requirements play havoc with iterative development methodologies that depend upon experiment, learn, then pivot based upon what's been learned. That, of course, causes no end of security/development friction.

The two strategies above are not mutually exclusive and, thus, can be used in conjunction. No matter what mix of critical and drop-in is used, there's a guarantee that some threat models will not get done or won't receive the attention that they deserve, which leads to missed security requirements.

If we allow neophytes to threat model, we are also guaranteed to miss security requirements. One way or another, requirements are going to be missed. For those efforts which do not receive a threat model or which receive only a cursory analysis, isn't it better if the neophytes at least try? Most likely, they will identify more security requirements than if they had ignored secure design altogether.

In fact, this gets to what I call the rule of "zero versus one." If a design has no attack and defense analysis, then zero security requirements will be identified, if you see what I mean. The outcome is going to be relatively insecure.

If we introduce threat modeling to development teams, then they will try. If they find a single additional requirement that brings the design one step closer to its intended security posture, isn't that a win over nothing?

The other side of this approach is that every time developers practice threat modeling, they are going to improve. Plus, they will be integrating security thinking into their standard practice, as a way of working, as a part of their skill set. Threat modeling becomes one of developers' "always do it" tools. They'll get better at identifying more requirements, and thus there will be continuous improvement in security posture over time.

I cannot see the downside here, not in the long term. The trick is to prevent really bad things from happening. That's where governance comes in as a safety net to prevent the truly catastrophic from going forward and where a program can most effectively deploy its most seasoned security architects as reviewers. Reviews take a lot less time than a threat model analysis.

I covered this in *Securing Systems* (pp. 372–373):

[P]eer review of assessments and threat models is essential. Responsibility can be overwhelming. By sharing that responsibility, architects can relieve some of the stress that responsibility may cause. Furthermore, the weighty decisions that must be made, the thoroughness that must be applied, the ease with which one can miss an attack surface or vulnerability are all mitigated by having several people look over the results of the assessment. It's just too easy to make a mistake, even for the most experienced architects. For the less experienced or junior practitioners, peer review can help fend off catastrophe.

What does a peer review process look like? When does an assessment require peer review? Who should perform the peer review?

For large, complex, and challenging systems, there's probably no substitute for a formal governance review. A common approach for this is to place senior and leader architects onto an architecture review board. The large or critical systems must pass through the review board and get approved before they can proceed. Sometimes, the review board will also have a checkpoint before deployment into production. This checkpoint helps to ensure that projects that haven't met their deliverables can't move to production to the harm of the organization. A senior security architect will be part of the formal review board and have a "no" vote if there is a significant risk that hasn't been sufficiently mitigated.

On the other hand, forcing every project, no matter how small, through a formal review board can quickly create a bottleneck to the velocity of project delivery. I've seen this happen too many times to count. The desire to have every project get checked by the most trusted and experienced architects is laudable and comes from the very best intentions. But unless an organization has an army of truly experienced architects to deploy, requiring every project to be reviewed by a small group of people who are generally overextended already is going to bring project delivery to a near standstill.

Instead, some other form of review that is more lightweight and nimble needs to be found. I've had success with the following approach.

I may be criticized for being too trusting. Certainly, considering some organization's missions, my approach will be too lightweight. But in the high-tech organizations in which I've worked, we have established a process whereby if the architect is unsure about an assessment for any reason, she or he must find a senior architect (senior to that architect), and an architect who is not involved in the project, to provide the required peer review of the assessment or analysis.

This process does presume that architects will seek peer review. Architects have to perceive peer review as valuable and not a hindrance. If the security architects understand the responsibility that they hold for the organization, my experience is that security architects generally like to receive some additional assurance on their assessments when they feel at all uneasy about what they've found.

I've used this same process four times now, at four different organizations. Those organizations were relatively similar, I admit. Still, in my experience, this works pretty well and catches most mistakes before serious harm takes place. One has to build a culture of support and collaboration or this approach cannot work. It is lightweight and dexterous enough not to interfere overly much with project delivery. And this lightweight peer review process does assume a level of competence of the architect to understand what is in her or his proficiency and what does not. We also encourage architects to seek subject matter expertise as a regular course of their assessments. Nobody knows it all.

The essence of my lightweight governance approach is peer review by one reviewer with more experience and one independent reviewer. If these cannot agree, then escalate to the next level of experience or seniority.

The final say, of course, belongs to management. But I've only seen these reviews get to management twice in nearly 15 years over four different organizations. It doesn't come to that among people who trust each other and have trust built from working through difficult technical questions.

For the most senior folks, they must turn to their peers, if there are any, or the next level down in the seniority or skill hierarchy. No one is above peer review; no threat model completes without a review. At the time I wrote *Securing Systems,* peer reviews might have been skipped in situations in which the threat model owner felt that the analysis lay completely within her/ his/their scope of practice and knowledge set. Further experience shows that this lightweight review process is highly effective and quite nimble. Today, every model goes through a review.

The advantage of the technical leader turning to the most skilled is that it establishes a culture of peer review. The senior person models what she/he/they expect from everyone else. Also, it's great training for one to become the next senior security architecture technical leader.

In other words, performing peer reviews is great training. Just as code reviews make a great coder, threat mode reviews make a great threat modeler."[*] (*Secrets,* pp. 90–92)

> *Using basic security principles as a starting point, coupled to strong mentorship, a security architecture and design expertise can be built over time. The other ingredient that you will need is a methodology for calculating risk.*
>
> *Generally, in our experience, information security risk[†] is not well understood. Threats become risks; vulnerabilities are equated to risk in isolation. Often, the very worst impact on any system, under any possible set of circumstances, is assumed. This is done rather than carefully investigating just how a particular vulnerability might be exposed to which type of threat. And if exercised, what might be the likely impact of the exploit? We have seen very durable server farm installations that took great care to limit the impact of many common Web vulnerabilities such that the risk of allowing these vulnerabilities to be deployed was quite limited. Each part (term) of a risk calculation must be taken into account; in practice, we find that, unfortunately, a holistic approach is not taken when calculating risk.*
>
> *A successful software security practice will spend time training risk assessment techniques and then building or adopting a methodology that is lightweight enough to be performed quickly and often, but thorough enough that decision makers have adequate risk information. (Core Software Security,* pp. 301–302)

Please see *Securing Systems,* Chapter 4, for a deep dive into risk rating, especially for software security purposes.

3.5 Testing

Designing and writing software is a creative, innovative art, which also involves a fair amount of personal discipline. The tension between creativity and discipline is especially true when trying to produce vulnerability-free code whose security implementations are correct. Mistakes are inevitable.

---

[*] Schoenfield, B. (2019). *Secrets of a Cyber Security Architect.* Boca Raton, (FL): Auerbach Publications/Taylor & Francis Group.

[†] Information security risk calculation is beyond the scope of this chapter. Please see the Open Group's adoption of the FAIR methodology.

It is key that the SDL security testing approach be thorough; testing is the linchpin of the defense in depth of your SDL. Test approaches must overlap. Since no one test approach can deliver all the required assurance, using approaches that overlap each other helps to ensure completeness, good coverage both of the code as well as all the types of vulnerabilities that can creep in. In our experience, test methodologies are also flawed and available tools are far from perfect. It's important not to put all one's security assurance "eggs" into one basket.

Based on a broad level of use cases across many different types of projects utilizing many of the commercial and free tools available, most of the comprehensive commercial tools are nontrivial to learn, configure, and use. Because testing personnel become proficient in a subset of available tools, there can be a tendency to rely on each tester's tool expertise as opposed to building a holistic program. We have seen one team using a hand-tailored approach (attack and penetration), while the next team runs a couple of language- and platform-specific freeware tools, next to a team who are only running static analysis, or only a dynamic tool. Each of these approaches is incomplete; each is likely to miss important issues. The following sub-sections contain suggestions for applying the right tool to the right set of problems, at a minimum.

As noted previously, we believe that static analysis belongs within the heart of your SDL. We use it as a part of the developers' code writing process rather than as a part of the formal test plan. Earlier, we explained the place of static analysis in the SDL. (Core Software Security, *pp. 302–303*)

Overreliance on single test approach or tool or, at best, a couple of approaches, continues to plague secure software development. What we wrote in 2014 remains just as true today, unfortunately. We cannot stress enough that no matter how proficient the tester in a particular tool or method, and in spite of how well tuned that particular tool may be, no single approach or method will be sufficient in the vast majority of cases. Multiple test approaches that use divergent but hopefully somewhat overlapping techniques continue to provide the best verification strategy. We warn readers to be wary of any vendor who claims that their product "solves software security." As far as we know, there is no such tool or technique.

3.5.1 Functional Testing

Each aspect of the security features and controls must be tested to ensure that they work correctly, as designed. This may be obvious, but it is important to include this aspect of the security test plan in any SDL. We have seen project teams and quality personnel claim that since the security feature was not specifically included in the test plan, testing was not required and hence was not performed. As irresponsible as this response may seem to security professionals, some people only execute what is in the plan, while others creatively try to cover what is needed. When building an SDL task list, clarity is useful for everyone; every step must be specified.

The functional test suite is a direct descendant of the architecture and design. Each security requirement must be thoroughly proved to have been designed and then built. Each feature, security or otherwise, must be thoroughly tested to prove that it works as designed. Describing a set of functional tests is beyond the scope of this book. However, we will suggest that using several approaches builds a reliable proof.

- *Does it work as expected?*
- *Test the corner and edge cases to prove that these are handled appropriately and do not disturb the expected functionality.*
- *Test abuse cases; for inputs, these will be fuzzing tests.*

Basically, the tests must check the precise behavior as specified. That is, turn the specification into a test case: When a user attempts to load a protected page, is there an authentication challenge? When correct login information is input, is the challenge satisfied? When invalid credentials are offered, is authentication denied?

Corner cases are the most difficult. These might be tests of default behavior or behavior that is not explicitly specified. In our authentication case, if a page does not choose protection, is the default for the Web server followed? If the default is configurable, try both binary defaults: No page is protected versus all pages are protected.

Other corner cases for this example might be to test invalid user and garbage IDs against the authentication, or to try to replay session tokens. Session tokens typically have a time-out. What happens if the clock on the browser is different than the clock at the server? Is the token still valid, or does it expire en route? Each of these behaviors might happen to a typical user, but won't be usual.

Finally, and most especially for security features, many features will be attacked. In other words, whatever can be abused is likely to be abused. An attacker will pound on a login page, attempting brute-force discovery of legal passwords. Not only should a test plan include testing of any lock-out feature, the test plan should also be able to uncover any weaknesses in the ability to handle multiple, rapid logins without failing or crashing the application or the authentication service.

In our experience, most experienced quality people will understand "as designed" testing, as well as corner cases. Abuse cases, however, may be a new concept that will need support, training, perhaps mentorship.

3.5.2 Dynamic Testing

Dynamic testing refers to executing the source code and seeing how it performs with specific inputs. All validation activities come in this category where execution of the program is essential.[*]

Dynamic tests are tests run against the executing program. In the security view, dynamic testing is generally performed from the perspective of the attacker. In the purest sense of the term, any test which is run against the executing program is "dynamic." This includes vulnerability scans, custom code vulnerability scans (usually called application scanning), fuzz testing, and any form of attack and penetration testing. We will examine the place of attack and penetration testing within an SDL in a subsequent section. Due to the skill required and the typical expense, we have reserved attack and penetration testing as a special case. However, we encourage any organization that can afford attack and penetration testing at scale to do as much of this as possible. In real-world tests, skilled attack and penetration testers always exceed the results of Web vulnerability scanners and typical fuzzing of inputs. For most organizations, the expense of the skilled practitioners and the fact that they can't be scaled across multiple organizations and multiple projects precludes attack and penetration testing at scale. (Core Software Security, pp. 303–305)

Penetration testing, and specifically, so-called "Red Teams" have become far more common than they were in 2014, when we drafted Chapter 9, as written above. Obviously, if circumstances preclude an investment in internal or external skilled, manual testing, it isn't going to take place. Still, we encourage organizations of all sizes to consider investing in skilled, manual testing, at least at some affordable periodicity, or for major change inflections (as was described, above, in the "Seven Determining Questions" section). There are so many benefits and, of course, a few downsides besides cost (we'll take those up below, in the dedicated section).

---

[*]   Singh, Y. (2011, November 14). *Software Testing*. Cambridge (UK): Cambridge University Press, p. 87.

Dynamic analysis is based on system execution (binary code), often using instrumentation.* The advantages of dynamic analysis are that it:

- *Has the ability to detect dependencies that are not detectable using static analysis—for example, dynamic dependencies using reflection dependency injection, etc.*
- *Allows the collection of temporal information*
- *Allows the possibility of dealing with runtime values*
- *Allows the identification of vulnerabilities in a runtime environment.*
- *Allows the use of automated tools to provide flexibility on what to scan for*
- *Allows the analysis of applications for which you do not have access to the actual code*
- *Allows identifying vulnerabilities that might be false negatives in the static code analysis*
- *Permits validating static code analysis findings*
- *Can be conducted on any application†*

3.5.2.1 Web [Protocol and Input] Scanning

Vulnerability scanners tend to fall into two categories: those with signatures to test against the runtime that supports execution of applications, and scanners that are focused on custom application code. The former are generally applied to infrastructures to assure that appropriate patching and configuration is done on a regular basis, and kept up to date properly. For those applications that will be hosted internally (as discussed in the section on the seven determining questions), runtime vulnerability scanners are essential to keep the infrastructure security posture maintained. Such a scanner might also be run against an appliance type of project to see that its default configuration is without vulnerability.‡ This type of vulnerability scanner might also be used against the running appliance to guarantee that the appliance presents an appropriate security posture for the intended deployment. However, for many software projects that do not fall into these categories, a runtime vulnerability scanner may be of limited value within the test plan. (Core Software Security, pp. 305–306)

Commercial cloud use has become regular, and for many organizations, expected and usual. Commercial cloud vendors scan and also maintain the infrastructure that is used. For at least the major commercial cloud offerings, vulnerability scanning and the resulting patching of findings can be assumed. There is little added security value for SDL scans of the cloud services that have been consumed to deploy and run software.

Of course, all the software supplied by the consumer of the cloud still requires vulnerability scanning and appropriate, risk-based patching of discovered (or announced) issues. Use of a cloud does not obviate scanning, though it does limit the requirement to the software that has been provided by the consuming organization. The cloud infrastructure may be assumed to provide this service as a part of the offering.

As we've noted several times already, cloud vendors have a commercial imperative to responsibly take care of what they supply. Any breach caused by vendor carelessness could cause a major hit to the

---

* Here, "instrumentation" is the addition of diagnostic messages and stopping points to code for the purposes of analysis.

† Wolff, B. and Zaidi, F. (2011, December 20). *Testing Software and Systems: 23rd IFIP WG 6.1 International Conference, ICTSS 2011, Paris, France, November 7–10, 2011, Proceedings*, p. 87. Berlin: Springer-Verlag.

‡ This is because an appliance will likely include a runtime stack, including a supporting operating system and its services. Unless the operating system is entirely proprietary, available tools will probably include appropriate vulnerability signatures against which to test. In the case of an entirely proprietary operating system, a specialized tool may have to be built for this purpose.

cloud vendor's credibility. For the well-known services (we have no preference between them), it may be assumed the vendor will deliver an issue-free and rapidly patched infrastructure.

It behooves the wise security practitioner to assess the practices of new or unknown cloud vendors. We never take on pure faith statements such as, "We take security seriously" or "Trust us to deliver best-practice security," and the like. Hand-waving statements such as these beg us to dig deeper to find out precisely what the vendor does or does not do. Due diligence demands a jaundiced eye.

Still, we have personally studied in some depth the practices of many of the major cloud vendors. We are convinced that they typically perform administration activities such as vulnerability scanning and patching as well as, or often much better than, many organizations can. A new cloud vendor must prove their capabilities and worth in likewise fashion.

In the following explanation, please let "Web server" denote all Web services, protocols, and inputs. Since 2014, the phrase "Web servers" has become archaic and only partially representative.

> *As described above, with respect to Web servers [and all other Web services, protocols, and inputs], a custom code or application vulnerability scanner is essential. If a Web server has been included in the software, an application vulnerability scanner will help smoke out those sorts of issues that attackers interested in Web application code will likely attack. We believe that every piece of content, whether dynamic or static, that is served through the software's Web server must be tested with an application vulnerability scanner. Considering the level of Web attack today, if that Web server is going to be exposed to the public Internet, we would never allow such an application to go live without such a scan. Attack is certain; it is just a matter of time. Current estimates as of this writing suggest that an attack will come in as few as 30 seconds, and not more than 8 hours after connection. Attackers are very swift to make use of newly found XSS errors and the like. These are precisely the sorts of errors that Web vulnerability scanners focus on.*
>
> *Effective use of a Web vulnerability scanner, however, is not a trivial operation. Skill with a particular tool is essential. Also, a strong familiarity with how Web applications are structured and built helps the tester refine the test suite in the tool. Further, a good familiarity with typical Web vulnerabilities will help in two ways: First, appropriate test suites can be configured with respect to the application and its intended use; and second, the results of the scan will likely need to be qualified. There are two issues with issue qualification. Depending on the application, the code, and the tool, the results might be "noisy." That is, there may be false positives that have to be removed. We have seen few runs of Web vulnerability scanners that were free of false positives, and some runs that had very high rates of false positives. In addition, most of the Web vulnerability scanners as of this writing attempt multiple variations of each type of issue. Most tools will report every variation as another vulnerability. Despite multiple vulnerabilities reported, all the variations may stem from a single bug in the code. For many tools, there is a many-to-one relationship between vulnerabilities and actual programming errors; a single input validation error may produce many "vulnerabilities." Hence, the tester and/or programming team need to qualify the results in order to find the actual programming errors.* (Core Software Security, pp. 306–307)

We note, with some amount of melancholy, that many scanners still record multiple findings against a single software bug. It is unfortunate that scanner makers don't seem to understand how multiple findings against a particular programming problem instance makes finding and fixing errors much more difficult. We have consistently asked vendors to shine a tightly focused beam on what needs to be fixed versus inflating findings counts with every potential variation.

It is an unfortunate assumption by many scan tool vendors that security people will both run scans and provide fixes. Neither of these assumptions may be true, depending upon how verification and the resulting remedies are handled. We security folk may be interested in each variation (which is how many scan products are offered). The people who deliver fixes don't need all of that information: They are highly concentrated on what's wrong and how to remedy it. We have long said that instead of results filled with variations why not increase a "confidence" score for each variation that has been found. If developers (or other users) want more information, variation data can be made available, say through a link. But developers don't need it to do their jobs; padding findings totals with exploitation variations overwhelms most developers, causing them to lose confidence in scan results. It's unfortunately quite counterproductive.

> *Training and practice need to be available to any testing personnel who will run the Web vulnerability scanning tools. Like static analysis tools, when Web vulnerability scanning tools are simply dropped on project teams, the results are likely to disappoint. Rather, an approach that we've found successful more than once is to start small and limited. Choose projects that are available for experimenting and will derive benefit from Web scanning. Find personnel who are intrigued by security testing, perhaps even hoping to enhance their career possibilities. Then, reduce the tool's vulnerability test suite to only those tests the tool manufacturer believes deliver extremely high confidence—deliver better than 80 percent results, that is, fewer than 20 percent false positives. We have even started with only those test suites that deliver fewer than 10 percent false positives.*
>
> *In this way, testers will be motivated to learn about the tool, and the tool will produce high-confidence results that can be relied on to find real bugs that need fixing. Everyone's confidence in the process and the tool will be high as a result. Starting from this strong place, testers and development teams will be much more willing to experiment with how many false positives they can tolerate and still get useful results. Different projects will need to find their own balance points.*
>
> *From these limited, pilot starting points, the team that is rolling out Web vulnerability scanning will gain valuable information about what works, what doesn't work, and what kind of resistance is likely to be encountered. Again, we caution against simply mandating the use of the tool and then tossing it over the wall without any experience and experimentation, without appropriate training and buy-in. We have seen too many programs flounder in exactly this way. Instead, start small, limited, and achieve success and confidence before expanding. A good tipping point for mandating any particular testing method is to achieve 60 percent voluntary participation before making any particular test a requirement.*

3.5.2.2 Fuzz Testing

> *Fuzz testing or Fuzzing is a Black Box software testing technique, which basically consists in finding implementation bugs using malformed/semi-malformed data injection in an automated fashion.*[*]

Because of the varied nature of non-Web inputs, finding a single type of tool that is good for each input method is not practical. Development teams may write their own test tool. However, to make that strategy a security strategy, the tool designers and implementers must have considerable knowledge about the sorts of attacks that can be promulgated against the input. The attack scenarios will have to be updated on a regular basis to account for new discoveries, tactic shifts, and changes to existing attacks. This is precisely what tool vendors do. Such a strategy may not be practical for most organizations.

Many attack methodologies are discovered by fuzzing, that is, using a fuzz tool against input attack surfaces. Once an unintended reaction is achieved from the program's input, the attacker (or

---

[*] Open Web Application Security Project (OWASP). (2013). "Fuzzing." Retrieved from https://www.owasp.org /index.php/Main_Page

researcher) can then examine the offending input and the program's behavior to determine what the vulnerability is and how best to exploit it.

Thankfully, software testers don't need to explore this far. If an input produces incorrect behavior, then the program is not defensive enough: A bug has been discovered. That's all that needs to be understood. This is the focus of fuzz testing: incorrect behavior upon processing an input. It can be argued that software, particularly secure software, must handle gracefully any data sequence through any of its inputs. To fail to handle improper or unexpected input gracefully will at the very least cause users concern. Further, the program is likely to expose a vulnerability.

Fuzzing each input of a program is a matter of writing a descriptor of the range of data inputs that will be tested. Most fuzzing tools handle many different kinds of inputs. The tester sets the type and series of inputs. The fuzz tool randomizes inside that range or series, continually sending improper inputs, just as an attacker might who is searching for vulnerabilities.

A fuzz tool automates the process of trying many variations to an input. Configuration files can be fuzzed, command-line interfaces can be fuzzed, APIs can be fuzzed, Web services, network protocols, etc. In fact, any type of input, including Web servers, can be fuzzed. Since there are numerous tools available for scanning Web servers in applications, we have focused on other types of inputs for fuzzing. If an organization develops strong fuzzing capabilities, there's no reason not to apply these capabilities against every input, including Web servers. In our experience, it may make sense to differentiate between Web inputs which can be scanned and other inputs for which there may be no direct scanning tools. It is these other inputs that must be fuzzed in the absence of a more focused tool.

Fuzzing is an undirected type of input validation, while vulnerability scanners are highly focused on known attack methods. A complete security test program will recognize the applicability of each of these techniques and apply them appropriately. There is some overlap; certain bugs will respond to both tool types.

3.5.3 Attack and Penetration Testing

Attack and penetration (A&P) testing involves a skilled human tester who behaves like the most skilled and sophisticated attacker. The tester will reconnoiter the target system, identifying attack surfaces. Then, the same tools as would be applied by a sophisticated attacker are run by the tester to identify not only the more obvious errors, but subtle logic errors and misses in the system. Logic errors are the most difficult to identify. All but the simplest errors in logic generally require a human to identify them.

We have separated out attack and penetration testing because it is usually rather expensive, both in time and effort. There's a reason that penetration testers receive premium salaries. It takes skill and understanding to deliver quality results. Alan Paller once casually suggested to one of the authors that there were not more than 1500 skilled penetration testers extant. We don't know the actual number, but there are not enough highly skilled penetration testers to deliver all the work that is needed. This situation will probably be true for some time. Due to the scarcity, we suggest that attack and penetration testing be reserved for critical components, and major releases that are expected to be under severe attack. (Core Software Security, pp. 307–310)

Six years later, the number of penetration testers, penetration test consultancies, members of Red Teams, etc., has grown dramatically. As far as we know as of this writing, there has been no definitive census of penetration testers, security architects, security analysts, or security engineers, etc. Still, the population of skilled penetration testers must certainly be far beyond Alan Paller's "1500" remark.

If your organization has sufficient attack and penetration resources, the skilled human element is the strongest testing capability in security. Everything that can be tested probably should be tested.

However, we have seen too many findings reports where the tester did not have this kind of skill, did not take time to understand the target of the test, ran the default tests, and reported hundreds of vulnerabilities. These sorts of tests help no one. Development teams may look at the first few vulnerabilities, declare them false positive, and stop looking. This is a classic, typical response to a report filled with possible vulnerabilities rather than real issues. Generally, in these cases, the attack test was not tuned and configured to the target, and perhaps the target was not properly configured as it would be when deployed. In our experience, this is a big waste of everyone's time.

Instead, focus your highly skilled resources or dollars on the most worthy targets. Critical code that must not fail can benefit greatly from an A&P test. And a strong return on investment can be made before major releases or after major revisions. This is where we suggest the most benefit can be gained from skilled attack and penetration testing.

Because an attack and penetration test can take considerable time to complete, the rate of code change must be considered when applying this intensive type of test. If the rate of change (update) is faster than the length of time to test the system, vulnerabilities may be introduced before the test even completes. These two factors must be weighed in order to get the most useful results. Generally, even if updating occurs every day, these will not be major releases, and certainly not major revisions. Hence, testing at the larger code inflections can be a better investment.

What is critical code? We have seen numerous definitions of "critical":

- *The highest-revenue system*
- *The most attacked system*
- *The largest system*
- *The system with the biggest investment*
- *The most strategic system*
- *The most regulated system*
- *The highest-risk system*
- *The system handling the most sensitive data*

Each one of these definitions can be blown apart easily with examples of the others. A practical approach is to let business leaders or other organizational leaders decide which systems are critical. Multiple factors may be taken into account. None of the definitions above are mutually exclusive; different factors may add weight to the criticality of a system. We suggest an open approach. A larger net, if the organization can afford it, is probably better in the long run. An organization doesn't want to miss an important system simply because it failed any single factor for criticality. (Core Software Security, pp. 310–311)

Penetration testers (and other security folk) must represent attacker risk during decisions. But we have found that fix decisions, which can be very complex problems involving business needs, customer requirements, level of fix effort, and probability of exploitation, are best left to those who can be held accountable for making risk and priority decisions. Decision makers must be supplied with coherent risk assessment, based upon solid risk methods (not risk based upon individual risk tolerances). In our programs, and to good effect, risk rating resides with security (red team members and other security practitioners). Having identified and rated a risk based upon a sound risk methodology, the red team is a fix priority stakeholder, but in most circumstances, not the decision maker.

Whether the penetration tester is internal or hired from a consultancy, or otherwise engaged, penetration testing also provides a "proof" of the threat model because the model produces a set of security requirements. The penetration test (and other tests, including scanning techniques, functional tests, fuzzing, etc.) validate whether the threat model's output was correct:

- Were all relevant attacks analyzed?
- Were all required protections and controls implemented? Were they implemented correctly?
- Do weaknesses still exist?

There is a natural and important feedback loop between the threat model (and modelers) and validations, especially skilled manual validators, which becomes a strong reason for combining the red team and defenders (blue team) into a "purple team."

Penetration testing is expensive; there will likely have to be a return on investment (ROI) analysis to justify the expenditure. As we wrote in 2014, a penetration test, often at each major inflection of software change, has proven a competitive advantage in many business contexts.

Since 2014, some organizations, especially larger ones and organizations whose goals demand a tighter security posture, have invested in so-called "red teams." These are essentially internal penetration testing teams. The advantage to a red team is that the team become familiar, often intimately, with the software against which they must test. That familiarity can lead to some cost savings and testing efficiencies. The downside from long-term familiarity may also lead the red team to become somewhat less thorough, having tested some of the software multiple times.

Another red team problem that has cropped up numerous times has been a tendency for the red team to take an adversarial role with developers. An adversarial relationship nearly always results in inter-team friction, and must be avoided.

To avoid friction, some organizations have collapsed their defending teams ("blue team") and their penetration team ("red team") into a single unit: "purple team." Whatever color we choose to associate with our security teams' functions, we have little doubt from experience that red teams cannot simply find issues and then "toss these over a wall" to developers and expect prompt, accurate fixes. We've found more efficiency when internal penetration testers also help to craft workable solutions. It's important that red team members not set priorities in the same manner as external security researchers and other issue reporters, who too often artificially and abstractly pick a fix time period out of thin air. A purple team combines defenders and attackers into a holistic security practice. Remediation priorities are best made taking a wide range of factors, including business objectives, into consideration, alongside and in concert with security concerns.

3.5.4 Independent Testing

There may be situations where it's advantageous to apply third-party security testing. If customers for a product are particularly security-sensitive, they may demand a third-party verification of the security health of the system before purchasing.

In the case of demonstrable customer demand for security verification, one successful approach that we have used is to have third-party testing be accounted for as a direct cost of goods sold. When systems can't be sold to many customers without third-party verification, third-party verification is considered a part of the cost of building the system for those customers. One report can typically be used for many customers.

Indeed, sometimes there are advantages to getting an independent view of the system. As in all human endeavors, if the evaluators are too close to the system, they may miss important factors. Applying some independent analysis will focus fresh eyes on the problems.

"Independent" doesn't necessarily mean outside the organization entirely. We have had success simply bringing in a security architect who hadn't looked at the system yet, who knew nothing about it. If the organization is big enough, there are usually resources tasked with alternative systems who can be brought in to check the work.

It is worth mentioning again that one of the strongest tools security architects have is peer review. It's easy to miss something important. We have instituted a system of peer review within multiple organizations at which we have worked, such that any uncertainty in the analysis requires a consensus of several experienced individuals. In this way, each assessor can get his or her work checked and validated.

If there's any uncertainty about any of the testing methodologies outlined here, getting an independent view may help validate the work or find any holes in the approach. (Core Software Security, pp. 311–312)

3.6 Assess and Threat Model Build/Release/Deploy/Operate Chain

Those who've been doing software security (or so-called "application security") may be somewhat surprised by our inclusion in our SDL of what has previously been grouped with operational functions.* Despite past categorizations, most seasoned software security practitioners know that they have to include in any comprehensive security analysis the chain of tools and set of processes that build, package, release, deploy, and then, where applicable, operate the software. Why hasn't this been a part of SDLs in the past? (We did include software maintenance and vulnerability management in *Core Software Security*, though Chapter 9 focused exclusively on software development security practices.)

As of this writing, and especially with DevOps, running software, packaging it, deploying it, and keeping it running is as much a part of "software development" as any other aspect or set of tasks. And much of the process will be automated through DevOps code (if not almost all of it). To us, it makes sense in a DevOps and cloud-hosted world to acknowledge the importance of the releasing end of development to the security posture of the code because an attacker can as surely compromise a system through leverage obtained through the build, release, and deployment chain as issues within the built software. Operations are routinely misconfigured to allow compromise. Administrative access problems get exploited. These are just as important as assessing the infrastructure's security on which the software will run, or strengthening design weaknesses, or fixing implementation issues. DevOps does not impose a hierarchy on development activities; neither do we.

It is imperative to understand how software moves from source code to execution. Numerous tools will be employed to achieve the executable program and then to deliver it to its usable environment. An assessment must analyze:

- The tools employed
- Tool configuration
- Who has access, at what privileges?
- How privileges are distributed and assigned
- How access is granted and for what purposes
- What validations exist to ensure that code is delivered as intended and that the tools function as intended, without compromise

Basically, the task is to threat model the tool chain and processes. Please see the threat model sections in this chapter and Chapter 4 for more information about threat models and the process of threat modeling.

3.7 Agile: Sprints

We believe that the key to producing secure software with an Agile process is to integrate security into the Agile process from architecture through testing. Rather than forcing Waterfall development on top of an Agile process, security has to become Agile; security practitioners must let go of rigid processes

---

* We reiterate that DevOps contains both software generation and operation under a single, holistic umbrella.

and enter into the dialog and collaboration that is the essence of Agile development. Recognize that we have to trust and work with Agile development teams, and make use of the Agile process rather than fighting the process and its practitioners.

 Requirements and architecture are a front-end process to Agile cycles, or "Sprints." Architecture feeds into the repeated Sprint cycles. At the end of a series of Sprints, prerelease testing is applied. All the other tasks in the SDL occur during each Sprint. (Core Software Security, p. 312)

It should be fairly clear by now to readers that architecture practice in relationship to Scrum Agile methods has matured since *Core Software Security* was published. Although one might start coding with no idea about the intended structure of the final software, it is generally believed that this is not a strong approach. Coding without structure does occur; the authors have experienced this personally. If the system has any complexity at all, the results of "code first, structure as you go" tend towards *ad hoc*, often what programmers call "spaghetti": code that has no discernable structure whatsoever, with a call tree resembling a plate of cooked, long pasta noodles, all intertwined. Hard to understand; wicked to maintain.

Noopur Davis, now Executive Vice President, Chief Product and Information Security Officer for Comcast Cable, Inc., and a dear friend to the authors, who has deep knowledge of Agile methods and has shepherded many Agile transformations, likes to state that there must be at least a "skeleton architecture" before coding. We find her statement to hold true in practice: There must be a sense of overall structure and sufficient structural detail to understand where to start and how everything will most likely fit together once built.

Some Scrum teams might choose to take all architecture tasks first; it's up to the team. Alternatively, we have seen excellent results from teams who architect while also designing, while also coding and testing. It's up to the Scrum team how they take the work. There are advantages to each approach: A more polished architecture and design may make coding easier, but can also be less flexible. On the other hand, when taking development aspects in parallel, there may be some code that has to be redone, due to structures that evolve. Still, the architecture benefits from what's learned through coding, and vice versa. Efforts for which less is understood may benefit from more flexibility. Highly innovative projects often face significant unknowns at the outset and, thus, require greater willingness to adapt to changing conditions and understanding. We point once again at Figure 3.1: parallel infinite loops held together through frictionless, constant communication and feedback.

In 2014, we were in step with thinking at the time when we declared that all security architecture would precede coding. As Agile has matured, we've learned that architecture preceding coding isn't necessary and, often, not the way Agile development works. Security, like all the other requirements, profits from flexibility. In fact, in our experience, letting security "breathe" with the development process allows teams to deliver security requirements that are more closely aligned with changes that occur during development than brittle, up-front requirements that cannot be changed, especially in the face of an Agile architecture and implementation that continuously revise and refine.

A Sprint is a cycle of development during which chunks of code—"user stories"—are built. Each Scrum team chooses the periodicity of the team's Sprints. Typically, Sprints last somewhere between 2 and 6 weeks. Each Sprint cycle is precisely the same length; this allows an implementation rhythm to develop. Whatever is not finished in its Sprint is put back into the backlog of items waiting to be built. At the beginning of a Sprint, some design work will take place; at least enough design needs to be in place in order to begin coding. Still, the design may change as a Sprint unfolds. Also, testing begins during the Sprint as soon as there is something to test. In this way, design, coding, and testing may all be occurring in parallel. At the end of the Sprint, the team will examine the results of the cycle in a process of continuous improvement.

In Scrum, what is going to be built is considered during user story creation. That's the "early" part. A close relationship with the Product Owner* is critical to get security user stories onto the backlog. This relationship is also important during backlog prioritization. During the Sprint planning meeting, the meeting at which items are pulled into the development process (each "Sprint") for build, a considerable amount of the design is shaped. Make security an integral part of that process, either through direct participation or by proxy.

Security experts need to make themselves available throughout a Sprint to answer questions about implementation details, the correct way to securely build user stories. Let designs emerge. Let them emerge securely. As a respected member of the Scrum team, catching security misses early will be appreciated, not resisted. The design and implementation is improved: The design will be more correct more often.

Part of the priority dialog must be the interplay between what is possible to build given the usual constraints of time and budget, and what must be built in order to meet objectives, security and otherwise. The security expert doesn't enter in with the "One True Way," but rather, with an attitude of "How do we collectively get this all done, and done well enough to satisfy the requirements?"

Finally, since writing secure code is very much a discipline and practice, appropriate testing and vulnerability assurance steps need to be a part of every Sprint. We think that these need to be part of the definition of "done." A proposed definition of "done" might look something like the following, based on the seven determining questions discussed earlier:

Definition of Done

1. *All code has been manually reviewed (and defects fixed).*
    a. *All code has been peer-reviewed.*
    b. *Critical code has been reviewed by a senior or security subject-matter expert.*
2. *All code has been statically analyzed (and defects fixed).*
3. *All functional tests have been passed.*
4. *Web . . . interfaces have been dynamically tested (and defects fixed).*
5. *All non-Web program input paths have been fuzzed (and defects fixed).*
6. Included and employed third-party software has acceptable software security practices.
7. All vulnerabilities in third-party software that have potential to significantly harm stakeholders have been patched, fixed, or otherwise mitigated.[†]

Each of the items designating a security definition of "done" is described in the relevant section.

In an Agile process, everyone is involved in security. Security personnel mustn't toss security "over the wall" and expect secure results. Development teams will likely perceive such a toss as an interjection into the work with which they're already tasked. Rather than collaborative security, the result is likely to be resistance on the part of the Agile team.

More effective is a willingness to enter into the problems at hand. Among those problems and important to the overall objectives of the project, security will be considered. The security experts will do well to remember that there are always trade-off decisions that must be made during development. By

---

*   The Product Owner is a formal role in Scrum. This is the person who takes the customer's and user's viewpoint. She or he is responsible for creating user stories and for prioritization. A Product Owner might be an independent member of the development team, a senior architect (though not typically) or a product manager, or similar. It should not be someone who has hierarchical organizational power over development team members.

†   Nos. 6 and 7 were added during the writing of this book.

working toward the success of all objectives, including security, security will be considered in its rightful place, and creative and/or innovative solutions are also more likely to be found by a collaborating team. Security people will have to get their hands dirty, get some implementation "grease" under their proverbial virtual fingernails in order to earn the trust and buy-in of Scrum teams.

Of course, setting the relative priorities over what will get built is one of the most difficult problems facing any development team. This is especially true with respect to security items. A strong, risk-based approach will help factor real-world impacts into the priority equation.

In our experience, if the Agile team has sufficient risk guidance to understand the implications for prioritizing security items against other tasks, we believe teams will make better decisions. The classic line, "It's a vulnerability that can lead to loss, so fix it now," has long since failed to sway decision makers. Let there be no FUD—fear, uncertainty, doubt.

Instead, consider loss not in terms of information security possibilities, but rather, real-world business impacts for the system under consideration as it will be used within the expected deployment. An approach focused on impacts will go much further in helping to make reasonable decisions. There may be items in the security queue that can be postponed in favor of other critical features. Team trust is built through everyone participating fully, which includes security expert participation. When a security expert becomes part of the Agile team, everyone wins; security wins. Indeed, when security is considered carefully and decisions are based on risk scenarios, there are two great wins for security:

1. *Security becomes part of the decision-making fabric, earning its rightful place. It's no longer an add-on or an unplanned extra. Thinking about security becomes part of the mindset of building software rather than an interjection from outside.*
2. *If risks are considered carefully, the item that has high risk will tend to be prioritized as it should. Giving up the idea that every security issue is equally important results in the items that truly are dangerous (these will be rare) getting the attention they deserve. Items bearing less risk can be scheduled according to their relative importance.*

For many organizations, there are too few skilled security experts. There aren't enough security experts that every Scrum team can include its own, dedicated security guru. Security experts must be matrixed across multiple teams. These experts will need to develop skills to "time-slice," to give a portion of their time to each of multiple projects. Context-switching time will need to be allotted so that matrixed personnel have adequate time in which to put down one project's context and remember another's. Excellent project management skills are required. These can be performed either by the security expert or through a project management practice. Project managers can be key to assisting with scheduling and deliverable tasks that make a matrix assignment strategy effective.

There are dangers, however, to assigning a single security expert to multiple projects. Foremost, overload is all too common. If a security expert has too many teams assigned, the expert may begin to "thrash"—that is, have just enough time to pick up the next project and retrieve context before having to switch projects again. No real work gets done. Not only is there no time to provide actual security expertise, security experts don't thrive without continual technical growth. If the security expert is overburdened, research time will be curtailed, which can lead to burn out. More important, without time to research problems properly and thoroughly, uninformed security decisions may be made.

Avoid overload; watch for the telltale signs, as each person has a different threshold for too many context switches.

With too much overload, projects will be delayed, as teams wait for the security expert to participate. The security expert then becomes a bottleneck to team velocity. Or worse, designs and implementations proceed without the required security expertise and help. This almost always leads to releases without appropriate security, security logic errors, or expensive rework. These are among the very problems that an Agile process is typically brought in to address.

Indeed, some overloaded security folks may compensate with ivory-tower pronouncements tossed out without appropriate participation. The collaboration and trust that are the hallmark and essence of Agile processes are skipped in favor of what is efficient for the security person. Without sufficient time to build team esprit de corps, an overly allocated security person is likely not to have the time to integrate into each Scrum team properly. As noted above, when the security person understands all the issues that must be solved by the whole team, security receives its rightful place and is not an interjection. It is security items as interjections into the functioning and autonomy of the Agile team that including a security expert in the team is attempting to prevent.

Still, it is possible, with just enough security people, to use virtual teams and multiple assignments. We have seen this done successfully multiple times. Just avoid overloading. Indeed, hold in mind that team spirit takes time, exposure, and experience to develop. Mistakes and missteps will occur during forming and learning periods. Build these into the process for success.

3.8 Key Success Factors and Metrics

3.8.1 Secure Coding Training Program

It is imperative that a secure coding program be implemented in an organization. It should cater to multiple stakeholders/groups and not just to development engineers. An effective security coding program will help a product manager to understand these practices, help polish skills of architects-in-training, and provide engineers with specific guidelines for writing correct code. Program modules should also be available for specific languages (e.g., Java, C, C++). Web Services architecture and proper use of cryptography must be part of any effective secure coding training program. (Core Software Security, pp. 312–318)

Please see the quote from *Secrets of a Cyber Security Architect* about short, discreet secure coding training that appeared earlier in this chapter under the heading, *"Effective Secure Coding Training."*

3.8.2 Secure Coding Frameworks (APIs)

In addition to secure coding, developers should be made aware of available secure coding frameworks that exist and any secured APIs that can be used as part of coding. This prevents ad hoc coding practices to solve well-known security problems (e.g., preventing XSS) and standardizes code— standardization helps to keep code maintainable over time. Different types of security testing will point out defects that result from improper use or failure to use secure coding frameworks (APIs). A secure coding training program should be offered periodically to reinforce best practices and should be updated to cover real defects that have resulted from improper use of APIs.

3.8.3 Manual Code Review

Every line of code that is committed for build should be at least peer reviewed. No matter how small a module or set of changes is, this is the "hygiene habit" of best practice. Comments from peer review should be taken not as a criticism but as a means to make the code more robust, readable, and secure. Critical code should be reviewed by someone who is well versed in security coding practices and the algorithms being implemented. In our experience, multiple code reviews can be quite beneficial.

3.8.4 Independent Code Review and Testing (by Experts or Third Parties)

Once code is complete, a comprehensive code review by third parties or independent experts should be performed. The idea here is to catch any remaining issues that were not identified during the SDL build and testing activities. Findings from independent review and penetration testing should be shared with the people who've performed the static analysis and code reviews. In the next round of development, many of these issues will then be addressed during peer review, by static analysis, or during the test plan.

3.8.5 Static Analysis

Before code is checked-in for manual review, it should be put through static analysis to find common errors and security best practices violations. This will help to reduce the number of comments during the manual and expert review phases. Performing static analysis on code before check-in should be mandatory and ideally should be tightly integrated into development environments and the developer work flow.

3.8.6 Risk Assessment Methodology

A risk assessment framework (RAF) is essential for the success of a SDL program. Threat modeling and architectural assessment feed into the RAF. The RAF helps to prioritize risks and enable decisions based on risk severity and impact. (Core Software Security, pp. 318–319)

Please see Chapter 4 of *Securing Systems* for a risk methodology based on Factor Analysis of Information Risk (FAIR), an Open Group standard that has been specifically designed for the needs and problems of software security.

3.8.7 Integration of SDL with SDLC

Integration of "determining" questions into the SDLC cycle will allow the SDL, that is, software security, to become easily integrated into project and development practices. The authors strongly emphasize creating an SDL program and mapping it into the SDLC cycle rather than making security requirements a project plan line item. Without proper guidance, pressed project teams are likely to invent their own interpretations of "minimum set of security activities."

3.8.8 Development of Architecture Talent

Security architecture talent is not easy to find, for it sits at the top of a skill set pyramid. Architects need to have background in software development and several different areas in security before they can take on an architect role. This often means a lack of competent candidates who are readily available. It is critical that a program be in place to develop and mentor resources that will eventually take on a security architect role. Hiring architects from outside is often less useful, given the time they will spend trying to understand an organization's software, the environments, and each organization's specific practices in order to apply real-world guidance. An architecture mentoring program will provide a clear return on the investment over time. (Core Software Security, pp. 319–320)

For readers who want more information on training security architects, *Secrets of a Cyber Security Architect* details the skills that security architects need (Chapter 1), and many techniques for teaching, coaching, and supporting learners (Chapter 5).

3.8.9 Metrics

This list is a compilation of useful metrics from the authors' experience applying SDL in the real world.

- *Maturity of security coding program*
- *Percent of vetted APIs used in the code*
- *Percent of software code manually reviewed at time of check-in*
- *Number of lines of code manually reviewed at time of check-in*
- *Percent of findings missed by manual review but found during expert review*
- *Percent of findings missed by static analysis but found during manual review*
- *Number of teams auditing software needed to be tweaked significantly during the SDL*
- *Percent of developers using integrated static scanning software from their integrated development environment (IDE)*
- *Number of defects found during manual review, static analysis, and expert review*
- *Percent of SDL phases "built in" to the SDLC*
- *Number of "upcoming" architects in the organization*
- *Percent of software systems assessed to systems produced (Are you reaching every project and every system?)*
- *Percent of security reviews completed for designs produced*
- *Maturity of security design review process*
- *Number of exceptions granted based on recommendations from design review**
- *Percent of Web servers covered by Web dynamic analysis*
- *Number of defects found by input fuzzing*
- *Number of major releases receiving independent A&P testing*
- *Number of externally reported security vulnerabilities (Core Software Security, pp. 320–321)*

3.9 Chapter Summary

As we have seen, there is a menu of security tasks which, taken together, build secure software, the sum total of an applied security development lifecycle. In order to get these tasks executed well, relationships among development team members and between security people and development teams make the difference between success and failure.

Engagement starts early during requirements gathering and continues throughout the SDL to the delivery of the finished software. Architecture and design-time engagement is meant to build the correct and appropriate security mechanisms into the software, which must be coded correctly and then proved to be functionally correct and free from vulnerability through a testing plan. The test plan includes multiple approaches, as appropriate to the attack surfaces exposed by the software. Security is an end-to-end process whose tasks overlap each other to provide continuity and assurance. No one task solves the security problem; there is no silver bullet. (Core Software Security, p. 321)

---

* We caution against overreliance on this seemingly innocent metric. Skilled security architects often employ exceptions to shift interactions from "fix or not" to "when to fix and how to fix."

In this chapter, we've described a generic SDL hopefully in the terms that we set out in Chapter 1 and which were reprised at the beginning of this chapter. In the chapter summary, which follows, each SDL activity will be summarized as an activity table for reader convenience and ease of use.

The attributes of each task in the generic SDL are set out through the following set of tables. Our hope is that presenting the SDL activities in this tabular form will more readily seed your software security practices. In our experience, a tabular form provides a ready-to-use SDL that can be easily consumed by security practitioners and developers, alike.

Each activity that was described in the text above is presented here as it will be enacted in concert by security and development people. We listed the qualities of an SDL that is independent and divorced from SDLC assumptions in Chapter 1, then reprised that list at the beginning of this chapter so that readers understand what a generic SDL must contain. The following tables condense to essentials the purpose of each activity—its preconditions that must be in place before it may be started (dependencies); when the activity may be considered to have been completed (until refined or renewed), the activity's outputs (which may be inputs for other activities); and the triggers for refinement, renewal, or review.

- Describe the SDL task's purpose
- State the necessary preconditions before the SDL task may be started, including any dependencies on other SDL task outputs, or the state of the software in development
- Describe those conditions that must be met to consider the task complete
- Explain the output(s), if any, of the task
- Describe any conditions that may trigger a refinement or review of the task's outputs

What follows in Tables 3.3 to 3.18 (and reprinted in Appendix A) comprises the essentials of a generic security development lifecycle (SDL).

When security people shift to a developer-centric focus, presenting security not as a deluge of vulnerabilities but rather as attributes that need inclusion for success and errors that developers wish to remove, developers and security people can work together tightly to craft appropriately secure

Table 3.3

	Begin Threat Model
Purpose	Begin a threat model to deliver a secure design based upon the security objectives for the software. Security objectives are based, in part, on the attacks the system must resist and the security expectations of the system's stakeholders, i.e., the system threat model.
Preconditions	The threat model may be started when there is an idea or concept to be realized through software. The threat model must be initiated when more than one structural element has been conceived as a solution to deliver the objectives of the software. When no threat model has been started for an architecture that is nearing or has been completed, and for mature systems, start the threat model immediately.
Definition of Done	Not Applicable—the threat model will be refined throughout development.
Results & Outputs	At concept time, output high-level security requirements and features. Identify additional security requirements and those structural elements/components and implementations that will deliver the security requirements.
Triggers for review or refinement	As architecture elements are added or conceived, refine the threat model. When security features are identified, refine the threat model. When new attack techniques or avenues of attack are discovered (threats), refine the threat model.

Table 3.4

	Refine Threat Model
Purpose	Refine a threat model to more clearly represent the attacks that the unfolding system will need to resist and to identify new security requirements, as well as to ensure that existing requirements remain synchronized with the architecture and the implementation of the software.
Preconditions	There must be an existing threat model. There must be at least some architecture (structural elements) that can be analyzed.
Definition of Done	The threat model is complete enough when all relevant attack scenarios have been considered, when scenarios have been risk rated, and when every attack scenario with potential for significant impact, as well as likelihood of exploitation, has sufficient security defenses to bring the system to the risk tolerance of the system's stakeholders.
Results & Outputs	A set of risk-rated attack scenarios and a set of defenses (including already-implemented and to be built) that together comprise an appropriate "defense in depth."
Triggers for review or refinement	Refine the threat model when there is a change to the architecture, when new exploitation types have been discovered, and when new defenses become available. Architectural changes might be any of the following: • Components or functions • Assets • Use cases • Lines of communication or data flows • Trust boundaries or levels of trust/distrust • Shifting the exposure of potentially vulnerable components

Table 3.5

	Conduct Privacy Impact Assessment (PIA)
Purpose	An analysis of the software to identify requirements (security and other) needed to protect the privacy of personal data and to comply with those privacy regulations to which the software will be subject. An essential part of the analysis will be threat modeling for privacy and data attacks. (Please see Begin Threat Model & Refine Threat Model activities, as well.)
Preconditions	There is a need to collect human entities' data. The data elements that are/will be collected must be known, as must the reasons for collecting the data. There must be an existing threat model. There must be at least some architecture (structural elements) that can be analyzed.
Definition of Done	The PIA is complete when all the privacy requirements (security and other) have been identified and the privacy-focused portions of the threat model are finished. (Please see Refine Threat Model activity.)
Results & Outputs	• A set of risk-rated attack scenarios and a set of defenses (including defenses already implemented and defenses to be built), which together comprise an appropriate "defense in depth" for privacy protection and privacy regulation compliance. • A set of non-security requirements to achieve privacy typically include legal, user interface, and privacy engineering needs.
Triggers for review or refinement	• Changes to the human entities' data elements • Use cases • Lines of communication or data flows • Trust boundaries2 or levels of trust/distrust • Shifting the exposure of potentially vulnerable components that handle privacy-related data

Table 3.6

	Threat Model Build, Package, Release, and Deploy Mechanisms
Purpose	To extend attack and defense analysis beyond the software development to include all mechanisms used to generate, run, and maintain the running software. Although a "comprehensive" threat model should include these aspects, particularly in DevOps where much of these functions will also be "coded," we call this threat modeling subtask out separately, since it is often skipped. But attackers don't skip it and compromise can allow the attacker to spoof or otherwise manipulate the software to their ends.
Preconditions	There must be build, package, release, and deploy mechanisms, code, and software components planned and existing.
Definition of Done	The threat model is complete enough when all relevant attack scenarios have been considered, when scenarios have been risk rated, and when every attack scenario with potential for significant impact, as well as likelihood of exploitation, has sufficient security defenses to bring build, release, deploy, and operations to the risk tolerance of the system's stakeholders.
Results & Outputs	A set of risk-rated attack scenarios and a set of defenses (including already implemented and to be built) that together comprise an appropriate "defense in depth."
Triggers for review or refinement	Refine the threat model when there is a change to the architecture, when new exploitation types have been discovered, and when new defenses become available. Architectural changes might be any of the following: • Components, functions, or tools • Assets used for build, release, deployment, and operating • Use cases • Lines of communication or data flows • Trust boundaries or levels of trust/distrust • Shifting the exposure of potentially vulnerable components

Table 3.7

	Assess Security of Hosting Infrastructure
Purpose	When unknown, any hosting infrastructure that will be used must have its security capabilities, security posture, and security practices assessed. Every infrastructure has security strengths and limitations. Software making use of an infrastructure must understand what it will gain and must take responsibility for the software's overall security posture. Threat modeling the infrastructure will be one of the foundational tasks of the assessment, but not the only one, since the software system to be deployed on the infrastructure may need to consume security services from the infrastructure. (Please see Begin Threat Model and Refine Threat Model activities.)
Preconditions	• A hosting infrastructure (planned, internal, external, commercial cloud, hybrid cloud, etc.) will be used by the software. • No previous infrastructure assessment has been undertaken, nor have significant changes occurred to the infrastructure.
Definition of Done	All services to be used or currently employed have been threat modeled and assessed for security tolerance, security posture, and security practices.
Results & Outputs	• A set of security requirements that the software will need to meet in order to run on the infrastructure and meet the software's security needs and objectives. • A set of the additional risks (if any) that running on the infrastructure adds to the operation and maintenance of the software.
Triggers for review or refinement	Review the assessment whenever unassessed infrastructure is added or changed (e.g., change of vendors or locations or services, etc.).

Table 3.8

	Review Threat Model
Purpose	To validate that a threat model is comprehensive enough, and that it is sufficiently complete for the state of development at this review moment.
Preconditions	A threat model that is believed to have been sufficiently completed. Each review should be made by a threat model practitioner who is independent of the target system and development and a reviewer who has more experience than those who generated the model. (In the case of the most senior threat modeler, peer review by other senior practitioners is sufficient.)
Definition of Done	The reviewers agree that the model is complete and comprehensive enough.
Results & Outputs	A risk-rated set of reviewed security requirements, including defensive measures and mitigations against attack scenarios.
Triggers for review or refinement	Whenever a threat model has been refined and the refiners believe that refinements are finished.

Table 3.9

	Secure Coding Training
Purpose	To prepare programmers (and other related staff) for generating code without security issues.
Preconditions	A need to generate or change software programming code.
Definition of Done	Demonstration of attendance and ability to apply the techniques that have been learned.
Results & Outputs	Programmers have been through appropriate training and can demonstrate secure coding practices.
Triggers for review or refinement	N/A

Table 3.10

	Manual Code Review
Purpose	Manual code review is used to find security issues that have been coded, as well as to ensure that security functionality has been coded correctly.
Preconditions	Code has been generated or changed.
Definition of Done	• Peer review has been performed and acknowledged by the programmer. • For security critical code, expert review has been performed and acknowledged. • Issues that have been agreed upon have been fixed. Code has been resubmitted for review and potential commit to build.
Results & Outputs	The security issues or incorrect implementations that have been identified are acknowledged and fixed.
Triggers for review or refinement	Code has been generated or changed.

Table 3.11

	Static Analysis Testing
Purpose	Static analysis for security testing (SAST) is employed to identify security errors that are contained in program source code.
Preconditions	Code has been generated or changed.
Definition of Done	• SAST has been performed over code modules containing changes and over all dependent and interacting modules. • Issues that have been found to offer potential attacker leverage ("true positives") have been fixed. Code has been resubmitted for analysis and potential commit to build.
Results & Outputs	The security issues or incorrect implementations that have been identified are acknowledged and fixed.
Triggers for review or refinement	Code has been generated or changed.

Table 3.12

	Assess Third-Party Code
Purpose	Third-party code assessment ensures that included code generated by external or outside parties (e.g., commercial and open source) meets similar SDL requirements as code produced under the organization's SDL.
Preconditions	Third-party code will be included.
Definition of Done	Third-party software security practices have been found to be sufficient so that inclusion of the code will not degrade the software security of the system or software. That is, the third-party execution of their SDL is similar to and meets the requirements of the organization's SDL.
Results & Outputs	An assessment as to whether third-party code may be included or must be avoided.
Triggers for review or refinement	• Third-party code proposed for inclusion/use. • Changes have been made to third-party used/included code.

Table 3.13

	Patch (Upgrade or Fix) Issues Identified in Third-Party Code
Purpose	Issues in third-party code become issues in the entire system or software. The task is to apply software upgrades ("patches") that fix issues in software produced by external parties.
Preconditions	Third-party software must be included or employed. And security issues (vulnerabilities) have been found or announced within the third-party software.
Definition of Done	All existing vulnerability patches whose issues may cause significant harm have been fixed or the risk has been accepted by risk decision makers.
Results & Outputs	Software patches have been applied or risk decisions recorded.
Triggers for review or refinement	• Announcement of issues in included/used third-party code. • Discovery of issues in included/used third-party code.

Table 3.14

Functional Security Testing	
Purpose	Functional testing of security functions and features ensures that these functions behave as intended and that they can handle error conditions and edge cases well.
Preconditions	• Completed realizations of security functions and features. • A set of tests designed to exercise the full range of behavior and error handling that is expected from each function or feature.
Definition of Done	Tests have completed successfully. All identified issues have been fixed.
Results & Outputs	Incorrect software behavior and improper handling of errors.
Triggers for review or refinement	• Tests must be rerun each time a feature or function has been changed. • Tests must be rerun to prove that issues have been fixed and new issues have not been introduced.

Table 3.15

Web Protocol and Services Dynamic Testing	
Purpose	Web protocol and services dynamic testing uses specialized tools to identify vulnerabilities and security weaknesses.
Preconditions	• Web protocol and services are included in the software, and the code has been completed sufficiently to execute in the intended execution environment or its simile. • The availability of tools (scanners, etc.) built to test the particular protocols and services that have been built.
Definition of Done	Tests have completed successfully. All identified issues have been fixed.
Results & Outputs	Incorrect software behavior. Vulnerabilities and weaknesses in the software.
Triggers for review or refinement	• Tests must be rerun each time changes are introduced. • Tests must be rerun to prove that issues have been fixed and new issues have not been introduced.

Table 3.16

Other Inputs Security Testing (e.g., Fuzzing)	
Purpose	Other inputs security testing uses fuzzing and potentially other specialized tools to identify incorrect software behavior when malformed data are input.
Preconditions	• Non-Web inputs are included in the software, and the code has been completed sufficiently to execute in the intended execution environment or its simile. • The availability of fuzzers capable of sending malformed data to each particular program input.
Definition of Done	Tests have completed successfully. All identified issues have been fixed.
Results & Outputs	Incorrect software behavior. Vulnerabilities and weaknesses in the software.
Triggers for review or refinement	• Tests must be rerun each time changes are introduced. • Tests must be rerun to prove that issues have been fixed and new issues have not been introduced.

Table 3.17

	Attack and Penetration Testing
Purpose	• Manual attack and penetration testing is used to find security issues whose discovery is not easily automated by commercial and open source vulnerability discovery tools. • Attack and penetration testing also proves/disproves the security assumptions and the sufficiency of the security requirements identified in the threat model.
Preconditions	Software capable of execution in its intended environment and the intended execution environment or an accurate simile.
Definition of Done	Tests have completed successfully. All identified issues have been fixed.
Results & Outputs	Vulnerabilities and weaknesses in the software. Proof of issue presence is provided by successful compromise.
Triggers for review or refinement	• Tests must be rerun each time changes are introduced. • Tests must be rerun to prove that issues have been fixed and new issues have not been introduced.

Table 3.18

	Assess and Threat Model Build/Release/Deploy/Operate Chain
Purpose	• Ensure that tools and administrative access do not offer attacker leverage to meet security posture needs. • Ensure that the software that is released contains only intended software.
Preconditions	Methods, processes, and technology used to build, package, release, deploy, and operate software.
Definition of Done	A comprehensive set of defenses has been identified (i.e., a completed threat model). (Please see Begin Threat Model and Refine Threat Model activities.)
Results & Outputs	A set of security requirements and controls that, when implemented, close or mitigate potential attacker leverage (threats).
Triggers for review or refinement	• Tool or technology changes. • Change to the number of administrators/administrative access types/points.

software. Security is not presented as a nonfunctional, top-down command. Instead, security takes its rightful place among the many attributes of complete software that must be considered and prioritized. Appropriate prioritization is achieved through deep and active engagement by security subject-matter experts throughout the entire SDL.

It is also true that each security activity is not appropriate to every project. Projects differ in size, criticality, and scope. A working SDL will scale to account for these differences. We offer seven determining questions as one formula for getting the right security tasks assigned to the appropriate projects.

Stepping back from the specific questions outlined here, instituting a set of project-specific questions that determine the appropriate security activities for each project has proven not only to ensure that the right security is performed for each project, but also to answer typical project management questions:

- *"What do we need to do?"*
- *"What is the minimum set of activities that we must perform?"*

Posing your SDL determining questions in a straightforward and easily understandable way will build trust between security and project teams. Ultimately, trust is key to building secure software, just as much as training in secure coding and rigorous security testing. Security must be considered from the beginning of the lifecycle in order to be factored into the design. Code must be written to minimize vulnerabilities and protect attack surfaces. The program's functionality and lack of vulnerabilities must be proven by a thorough series of tests: architect, design, code, test.

Secure software must:

- *Be free from errors that can be maliciously manipulated—ergo, be free of vulnerabilities*
- *Include the security features that customers [stakeholders] require for their intended use cases*
- *Be self-protective—software must resist the types of attacks that will be promulgated against the software*
- *"Fail well," that is, fail in such a manner as to minimize the consequences of a successful attack*
- *Install with sensible, "closed" defaults*

Failure to meet each of these imperatives is a failure of the software to deliver its functionality, a failure to deliver the safety that should be implicit in a world beset by constant digital attack. There are two important and interlocking paths that must be attended to: building the correct features so the software can protect itself and the software's users, and removing the errors that inevitably creep into software as it's being built. Incorrect implementations (logical errors) must be caught and removed. Any vulnerabilities that are introduced must be discovered and eradicated.

The security development lifecycle is a relationship-based, real-world process through which teams deliver secure software. (Core Software Security, pp. 321–323)

Chapter 4

Secure Design through Threat Modeling

4.1 Threat Modeling Is Foundational

It has been common in security development lifecycles (SDLs) to provide multiple activities for secure design. Typically, each of these activities uses a different name and scope, and timing is explicitly stated: The first engagement will be an Architecture Risk Assessment. Where potential security risk has been uncovered during the review, an Architecture Review will be scheduled, eventually completing a Threat Model, and finishing secure design tasks with, perhaps, a Design Review. Different SDLs may name design activities differently and might break down into just three, or two activities, or there may be more than the four that I've listed. Therefore, significant SDL variation remains surrounding secure design activities.

In *Core Software Security: Security at the Source*,[*] we provided the above four activities, though we provided a set of conditions and triggers for practitioners to identify those activities that would be applicable to a particular set of changes, while also eliminating irrelevant activities. We called these the "The Seven Determining Questions" (Chapter 9: Applying the SDL Framework to the Real World, pp. 277–278 [Section 9.2.1]). Our activities were in line with the software security thinking at the time that we wrote the book.

Since publishing *Core Software Security*, we've revisited our assumptions; we believe that secure design process complexity can be significantly reduced through a clearer understanding about what we are trying to achieve. We have increased effectiveness since then through a simpler approach. As Brook wrote in *Secrets of a Cyber Security Architect*,[†]

> Attacks and their defenses are the value proposition that security architects bring to the design and implementation of software—that is, development, engineering, or research and development. Over the years, "threat modeling" has gone by various names:

---

[*] Ransome, J. and Misra, A. (2014). *Core Software Security: Security at the Source*. Boca Raton (FL): CRC Press/ Taylor & Francis Group.

[†] Schoenfield, B. S. E. (2019). *Secrets of a Cyber Security Architect*. Boca Raton (FL): Auerbach Publications/ Taylor & Francis Group, p. 177.

- Architecture risk assessment (ARA)
- Architecture review or security architecture review
- Security architecture assessment
- Security engineering
- [Secure] design review
- Secure design checkpoint
- Security requirements

And quite possibly, a few other terms that are, by now, lost in the mists of time.

Although practitioners are certainly free to disagree with our collapsing all the above terms into one analysis that in their processes seem quite distinct, I came to realize how threat modeling analysis actually underlies what may appear on the surface to be different analyses. Threat modeling is the method that practitioners must apply no matter at what point in development a security analysis is taking place, no matter whether completed or initial or inflight a project or effort may be.

For a couple of years, my duties as a Principal Engineer for software security at Intel® included sitting on Intel's software security review panel, SAFE (Security Architecture Forum). We reviewed projects from initial concept through the completion of the design. At Intel, there are several review stops for security; more or less the same body of people would engage across projects and at these different review points during development.

Of course, I was a full participant, attempting to apply my best understanding of security architecture to each project as it came before the SAFE board. At the same time, as I often do, I was a participant observer, considering what I heard during the interactions between development teams and board members, assessing the efficacy of our process (or not) as reviews proceeded. I found the experience of watching my peers—that is, other Principal Engineers—practice security architecture very enlightening, not only to refine my own craft, but also in stepping back from the content of the work to observe how we do what we do. The projects ranged across myriad and often vastly different architecture types, projects at every stage of development, using nearly every type of software development methodology (Waterfall, Agile, Extreme, etc.) SAFE would typically interact with two to four projects each week of the year. That's a lot of projects in any given month, quarter, or year to observe and from which to learn.

As I watched the SAFE review process unfold, it became crystal clear to me that no matter at what stage or in which review point we board members were with a project, in order to complete the review, we were all threat modeling in our heads, call the review what you will. This was quite a revelation.

What differed was the level at which the threat model analysis occurred.

For instance, during an official threat model review, we had to dig deep, to attempt to cover every credible attack via every reachable attack surface (exposure) and find reasonable, workable, implementable defenses that could be built by the team presenting their project.

However, if a project had just been initiated, the level of threat modeling was vastly different. All we needed was to think through a few gross possibilities in order to derive the very broad security requirements and to understand the risk posture that the effort would need in its usage and deployment context.

The architecture assessment phase in the Intel Security Development Lifecycle (SDL) is intended to identify those efforts that will require deeper security analysis, while at the same time passing those efforts whose security architecture needs will likely be (comparatively) minor. The threat model analysis for this review needs only to determine the credibility of a significantly impactful successful attack. One credible attack that might cause Intel's or the product's stakeholders significant harm is all that was required to flag the project for further engagement. The analysis technique is threat modeling, nevertheless. (*Secrets*, pp. 26–28)

In other words, and very important for matching Agile and DevOps SDLC methods, there is no reason to complicate matters with a series of individually named activities in order to achieve appropriately secure designs.

Instead of distinct activities, today, our practice emphasizes the primacy of threat modeling. To wit, threat models start at a very high level and are refined in detail and comprehensiveness, as conditions change. The triggers for defining, continuing, refining, and reviewing the threat model turn out to be deterministic. We will take those up below.

There was nothing wrong with the triggers and dependencies that we were using (effectively) at the time of *Core Software Security*. But since then, we have realized that each of the activities we had described as separate and distinct were, in fact, different levels of specificity and depth of threat modeling. Isn't it simpler and more direct to acknowledge that it is threat modeling that we are performing, rather than a series of what may seem, at first glance, to be several different activities? (Brook notes that even our most experienced SAFE board members would sometimes lose the difference between Architecture Risk Review, Architecture Review, and Threat Model. We often relied upon a process facilitator to bring us back on track.)

Simplifying to the essentials allows the threat model process to unfold as discreet engagements, at appropriate levels of analysis, and to integrate well with continuous software development practices. (Differentiating aspects of secure design activity doesn't integrate well—requiring developers to perform individually conceptualized architecture and design activities proves to be overly confusing. Developers then struggle with what the activity is supposed to produce and its value to their development).

Secure design is our goal, that is, building appropriate security and avoiding security design weaknesses. Threat modeling is the technique that we employ in order to ascertain what we must guard against (attacks). For secure design, a threat model's output will be the set of defenses that will achieve a system's (or set of changes, or organization's) desired security posture.

What is meant by "secure design" and why must that be a key objective?

- It's much harder to defend poorly designed software.
- With all due respect to commercial defense vendors, the products are software, which must be inherently flawed.
- Defenses generally do a thing reasonably, but imperfectly. They're no panacea, despite what vendors may claim in their marketing.
- To remain defendable, we must try to avoid known weaknesses that attackers may use to walk right through our well-laid defenses.

A Real-Life Example:

Imagine a business customer recognition system whose identifier is made up of calculated values based in a fairly straightforward algorithm from data that are ordered and, thus, guessable. Imagine that the identifier is then used throughout a complex system to separate processing and data flows between customers. The customer is responsible for protecting the value that is assigned by the system owner. We're not making this up.

If an attacker can discover (or steal) a relatively small population of identifiers, they will, with today's tools, fairly quickly reverse engineer the construction of the value, which then means that attackers now have significant leverage, not only to get into the system but also to correlate processing flows, that is, data for each customer. That's bad! The potential for negative impact increases where customer data are more critical or sensitive.

A long period of apparent failure by attackers to misuse this weakness might mean that the system owner has been lucky. Luck! = Security. Or attackers simply haven't been discovered or have hidden their compromise well. We've seen attacks that haven't been discovered for many years.

This example is a design weakness. This is what secure design practice based in threat modeling is trying to prevent from getting into releases, from being deployed into service. There are alternate design choices that would make it much harder to gain this leverage and that would be far easier to defend. In addition, a stronger design becomes much more resilient to successful compromise of any particular customer or any portion of the system. A desirable trait of a defensible system is that even sophisticated, targeted compromises can be contained and damage held to a minimum, thereby ensuring survival from an attack.

4.2 Secure Design Primer

As explained in *Secrets of a Cyber Security Architect*:

> We know with fair certainty that credentials (secrets) that are placed in the binary executable of software are relatively easy to uncover, given today's reverse engineering tools. For commercial software whose distribution involves execution within third-party environments—say, commercial off-the-shelf (COTS) software that is run by the purchaser—distributing a secret tucked away in the static data of an executable has proven to be a very poor design choice.
>
> Secrets placed into executable data areas are routinely discovered by both attackers and researchers. Once held by an attacker (whether through discovery or published research), the attacker then has the ability to wield the secret successfully against whatever challenge it was meant to protect. If there are 10,000 copies of that executable in use, attackers can undo at least one aspect of the security for all 10,000 of those installations. Unfortunately, this design mistake happens far too often, with the resulting consequences.
>
> How do our secure software principles apply? If programmers have coded the credential into the binary with correct language semantics (easily coded—for most languages, this is just a declaration), then there is no "implementation error." This is a design error. It's a failure to have the security features that stakeholders expect—that is, credentials have sufficiently been protected.
>
> Furthermore, attempting to "hide" a secret as static data in an executable isn't self-protective. Quite the reverse, given the binary exploration and execution analysis tools that exist today.
>
> Often this design miss assumes that the credential is "safe enough," so the use of the credential (which is legal) and the actions taken after the challenge has been passed will not be monitored; there is no failure—the credential is working as expected, but in the hands of adversaries. So, the "fail well/fail closed" principle doesn't really apply. It would depend upon the installation and configuration sequences of the software as to whether the placement of the credential in the binary is a "sensible, closed default."
>
> I hope that the preceding trivial example demonstrates how the software security principles are meant to provide appropriate targets for deriving a secure architecture. The design patterns that will achieve these results require quite a bit more detail, which then must be applied in context.
>
> A high-level set of secure design patterns and their application can be found in IEEE Center for Secure Design's "Avoiding the Top 10 Software Security Design Flaws."[*] This booklet is free, under The Creative Commons license. (Disclosure: I'm one of the co-authors.[†]) The design patterns discussed in the booklet are:

---

[*] IEEE, 2014.

[†] Iván Arce, Kathleen Clark-Fisher, Neil Daswani, Jim DelGrosso, Danny Dhillon, Christoph Kern, Tadayoshi Kohno, Carl Landwehr, Gary McGraw, Brook Schoenfield, Margo Seltzer, Diomidis Spinellis, Izar Tarandach, and Jacob West.

- Earn or give, but never assume, trust.
- Use an authentication mechanism that cannot be bypassed or tampered with.
- Authorize after you authenticate.
- Strictly separate data and control instructions, and never process control instructions received from untrusted sources.
- Define an approach that ensures all data are explicitly validated.
- Use cryptography correctly.
- Identify sensitive data and how they should be handled.
- Always consider the users.
- Understand how integrating external components changes your attack surface.
- Be flexible when considering future changes to objects and actors.

Each of the design patterns explained in the booklet is meant to fulfill one or more of the software security principles listed above. First, we define how we intend secure software to behave (secure software principles) and then set out the means through which those aims are to be achieved (secure design patterns). With software security principles and design patterns, we know what we are to build when we wish to build "secure software." (*Secrets*, pp. 30–31)

Threat modeling helps us avoid design weaknesses. For instance, if software can be subjected to reverse engineering techniques, and most released software can be, then placing a secret into the static data of a program provides poor, if any, protection for the secret. Reverse engineering tools continuously gain sophistication and ease. As of this writing, it's become relatively trivial to find secrets in the data portions of programs. There are better ways to create and then protect a secret, such as a credential, than sticking the secret into the code's data area, which can then be fairly trivially found with today's tool set. After discovery, since it's the same secret for every run and instance of the software, attackers then have the key to whatever that secret was supposed to protect, in every running instance of the software. Threat modeling is our state-of-the-art analysis for finding potential issues and weaknesses and then designing something better.

Hence, the authors have abandoned a series of secure design activities and replaced these with threat modeling at successively specific levels. We begin the threat model at a very high level: What are the typical, successful attacks against systems of this nature, and what are those attackers' ultimate objectives? We answer the questions:

- Who might attack this software?
- How have attackers been successful in the past against systems/software of this type and against similar technologies?
- If successful, what will attackers achieve?
- How will a compromise hurt the system and its stakeholders?
- What can we do to thwart these expected attacks—that is, prevent, make more difficult, mitigate effects, and discover attacks in process (ergo, defenses)?

The beginning analysis doesn't have to be detailed. At this early and very high-level stage, every attack doesn't have to be thoroughly understood. A single example that leads to understanding the sorts of defenses that are likely to be necessary is sufficient. We are analyzing for general guideposts and directions. Specifics come later. The threat model will be refined.

As the structures that will meet system objectives get defined, we revisit the threat model in light of the structural (architectural) considerations. Architecture needn't yet be fully determined.

- Which architectures provide appropriate security?
- Are there needed defenses that will be structural? Which defenses will be consumed or inherited?

As we architect, we figure out what security structures will need to be built and/or included. Security architecture proceeds as an integral part of the creation of the entire architecture; security architects are key members of the architectural team.

When security architecture is treated as some discreet, separated process, it becomes ill-timed and out of joint with the unfolding architecture. This leads to effects such as attempting to provide security structure after all architecture decisions have already been made, maybe after integrations and coding have begun. At that point, the security features of the system that haven't been considered yet will likely not be fully integrated into the already-completed architecture, that is, they will be "bolted on" rather than "built in." Another typical effect will be rework, as assumptions made without security consideration may then need to be rethought, work in process will contain weaknesses that cannot be tolerated, etc.

Instead, we have seen great success through treating security as one of the necessities of the entire planning and architectural process, not a special, point-in-time, add-on process. Jettisoning a set of discrete activities in favor of treating threat modeling and its associated attack and defense knowledge as a key input throughout the formulation of new software and change plans means that security is taken as a part of what must be considered.

That doesn't mean that security always wins, that is, trumps other necessities. There are always trade-offs, security and otherwise. Decisions will need to be made, hopefully based upon reasonable risk analysis. (A deeper treatment of risk methods can be found in Chapter 4 in *Securing Systems: Applied Security Architecture and Threat Models.*[*]) At our current state of the art, the best that one may reach for will be to supply decision makers with sound risk advice from which they may make appropriate decisions about security versus other business and technological demands.

At some point, people have to actually build the architecture, whether that is through integration of existing or new systems and/or coding. This is true whether the coding process runs alongside of and in parallel to architecture or if these are treated as separate "phases," that is, the system must be implemented through whatever software development life cycle (SDLC) methodology (if any) is used.

As major architectural decisions get made, system structures become relatively well defined. In parallel, and, hopefully, as an integral part of the structuring and planning process, we refine and revise the accompanying threat model. We refine in order to understand the steps that a successful compromise will have to complete, thus informing how we will defend against each step in the set of likely attacks.

As structure understanding unfolds, the attack scenarios (often called "threats") become far more specific, drawing upon our knowledge of attacks and such resources as MITRE's ATT&CK® and Common Attack Pattern Enumeration and Classification (CAPEC™). (More information on how these resources can be used as a catalog of attack types can be found in Chapter 5: Learning the Trade and, specifically, Section 5.1 Attack Knowledge, in *Secrets of a Cyber Security Architect* [pp. 116–123].)

We don't have to invent new attacks. But we do assume that even though typical weaknesses and vulnerabilities may not exist presently, they will show up at some point in the future. This is a very key part of a threat model analysis that may seem, at the outset, somewhat counterintuitive? Why are we worrying about issues that haven't yet occurred?

We build defenses against both the known and the expected. This is perhaps one of the most misunderstood points in threat modeling—the anticipation of future weaknesses based upon past discoveries of similar issues. Certain types of security weaknesses occur regularly in their associated technologies. For example, Cross-Site Scripting (XSS) errors are legion in Web applications irrespective of the underlying language in which the application has been written. And vulnerable memory conditions continue to be released in C/C++ (and other memory handling languages) despite the best efforts to eliminate these.

---

[*] Schoenfield, B. S. E. (2015). *Securing Systems: Applied Security Architecture and Threat Models.* Boca Raton (FL): CRC Press/Taylor & Francis Group.

Thus, it isn't a big stretch to mitigate tomorrow's XSS or C buffer overflow today. There are lots of recurring types of issues. We don't have to look far and wide. In fact, there are several public resources devoted to capturing these:

- MITRE's ATT&CK collection of attack techniques
- MITRE's CAPEC database of software security issues
- The Common Weakness Enumeration (CWE)

Although each of the above collections was not designed or organized with threat modeling in mind, still, below (as well as in *Secrets of a Cyber Security Architect*, Section 5.1, beginning on p. 116), we point to ways that these resources can be used to identify a relevant set of attack techniques.

> A security architect must assume that at least one vulnerability of the sort that commonly occur in any particular language, execution environment, and operating system will fail to be identified through testing. Each class of vulnerabilities can be exploited with one or more known sets of exploit techniques.
>
> Although new attack techniques do arise and will have to be understood and then defended, variations on a known technique usually don't require new defense techniques. By understanding exploitation techniques and their system objectives, a defense can be built to stop or at least delay exploitation of potential weakness types that typically appear in particular systems and collections/integrations of systems (as in an enterprise's collection of systems). The mental trick is to assume that typical weaknesses known to have appeared in the past will appear in the future. That is, all software has bugs. (*Secrets*, p. 56)

Simply put, software must be expected to contain errors, if not discovered or present now, then as changes are made. Current errors as yet unknown will eventually be discovered, and new errors will eventually be created (especially of the types that repeatedly occur in the technologies employed). Some errors will offer leverage to attackers of one kind or another and, therefore, will have security consequences.

> *Our ability to develop complex software vastly exceeds our ability to prove its correctness or test it satisfactorily within reasonable fiscal constraints . . . complex software is difficult to write and to test, and will therefore contain numerous unintentional 'bugs'[.] It would be extremely difficult and expensive to determine with certainty that a piece of software is free of bugs[.] Given the relatively small amounts of funding allocated for developing and testing . . . software, we may safely consider it as effectively impossible.[*]*

> Still, it remains that software has vulnerabilities, and will continue to have for the foreseeable future. The plain truth of it is, human endeavor is filled with errors, and software creation and implementation are a human endeavor. Whether the vulnerabilities are caused through poor design choices or through implementation, there will be errors even after the most robust security development lifecycle (SDL, or secure software development life cycle, S-SDLC), with equally rigorous validation. "To err is human . . . ," as Alexander Pope so famously wrote.[†] (*Secrets*, p. 56)

---

[*]   Rivest, R. L. and Wack, J. P. (n.d.). "On the Notion of 'Software-Independence' in Voting Systems." Cambridge (MA): Computer Science and Artificial Intelligence Laboratory Massachusetts Institute of Technology (MIT), pp. 3–4. Retrieved from https://people.csail.mit.edu/rivest/RivestWack-OnTheNotionOfSoftware IndependenceInVotingSystems.pdf

[†]   Pope, A. and Johnson, S. (1836). *The Poetical Works of Alexander Pope, Esq., to which is prefixed A Life of the Author,* Vol. 1. Bristol: J. Gladding & Co., p. 89.

. . .

Furthermore, an analyst also applies relevant past exploit/vulnerability pairs even if such vulnerabilities have not yet been found in the system. It's important to understand that even the most rigorous testing, as Edsger Dijkstra so famously quipped, "proves the system has bugs, not that it doesn't."* If there have existed exploitable vulnerabilities in any component within the system under analysis, even though fixed in the versions included, then the analysis must assume that at least some similar issues will likely be found in those components at some point in the future. (*Secrets*, p. 75)

Since errors are unavoidable, security demands that we plan for them. But how to plan for the currently unknown? It turns out that certain types of security effects are routinely found in particular technologies.

For instance, as we noted previously, the C/C++ programming languages must directly handle program (sometimes system) memory. Therefore, we can expect memory errors to occur. When C/C++ is used, we must assume that, eventually, there will be memory errors that offer attacker leverage. Even some of the most robust and mature SDL programs still suffer the occasional release of software containing a C/C++ memory condition that allows security effects.

For another example, although not particularly common, every virtual runtime environment has suffered a vulnerability that has allowed code in the guest (virtualized environment) to escape the guest and run in the host environment. Doing so breaches the protections that are expected of virtual environments. When an attacker can supply the code that will escape the guest to be run in the virtual environment's host runtime, the attacker's code then runs with the higher privileges required by the hosting environment. That is bad. It usually spells complete compromise of all the virtual environments that the host supported.

Despite virtual environment coders' best efforts, guest escapes, while not common, have occurred. It is wise to assume that even though there may be no known guest escapes currently present, eventually, at some point in the future, there will be one in whatever virtual environment has been chosen. In the threat model, we can then think through how a guest escape might be contained, if and when such an issue appears. Perhaps we have the host run with limited privileges such that the guest escape doesn't allow complete compromise but, rather, is tightly limited in what the attacker may gain.

Threat modeling analysis requires that we consider future issues, even those that don't commonly occur, such as guest escapes. There are defensive actions that can be deployed to limit the impact of a guest escape. Running the virtual environment at low and constrained privilege levels means that even in the event of a successful guest escape, the damage can be contained to a single virtual host or host type.

Of course, it is possible that the stakeholders of the software will choose to take the risk that a new guest escape vulnerability won't occur in the immediate future, since these are not particularly common errors. These should be risk-based decisions. Arriving at a realistic risk rating for the various types of weaknesses and attacks is one of the key outputs from threat modeling.

C programming language memory errors are common; it would be foolish to assume that these cannot emerge. Experience demonstrates that such errors leak through even the most rigorous SDL regimes, though their frequency in releases will certainly be significantly reduced. Threat modeling must take into account the probable future occurrence of such issues as well as the SDL steps that have been taken to reduce their occurrence. Both of these would be factored into a risk rating. On the other

---

* Dijkstra, E. (1969, October). NATO Science Committee. Software Engineering Techniques. Report on a Conference Sponsored by the NATO Science Committee, p. 16. Rome, Italy. Retrieved from http://homepages .cs.nci.ac.uk/brian. randell/NATO/nato 1969.pdf

hand, guest escapes are fairly rare, by comparison, which must also be taken into consideration. Which would you address immediately?

Either a memory error or a guest escape can lead to full compromise of the system, the operating environment, the runtime, or even entire classes of systems and networks (depending upon what further compromises the adversary has successfully managed to execute), so the ultimate security effects may end up being critically important from either condition that we've been considering. Analysis of these three angles (and more) must be part of a threat model.

After enumerating the types of weaknesses that have occurred in the technologies in use, consider:

- What has been the observed recurrence rate of each issue as reported in the public announcements and databases (e.g., National Vulnerability Database—NVD)?
- What SDL activities (if any) are employed in this case to catch and/or prevent each issue?
- When each issue has been successfully exploited, what are the potential gains for the attacker and potential damages to system stakeholders?

As Brook stated in *Secrets:*

In practice, when practitioners are performing an Architectural Risk Analysis (ARA) or an initial or final Security Review (SR) in their heads, the reviewers will be threat modeling as a part of the analysis:

- Who's going to attack this system?
- To achieve what purposes?
- With what techniques?
- Through what vectors?
- Exercising what potential conditions?
- Causing what harm? (p. 71)

Let's do away with complex SDL design-time activities. We hope that you can see that underlying all of these differently named activities, practitioners are threat modeling at varying levels of specificity and detail. As development proceeds, we repeatedly revise the threat model based upon current knowledge, whether the knowledge is design-time structural understanding, lessons gained through attempting to implement (coding), knowledge gained through verification, and any observable changes to the threat "landscape," ergo new, relevant attack techniques. The threat model is a living document that reflects whatever attack and defense comprehension has been attained at the time of threat model revision or review.

4.3 Analysis Technique

Hopefully, through the preceding section, you've been convinced that threat modeling is nothing more (nor less) than considering attacks and their best defensive measures? Conceptually, threat modeling isn't particularly obscure.

In fact, threat modeling analysis can be reduced to the following simple steps:

- "Apply known, successful attacks in system's technologies
- To points on a system that attackers might reach
- Rate the potential (negative) impacts
- Rate the risk for each attack scenario

- Identify appropriate defenses
  - (sometimes, support implementation of defenses)"*

Brook has had 1000s of attendees in his threat modeling classes. Most participants quickly grasp the above steps. Classes often begin with a nontechnical example: home delivery of restaurant food when the deliverer takes payment. For most people, it isn't hard to identify who and what is at risk and how an attack might be carried out.

Threat model subtleties lie in each of the above steps:

- What is the set of relevant attacks that have some likelihood of being attempted?
- Given that set of attacks, where can attackers begin, and how?
- What are the likely impacts from successful compromise? The valuations of impact are a key input to risk rating.
- Which defenses will mitigate the attack scenarios that are deemed too risky to tolerate?

The major problem is that each of these questions has dependencies, each question's definitive answers are related to the answers of the others! For instance, whereas there may be a set of attacks that can be determined, what exposed opportunities a system allows to attackers, and particularly, which of those exposures offer relatively easier access will influence which attacks are going to be the most likely, at least in the short term. The set of relevant attacks will be partially determined by those points in the system that attackers can more easily get at. Usually, these are system inputs of one kind or another. Places on a system exposed to larger populations generally have higher potential for exploitation than those exposed to smaller ones. The more people who have access, the more likely that one of them will try to attack an interface. Obviously, the Internet, with several billion people is much more exposed than a home computer not connected to any networks.

Points at which attacks can be initiated are called "attack surfaces." One of the key steps in a threat model will be to enumerate the attack surfaces offered by a system. Attack surfaces typically map to system inputs—places where the system accepts data, any data. The amount, if any, of potential attacker control over data is one of the dimensions that will be considered to answer the second question above: "[W]here can attackers begin, and how?"

If the system can somehow establish some assurances that data received are not likely to be under attacker control, then the data might be considered as "trusted." If less or not assured, then data is "tainted," that is, potentially containing malicious exploitation attempts. Assurances must be designed into the system; establishing assurance might be one of the outputs of the threat model, one of the security requirements that will be built into the system.

The type of input (network connection, user interface, command line, programmatic data interchange) helps to define which attacks out of the range of all that are possible, can proceed through that type of input. All attacks cannot be leveraged through every input. Some attack types are eliminated based upon the allowances and limitations of each particular type of input. Other attacks are made much easier and, thus, more likely. There is a set of dependencies and interactions between attack type, input type, and weakness: These are related, sometimes tightly coupled.

Likewise, different exploitations produce different effects. The constellation of attack manipulation type, attack surface (which is partly determined by architecture), and type of asset compromise or breach determine the impact from that type of attack in the target system. We often hear sophisticated,

---

* Schoenfield, B. S. E. "An Introduction to Threat Modeling," Secure Design and Secure System Architecture Webinar Series, Part 1, July 23, 2019. Retrieved from https://acton.ioactive.com/acton/fs/blocks/showLandingPage /a/34793/p/p0054/t/page/fm/0?utm_term=Access%20Part%201&utm_campaign=IOActive%20Webinars%20 and%20Videos&utm_content=landing+page&utm_source=Act-On+Software&utm_medium=landing+page &cm_mmc=Act-On%20Software-_-Landing%20Page-_-IOActive%20Webinars%20and%20Videos-_-)

ethical hackers proclaim that nearly every attack will eventually lead to full compromise of nearly every asset. They are performing the mental arithmetic that strings together many of the attacks that are cataloged in MITRE's ATT&CK collection. ATT&CK shows the techniques used by many examples of publicly reported, successful attacks. And indeed, given the correct set of system opportunities, weaknesses, and attacker sophistication, almost any leverage, coupled to many others, will lead to full compromise.

But, and this is key to building a realistic threat model, every attacker opportunity may not line up advantageously. An information disclosure of technical details about a system may lead solely to information that's valuable to the attacker. It may be very difficult to misuse the information due to a lack of additional opportunities, the presence of defenses raising exploitation cost beyond that which the attacker is willing to afford, etc. Assessing attacker effort to gain a next step toward the attacker's goal(s) is a core part of what one does during a threat model: How realistic is it that the presence of a technical information disclosure can lead to worse impacts? What else does the attacker need in order to proceed? Is the exploitation of these available in this system? How much work is the exploitation compared to less well-defended systems, and so forth?

In Brook's threat modeling classes, he presents the touchstones that every threat model must assess, as presented in Figure 4.1.

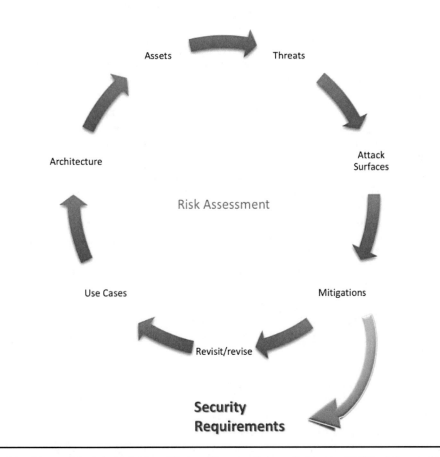

Figure 4.1 Threat Model Activities Circle. (*Source:* Schoenfield, B. [2017]. "Threat Modeling Demystified." RSA Conference, p. 9. Retrieved from https://published-prd.lanyonevents.com/published /rsaus17/sessionsFiles/4957/LAB3-W04_LAB3-W04_Threat-Modeling-Demystified.pdf)

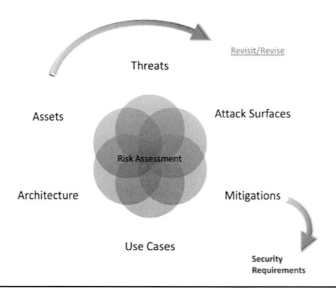

Figure 4.2   Interdependent Threat Model Activity Circle. (*Source*: Schoenfield, B. [2017]. "Threat Modeling Demystified." RSA Conference 2017, Slide 38. Retrieved from https://published-prd .lanyonevents.com/published/rsaus17/sessionsFiles/4422/LAB3-W04_Schoenfield.pptx)

Figure 4.1 is the result of a conversation (over enchiladas and beer) with David Wheeler (co-author of *The IoT Architect's Guide to Attainable Security and Privacy* (Auerbach Publications, 2019) and Principal Engineer, Intel, Inc.). Dave reminded Brook that there is a set of analysis assessments, each from a slightly different perspective, that every threat model must perform. However, the order of assessment isn't significant in any way. Security Architect Sung Lee (Intel, Inc.) then drafted the first version of the threat model activity circle for the Intel threat modeling classes that eventually gave rise to Brook's Participatory Threat Modeling class syllabus.

After reflection, Brook realized that not only must all assessment points be touched, but they are also highly interdependent and interacting. Thus, we see in Figure 4.2 that each activity depends upon the others for correctness and thoroughness. This is the nonlinear, fractal character of threat model analysis that we have mentioned previously. No matter where one starts on the circle, one will have to touch other areas in order to fully understand which assets are more likely to be attacked, and through which attack surfaces. Use cases help to determine how attackers might proceed. They will use their available capabilities—"Threats" upon the weaknesses in the "Architecture." The analysis must lead to those mitigations that prevent, or make too difficult, use of the threats.

For example, Figure 4.3 illustrates how an analysis that begins from architecture (structures and components) then proceeds through other views of the system to arrive at the appropriate mitigations. It should be noticed that risk assessment is assumed in the flow. That is, in order to derive the right set of defenses, risk must be graded for every attack scenario that is deemed to be credible (have some likelihood of success). After attack scenarios are developed, each must be rated for risk. We will come back to that problem below. We wanted to keep the number of arrows in Figure 4.3 visually sparse. In reality, during analysis, as new information is uncovered, one may bounce back and forth repeatedly between viewpoints.

In Figure 4.3, the analysis begins with understanding the structure of the system under analysis (target system). Starting at architecture is the flow map mapping suggested by Brook's ATASM threat modeling approach, as proposed in *Securing Systems*. For many practitioners, the first place to start an analysis is by understanding the overall function of the system, its purpose(s), each major technology employed divided up into logical or functional components (the structure of the system), what the data

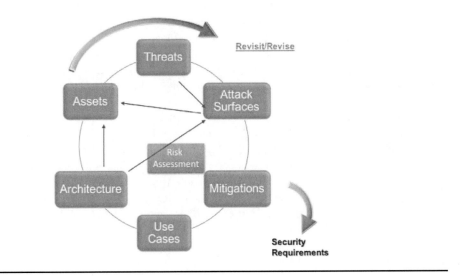

Figure 4.3   Threat Model Activity Flow.

are and how important to protect (sensitivity), and how data moves between components and with other entities, be these human or digital. That is, "architecture."

An architectural analysis will uncover assets. Figure 4.3 has an arrow from Architecture to Assets. Assets are of interest when they have value to system stakeholders. We must also identify the assets that are targets of attack. These two sets are intersecting but may not be entirely coherent. For instance, botnet attackers are interested in hosts and operating systems. In horizontally scaled systems, hosts may seem insignificant to many stakeholders. Brook has encountered exactly this disconnect many times when reviewing systems with development teams.

An architecture analysis will also reveal those points on the system through which attackers may proceed—the "Attack Surfaces." Figure 4.3 also has an arrow from Architecture to Attack Surfaces to indicate that when one starts with Architecture, one will then cross into attack surface enumeration.

Each attack surface will offer attackers a collection of potential exploitation possibilities unique to that surface. Every attack cannot work on every attack surface and its associated data flows (usually inputs, but outbound may also need to be considered). Figure 4.3 diagrams an arrow from Threats to Attack Surface, indicating that attackers apply threats at points that can accept these and are sufficiently available (exposed) to attack. As we consider attack surfaces, the various potential threats are "applied," that is, thought through for possibility, potential success, and attacker activity level (which leads to likelihood, a key component of risk rating). We take up threat research and libraries in further detail below.

Of course, attackers' objectives may include Assets, so there is an arrow in Figure 4.3 completing this part of the analysis, from Attack Surface to Assets.

Ultimately, though this is not diagrammed in Figure 4.3, the above analysis will lead to Mitigations through Risk Assessment. We cannot divine the right set of mitigations without first ranking attack scenarios for both likelihood (probability) and impact. Generally speaking, organizations can't afford every possible defense. Instead, we reach for that "desired defensive state" from the definition of threat modeling (given previously). Hence, risk assessment is critical to identifying those attacks that are worth defending, as well as the priorities of building defenses: Which must be in the system as soon as humanly possible, and which may wait, and for how long?

Figure 4.3 diagrams an ATASM flow. But one must not be pedantic about starting or the analysis flow order. Brook's colleague at Intel, Inc., Sung Lee, who is an expert threat modeler and helped refine some of the early versions of the participatory threat modeling class, prefers to begin from use cases. Other practitioners like to begin at assets since these will be among attackers' most sought-after objectives.

Many practitioners prefer to begin with a set of relevant threats. In fact, the famous and oft-used Microsoft® method, STRIDE (Spoofing, Tampering, Repudiation, Information disclosure, Denial of service, Elevation of privileges), is a compact set of potential threats from which to start. STRIDE is particularly useful for those without deep experience in attack types, as STRIDE provides an easy-to-understand framework from which to begin to identify relevant threats. Or, as author and world-renowned threat modeling teacher, Adam Shostack, so pithily puts it, "What can go wrong?" Starting with Threats begins the threat model with "What can go wrong?" From Threats, the analysis then proceeds to apply each "go wrong" to its associated Attack Surface(s), which, of course, then leads one to consider the Architecture and the Assets, and probably also Use Cases that allow the Threat to proceed or gain access. As we noted in Figure 4.2, each analysis perspective of the target system provides yet more depth and refinement for the analyst to reach for that set of defenses (Mitigations) that will bring the system to its "desired defensive state."

In *Securing Systems*, Brook attempted to visually show the recursive nature of threat modeling through Figure 4.4 (formerly Part II-Figure 1).

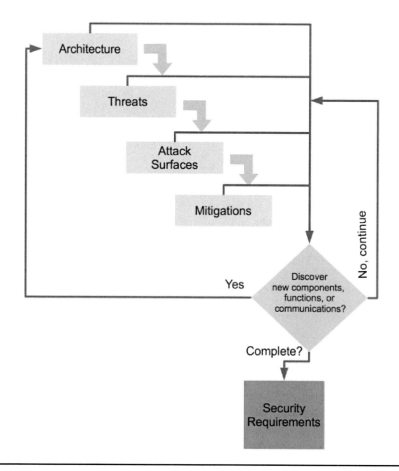

Figure 4.4   Recursion While Threat Modeling. (Source: Modified from Schoenfield, B. S. E. [2015]. *Securing Systems: Applied Security Architecture and Threat Models.* Boca Raton [FL]: CRC Press/ Taylor & Francis Group, p. 188, with permission.)

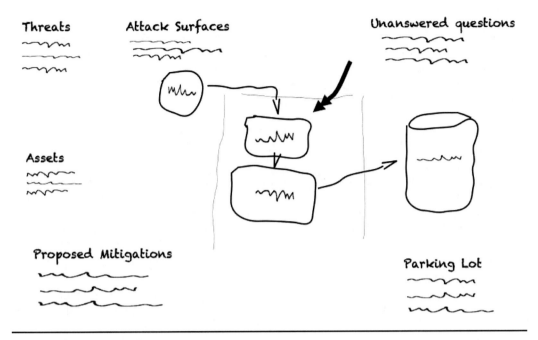

Figure 4.5   Threat Model Notes Example.

Gary McGraw, PhD (author, researcher), puts the problem even more succinctly: "[T]hreat modeling is fractal." Our experience from 1000s of threat models confirms that though we'd like to impose an order to threat modeling analysis, if for no other reasons than to explain and teach it easily, actual threat model analysis resists strict, linear order. In the foregoing discussion, we've attempted to provide a more realistic picture for readers. We find that it helps (tremendously) to keep really good notes as one goes along.

Perhaps Figure 4.5, demonstrating how we prefer to document our threat models as we proceed, will offer a ray of hope to provide some order to this potentially chaotic and notoriously difficult-to-wrangle process?

We keep a running account of what has been discovered and our assumptions in each area. Nothing is considered final until we believe that we have developed a comprehensive list of attack scenarios that can lead us towards the "right" set of defenses and mitigation strategies. The Unanswered Questions list always indicates that we have more to investigate but may not have sufficient information at the point at which the question has been posed.

When the threat model has been completed as far as it can be (which depends upon the level of detail known at the time of analysis), the Unanswered Questions list should be empty. Even so, oftentimes there are areas that should be explored that have implications for our underlying assumptions. These areas are queued for background research in the Parking Lot. Parking Lot items are topics that we hold some doubts about regarding our knowledge or grasp; due diligence demands more assurance.

4.3.1 Before the Threat Model

Threat modeling normally requires considerable contextual and background knowledge, as the following example may show.

At one of the organizations at which the authors worked together, Cross-Site Scripting (XSS) errors were sometimes reported in the administrative interfaces of that company's products. XSS errors continue as one of the banes of Web development. It remains difficult for Web programmers to avoid, unless they are fairly security conscious or they have a sufficient level of support to avoid allowing XSS in their code, especially input code. XSS is a pretty big problem, sadly, having been on the OWASP Top 10 Vulnerabilities* list for as long as it has existed.

XSS allows an attacker to vector their attacks through a Web application to the users through outputs of the server. The Web application itself is not the target. Its users, or perhaps other downstream automation are the victims of successful XSS. If an organization cares about its users, it probably should invest in avoiding XSS in its Web code.

But, as nasty as XSS is, the effects may be contextually irrelevant, which brings us back to an XSS in an administrative portal.

A very worrisome problem exists if an attacker can set up or promulgate the XSS remotely, without authentication. The effects of XSS often include reading the victim's browser cache of cookies and other server-related data, which means that authentication tokens can be stolen (among lots of other potentially damaging data), which then can be used to access the administration functions. That's bad; there can be no doubt about it.

On the other hand, if the XSS can only be leveraged *after* authentication, in the event of a successful XSS exploitation, the administrative portal must already be completely compromised, at least to the privileges allowed to that user. Although the attacker might also wish to leverage the XSS to gather any sensitive or other useful information from the administrator's browser cache, from the perspective of the portal's owners, they have far worse problems having lost an administrative login to an attacker. The loss of the account will most likely be the more important attack, not a subsequent XSS exploitation. In this case, the XSS isn't the most dangerous piece of the attack puzzle.

We aren't suggesting that the XSS shouldn't be fixed; one mustn't leave any easily remedied attacker leverage lying about.† The second situation described in our example, however, is less dangerous to the owner of the administrative software, as the precondition of exploitation is loss of sensitive privileges. In addition, if sufficient protections of administrative privileges have been put into place and are believed to be functioning as designed, the XSS isn't an immediate concern. The foregoing is the sort of risk-based analysis that threat modeling must include.

4.3.2 Pre-Analysis Knowledge

Just as a good cook pulls out all the ingredients from the cupboards and arranges them for ready access, so the experienced assessor has at her fingertips information that must feed into the assessment. In Figure 4.6 [formerly Figure 2.2], you will see the set of knowledge domains that feed into an architecture analysis. Underlying the analysis set are two other domains that are discussed, separately, in subsequent chapters: system architecture and, specifically, security architecture and information security risk. Each of these requires its own explanation and examples. Hence, we take these up below.

The first two domains from the left in Figure 4.6 are strategic: threats and risk posture (or tolerance). These not only feed the analysis, they help to set the direction and high-level requirements very early in the development lifecycle. For a fuller discussion on early engagement, please see Chapter 9, "The SDL in the Real World," in *Core Software Security*. The next two

---

* "OWASP Top Ten." "The OWASP Top 10 Project." The OWASP® Foundation. Available at https://owasp.org/www-project-top-ten/

† The organization for whom we worked, of course, fixed any reported administrative Cross-Site Scripting (XSS) errors.

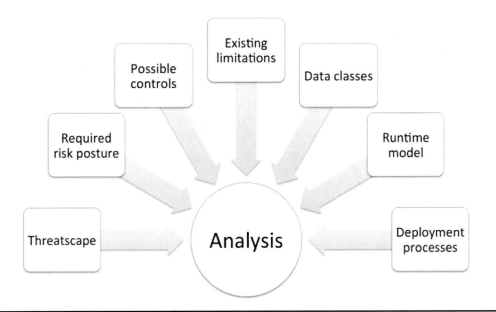

Figure 4.6   Knowledge Sets That Feed a Security Analysis. (Source: Reprinted from Schoenfield, B. S. E. [2015]. *Securing Systems: Applied Security Architecture and Threat Models*. Boca Raton [FL]: CRC Press/Taylor & Francis Group, p. 33, with permission.)

domains, moving clockwise—possible controls and existing limitations—refer to any existing security infrastructure and its capabilities: what is possible and what is difficult or excluded. The last three domains—data sensitivity, runtime/execution environment, and expected deployment model—refer to the system under discussion.

Figure 4.7 [formerly Figure 2.3] places each contributing knowledge domain within the area for which it is most useful. If it helps you to remember, these are the "3 S's." Strategy, infrastructure and security structures, and specifications about the system help determine what is important: "Strategy, Structures, Specification." Indeed, very early in the lifecycle, perhaps

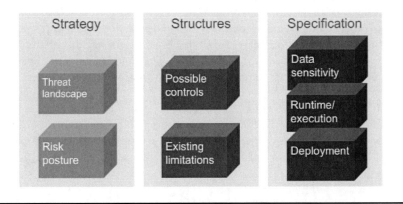

Figure 4.7   Strategy Knowledge, Structure Information, and System Specifics. (*Source*: Reprinted from Schoenfield, B. S. E. (2015). *Securing Systems: Applied Security Architecture and Threat Models*. Boca Raton [FL]: CRC Press/Taylor & Francis Group, p. 34, with permission).

as early as possible, the strategic understandings are critically important in order to deliver high-level requirements. Once the analysis begins, accuracy, relevance, and deliverability of the security requirements may be hampered if one does not know what security is possible, what exists, and what the limitations are. As I did in my first couple of reviews, it is easy to specify what cannot actually be accomplished. As an architecture begins to coalesce and become more solid, details such as data sensitivity, the runtime and/or execution environment, and under what deployment models the system will run become clearer. Each of these strongly influences what is necessary, which threats and attack methods become relevant, and which can be filtered out from consideration.

It should be noted that the process is not nearly as linear as I'm presenting it. The deployment model, for instance, may be known very early, even though it's a fairly specific piece of knowledge. The deployment model can highly influence whether security is inherited or must be placed into the hands of those who will deploy the system. As soon as this is known, the deployment model will engender some design imperatives and perhaps a set of specific controls. Without these specifics, the analyst is more or less shooting in the dark. (*Securing Systems*, pp. 34–35)

We find that the security researcher's mental path toward complete system compromise is based upon a set of assumptions about attack resources, privileges, and target weakness or vulnerability that may or may not be valid and should be considered for each attack vector. We have previously proposed that those attack scenarios that pass this "sniff test" for real-world validity be called "credible attack vectors" or CAV.[*] In threat modeling, it helps tremendously to focus on CAV and to filter out those attack scenarios that aren't all that likely, whose impact is negligible, and whose technical sophistication exceeds that value of the compromise to the attacker.

Through our examination of the process of threat modeling, we perhaps can arrive at a formal definition (as was stated in *Secrets*):

Threat modeling is a technique to identify the attacks a system must resist and the defenses that will bring the system to a desired defensive state.

"System" in the above definition should be taken inclusively to mean any organization, architecture, system, set of processes, whether manual or digital.

My definition highlights a few key points. First, threat modeling is not a design or an architecture, it is an analysis technique. Next, its purpose is identifying attacks and defenses.

Third, and this is key, the defenses bring the system to its "desired defensive state." That is, not to bring the system to an ivory tower security perfection (which, of course, doesn't actually exist in the real world, anyway).

In order to complete a threat model, one must first understand what defensive state a system's stakeholders expect the system to achieve. To put that in a different way, a priori to analyzing the attacks and specifying the defenses, the analyst must understand against what the system must defend and to what level—what is commonly termed its "security posture." (*Secrets*, pp. 73–74)

"A number of methods have been proposed to achieve the goals of threat modeling; some of these are more formal than others." Izar Tarandach and Matthew Coles, in *Threat Modeling: A Practical Guide for Development Teams*,[†] assess for their effectiveness several of the most well-known methods. We have no preference for any particular methodology or approach, having found that employing a

---

[*]   Schoenfield, B. S. E. (2015). *Securing Systems: Applied Security Architecture and Threat Models*. Boca Raton [FL]: CRC Press/Taylor & Francis Group, p. 105.

[†]   Tarandach, I. and Coles, M. J. (2021). *Threat Modeling: A Practical Guide for Development Teams*. Sebastopol (CA): O›Reilly Media, Inc.

method for ordering the analysis seems to help. Brook's ATASM formula provides a high-level mental structure for threat modeling. ATASM focuses on what must be done, rather than results or details. In that, ATASM is inclusive, in that many other methods will fit under the rubric of ATASM. For instance, STRIDE can provide a window into potential threats and has no tension as the threat identification method for ATASM. The next section defines and describes ATASM.

4.3.3 ATASM Process

In *Securing Systems*, Brook offered a mnemonic: ATASM, which stands for Architecture, Threats, Attack Surfaces, Mitigations. Figure 4.8: Architecture, Threats, Attack Surfaces, Mitigations illustrates ATASM as a linear flow, to show the tight relationship between each area of analysis. As we shall see through subsequent figures and discussions, the relationships are not particularly linear. Each area comprises a large area of discovery, research, and analysis. (Figure 4.9 breaks activities down in sub-steps.) Figure 4.8 shouldn't be taken literally so much as a simplified visual representation of a complex process.

ATASM is not really a method as much as a reminder to consider several different angles to achieve a more complete analysis. ATASM was invented as a pedagogical technique for helping people climb into the threat modeling process. It isn't meant to replace other methods but, rather, to simplify and augment the process. Each component of ATASM—Architecture, Threat, Attack Surface, and Mitigation—may be broken down into component steps, as was done in *Securing Systems* (pp. 133–134).

There is, perhaps, a nearly infinite breakdown of steps into ever finer gradation of activity. In our threat modeling classes, we have found that breaking down ATASM much further than Figure 4.9 provides little benefit. Most learners seem to fairly quickly grasp ATASM, once they are given example target systems with which to practice.

The following subheads in *Securing Systems*, Chapter 5, supply a very high-level set of steps that we hope provide the reader with what must be accomplished to deliver a reasonable threat model. We reiterate them as a collection of tasks that give some detail to ATASM:

Architecture and Artifacts
    Understand the Logical and Component Architecture of the System
    Understand Every Communication Flow and Any Valuable Data Wherever Stored
    Threat Enumeration
    List All the Possible Threat Agents for This Type of System
    List the Typical Attack Methods of the Threat Agents
    List the System-Level Objectives of Threat Agents Using Their Attack Methods
Attack Surfaces
    Decompose (factor) the Architecture to a Level That Exposes Every Possible Attack Surface
    Filter Out Threat Agents Who Have No Attack Surfaces Exposed to Their Typical Methods
    List All Existing Security Controls for Each Attack Surface
    Filter Out All Attack Surfaces for Which There Is Sufficient Existing Protection

Figure 4.8 Architecture, Threats, Attack Surfaces, Mitigations. (Source: Reprinted from Schoenfield, B. S. E. (2015). *Securing Systems: Applied Security Architecture and Threat Models*. Boca Raton [FL]: CRC Press/Taylor & Francis Group, p. 133, with permission).

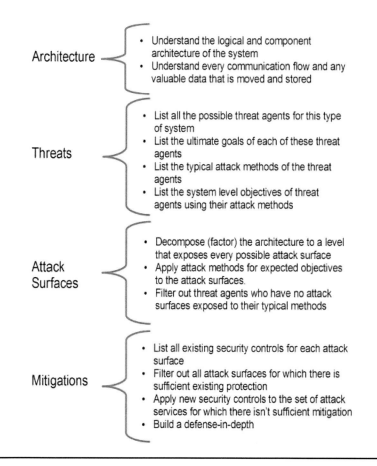

Architecture
- Understand the logical and component architecture of the system
- Understand every communication flow and any valuable data that is moved and stored

Threats
- List all the possible threat agents for this type of system
- List the ultimate goals of each of these threat agents
- List the typical attack methods of the threat agents
- List the system level objectives of threat agents using their attack methods

Attack Surfaces
- Decompose (factor) the architecture to a level that exposes every possible attack surface
- Apply attack methods for expected objectives to the attack surfaces.
- Filter out threat agents who have no attack surfaces exposed to their typical methods

Mitigations
- List all existing security controls for each attack surface
- Filter out all attack surfaces for which there is sufficient existing protection
- Apply new security controls to the set of attack services for which there isn't sufficient mitigation
- Build a defense-in-depth

Figure 4.9 ATASM procedure steps. (Source: Reprinted from Schoenfield, B. S. E. [2015]. *Securing Systems: Applied Security Architecture and Threat Models.* Boca Raton (FL): CRC Press/Taylor & Francis Group, p. 136, with permission).

Data Sensitivity
Risk Rating*
Possible Controls
   Apply New Security Controls to the Set of Attack Services for Which There Isn't Sufficient
      Mitigation
   Build a Defense-in-Depth" (*Securing Systems*, pp. 137–169)

In order to threat model, one must tease out background information—what Brook has termed "The Three S's" (*Securing Systems*, p. 135):

Strategy:
   Threat landscape
   Risk posture

---

* The original header from *Securing Systems* was "A Few Additional Thoughts on Risk." But we are not offering "additional" thoughts about risk in this book. Rather, in this book, we must explain risk-rating techniques, as these can be used when executing SDL activities. Because the subject matter has changed between the books, we've taken the liberty to change the header to more accurately reflect what we are presenting here.

Organizational
For the target system

Structures:

The set of security controls that are possible to implement for this system and organization
and at the current state of the art

All existing limitations designed, unintentional that will prevent controls from being used
with the target system

Specifications:

The technologies that will be and have been used to build the target system and any
underlying or foundational infrastructure

The highest data sensitivity for each data interchange both within the target system and
with other systems and for each point of storage, even if temporary or ephemeral

All runtime and execution environments including all operating systems used

Deployment and build chains, pipes, technologies and how these are administered and
maintained

As we will see, an architectural review will usually include much of the technical material required.
Still, depending upon how the software and operations organizations are put together, the analyst may
need to talk to different teams in order to uncover some information.

One needs a working knowledge of threat agents and their techniques as applied to the technologies
employed in the system under analysis (the target system). Sometimes, analysts specialize in particular
types of systems and thus have the right set of threats and active threat agents that typically attack those
systems that the analyst is experienced with. For instance, an analyst might work with a particular technology stack that supports public cloud–run Web applications. Another might specialize in firmware or
operating system kernel threats. If the analyst isn't familiar with the types of threats that will be levied
against the target system, research will be required.

As to organizational risk posture, we've only found one way to get a feel for the sorts of risks an
organization will take and those that are too much: The analyst has to canvas executives and other risk
decision makers about those risks that they may be willing to take (tolerate) and those that must be
mitigated to within tolerable levels. One of the first things that Brook does when taking a new role is
to take a look at the existing exceptions, if these have been documented. Exceptions are the data pool
describing what decision makers were willing to risk. Still, even with documented exceptions, we've
found no substitute for actually taking the risk pulse of those people who ultimately must make the
hard risk decisions: What's okay? And what is scary? What are the most important assets to protect,
including intangible assets like customers' goodwill, and brand protection?

Because security controls will actually have to be built, whether as a part of the software to be
fielded or in foundational infrastructure, it is key to understanding what security is available:

- Authentication systems
- Network architectures, restrictions, and protections
- Security monitoring capabilities, both technical and human
- Incident response teams and processes
- And more

Sometimes, an existing design precludes the usual controls. In that case, we will have to find alternatives. Or existing capabilities might be critical to the business and, thus, not interruptible. The system may be old, what we call "legacy." If so, then the design might have been made against a long-past
(hence, simpler) threat landscape, which would make the defenses weak for current needs. The analyst
must understand these limitations, or they might specify "ivory tower" solutions that cannot and will

not be implemented. A comprehensive threat model must account for weaknesses in the defensive control set. A fairly thorough understanding of what has been built and what cannot be implemented, given the current design(s), is critical to a set of security requirements that are implementable* and which, when built, will enact the desired security posture for the target system and the stakeholders.

4.3.4 Target System Discovery

Part of the threat modeling process is discovery:

- What does the target system do?
- What services, functions, benefits does the system provide to its owners? It's users? Other stakeholders: Why will/has this system been put into service? How does it contribute to larger strategic goals?
- What are the system's major functions?
- What are the system's lines of communication? User inputs? Internal? External?
- Are there levels of trust and distrust between communicating portions? Are there levels of criticality and/or differing security postures? Why?

Very occasionally, a target system or project team will be able to articulate definitive answers to all the questions listed above. Or perhaps the system is so simple as to have obvious answers. Both of these situations do occur, although based upon experience with 1000s of threat models, we can say with some certainty that having all the required information up front is rare, indeed.

Usually, analysis requires discovery. Discovery may constitute the most time-consuming, even the most demanding, task for a particular threat model. The required information without which the threat model cannot be completed often takes considerable time and effort, as partial responses elicit more questions. Those new questions uncover more information that may lead to new questions, or refinements to existing ones, and so on as a threat model analysis proceeds towards sufficient answers to the questions we pose above.

Gary McGraw (author and frequent industry speaker, board member of Berryville Institute of Machine Learning and several security startups) likes to say, "Threat modeling is fractal." Truer words have not been spoken.

The analyst learns enough to make some assumptions and perhaps to identify a few possible attacks and their defenses. The project team may correct an assumption, which then indicates some adjustment in attacks and defenses. Next, a major function is "decomposed," that is, broken down into its constituent parts in order to further identify potential attack surfaces. One or more constituent parts throw several early assumptions into disarray or uncover data that require a stricter security posture, or some such change. Necessarily, new attacks will be added, and early ones shifted, which leads to a different set of defenses, and so forth. This game can go on for quite some time before everyone agrees that the target system is sufficiently understood such that an appropriate threat model can be stated.

Any decomposition, or addition (perhaps missed in a previous round of analysis), will, quite possibly, shift the threat model in substantive ways. To paraphrase Shakespeare, rarely does the course of

---

* Certainly, there are "best practice" methods. Many of these can be found in standards and publications. Given design choices, "best practice" solutions may not be possible. When we insist on a standard best practice, although it cannot be built given current capabilities and resources, we (greatly) risk not achieving any mitigation. In addition, we may waste much organizational time in conflict that may end up being unproductive. Luckily, there are often multiple ways to get similar security control and mitigation. Sometimes, one must be creative and resourceful, pulling multiple controls together into a defense-in-depth that comes close to, or even matches, a best practice method.

true threat modeling "run smooth." More typically, it's fractal, which implies recursing back to some previous point of analysis and starting the process again, in light of newly discovered information.

There have been a number of methodology proposals, PASTA (Process for Attack Simulation & Threat Analysis*), STRIDE (which will be covered in Chapter 4), and so forth (please see Izar Tarandach and Matthew Coles' survey of methods and their relative effectiveness in *Threat Modeling: A Practical Guide for Development Teams.*[†] All of the methods reviewed in that book attempt to hide or paper over the fractal nature of the analysis. This is why Brook proposed ATASM as an attempt to at least lend some sense of order to a process that can seem frustratingly chaotic at times.

We find (and have experienced) value from those methods with which we've worked. But we caution those who are new to threat modeling to remain open to its fractal nature—to not let a method, whichever one helps, to overrule an open, inquisitive mindset. Thorough and comprehensive threat models require a readiness to go beyond method, reaching for that "desired security posture," rather than completing a list or collection of patterns or attack types, such as the set of exploitation techniques contained in the STRIDE acronym. Collections like STRIDE will nearly always be somewhat (or quite) incomplete, given the complexities and, perhaps, innovations of the system under analysis.

As my friend and colleague, Lance Reck (Senior Consultant, IOActive, Inc.) likes to say, "It's easy to say in words, it's much harder to actually build." ATASM assists those unfamiliar with threat models to conceptualize what is required. We take up a short survey of how we do it, in the next section.

4.4 A Short "How To" Primer

An exhaustive threat model approach is beyond the scope of this work, which is focused on software security as a whole. We refer the reader to the entirety of *Securing Systems*. That book includes both fairly exhaustive explanations of each skill required, as well as six cases studies and their threat models. The case studies are intended to demonstrate the application of threat modeling skills to fictional systems whose structures and situations were drawn from real systems with which the authors have worked together, and Brook, alone.

Readers may wish to study Chapter 5 in *Securing Systems* in which the details of ATASM are explained through a fictional e-Commerce website. In the following section, we will touch on each required skill and activity.

4.4.1 Enumerate CAV

The analyst's knowledge of attack types, including strong and weaker areas, determine the comprehensiveness and relevance of the attack scenarios. This is where the analyst's craft ("art") either helps or detracts from the quality of the threat model. If knowledge of which attacks are relevant and likely to be tried by active threat agents is sufficient, this speeds up the analysis, as well as ensuring that the analysis covers a reasonably complete set of CAVs.

Observing thousands of participants learning threat modeling suggests that thinking through the right set of attacks, given the thousands that are known, remains one of the most difficult challenges for those with less experience and limited knowledge. In this section, we suggest a few approaches for bridging this key gap.

---

[*] UcedaVelez, T. and Morana, M. M. (2015). *Risk Centric Threat Modeling: Process for Attack Simulation and Threat Analysis.* Germany: Wiley.

[†] Tarandach, I. and Coles, M. J. (2021). *Threat Modeling: A Practical Guide for Development Teams.* Sebastopol (CA): O'Reilly Media, Inc.

One approach that organizations may take is to build a relevant threat library from which to draw on. Public resources tend toward the encyclopedic. (We'll delve into a couple of these below.) Unfortunately, when focusing on a particular type of architecture, with a constrained set of technologies, much of what has been catalogued will be extraneous or irrelevant.

Worse, the public threat collections aren't organized by architecture or technology type. Such an additional set of views into the collections would make these resources far more useful for threat modeling than they are today. It can be maddening to wade into one of the public collections of exploit types and then find that much that one has retrieved can't be leveraged against the system at hand. This is why we keep emphasizing that threat modeling involves significant "art," that is, knowledge by the practitioner who knows what's relevant and what's not, based upon the practitioner's experience.

For this reason, organizations can help threat modeling along by compiling those threats that are relevant to the software purposes, architectures, and technologies in use. These are typically called "threat libraries." Practitioners use the list of weakness/exploitation pairs contained in the "threat library" to create relevant attack scenarios in the target software. Each weakness/exploitation pair must be described well enough that threat modelers can identify the credible attack vectors, that is, construct appropriate attack scenarios for the software under analysis. Employing a threat library simplifies one of the hardest tasks in threat modeling: identifying attack scenarios.

Please take our guidance with a grain of salt; there are a couple of gotchas that must be considered when embarking on building threat libraries.

First and foremost, in situations where there are few or no "typical" architectures, where a broad set of technologies have been used, building a comprehensive threat library is akin to maintaining the public resources. We have found that the energy involved is not worth the output. It's proven more effective to train practitioners to build the necessary analytic skills than to waste time on a comprehensive enough threat library that may well become obsolete before it's even been completed.

Another consideration is the checklist nature of threat libraries. If teams merely work with the checklist, any unique or new situation might get overlooked. Developers are busy. Give them a list for a task that they consider secondary to other responsibilities and they are very likely to constrain themselves to the list in order to call the task "done." We remain rather suspicious of checklist approaches. Time and again, we've seen strict adherence to the list without any further analysis, thus missing key issues that weren't on the list.

When employing threat libraries, we strongly recommend that these are the starting point for analysis. Threat libraries must not be used as the "correct and official checklist." The common issues can then be easily identified, reserving human analysis for the more difficult, the unique, the local, the complex. This is how we encourage the use of threat modeling automation, as well (as we shall see in that section below).

The perhaps nonintuitive trick with developing a comprehensive set of attack scenarios is that one needs a single, credible attack scenario to mentally "prove" that adversaries have the means to exercise the opportunity and to identify at least a single method through which there will be significant harm. When constructing attack scenarios, one needn't be exhaustively thorough, since given that after one has been convinced that a particular attack scenario is at least possible, and perhaps likely, one can readily add defenses to other attack types that may be related to the scenario, that take advantage of similar issues, or exploitation types that are aimed at the same targets in the system under analysis.

Defenses don't typically have a 1-to-1 (1:1) match to exploits. Some attack scenarios will require several defenses, others exactly one; in general, exploits and defenses have a many-to-many relationship. This implies that building a reasonable set of defenses against one credible, well-thought-out attack scenario will also defend against a host of similar exploitations and assist in mitigating other types, as well.

If one has enumerated at least one attack scenario for each likely harm, the collection of defenses, a "defense in depth," will generally suffice to mitigate most, maybe all, of the relevant attacks.

This is why the authors find less value in exhaustive attack trees, since many of the branches will lead to attacks that have little likelihood of succeeding or may not result in significant harm. In our practice, we feel that time is better spent thoroughly considering types of attacks that have the potential for harm. We focus on exploitations that are known to be used by attackers against the technologies in the target system. Frequency of attack (if known) helps to rate the probability of attack within each particular period (e.g., software release cadence, business period, annually, expected life of the system, etc.—whatever periodicity makes sense for the analysis). One or two example attack scenarios through each attack surface that reveal potential harm (impact) are sufficient through which to generate a thorough defense.

4.4.1.1 STRIDE

Microsoft's STRIDE method is perhaps the easiest and most straightforward angle from which to divine Adam Shostack's wry starting point: "What can go wrong?" We know, intuitively, that people attack systems. Experience shows that even well-designed and thoughtfully implemented systems can still contain attacker leverage and vectors through which the leverages may be found and then exploited. Table 4.1 introduces the STRIDE attacker exploitation techniques and defines each STRIDE security property.

Table 4.1 Microsoft's STRIDE

Threat	Security Property	Description
Spoofing	Authentication	The identity of users is established (or you're willing to accept anonymous users).
Tampering	Integrity	Data and system resources are only changed in appropriate ways by appropriate people.
Repudiation	Non-repudiation	Users can't perform an action and later deny performing it.
Information disclosure	Confidentiality	Data is only available to the people intended to access it.
Denial of service	Availability	Systems are ready when needed and perform acceptably.
Elevation of privilege	Authorization	Users are explicitly allowed or denied access to resources.

Source: Data derived from Hernan, S., Lambert, S., Ostwald, T., and Shostack, A. "Uncover Security Design Flaws Using the STRIDE Approach." Retrieved from https://docs.microsoft.com/en-us/archive/msdn-magazine/2006 /november/uncover-security-design-flaws-using-the-stride-approach

Can an attacker pretend to be an authenticated and authorized user? That would be Spoofing. A classic Web spoof technique is Cross Site Request Forgery (CSRF). CSRF is an exploit that allows the attacker's transactions to ride alongside the user's input into a system that has not prevented two or more transactions occurring at the same time for the same user from the same source.

Each of the STRIDE threats represents a class of exploit types. While far from exhaustive, STRIDE provides a reasonable set of exploitation types with which to begin. That was the idea behind STRIDE: hand developers just enough to get them to consider how their system might be misused so that they might generate attack scenarios against which they (developers) will then implement reasonable defenses. STRIDE is quickly understood and then practiced. Hence, it is easy to understand STRIDE's popularity.

As Brook stated in *Secrets*:

STRIDE is interesting for a few reasons:

- It was the first published attempt to make threat modeling accessible to development communities.
- It finally gave security and development some common language to discuss potential attacks.

- It's easy to understand, especially for developers with little security knowledge.
- It has become security industry "folklore," in that nearly everyone who's had any experience of threat modeling has heard of it.
- STRIDE is often treated as though it were a canonized standard; it isn't and has never been.

However, STRIDE has some significant problems when taken beyond its intended purpose: an initial opening for developers to grasp the importance of considering how their software may be attacked. STRIDE provides a gateway to the art of threat modeling software.

Most importantly, STRIDE is far from comprehensive; a glance through the ATT&CK column headers ought to show the range of attack types that may have to be considered. STRIDE is more or less focused on application and operating system development for developers of these types of software. STRIDE may be less applicable to other types of software.

Because of STRIDE's prevalence, threat model findings are often couched in STRIDE terms. I've seen numerous models in which the many complex attack vectors that have been considered are tortured into conforming to one or more of the six STRIDE categories. Why is this even useful? (In my experience, conforming all attacks to STRIDE provides zero value and may, in fact, obscure details necessary to build effective defenses). (*Secrets*, p. 117)

STRIDE provides a further example of the problems with existing threat modeling methods. Its primary contribution is a structure for identifying attack scenarios. In fact, that's just about all STRIDE provides, in and of itself. In order to operationalize STRIDE, one must then place STRIDE within a threat modeling armature, that is, all the other tasks, analyses, information needed to build and then complete a threat model. It may be useful to repeat the high-level outline from earlier in the chapter that we quoted from *Securing Systems*:

Architecture and Artifacts
Threat Enumeration
Attack Surfaces
Data Sensitivity
Risk Rating*
Possible Controls (*Securing Systems*, pp. 137–169)

STRIDE solely addresses Threat Enumeration. Dozens of papers, guides, presentations, and a couple of books describe in gory detail where STRIDE (Threat Enumeration) fits in a threat model process, let's call it, the threat model process armature.

4.4.1.2 ATASM

This is why Brook proposed Architecture, Threats, Attack Surfaces, Mitigations (ATASM) in *Securing Systems*. ATASM is a process armature. Reading other approaches, each seems to focus on one aspect, while then placing that rigorous aspect within its larger threat modeling armature. For instance, PASTA provides fairly rich risk analysis. But to only perform that risk analysis would not produce a threat model: All the tasks must be completed.

In fact, perhaps ATASM would be more complete if given by "Purpose, Architecture, Threat, Attack Surface, Risk Rating, Mitigations," PATASRM, which is rather difficult to pronounce, at least in English. Any threat modeling process must:

---

* Please see footnote on p. 204.

- Understand the purpose of the target system, its uses, what problems it solves, the functions of the system (the "Three S's").
- Understand the functional pieces of the system, the technologies employed to deliver those functions, and the logical grouping of functions and technologies: architecture.
- Discover or analyze for those threat actors and their methods (threats) that are likely to get thrown at the system.
- Figure out where the threats will have an opportunity to begin, those points of the system that are exposed in some way to the threats: attack surfaces.
- Rate the risk of each attack scenario (threat against attack surface) such that mitigations can be prioritized and the most likely attacks defended against first.
- Build a defense in depth to prevent, render too difficult, slow down, and catch threats: mitigations.

The above should be considered a reasonable statement of the armature of the threat modeling process: those analyses that must be completed in order to generate a comprehensive threat model. With ATASM (or PATASRM, if you will) in hand, readers will have a better yard stick against which to measure the various threat modeling techniques and methods. No matter the focus, every method must execute the complete armature: PATASRM, or it is obviously incomplete.

Of course, PATASRM or ATASM is not intended to be a method. As we've noted, it's the armature, the collection of things that must be done by any method adopted.

4.4.1.3 Elevation of Privilege Card Game

One excellent place in which one may play with technical attacks is Adam Shostack's card game, "Elevation of Privilege."* I believe that when Adam teaches, he has participants play the game. We used it a bit in the first term of Michele Guel's National Cybersecurity Award (2011)–winning education class, Security Knowledge Empowerment (SKE), at Cisco (Michele Guel is Cisco Distinguished Engineer and 2011 National Cyber-Security Award Winner). Playing the game, or at the very least, glancing through the cards, can provide a pretty comprehensive (if not always up to date) introduction to the techniques that attackers employ. Elevation of Privilege, to my mind, puts the meat on the bones of STRIDE.

However, I've found that there are too many cards to use when actually threat modeling a system. (Although, I wonder if Adam Shostack uses the cards in some effective manner in his threat modeling classes?) As far as I know, Elevation of Privilege wasn't meant for building attack scenarios; it's a teaching tool, for which it works admirably. However, if running through the deck helps threat modelers identify relevant attack possibilities, then please, by all means, use any and all tools available. (*Secrets*, pp. 119–120)

4.4.1.4 ATT&CK & CAPEC (from *Secrets*)

MITRE's Common Attack Pattern Enumeration and Classification (CAPEC)

The MITRE® Corporation has sponsored a collection of adversarial attributes called MITRE ATT&CK®,† which groups the steps and techniques of known, multi-step attacks, such as various Advanced Persistent Threat (APT) and ransomware campaigns. One can go to the ATT&CK

---

* https://social.technet.microsoft.com/wiki/contents/articles/285.elevation-of-privilege-the-game.aspx

† ATT&CK® may be found at https://attack.mitre.org/wiki/Main_Page

Navigator* and select one or several known campaigns, and the Navigator will highlight—that is, show in visual form—the various techniques that were known to have been employed by that campaign. ATT&CK, like most of the tools, analysis systems, and ontologies that I've seen, is focused on the problem of attack analysis intended for use by incident responders—the analysis that must be done when presented with one or more indicators of compromise (IoC). Based upon my classes, I now believe that ATT&CK can prove useful for security architecture practitioners to familiarize themselves with the tools, tactics, and procedures (TTP) that make up a multi-step attack scenario.

Beyond the details of multi-step attacks, glancing through the high-level categories . . . may offer a useful mental classification system of the various types (and, implicitly, the attacker's desired effects) of attacks, without which, as I've noted, no security architect can practice. ATT&CK may offer a leg up for beginners, as well as filling in attack categories and exploit types for those who are more experienced. ATT&CK could provide an industry-wide organizing principle, which is presently lacking. (*Secrets*, p. 116)

Table 4.2 reproduces the matrix's column headers from MITRE's ATT&CK (attacker) tools, tactics, and processes (TTP) collection. The header titles provide a threat modeler's organization of the purposes to which attackers apply their techniques. We can call these "attacker intentions." Figure 4.10: ATT&CK* Headers Combined with CAPEC™ Categories adds mechanisms of attack to attacker intentions for a more complete picture of what must be considered to develop attack scenarios.

As presented in *Secrets*:

ATT&CK headers coupled to CAPEC top-level categories (Mechanisms of Attack) might just provide the set of relevant information to make threat modeling easier. And that's how I present these to my classes: ATT&CK column headers and CAPEC's categories linked together.

Table 4.2 MITRE ATT&CK® Column Headings

Category
Initial Access
Execution
Persistence
Privilege Escalation
Defense Evasion
Credential Access
Discovery
Lateral movement
Collection
Exfiltration
Command and Control

Source: Data derived from MITRE ATT&CK® Navigator. Available at https://mitre-attack.github.io/attack-navigator/enterprise/, with permission from © 2019 The MITRE Corporation. All rights reserved. Matrix current as of May 2019.

---

* Retrieved from https://mitre.github.io/at tack-navigator/enterprise/

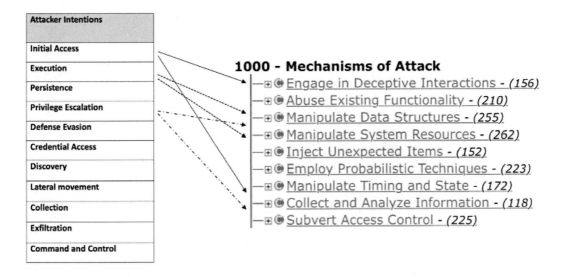

Figure 4.10   ATT&CK® Headers Combined with CAPEC Categories. (Source: Modified from © 2019 The MITRE Corporation, with permission. All rights reserved. Matrix & Mechanisms of Attack current as of May 2019.)

ATT&CK's column headers provide attacker intentions. CAPEC's categories provide the methods to achieve those intentions (right side of Figure 4.10 [formerly Figure 5.3]).

In Figure 4.10 [5.3], I've drawn arrows between "Initial Access" and a couple of the techniques that attackers use to gain access to systems: "Collect and Analyze Information," then "Engage in Deceptive Interactions." These two mechanisms don't comprise the universe of "Initial Access" techniques, but they are commonly employed.* Likewise, "Execution" is gained through "Inject Unexpected Items" and "Manipulate Data Structures" (again, not an exhaustive set).

In order to keep Figure 4.10 [5.3] readable, I used only two arrows and linked directly from only three of the categories. The relationships are more complex than those shown here. Still, I hope that this simple graphic demonstrates visually how ATT&CK column header intentions are achieved through the mechanisms (techniques) in CAPEC.

When building defenses, we want to prevent or increase the cost of prosecuting the mechanisms, thus preventing or slowing down ATT&CK's (attacker's) intentions (column headers). In order to build the correct set of defenses, it's helpful to understand what the attacker is trying to achieve (intentions). Preventing successful prosecution of the mechanisms becomes the purpose of each defense. Defenses, as we have seen previously, are not tied one-to-one (1:1) to exploits. Some defenses close off several mechanisms, whereas others may solely warn that an attack technique has been tried. Nevertheless, without understanding the actual mechanisms (and sometimes, the details in the branches that lie within each high-level category's tree of entries), one will be forced to guess.

"Encryption is secure; maybe we should encrypt data in motion." Unfortunately, such statements too often are made during development. Instead, wouldn't it be useful to know that data are moving over untrusted networks? Or not? And that attackers might "Collect and

---

* A more comprehensive listing of Initial Access techniques can be found by perusing attacks that have been added to ATT&CK® Navigator.

Analyze Information" by "Subvert(ing) Access Control"? Now we know that bi-directionally authenticated TLS might be worth consideration as a defense mechanism. The attacker will have to "Engage in Deceptive Interactions" (Man in the Middle), which will raise errors on both sides of the connection if the X.509 certificates tendered during a TLS authentication exchange are being handled correctly. My sincere hope is that these two readily available resources, when combined in this somewhat unexpected manner, might provide that bit of organization and insight—the guidance necessary to properly identify those attacks that systems will need to resist. I'm using this paradigm regularly in my threat modeling classes; anecdotal evidence suggests that the approach is proving useful to attendees.

In order to take over a machine so that it can be used without the knowledge of its ordinary user or owner (for instance, as part of a botnet), an attacker will have to piece together one or more stepping-stones, system objectives, such that the attacker will gain sufficient privileges on the host and its operating system in order to install command and control software that will persist across restarts (reboots). The goals are the attacker's "intentions" to be gained through prosecution of technical "mechanisms."

For instance, a vulnerability that allows "code of attacker's choosing" isn't actually sufficient until that exploitation can be coupled with an escalation of privileges in order to take control of an operating system (and, thus, the host). (In a scenario in which the attacker is starting at a high level of privilege, escalation is not needed.) In a situation in which the victim is not running at sufficient privileges to install high-privilege software, an attacker must not only execute code but also find a way to increase privileges such that the attacker's command-and-control software can be installed and run. In this trivial example, an attacker might need to exploit as many as three or four system objectives in order to successfully gain persistent control of the machine:

1. Find a way to deliver the attack code payload.
2. Get the payload to run on the victim's machine.
3. From the "code of the attacker's choosing" payload, exploit a second vulnerability that increases privilege level above that of the operating system's current user.
4. Establish communications with the attacker.
5. Potentially download additional code for permanence across restarts.

Of course, one may dig into ATT&CK to find the techniques used in each category (Intentions or System Objectives). MITRE's ATT&CK Navigator contains templates for many of the most well-understood attack sequences. By selecting a named campaign such as "APT1," the Navigator will highlight those TTP that the APT1 attackers employed. Exploration of well-known attacks could offer invaluable insight into how attacks proceed. It should be obvious through taking a look at just a few of Navigator's attack templates how multi-step attacks advance. An understanding that attacks often comprise a string or collection of exploitations is important, perhaps key.

In parallel, I believe that it is useful for practitioners to understand at least a few of the techniques described in each of the CAPEC mechanism trees. CAPEC entries describe the technical details used in each mechanism. By understanding in computer science terms, we can more readily derive the right defenses to prevent or at least slow down the attacks.

A bit of study of both ATT&CK and CAPEC, I hope, might shorten the learning curve about attacks without which security architecture cannot be practiced. Combining the two organizing principles—ATT&CK highlighting that which attackers need to accomplish and CAPEC the techniques to achieve these goals—seems to help my class participants to widen their understanding of attacks. (*Secrets*, pp. 120–123)

4.4.1.5 Continuous Threat Modeling Project

One of Brook's favorite, relatively new threat modeling approaches is Autodesk®'s Continuous Threat Modeling Project. This project has several interesting aspects; we recommend that those wishing to increase depth in threat modeling take a look at all the resources available from https://github.com/Autodesk/continuous-threat-modeling. Of particular note is Izar Tarandach's pytm threat modeling tool. Contributors are adding new threats to the tool to increase its coverage.

We believe that the project's "Secure Developer Checklist" provides a valuable and much-needed resource for design-time security decision making. The Secure Developer Checklist takes another approach to threat modeling: design patterns versus attack modeling. Most designs encounter common security problems:

- "added functionality that changes sensitive properties or objects in the system
- created a new process or actor
- used cryptography
- added an embedded component
- received uncontrolled input from an untrusted source
- added Web (or Web-like, REST) functionality
- transmitted data over the network
- created a computationally- or storage-bound process
- created an install or patching capability
- created a command interpreter (CLI) or execute a system command as part of a process
- added a capability that can destroy, alter or invalidate customer data and/or system resources
- added a log entry"[*]

These recurring design situations have common, well-understood, and vetted engineering solutions, often called, "secure design patterns." The checklist enumerates commercially reasonable security solutions to each of the problems quoted above.

This checklist provides secure design patterns that will result in security strength and that will avoid building weaknesses in. The list is composed of typical problems and areas that crop up repeatedly in software designs, as well as the associated methods and approaches that will offer the industry best practice defenses to the design-time problem. "If you have this, then do this." The first problem and associated solution is given below:

If you did THIS: added functionality that changes sensitive properties or objects in the system, then: Protect with authentication—You must make sure that all new functionality is protected with authentication. Validate that an individual, entity or server is who it claims to be by using strong authentication mechanisms like SAML, OAuth, etc.[†]

In the foregoing quotation from the checklist, the secure pattern is one of six patterns that have been gathered as solutions to the first problem. That is, for changes to sensitive properties or objects, and depending upon the details of the change, any one or more of the six solutions might be applicable.

The Secure Developer Checklist does not eliminate the need for threat modeling. What it eliminates is the need to model every potential weakness. Instead, typical weaknesses can be avoided, such

---

[*] Tarandach, I., Schoenfield, A., and the Autodesk Product Security Team, et al. (2019). Retrieved from https://github.com/Autodesk/continuous-threat-modeling/blob/master/Secure_Developer_Checklist.md)

[†] Ibid.

that the threat model can concentrate on the unique, the local, the complex, the unusual, that which is entirely new (or is simply not in the checklist!).

The authors have been wishing that someone would publish a set of secure design patterns. The Secure Developer Checklist is a positive start towards that goal.

4.4.1.6 OWASP® Threat Modeling

For Web architectures, the Open Web Application Security Project (OWASP) threat modeling resources can be of great help. OWASP have compiled quite an extensive set of threat modeling documentation, consisting in tutorials, guides, threat libraries, and even an open source threat modeling tool, Threat Dragon. (As of this writing, however, Threat Dragon remains fairly limited in the number of threats that are available. Generally, one must program one's own threat library.) (Please see https://owasp.org /www-community/Application_Threat_Modeling)

4.4.2 Structure, Detail, and Abstraction

[S]killed security architects usually have at least some grounding in system architecture—the practice of defining the structure of large-scale systems. How can one decompose an architecture sufficiently to provide security wisdom if one cannot understand the architecture itself? Implicit in the practice of security architecture is a grasp of the process by which an architect arrives at an architecture, a firm grasp on how system structures are designed. Typically, security architects have significant experience in designing various types of computer systems. (*Securing Systems*, p. 10)

As we've already noted above, we first must understand the structure of the target system (the system under threat model analysis). Identifying areas and languages that have proven to harbor repeating weaknesses and vulnerabilities focuses the analysis. The following is a good list to draw from:

- **Old code:** Older code may have more vulnerabilities than new code, because newer code often reflects a better understanding of security issues. All "legacy" code should be reviewed in depth.
- **Code that runs by default:** Attackers often go after installed code that runs by default. Such code should be reviewed earlier and more deeply than code that does not execute by default. Code running by default increases an application's attack surface.
- **Code that runs in elevated context:** Code that runs in elevated identities, e.g., root in *nix, for example, also requires earlier and deeper review, because code identity is another component of the attack surface.
- **Anonymously accessible code:** Code that anonymous users can access should be reviewed in greater depth than code that only valid users and administrators can access.
- **Code listening on a globally accessible network interface:** Code that listens by default on a network, especially uncontrolled networks such as the Internet, is open to substantial risk and must be reviewed in depth for security vulnerabilities.
- **Code written in C/C++/assembly language:** Because these languages have direct access to memory, buffer-manipulation vulnerabilities within the code can lead to buffer overflows, which often lead to malicious code execution. Code written in these languages should be analyzed in depth for buffer overflow vulnerabilities.
- **Code with a history of vulnerabilities:** Code that has shown a number of security vulnerabilities in the past should be suspect, unless it can be demonstrated that those vulnerabilities have been effectively removed.

- **Code that handles sensitive data:** Code that handles sensitive data should be analyzed to ensure that weaknesses in the code do not disclose such data to untrusted users.
- **Complex code:** Complex code has a higher bug probability, is more difficult to understand, and may be likely to have more security vulnerabilities.
- **Code that changes frequently:** Frequently changing code often results in new bugs being introduced. Not all of these bugs will be security vulnerabilities, but compared with a stable set of code that is updated only infrequently, code that is less stable will probably have more vulnerabilities.[*]

Increased scrutiny of each of the items in the preceding list will identify those places within a particular system that will have a higher likelihood of attackers leveraging any weaknesses and issues. If any of these conditions exists, those are the points in the system and technologies to dive deep, to understand thoroughly. We add that all languages that allow or worse, require direct manipulation of memory present many of the same opportunities as C/C++/assembly, named in the above list by Michael Howard.

The art of architecture analysis and decomposition is fundamental to threat modeling. We must figure out the avenues of attack, to what places, then how those "places," attack surfaces, allow an attack to proceed onwards toward intermediate "system objectives" and, when successful, to the attacker's ultimate goals.

"Threats are applied to the attack surfaces that are uncovered through decomposing an architecture. The architecture is "factored" into its logical components—the inputs to the logical components and communication flows between components." (*Securing Systems*, p. 32)

The question that needs answering in order to factor the architecture properly for attack surfaces is at what level of specificity can components be treated as atomic? In other words, how deep should the analysis decompose an architecture? What constitutes meaningless detail that confuses the picture?

[A]ny executable package that is joined to a running process after it's been launched is a point of attack to the executable, perhaps to the operating system. This is particularly true where the attack target is the machine or virtual machine itself. Remember that some cyber criminals make their living by renting "botnets," networks of attacker-controlled machines. For this attack goal, the compromise of a machine has attacker value in and of itself (without promulgating some further attack, like keystroke logging or capturing a user session). In the world of Advanced Persistent Threats (APT), the attacker may wish to control internal servers as a beachhead, an internal machine from which to launch further attacks. Depending upon the architecture of intrusion detection services (IDS), if attacks come from an internal machine, these internally originating attacks may be ignored. Like botnet compromise, APT attackers are interested in gaining the underlying computer operating environment and subverting the OS to their purposes.

Probing a typical computer operating system's privilege levels can help us delve into the factoring problem. When protecting an operating environment, such as a user's laptop or mobile phone, we must decompose down to executable and/or process boundaries. The presence of a vulnerability, particularly an overflow or boundary condition vulnerability that allows the attacker to execute code of her or his choosing, means that one process may be used against all the others, especially if that process is implicitly trusted." (*Securing Systems*, pp. 81–82)

In *Securing Systems*, Brook proposed that architecture decomposition is to two sometimes intersecting, but in other circumstances into different views (and specificity) of structural details:

---

[*]   Howard, M. (2006, July–August). "A Process for Performing Security Code Reviews." *IEEE Security & Privacy*, pp. 74–79. Reprinted in *Core Software Security*, as well as in Chapter 2, in the current book.

- Attackable surfaces: points on the system attackers may enter to start their exploitation process)
- Defendable boundaries: those points in the system or in its boundaries where defensive mechanisms (controls) and mitigations can be implemented

When we consider which attacks might have some potential for success (and resulting harm), we think like an attacker who must first get at any weaknesses. Where do they start? Having established a beachhead, what's next, and importantly, where? Brook proposed some guidance in *Securing Systems*:

[O]ne must factor an independently running endpoint architecture (or subcomponent) down to the granularity of each process space in order to establish trust boundaries, attack surfaces, and defensible perimeters. As we have seen, such granular depth may be unnecessary in other scenarios. If you recall, we were able to generally treat the user's browser atomically simply because the whole endpoint is untrusted. I'll stress again: It is the context of the architecture that determines whether or not a particular component will need to be factored further.

For the general case of an operating system *without the presence of significant, additional, exterior protections*, the system under analysis can be broken down into executable processes and dynamically loaded libraries. A useful guideline is to decompose the architecture to the level of executable binary packages. Obviously, a loadable "program," which when executed by the operating system will be placed into whatever runtime space is normally given to an executable binary package, can be considered an atomic unit. Communications with the operating system and with other executable processes can then be examined as likely attack vectors. (*Securing Systems*, pp. 83–84)

In short, when protecting endpoint software, intercommunicating pieces of the collection we typically refer to as "the application" present attack surfaces and defensible boundaries. For a cloud application, each logical function and communication layer may be sufficient, since the cloud provider should be doing their utmost to obscure underlying, supporting technologies and components. Virtual layering by the major cloud vendors is designed to prevent hosted components from getting beyond the boundaries of the virtual environment. Since components are generally horizontally scaled, that is, repeated exactly in as many instances as necessary to support required loads, we treat each component as sufficiently decomposed. Instances are unimportant. Break one, you've broken them all.

In the case of managed server environments, the decomposition may be different. The difference depends entirely upon the sufficiency of protections such that these protections make the simple substitution of binary packages quite difficult. The administrative controls placed upon such an infrastructure of servers may be quite stringent:

- Strong authentication
- Careful protection of authentication credentials
- Authorization for sensitive operations
- Access on a need-to-know basis
- Access granted only upon proof of requirement for access
- Access granted upon proof of trust (highly trustworthy individuals only)
- Separation of duties between different layers and task sets
- Logging and monitoring of sensitive operations
- Restricted addressability of administrative access (network or other restrictions)
- Patch management procedures with service-level agreements (SLAs) covering the timing of patches
- Restricted and verified binary deployment procedures
- Standard hardening of systems against attack

The list given above is an example of the sorts of protections that are typical in well-managed, commercial server environments. This list is not meant to be exhaustive but, rather, representative and/or typical and usual. The point being that when there exist significant exterior protections beyond the operating system that would have to be breached before attacks at the executable level can proceed, then it becomes possible to treat an entire server, or even a server farm, as atomic, particularly in the case where all of the servers support the same logical function. That is, if 300 servers are all used as Java application servers, and access to those servers has significant protections, then an "application server" can be treated as a single component within the system architecture. (*Securing Systems*, p. 93)

. . .

Special cases that require intra-executable architectural decomposition include:

- Encryption code
- Code that handles or retrieves secrets
- Digital Rights Management (DRM) code
- Software licensing code
- System trust boundaries
- Privilege boundaries

Wherever there is significant attack value to isolating particular functions within an executable, then these discreet functions should be considered as atomic functions. Of course, the caveat to this rule must be that an attacker can gain access to a running binary such that she or he has sufficient privileges to work at the code object or gadget level. As was noted above, if the "exceptional" code is running in a highly protected environment, it typically doesn't make sense to break down the code to this level (note the list of protections, above). On the other hand, if code retrieving secrets or performing decryption must exist on an unprotected endpoint, then that code will not, in that scenario, have much protection. Protections must be considered then, at the particular code function or object level. Certain DRM systems protect in precisely this manner; protections surround and obscure the DRM software code within the packaged executable binary." (*Securing Systems*, pp. 94–95)

The foregoing illustrates why the amount of decomposition is dependent upon the system under analysis. There's no "one size fits all." Indeed, though there are some general guidelines, the desired security posture of the system will also be a factor in how deep to investigate.

We hope that we've, at the very least, introduced readers to the fine art of architecture analysis and decomposition. It should be obvious that threat modeling effectiveness stands on the shoulders of software and system architecture practice. Those who wish to pursue skills further are advised to study the science, engineering, and art of architecture as it applies and is practiced for software. Particularly, as Brook has mentioned elsewhere, the practice of enterprise architecture is well-documented, as well as having experienced practitioners who can help. We, the authors, have benefited greatly from the many fine enterprise architects with whom we've had the privilege to work.

4.4.3 Rating Risk

The success of the assessment depends greatly upon the assessor's ability to calculate or rate the risk of the system. There is the risk of the system as it's planned at the moment of the assessment. And there's the risk of each attack vector to the security posture of the system. Most importantly, the risk from the system to the organization must be determined in some manner. If computer security risk cannot be calculated in a reasonable fashion and consistently over time, not only does any particular assessment fail, but the entire assessment program fails. An ability to understand, to interpret, and, ultimately, to deliver risk ratings is an essential task of the architecture risk assessment (ARA) and threat modeling.

The word "risk" is overloaded and poorly defined. When discussing it, we usually don't bother to strictly define what we mean; "risk" is thrown around as though everyone has a firm understanding of it. But usage is often indiscriminate. A working definition for the purposes of security assessment must be more stringent . . . [L]et's explain "risk" as Jack Jones does: "the loss exposure associated with the system."* This working definition encompasses both the likelihood of a computer event occurring and its negative impact." (*Securing Systems*, p. 101)

. . .

What is "risk"?

An event with the ability to impact (inhibit, enhance or cause doubt about) the mission, strategy, projects, routine operations, objectives, core processes, key dependencies and/or the delivery of stakeholder expectations.[†] (*Securing Systems*, p. 107)

But how to effectively and consistently rate risk across projects, architectures, and importantly, by multiple practitioners? This question has bedeviled information security practitioners for as long as the authors have been involved. Too often, rating has come down to how uncomfortable the situation makes the rater. Personal risk tolerance is neither consistent nor repeatable. We have experienced the results of that inconsistency: project teams "shopping" security people for the best, most advantageous (usually, lowest) risk rating. That's not a good situation.

Microsoft used DREAD alongside STRIDE, which we have already examined. DREAD has found wide adoption, especially at larger organizations.

- **D**amage potential (How much are the assets affected?)
- **R**eproducibility (How easily the attack can be reproduced?)
- **E**xploitability (How easily the attack can be launched?)
- **A**ffected users (What's the number of affected users?)
- **D**iscoverability (How easily the vulnerability can be found?)

Ratings do not have to use a large scale because this makes it difficult to rate threats consistently alongside one another. You can use a simple scheme such as High (1), Medium (2), and Low (3).

After you ask the above questions, count the values (1–3) for a given threat. The result can fall in the range of 5–15. Then you can treat threats with overall ratings of 12–15 as High risk, 8–11 as Medium risk, and 5–7 as Low risk.[‡]

DREAD is an attempt to allow teams to come to a consensus on the potential for harm. Most methods, short of the casino mathematics used by Factor Analysis of Information Risk (FAIR), the Open Group standard, will likely still require some qualitative judgement; there seems to be no way out of qualitative rankings, given the state of information risk practices today. Furthermore, in threat modeling we find a necessity to risk rate any number, often more than a few of the CAVs quickly.

---

* Jones, J. A. (2005). "An Introduction to Factor Analysis of Information Risk (FAIR)." Risk Management Insight LLC. Retrieved from http://riskmanagementinsight.com/ media/documents /FAIR_Introduction.pdf

† Hopkin, P. (2005). *Implementing Effective Risk Management,* 2nd ed. Institute of Risk Management (IRM). Kogan Page, p. 14.

‡ Meier, J. D., Mackman, A., Dunner, M., Vasireddy, S., Escamilla, R., and Murukan, A. (2003, June). Microsoft Corporation. Retrieved from https://docs.microsoft.com/en-us/previous-versions/msp-n-p/ff648644(v=pandp .10)?redirectedfrom=MSDN

Unfortunately, the setup required for something like a FAIR risk simulation run will be too lengthy for most organizations' threat modeling needs, which is probably why DREAD has been adopted.

A method that should not be used under any circumstances is Common Vulnerability Scoring System (CVSS), as it was not designed for risk rating but, rather, consistently scoring vulnerability severities as a quick indicator of potential seriousness. CVSS' designers never imagined that it would be taken as substitute for risk.* Unfortunately, and rather sadly, CVSS enjoys wide adoption as a risk rating. We wish this weren't so because CVSS has several rather important limitations. Brook has written about the problems with CVSS elsewhere. Interested readers are encouraged to Web search for blog posts or to read the CVSS analysis in *Secrets of a Cyber Security Architect* (p. 72 and Appendix C). To keep this risk tutorial brief, we will simply note that CVSS is not suited to the task of threat model risk rating without significant additions and amendments.

In *Securing Systems*, Brook offered the simple but field-tested and proven rating method—Just Good Enough Risk Rating (JGERR). JGERR was invented as a simplification of FAIR by Brook and Vinay Bansal (Distinguished Engineer, Cisco Systems, Inc.)

Credible Attack Vector * Impact = Risk Rating

where

> *Credible Attack Vector (CAV) = 0 < CAV > 1*
> *Impact = An ordinal that lies within a predetermined range such that 0 < Impact >*
> *Predetermined limit (Example: 0 < Impact > 500) (Securing Systems, p. 105)*

CAV is composed of a set of terms. In *Securing Systems*, these terms were given as:

- Threat
- Exposure
- Vulnerability
- Impact

Since that time, Threat has been broken into "Threat Agent" and "Capability," redefining CAV as:

- Threat Agent
- Capability
- Exposure
- Vulnerability
- Impact

Since creating JGERR,[†] and then explaining it more fully in *Securing Systems*, Chapter 4, we've found that the term "Threat" was actually overloaded. Threat encompasses two distinct components: an active human entity (person, organization, enterprise) who is motivated to attack (for a particular set of reasons and goals, please see the attacker matrix in *Secrets of a Cyber Security Architect* [Chapter 2]) and a threat agent who must have the technical capabilities to exploit a weakness before proceeding. For instance, where no exploit has yet been invented and threat agents are not yet aware of a vulnerability,

---

[*] The authors have been using CVSS since before its first version. One of the original designers was on the same team as Brook, where they conversed about CVSS' purposes. In that role, Brook was required to score incoming vulnerabilities as a pre-version 1.0 beta test of CVSS.

[†] Co-creator and co-author Vinay Bansal and Brook formalized JGERR for a SANS Institute Smart Guide in 2011. JGERR became, and still is, the risk rating method used for Cisco® Infosec's application security. JGERR or descendent methods are used at other enterprises, as well. Since both James and Brook worked at Cisco, we know with certainty that thousands of JGERR scores have been collected—the ratings used effectively since 2009.

we may relatively, safely assume that even motivated, active threat agents don't yet have the capabilities to prosecute the unknown and not yet exploited weakness. Ergo, the threat agent has not yet acquired the requisite capabilities for exploitation.

Indeed, some threat agents focus on (and perhaps prefer or must use) well-known and programmed exploit code. Such code, termed "weaponized," may be found in exploit kits (EK), which may be open source, but which are also for sale on the Dark Web. The threat agents may lack the technical sophistication to generate their own exploits and, hence, are forced to use those that have already been coded. Another driver for reliance on EK is the expense of research and development (R&D). For cyber criminals, it's cheaper to use EK rather than to invest in developing exploits. Exploitable conditions continue to be abundant on the Internet, and unpatched operating systems and applications are common. Why waste time and money trying for something new when old tried and true will deliver substantial financial returns?

Hence, Capability is an important dimension within the rating of the likelihood of any particular attack scenario.

> There is a collection of conditions that each must be true in order for there to be any significant computer security risk. If any one of the conditions is not true, that is, the condition doesn't exist or has been interrupted, then that single missing condition can negate the ability of an attack to succeed.
>
> "Negate" may be a strong term? Since there is no absolute protection in computer security, there can be no surety that any particular exploit against a known vulnerability will not take place. Although Internet attack attempts are certain, there is no 100% guarantee about which will be tried against a particular vulnerability and when that particular attempt will take place.
>
> However, even in the face of intrinsic uncertainty, we can examine each of the conditions that must be true and thus gain a reasonable understanding of whether any particular attack pattern is likely to succeed. "True" in this context can be thought of as a Boolean true or false. Treating the sub-terms as Boolean expressions gives us a simple way of working with the properties. But please bear in mind that because there is no absolute surety, these conditions are not really binary, but, rather, the conditions can be sufficiently protected to an extent that the probability of a particular attack succeeding becomes significantly less likely. (*Securing Systems*, pp. 108–109)

A "finger to the wind" rating can be made very easily by checking if each term is true (at the moment of rating) in a probability substitution set: Threat Agent, Capability, Exposure, Vulnerability. When every condition to exploitation lines up, those are the attack scenarios most likely to be tried and, perhaps, soon. But we still don't have a risk rating, as exercise of an issue isn't the sole component of risk: There must be significant impact about which we care. We'll take impact up in a moment. However, it should now be obvious that, for a quick-and-dirty rating, any CAV where all terms are true and successful exercise will cause significant harm, pose a level of risk, that is, loss exposure.

Defenses for "CAV all terms true delivers harm" conditions must be prioritized above any other potential security work. These are the attack scenario defenses that are worth pushing, and probably pushing hard for: highest potential for damage that we care about.

For any term not true at the moment of rating, the next still fairly simple step will be to consider the ease or regularity with which similar agent activity, capability, exposure, and vulnerability turns up or is discovered and then used. Given that exploitation will lead to a loss event, then these would be the next priority down.

Readers will perhaps notice that, so far, we haven't tried to quantify the rating. JGERR allows levels of rating from a quick-and-dirty assessment to identify what's most important to a formalized rating system, producing a comparable and, typically, fairly consistent set of ratings. However, this requires more work.

A next step will be to consider each term in CAV as a range of conditions:

- Threat Agent (activity+motivation): Rare, occasional, common, abundant, continual
- Capability: Unknown/requires significant resources and knowledge to develop, researchers are working on or have published a proof of concept, commonly understood technique, weaponized/EK
- Exposure: Must circumvent a defense-in-depth and/or requires artificial preconditions, protected by at least a single defense, open to public probe
- Vulnerability: Rarely occurs in similar systems—doesn't currently exist in target system, occurs with some regularity—expected to occur in target system within the expected life of the system, common mistake or weakness—not observable in target system (but may exist)—to be expected, repeatedly occurs in target system or its technologies—occurrence can be expected regularly, proven to exist in target system

By then, rating the potential for harm and taking each term's expectations for occurrence, one can fairly easily spot the important attack scenarios and deprioritize those less risky. We still haven't calculated a number. But we can now easily add this, if needed.

Divide each CAV term's continuum—from rare to expected—into slots. When Vinay Bansal and Brook proposed JGERR for a SANS Smart Guide (2011), they divided the CAV (probability) terms equally. Some situations might want to weigh heavily toward one side of the continuum or the other, as required by local risk tolerances. However, one assigns a number to each condition, all numbers must be $0 > N < 1$, that is, a decimal between 0 and 1. Divide by the number of CAV terms for a probability substitution term:

Probability Substitute = (Threat Agent + Capability + Exposure +Vulnerability) / Terms Comprising CAV

Terms Comprising CAV = 4

We're taking the average of our probability ratings. That's because if threat agents appear to be very active (let's say, .9) against an existing weakness (again, let's say, .9), that may be mitigated by the difficulties of obtaining an exploit and an existing set of defenses preventing or slowing exercise of the issue (let's say each of those is .2), which will lead to a rating of

.9 + .9 + .2 + .2 / 4 = .775

But we haven't calculated a rating yet.

Risk = Probability * Loss

Or, in the JGERR case

Risk Rating = CAV * Impact Harm Level

We find that it's fairly easy to build a set of impact harm ratings. One chooses a scale. The range of the scale is unimportant: 1–10, 10–100, 1–500, $5million–$1billion.* Choose a granularity. The wider the scale, the greater granularity one achieves. But a wider range may not deliver truly greater

---

* When Brook led Web Application and Infrastructure security at Cisco Systems, Inc., Cisco Finance told him that losses less than $5 million were essentially insignificant at the enterprise level. We've reproduced the financial scale from those days at Cisco. Things may have changed since then.

granularity, as it turns out to be more intuitive to establish buckets of harm across whatever range has been selected. In practice, people quickly get used to whatever scale is chosen. We don't find that the range decided upon for the impact scale really matters much so long as impacts are rated consistently for the organization's needs.

On a scale of 1–10, let's say that harm to one or two users might be rated 1, while loss of most customer-facing services for a week would be rated 10. One would identify potential organization impacts and those unique to a system in this fashion on whatever scale had been chosen.

As a risk rating aside, much of the harm rating can be done a priori, before threat modeling. There may be a few harms specific to a system. But we find that many harms are obvious and, thus, can be rated during the period one is ramping up a threat modeling program. Experience teaches that harm ratings aren't that hard to create; the effort just requires some time and attention.

JGERR risk then can be consistently quantified:

Risk Rating = CAV * Impact Rating

JGERR makes no pretensions to be an actual risk calculation. In the absence of actuarial tables built up from a body of successful compromise data, we either have to do some clever mathematics such as those used by FAIR or be clear about exactly what one is quantifying and how that's being done. JGERR offers a consistent approach based upon solid risk concepts. Still the number you get (or a JGERR unquantified rating, for that matter) isn't "risk." It's merely a diagnosis of the situation specific to threat modeling.

JGERR can also be tweaked for vulnerability analysis, if desired. The CAV buckets would need to be changed somewhat from those we've presented in this section. As a practice, every vulnerability management method must start with a Common Vulnerability Scoring System (CVSS). CVSS is the industry standard, the *lingua franca*, of vulnerability interchange and discussion. We have always used CVSS as our starting point, and then amended it or folded CVSS into another rating system, such as JGERR, for vulnerabilities. We'll take up vulnerability management further in later chapters.

We advise (as we've done above) that the most important first vulnerability analysis will always be for attacker utility/value from exploitation. We've used that dimension to filter out attack scenarios and vulnerabilities that won't get over the bar of utility that attackers require. With low or no attacker value, exploitation doesn't offer enough gain to be worth the effort. In our programs, we try not to waste time on issues whose exploitation returns minimal or insignificant gains to an attacker.

4.4.4 Identifying Defenses

Which Defenses for What System?

A skilled security architect must also know how to prevent successful attacks. The other side of the attack coin is the face of defense. The complete security architecture cycle involves planning for attack and specifying those defenses that will either prevent particular attacks or, at the very least, make the prosecution of the attack sufficiently difficult as to either prevent success or at the very least, slow an attack down enough to catch the compromise before it has been completed. (*Secrets*, p. 47)

Once we have identified a set of credible attack scenarios, we have to fully understand the technical mechanisms that the steps in the attack scenarios will employ. We needn't understand exploitable detail about the precise computer instructions that will take advantage of a specific weakness. That detail is critical to building security technology, such as scanners, and to skilled, manual penetration testers. For the purposes of finding reasonable defensive measures, we need to understand mechanisms and how these work and, just as important, the sorts of measures that will prevent, increase the difficulty of exploitation, or, at the very least, alert that an attack is in process.

Understanding mechanisms of exploitation comprises one aspect of threat modeling engineering, the "science" of threat modeling. Unless we understand what the attacker is misusing or abusing in our system, the computer science of the exploitation, and who the victim is, we may not apply the correct defense for that attack scenario.

As an example, architects unfamiliar with the details of attacks might assume that using Secure-Hyper Text Transfer Protocol (HTTPS), which relies upon the Transfer Layer Security (TLS) services, "secures" their application. However, the standard HTTPS used by most websites only protects data in transit between the user's browser and the server, if used correctly on both sides, including being used correctly by the user! That may come as a surprise to those unfamiliar with HTTPS.

HTTPS is woven so deeply into our Web use, that users don't typically understand what it's providing and what it's not. When one gets one of those, "can't identify server" errors from the browser, it might just be a mismatch between server IP address and certificate because the service provider hasn't registered all of the addresses that they are using. That isn't really a worry, if the IP does, in fact, belong to the service.

But the "invalid certificate" error could indicate a man-in-the-middle (MitM) attack. You'll see these errors pop up fairly commonly at hotels and airports, where the WiFi is capturing the traffic before passing it on to the Internet (e.g., before having provided one's email to the service for their advertising sponsors). Applications on the connecting machine will get the WiFi's self-signed certificate before the connection process completes. In this situation, an attacker might control the intermediary WiFi. There is a distinct MitM potential that a malefactor has control over the certificate and thus the supposed protections.

Furthermore, all that standard HTTPS provides is an assurance that the IP address(es) registered with the certificate are supplying the certificate issued for those IP addresses to the browser. What with free HTTPS certificates readily available, attackers have no trouble acquiring both IP addresses and matching certificates. Certificate authorities make no representations about the trustworthiness of the holder of the certificate nor about the servers sending it! HTTPS is actually a house of cards that more or less works, most of the time, for most sites, because well-known sites such as big banks and social media sites guard their certificates fairly well (or should!).

For lesser-known sites, there's not much assurance that someone isn't decrypting traffic in the middle or is out-and-out evil. Web user: Beware! Don't just accept that certificate error if you don't understand X509 certificates and their usage for server assurance. That little browser lock icon doesn't mean very much, we're sad to relate.

Typical HTTPS, if done correctly, provides server-side IP address assurance, which can then result in encryption protection across untrusted networks, such as the hostile Internet. But even that may not provide what it seems since browsers can negotiate downward to vulnerable versions of TLS/SSL, and weaker or even broken encryption standards. A software architect must not believe that just because some form of HTTPS has been implemented that their application is, thereby, "secure." We hope this long example demonstrates that the devil is in the technical details. One must understand the attack mechanisms. Presenting an alternate certificate as an HTTPS intermediary, for instance, allows a MitM attacker to view and even take control over the traffic between browser and service.

Chapter 3 of *Secrets of a Cyber Security Architect* is focused on precisely this question: What do threat modelers need to technically understand, and what is irrelevant? We suggest that readers who wish to delve more deeply into this subject begin with that chapter, which uses the famous Heartbleed vulnerability as its example.

> [W]e cannot expect a 1-to-1 mapping of control, of mitigation to attack, though of course, some mitigations will be 1-to-1. (*Securing Systems*, p. 165)

Unfortunately, the lack of 1:1 mapping between the mitigations that happen to be available in any particular situation and the attacks we must counter presents the threat modeler with a fairly nasty problem. Complexity quickly increases due to the interaction between various levels in the software stack at which attacks may be vectored. Defenders must account for the foundational fact that attackers seek varying targets, but are also opportunistic. Should an unplanned target become available, attackers may take advantage of the extra opening. As we've noted in our books, papers, and presentations from stages worldwide and in our university guest lectures: Attackers are adaptive and creative. Attacks aren't necessarily single-minded, or tightly focused: some are, some aren't. Therefore, we cannot fall into a trap that only considers a single angle.

Protecting against any particular attack scenario might involve security controls placed along the route the attack is expected to take. Some controls, such as firewalls, will be at the perimeter, in the network plumbing, whereas others may have to be individually coded in the application, or anywhere else in the set of technologies employed. East-West, North-South, Back-Front, Top-Bottom: Controls may need to exist anywhere, in whatever dimensions are used to visualize and discuss the system(s) to be protected.

Chapter 5 of *Securing Systems* introduced a fictitious Web store, Web-Sock-A-Rama, to provide an example system for exploring threat modeling through ATASM structure. Although completing the defenses and mitigations for a threat model of such a system is far beyond the scope of this introduction to threat modeling, we can use the Web store example to illustrate the complexities of attack scenarios to defenses. Figure 4.11 (formerly Figure 6.7) provides a high-level diagram of a typical Web store.

Websites have figured prominently in threat modeling literature as a "simple" system from which to start. This is partly because most people who want to learn threat modeling also use the Web and are, thus, familiar (more or less) with the idea that there's a server out there somewhere on which we browse and from which we download content. One often sees diagrams containing a browser, a Web server, and a double-headed arrow between them. The reality of websites, especially those expecting to sell things online, is considerably more complex. Even Figure 4.11 fails to represent many aspects of modern websites, since these will likely have components that are offered through some public cloud provider. We've kept Web-Sock-A-Rama purposely constrained to what turns out to be the less complex case, despite what may seem by glancing at the diagram.

A scan of Figure 4.11 with an eye toward what may be most critical to the website, or most interesting to an attacker, will likely focus on the data stores containing customer profiles and customer financial information. Threat modeling class participants never fail to identify these as likely attack targets. Obviously, criminals will be interested in financial data and personal information that may lead to other financial data elsewhere. In Figure 4.12, we've circled these two patently important data stores.

There is no doubt that protecting the two obviously sensitive data collections must be important for any business that expects to survive and thrive and which intends to maintain its customers' goodwill. If defenses could be applied such that there existed a single defensive measure that would protect these data resources, threat modeling will be a lot less complex. In the following paragraphs, we hope to highlight just a few of the complexities that force us to think nonlinearly, identifying patterns of attack that do not proceed in a stepwise fashion, from initiation, marching straight toward the attacker's objective.

Let's say, for the sake of example, that we focused on the data themselves. Obviously, we would want to avoid passing attacker-defined Structured Query Language (SQL) commands to our database. Preventing SQL injection might be top of mind. Many designers would insist upon user authentication before allowing a customer to access their data and require that applications authenticate before accessing databases, as well. Would the foregoing security measures suffice? No, not in the real world of adaptive, creative, opportunistic attackers. We'll try to explain an avenue of attack requiring further analysis on the part of the defenders.

There are attackers whose primary objective is networking equipment. They may sell captured equipment to hide malicious email forwarding and other malicious activities. These attackers' primary first objectives will not include the financial data for our mythical Web store. Similarly, attackers

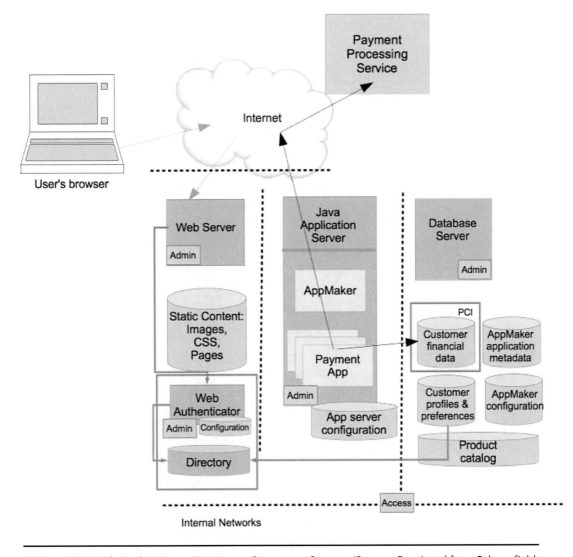

Figure 4.11   Web-Sock-A-Rama Ficticious eCommerce System. (Source: Reprinted from Schoenfield, B. S. E. [2015]. *Securing Systems: Applied Security Architecture and Threat Models.* Boca Raton [FL]: CRC Press/Taylor & Francis Group, p. 204, with permission.)

running botnets composed of compromised hosts that are rented on the Dark Web for malicious activities wouldn't aim their first attacks at the store's customer financial data, either. In neither of these cases are the attackers focused on the financial or customer profile data as they begin.

However, having captured a couple of the hosts or a router or two on the eStores's DMZ network, should these attackers poke around to see what else is available, they are very likely to go beyond their initial targets. If there's financial data to be grabbed as well, why not? After all, selling valuable data on the side increases revenue; we must remember that cybercrime is a business whose ultimate objective is to make money, as much money for as little work as possible.

The security measures outlined above assumed that attacks will all be vectored from the user through expected flows that must go to the database. Certainly, those flows must be protected; let there be no doubt about the defenses already described.

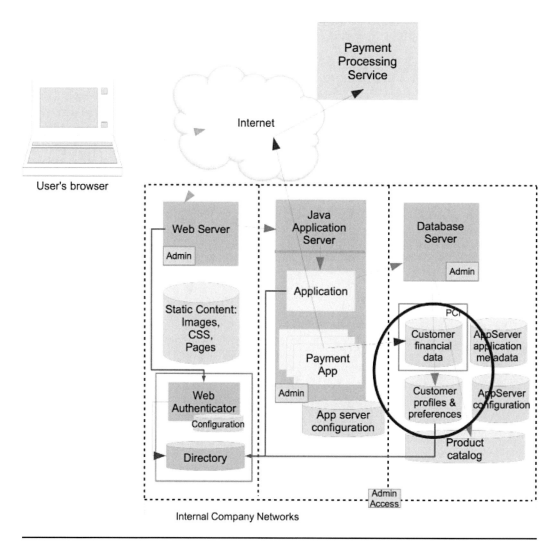

Figure 4.12   eCommerce Obviously Critical Data. (Source: Modified from Schoenfield, B. S. E. [2015]. *Securing Systems: Applied Security Architecture and Threat Models.* Boca Raton [FL]: CRC Press/ Taylor & Francis Group, p. 204, with permission.)

Still, there are other attack vectors that should be considered carefully. Our network and host attackers aren't going to route their attacks through usual and expected channels. Once having a beachhead on networking equipment and/or hosts, they may start probing to see what else they can find. They may capture authentication traffic. Such traffic typically contains some form of a credential, whether that be an X509 certificate, a hash of the password, or some other credential. (Once in possession of password hashes, current brute force password cracking techniques generally make quick work of all but the strongest passwords.) Attackers might listen to data exchanges. In our fictitious website, updates to the authentication database get pushed on a periodic basis from the user profile store. The attacker needn't compromise either the source data or the destination repository if they have possession of the networking equipment over which the data must flow. Being inside what may be considered internal networks, attackers might listen to administrative authentications and thus gain control of even more sensitive equipment, such as the application server itself. None of the foregoing makes any use whatsoever of the expected customer use cases of the system.

To protect networking equipment, we would make it difficult to access user interface and administrative components, require multiple authenticators before allowing access, perhaps restrict networks that can access the equipment, and most certainly restrict user access to only those people with the proven skill to protect their access well. This explanation is too short to exhaustively list all the typical measures for protecting networking equipment. (Please see *Securing Systems*, Chapters 5 and 6, for more detail.)

Besides restricting user access, we would also employ network restrictions such that only those hosts, and better, applications that have a specific need can access sensitive data. All others are disallowed. In this way, even a loss of some relatively unimportant and uninvolved host that has some other purpose (say, company blog) can't be misused to get at the data stores we must protect.

We have to think laterally about attack scenarios that are outside the use cases of the system. Our defenses have to account for protecting our infrastructure, as well as opportunistic compromises that might offer themselves to attackers interested in other goals.

Underlying a thorough set of defenses is a comprehensive understanding of the range of attack types and attacker goals that have been seen against similar systems, in this case, Web stores. Each attacker type has typical goals (please see the Attacker Matrix, Table 1.2, p. 14 [Chapter 1], in *Secrets of a Cyber Security Architect*, for a deeper analysis of attacker goals and capabilities). Some attacker goals are mapped to abusing the intended functions of the target system. But others have nothing to do with the purposes of a system, its use cases, or even its stakeholders' interests in the system (as we saw with router and botnet renting schemes above). Yes, the analyst must consider how the functions of the system can be misused. In addition, other typical attacker goals must also be considered. If any of these turn out to be relevant and thus worth defending against, defenses will have to be thought through.

We hope that the foregoing illustrates, at least a little bit, the complexities of building a true defense in depth. As we've noted above, defenses and attacks don't necessarily lineup 1-to-1, a single defense for each type of attack. We have to look for ways to raise the cost of exploitation, techniques for closing off attack possibilities, make attackers switch tactics, make them puzzle over their next steps, and at the very least, try to catch them in the act before significant damage has been done.

As we've seen previously, once we identify the attacks that we believe will be levied against a system, the next task is to build the best set of appropriate defenses. But how does one acquire this knowledge set?

One might take a "follow-the-herd" approach. There are plenty of standards one could follow: just do everything in the standard, as well as everything humanly possible. Venerable NIST 800-53 (revision 53ARev4[*]) contains 170 controls. Implementing each of these might be a way to play it safe, to avoid additional analysis. But it would be expensive to implement each of 800-53's controls well, probably prohibitively so. Plus, without additional analysis, there's no way to know which controls apply and which might be irrelevant in context.

NIST 800-53 is a hodgepodge of nearly everything that comprises information security's controls and processes. AC-5, Separation of Duties, is a design principle aimed at foiling fraudulent and collusive behavior. The idea is that it's harder to get a *group* of people to act fraudulently, especially when the group is not particularly cohesive. AC-7, within the same control family, Unsuccessful Logon Attempts, is a common abuse indicator: when attackers are attempting to brute force a password, there will be an unusual number of unsuccessful logons. The control is to limit the number of attempts, usually within some given time period.

For a very small company, separation of duties doesn't make much sense. Everyone already knows what everyone else is doing. A person behaving poorly will often get caught by the

---

[*] Retrieved from https://nvd.nist.gov/800-53/Rev4/impact/HIGH

other principals, who usually watch each other's actions pretty closely. I call that "eyeball-to-eyeball security." It works reasonably well in small, tightknit, closely coordinating teams. Besides, during the startup phase it is very typical for each person of the very small founder team to fulfill multiple organization roles. There aren't enough people to "separate" the duties between. But eyeball-to-eyeball security doesn't work well at all at enterprise scale, where formal separation of duties access policies apply.

Although a standard like 800-53 sets out a universe of information security typical practices, it does nothing to define what applies to particular contexts.

Still, I believe that in order to apply defenses appropriately, a practitioner would need to understand the function of just about every control named within NIST 800-53 and similar standards. Such standards, at the very least, set out the well-understood universe of stuff that people do to secure their organizations.

Something like the BSIMM™ (Building Security In Maturity Model)[*] software security measurement is also an example of follow-the-herd. In the case of BSIMM, the measurement is of companies that take software security seriously enough to pay for a BSIMM assessment. It's not (yet) a measurement of the universe of what organizations in general do or do not do. It's not a random sampling of organizations; there is no attempt at generating a statistically valid sample (though, to be sure, the designers have put a lot of thought into how to measure what they measure). BSIMM's measurement is of companies willing to pay for a BSIMM measurement—ergo, companies that care about software security.

I don't mean to imply that BSIMM tells us nothing. It tells us what companies that have sufficient resources already dedicated to software security are doing and evaluates how mature those practices are. That is certainly valuable: what do the leaders do and how mature are they at doing what they do?

What BSIMM does not tell us is how effective their software security programs have been at preventing harm from security incidents caused by issues in software that the measured companies have built or deployed. Is what BSIMM companies do effective? Since the total list of BSIMM companies is not public, there's no way to match known incidents against BSIMM participants[†]. . . .

But just maybe, the practices outlined in BSIMM constitute a fair sample of reasonable software security practices.

My point in all of the foregoing is that we do have examples of what organizations try. We do have pretty concrete descriptions of the sorts of controls that at least NIST thinks make up a robust security program. Familiarity with a few of the available standards might help someone new to defenses build the requisite knowledge to apply particular defenses to particular security needs. . . .

A quick Web search for Massively Open Online Course (MOOC) returns dozens of hits.[‡] There appear to be lots of offerings available to the willing student. I make no representation as to which MOOC might be any good. Obviously, a lot of MOOCs are for-profit operations. Buyer beware, always. Still, today it's not that hard to find an introductory course in information security. Any decent survey course must include typical security controls and their application. Probably, for those living near to a university, college, or other post–high-school institution, such institutions also offer some intro to cyber security that might prove useful.

---

[*] Retrieved from https://www.bsimm.com/about/membership.html

[†] If I knew anyone who was at one of these two firms, I wouldn't be able to relate what they may have told me, anyway. All BSIMM conferences (I've attended three and spoken at two) are strictly held under a Non-Disclosure Agreement (NDA).

[‡] You can find two example listings in the following two links: https://www.mooc-list.com/tags/information -security and https://www.coursera.org/courses?query=information%20security

One other public resource may be worth considering. Each individual attack pattern in MITRE's CAPEC™ collection has a set of preconditions that must be met before the attack pattern can be exploited successfully. Although each attack pattern's preconditions aren't themselves defenses, any tactic or control that removes a precondition is, in fact, a defense against that attack pattern. I suggest that if there is any doubt about what defenses may counter a particular attack, a study of the preconditions listed in its CAPEC entry may point toward the right set of defenses.

Whatever the media, one must eventually learn those controls (NIST 800-53 listing or similar) that will apply to the systems one will be analyzing. To be honest, depending upon the situation, I've been called upon to analyze controls that have included:

- Network restrictions
- Traffic analysis
- Memory protections
- Operating system privileges
- Coding practices
- Testing strategies
- Boot loaders
- Disk protections

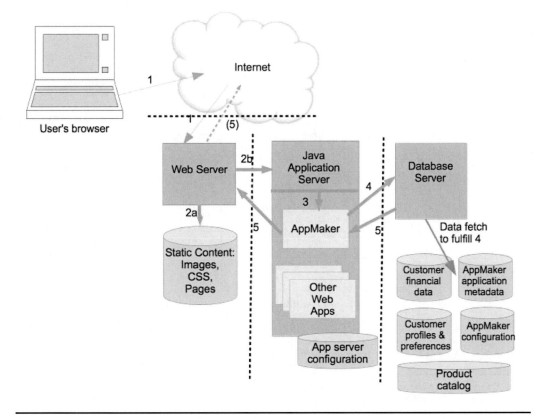

Figure 4.13   Sample Web Architecture Web-Sock-A-Rama. (Source: Reprinted from Schoenfield, B. S. E. [2015]. *Securing Systems: Applied Security Architecture and Threat Models.* Boca Raton [FL]: CRC Press/ Taylor & Francis Group, p. 155, with permission.)

(A description of Figure 4.13 can be found on page 233.)

Table 4.3 (formerly Table 5.6) Attacks and Controls

Specific Attack	Attack Surface	System Objective(s)	Control
SQL and LDAP injection	Applications via HTTP	• *execute unintended commands* • *access data without proper authorization*	• Design application code such that dynamic requests to LDAP and to databases are built within the application and not received from users • Dynamic input from users, such as user name or item numbers, must be validated to contain only expected characters • Input not matching precisely constrained values must return an error to the user
Cross-Site Scripting (XSS)	Web server and applications via HTTP	• *execute scripts in the victim's browser* • *hijack user sessions* • *deface web sites* • *redirect the user to malicious sites*	• Dynamic input from users, such as user name or item numbers, must be validated to contain only expected characters • Input not matching precisely constrained values must return an error to the user • Response generation must clear all scripting tags found within stored content
(exposed) Direct Object References	HTTP responses from applications and application server	*manipulate . . . references to access unauthorized data*	• Do not use object revealing protocols similar to Java Remote Method Invocation (RMI) in communications with the user's browser • Remove all debugging and coding information from errors and other user content. Errors shown to user must be user-centric, in plain (nontechnical) language • Do not expose any debugging, configuration, or administrative interfaces over customer/public interfaces • *Use per user or session indirect object references* • Authorize all direct object accesses
Cross-Site Request Forgery (CSRF)	Application server via HTTP (in this case, AppMaker)	• *force a logged-on victim's browser to send a forged HTTP request* • *generate requests . . . [that appear to be] . . . legitimate requests from the victim*	Include a nonpredictable nonce in the response to a successful user authentication. Return the nonce for the session with every authenticated response in a hidden field. Before processing an authenticated request, validate the nonce from the user's session
Unvalidated Redirects and Forwards	Web server and applications via HTTP Possibly also the application server	• *redirect and forward users to other pages and websites* • *use untrusted data to determine the destination pages* • *redirect victims to phishing or malware sites* • *use forwards to access unauthorized pages*	• *Simply avoid using redirects and forwards* • *If used, don't involve user parameters in calculating the destination. This can usually be done* • *If destination parameters can't be avoided, ensure that the supplied value is valid, and authorized for the user* • Employ an indirect reference to URLs between client and server rather than sending the actual value to the user

SQL = Structured Query Language; LDAP = Lightweight Directory Access Protocol.
Source: Data set in italics is from the Open Web Application Security Project (OWASP) (2013). *OWASP Top 10 List.*[*]

---

[*] Open Web Application Security Project (OWASP). (2013). *OWASP Top 10 List.* Retrieved from https://www.owasp.org/index.php/Top_10_2013-Top_10

- Network storage configurations
- Website configurations
- Administrative controls and restrictions
- Monitoring and logging

(*The above list should not be considered exhaustive.*)

Basically, I've dealt with a potpourri of the length and breadth of information security practices. Eventually, I fear that if one examines enough systems and organizations, one will encounter just about everything described in NIST 800-53 and similar at one point or another. I don't think that there's a quick path to such exposure. I'm lucky to have always had brilliant practitioners around me who could help me to understand the problems and help craft reasonable solutions within each diverse context. (*Secrets*, pp. 123–126)

What follows is the defenses summary from Chapter 5 of *Securing Systems* to demonstrate a set of defenses for the fictional eStore that we've used as an example throughout this section. The eStore's high-level architecture can be viewed in Figure 4.13 [formerly Figure 5.5].

Table 4.3 (formerly Table 5.6) adds defenses to each of the attack methods that we enumerated in previous ATASM steps. These are the five attacks and their associated attack surfaces (the CAVs) that we believe are applicable to this system, in this organizational context.

Some of the defenses are programming requirements. For instance, rewriting errors that will be returned to users in plain language easily understood by users and not containing any programming information is something that will have to be programmed into the applications. Likewise, input validation, which is required to prevent the two injection errors, must be done within code.

Contrast the coding defenses with not using an object referencing or serialization protocol (RMI) to prevent direct code references from escaping to the user. This, like building nonces into responses or using no redirects or forwards, is a design issue. The applications making up the Web-Sock-A-Rama store will have to be designed such that redirects are unnecessary, such that appropriate protocols are used for any code that runs in the user's browser . . .

In reality, there are many more attacks that will be received from the public Internet. Because we are exploring the ATASM process, the list of attacks has been truncated to keep the discussion manageable. Network-based attacks, such as distributed denial of service (DDoS), have not been discussed. However, for a real site, these and many other attacks must be defended, as well.

For example, the networking equipment that routes traffic into the site and between its various layers would all be subject to attack. We have not examined the physical network architecture. But in a real analysis, we would examine everything from top to bottom. Such an examination would, of course, include the networking equipment, the operating systems of the servers running AppMaker, the database servers, the Java application server, and so on. (*Securing Systems*, pp. 166–168)

Please refer to the case studies provided in Chapters 6–11 (*Securing Systems*) for detailed defenses derived through threat modeling analysis.

4.5 Threat Model Automation

At the time of *Securing Systems*, there was one existing commercial threat modeling tool. Brook mentioned it in the Afterward as a hopeful sign. In *Secrets of a Cyber Security Architect*, Chapter 6, Brook discusses the making of a threat modeling tool market by the entry of two additional threat modeling tools, and several open source projects. As of this writing, the threat commercial offerings still exist and are doing reasonably well. A couple of the open source projects are maturing. It would seem that automated threat modeling is coming of age?

We believe that there is little reason for human analysts to repeat the same tired requirements, time after time, project after project. A great number of security requirements have become standard, which means that these can be automated. In our opinion, these should be!

In a DevOps world, we should be reserving human analysis for that which truly requires it. There is no need to reiterate that Web inputs must be escaped to prevent Cross-Site Scripting (XSS) vulnerabilities. Automation can deterministically identify Web inputs, either for code or from diagram artifacts in parsable languages such as UML, to output the "escape inputs" requirement, which is well-understood and basic to Web programming. Free tools such as Microsoft's Threat Modeling Tool (commonly referred to as "TMT") readily find such issues, as does the Continuous Threat Modeling Project's pytm.

Hence, we would like to see far more automation of threat modeling wherever it can be applied. Let's apply human analysis to the complex, the sophisticated, the unique, the innovative, where automation hasn't yet caught up. In the foreseeable future, we see a continuing need for human threat modeling analysis, even in DevOps.

> If development is constrained to a well-understood and defended set of technologies, languages, infrastructures, and platforms, I believe there's significant benefit to automate at least part of the threat modeling process. The security requirements can be scoped and bounded such that many basic requirements will be identical for sets of applications—maybe all.
>
> As an example, imagine generating new business logic for applications that will run in a carefully designed and managed cloud platform. In this case, the application programmers will be defended, as least in part, by what's been built into the platform. . . . In a tightly constrained environment, hewing to standards will take care of a lot of, perhaps most, ongoing security needs. In such systems, questionnaires/surveys about use cases and technology uses will be sufficient for much new development. Commercial requirements tools might help generate the needed requirements surveys. . . . Where development is less constrained, but there are still well-understood patterns, perhaps because various implementation elements can be reused (let's call them "ingredients"), automation might still be applied, at least for those systems that will be consumed by additional development as ingredients. (*Secrets*, p. 151)

. . .

> Reserve manual analysis for difficult, atypical, and unique problems. Either purchasing or documenting the well understood will eliminate unnecessary analysis to improve velocity and agility. Besides, repeating "escape your Web inputs" and "validate the adherence of your messages to expectations" is boring: these security defenses are well described in multitudes of literature, standards, and in all the tools. As Cristoph Kern did at Google*, make it impossible to release code that doesn't adhere to the obvious security standards.
>
> Instead, let's focus on one-of-a-kind problems and designing build/deployment systems that ensure defensive code. That will surely be faster. (*Secrets*, p.153)

There are open source tools that detect changes in architectural diagrams that have been written into one of the diagramming languages. In a DevOps chain, user stories (or task tickets) to review the threat model might be placed on the backlog thus forcing iterative threat modeling in response to architectural changes. Even if the threat modeling analysis is not automated, using automation to initiate human analysis is well within the DevOps spirit to "automate everything" (possible). We believe that threat modeling should never be seen as a heavy-weight, time-consuming, and agility-killing task. Think iterative. Build the threat model alongside structural definition and change. Automate standard and well-understood requirements.

4.6 Chapter Summary

We have replaced old-fashioned and outdated design-time security activities geared to a separate security function that is disconnected with development and replaced these with threat modeling at various levels of specificity, from very high-level to detailed requirements that will be coded (design specifications).

Threat modeling must become iterative and easy to integrate with modern development methods. It must be readily learned, understood, and practiced by developers and, probably, as least during study and learning phases, by skilled threat modelers who also like to teach and empower. That's the only way that threat modeling will scale to large numbers of developers working complex software projects. Our own experience building and running threat modeling as secure design programs indicates that this works and has side benefits, such as fostering a developer culture of security.

Whatever methods are employed, these must account for PATASRM: Purpose, Architecture, Threats, Attach Surfaces, Risk, and Mitigations. We surveyed each of these areas to help readers understand the importance and the practice of threat modeling.

Finally, we believe that some of the burden of threat modeling can and must be automated to keep pace with modern developer agility, velocity, and delivery, that is, threat modeling at DevOps speed.

Chapter 5

Enhancing Software Development Security Management in an Agile World

5.1 Introduction

Within software development, the weakest link is still the human and, in particular, the managers of those humans and the processes and tasks they are expected to carry out. Chapter 2 focuses on what humans can do to control and manage a secure software development process and its adjacencies within an Agile and DevOps environment and an awareness of what managers can do to help them deliver secure software at Agile speed. This chapter addresses the same areas covered in Chapter 2, but rather than a baseline discussion, it is a follow-on to the new SDL model proposed in Chapter 3 as well as some of the discussions in Chapter 4. Specifically, we will discuss a future state in which security tools, technology, and people are integral to the DevOps pipeline and used to fully integrate software security into the DevOps environment. This includes automating much of the code check-in with software security checkers as you write source code; static code analysis after each check-in; and security reviews by software security experts for requirements, design, and threat modeling documents. The approach will also use static code analysis and dynamic analysis to link the software security defects from the outside in and inside out. In the outside-in security approach, most of the resources are focused on identifying potential software vulnerabilities that can be exploited from an outside attacker, which means you are only looking to stop potential external threats to your software. In today's environment, a significant amount of exploitation of software vulnerabilities can happen from insiders or attackers within a hosted network, which requires you to look from an inside-out perspective. Although most of this analysis is covered as part of the threat modeling process described in Chapter 4, it is important to enhance and automate this process with static and dynamic code analysis tools, where possible. The different tools used for source code analysis and secure software design must integrate those bugs in one central repository integrated into the Agile development process. People actually writing the policies understand software development along with the implementation of only those standards that can be adopted and modified for use in an Agile environment. As discussed previously, this will require

Table 5.1 Key Elements of the DevSecOps Manifesto

Should be	Rather than
Leaning in	Saying "No"
Data and Security Science	Fear, Uncertainty, and Doubt
Open Contribution and Collaboration	Security-Only Requirements
Consumable Security Services with APIs	Mandated Security Controls and Paperwork
Business-Driven Security Scores	Rubber Stamp Security
Red and Blue Team Exploit Testing	Relying on Scans and Theoretical Vulnerabilities
24×7 Proactive Security Monitoring	Reacting After Being Informed of an Incident
Security Threat Intelligence	Keeping Information to Themselves
Compliance Operations	Clipboards and Checklists

a new mindset for security as reflected in the DevSecOps Manifesto[*] highlighted in Table 5.1. These key changes are required so that security teams can maximize their value in the DevOps process by protecting the business and ensuring secure development, delivery, and that the security bugs are fixed.

Table 5.1 highlights a better way for security practitioners to operate and contribute value with less friction by:

- Creating better products and services; providing insights directly to developers;
- Favoring iteration over trying to always come up with the best answer before a deployment;
- Operating like developers to make security and compliance available to be consumed as services; unlocking and unblocking new paths to help others see their ideas become a reality;
- Not just relying on scanners and reports of findings.
- Attacking products and services like an outsider to help you defend what you've created;
- Learning the loopholes, looking for weaknesses, and working with developers to provide remediation actions instead of long lists of problems for them to solve on their own;
- Not waiting for our organizations to fall victim to mistakes and attackers;
- Not settling for finding what is already known; instead, looking for anomalies yet to be detected
- Keeping up with new threat research to plan for future attacks; and
- Striving to be a better partner by valuing what our developers value.[†]

Although many of the attributes of what security should be in the DevOps environment as highlighted in the DevSecOps Manifesto above were discussed in Chapter 2, this chapter will focus on evolving those practices to support the model visualized in Figure 5.1, which is described in Chapter 3 (Figure 3.1). The challenge and way forward are perhaps represented best in the following quote from *The DevOps Handbook*:

> One of the top objections to implementing DevOps principles and patterns has been, "Information security and compliance won't let us." And yet, DevOps may be one of the best ways to better integrate information security into the daily work of everyone in the technology value stream.[‡]

---

[*] DevSecOps. (2020). *DevSecOps Manifesto*. Retrieved from https://www.devsecops.org
[†] Ibid.
[‡] Kim, G., Humble, J., Debois, P., and Willis, J. (2016). *The DevOps Handbook: How to Create World-Class Agility, Reliability, and Security in Technology Organizations*. Portland (OR): IT Revolution Press.

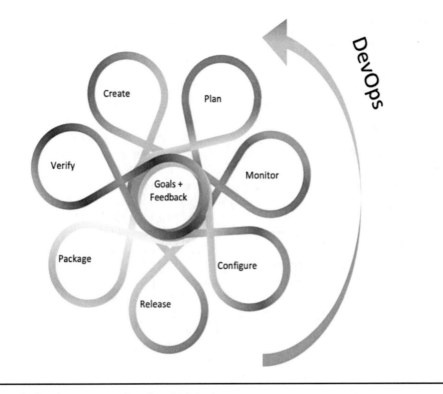

Figure 5.1   Idealized Continuous DevOps Activity Loops.

The 2019 State of Agile Survey states that, "While buy-in and support for Agile continues to grow, most respondents (78%) state that not all of their company's teams have adopted Agile practices, an indication that most enterprise Agile adoptions are still in flight."* Although there is an aggressive move to Agile and DevOps by organizations, we have seen them invest heavily in DevSecOps toolchains and only to replicate legacy processes. DevSecOps is more than just deploying tools; it includes pipeline automation processes with practices that will take many software changes required all the way through production. Unfortunately, many vendors are using snake-oil–type pitches to companies trying to convince them that tools will solve all their problems in developing and delivering secure software. This is an antithesis to DevOps transformation, which requires a culture of continuous learning and improvement, as well as DevSecOps that, as discussed previously, incorporates security into the culture, principles, and processes created to streamline software release cycles. As discussed earlier in this book, the founders of DevOps envisioned a multidisciplinary approach grounded in communication, domain understanding, and passion for the underlying business. These are, of course, human characteristics that cannot be automated but are rather the qualities cultivated through a strategic vision, transformational leadership, and employee empowerment. This culture challenge and change is something we will continue in this chapter, as we discussed in Chapter 2.

The evolution of those practices discussed in Chapter 2 required to support the model described in Chapter 3 will be discussed in this chapter. Specifically, how to enhance software development security management in an Agile world to facilitate continuous security in an DevOps environment.

---

* CollabNet® VersionOne. (2019). "13th Annual State of Agile™ Report." Retrieved from https://www.stateofagile
  .com/#ufh-i-521251909-13th-annual-state-of-agile-report/473508

5.2 Building and Managing the DevOps Software Security Organization

5.2.1 Continuous and Integrated Security

There are continuous insertions of security into the development process, whether it is technology, requirements, or people. The development and security lifecycles must be combined to increase efficiency and to avoid redundancy and unnecessary silos. As an analogy, you can't create an assembly line, then bolt on security off to the side that is out of band, out of process, and not part of the flow, which creates friction and problems in the organization.

There are so many variations of development programs and use cases that there isn't a one-size-fits-all solution. What works for Company "A" may not work well for Company "B." This is why building security into the process as part of the same team makes security more flexible and relevant no matter what type of program and use cases are used in an organization.

Perhaps the most challenging part of moving to the next level of security in the DevOps environment is that you must add the element of continuous and integrated security to what is already being done in continuous integration (CI) and continuous delivery (CD). For this chapter, the focus will be on managing the elements of security that will facilitate continuous and integrated security (CIS) providing the basis for CI/CD/CIS within the "Idealized Continuous DevOps Activity Loops" model shown in Figure 5.2. This arguably goes beyond what is currently called DevSecOps in today's operational environments. In essence, doing DevOps securely, fully integrated, and continuously. To do this, security must:

- Cross every domain.
- Be integrated and underscore every activity.
- Have adoption top down and bottom up.
- Be automated as much as possible.
- Integrate its tools with implementation and test flows.
- Enable innovation without compromising build.

DevOps Pipeline

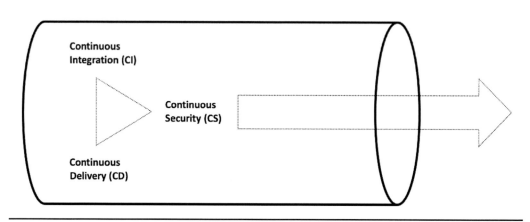

Figure 5.2   Continuous and Integrated Security Is Integral to the DevOps Software Development Process.

- Be sustained.
- Be continuous, integrated, and part of interdependent infinite loops.
- Bring individuals within the DevOps organization at all levels of experience and ability to a high level of proficiency in security in a short period of time, as well as the understanding that security is everyone's responsibility.

As mentioned earlier in this book, we have to stop jumping from threat modeling to penetration testing to secure coding as though these are all equivalent. They are not. Each of these activities is a discreet dimension of software security, especially when software security is considered as a holistic problem. Each technique at this state of the art is quite distinct from the others.

Continuous and integrated security is integral to the DevOps software development process (see Figure 5.2). To achieve integration, our experience suggests that security has to give up its primacy and take its rightful place among the other attributes that must be delivered. To that end, Brook offered a set of behaviors earlier in this book that define what "security" means in software. The extent of these behaviors will, of course, be contextual. But these five behaviors define what secure software should do. Having defined security as "continuous and integrated" makes security a part of the fabric of the activities and considerations. Old school security was fighting for its empowerment, for a voice, to be heard. We often adopted the attitude that security trumps other dimensions—security risks are the most important risks. We need to shift the mindset that security is important. As important as revenue, as stakeholder usefulness, as performance, as scalability, etc. Security becomes one of the liabilities, not more, and certainly not less. Continuous Security must be fully integrated into the People, Process, and Technology components of DevOps (Figure 5.3).

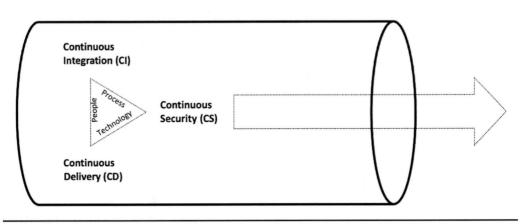

Figure 5.3 Continuous Security Must Be Fully Integrated into the People, Process, and Technology Components of DevOps.

5.2.2 Security Mindset versus Dedicated Security Organization

Within DevOps, security as a mindset is more important than a separate security organization. Arguably, as security is truly built into the software development process, the term DevSecOps will no longer exist and it will just be DevOps. This will require trained security development architects and engineers, security practices and requirements fully built into the software development lifecycle rather than as a separate security development lifecycle, and the security tools managed by the development organization as part of their overall tool management program. This will require that security operational leadership, security operations, and governance and associated staffs be substantially reduced through outsourcing their responsibilities to the development teams and automating tasks and deliverables, whenever possible.

Security as a mindset means moving as much security as possible from operations to development. This will minimize security within the operations side of the organization. Security Operations Leadership and staffs will be minimized along with the Product Security Incident Response Team (PSIRT) and GRC teams by cross-training development engineers or hiring development team members solely responsible for product security, PSIRT, or security-related GRC tasks (Figure 5.4), with dotted-line reporting relationships to the limited security operations positions remaining. These development organization security experts will also function as change agents working with the senior product security leader and evangelist to facilitate the cultural transformations necessary to manage security from within the development organization.

The senior product security leader will likely remain in the operations organization but could also be in development. This position will be responsible for transformational leadership to include the vision, inspirational communication, intellectual stimulation, and supportive leadership to lead the cultural change required for security to be managed and delivered within the software development teams as well as building relationships with other leaders on the journey to secure software delivery.

One of the biggest hurdles in product security within the development teams is that they believe security leaders and engineers "have never worked in software development and do not understand how

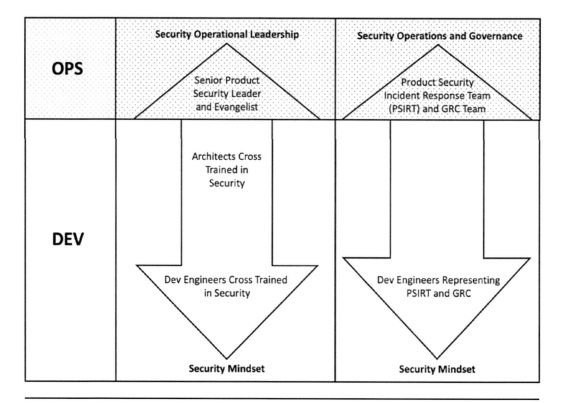

Figure 5.4 Security as a Mindset: Moving Security from Ops to Dev.

a Sprint team delivers software." Although that may be true in many cases, that is why it is important to recruit security leaders and engineers who have this experience. These folks exist and are growing in numbers every year. This is imperative to be able to forge some much-needed common ground between development, operations, and security.

One of the other issues is the reporting structure for the senior product security leader. To facilitate the best use of the people responsible for software security, they must be part of the right organization. Having been in seven Chief Security Officer (CSO) and Chief Information Security Officer (CISO) roles as well as several Senior Product Security Executive roles, I, James Ransome (co-author), have had software security reporting to me in several of my roles. Based on both my experience and communication with my peers in the industry, it is clear that the software security function ideally should fall within the software development function. Although this position can be a "dotted-lined" relationship to the CIS or CSO, it should be a direct report to the head of the engineering or software development organization. The general consensus is that the application security role typically reports to the centralized information security role (CSO/CISO) position, which should not be confused with the software security function responsible for developing and delivering software products to external customers. This will result in enhanced empowerment, credibility with the development teams, and budgetary ownership.

For the most part, the roles for security architects and engineers will have the same responsibilities described in Chapters 2 and 4. The most significant change will be that they will be part of and integral to the software development organizational product teams.

Earlier in the book, we discuss our success in the creation of Security Champions within organizations we have been responsible for and security experts within development teams who convey security priorities to colleagues. We did this successfully in order to meet the challenge of transforming DevOps to what is now called DevSecOps. These Security Champions took on the role of "local" experts who can answer questions, recommend training, and interface with security experts to find answers to deeper questions. Although they served as a powerful transformational force to deliver higher-quality, secure code, we are now suggesting that solely dedicated product security professionals with backgrounds in software code development reside within each development team with dotted lines to the senior product security executive but reporting directly to a development team. In addition, a dedicated security professional with a background in managing software development teams for divisional engineering/development groups should represent security for the multiple products being developed from that group while also reporting to the business owner for the same group. James used this model in his most recent position at a Fortune 100 company and found it very successful if the function is empowered by the CEO and Board of Directors. Ideally, the product security executive should report to the General Manager of the Business Unit responsible for product development or the company's Head of Engineering, who is responsible for developing software products.

The enhanced organizational roles and responsibilities for PSIRT and GRC to support the model discussed so far and highlighted in Figure 5.4 will be described later in this chapter. As with the centralized product security role, much of these responsibilities will be transitioned to partner positions within the software development teams.

5.2.3 Optimizing Security to Prevent Real-World Threats

Before moving beyond optimizing organizational structures to move traditional operations security organizational responsibilities into the development organization, it is important to discuss why optimizing, streamlining, and making software development becomes more efficient by making this move. This move not only reduces overhead and overall costs of software product development, and improves efficiencies, but it also optimizes our ability to protect countries, companies, and critical infrastructures from real-world threats.

Cyber threats result from software flaws, which are weaknesses that can be exploited by cyber attacks or exploitation of a software application or system. In this book, we have covered strategies for implementing specific aspects of software security in the form of SDL best practices to assist software development organizations in avoiding and reducing software flaws as an essential element of effective core software security by providing security at the source.

Although achieving a vulnerability-free product is exceedingly difficult, maybe even impossible, it should always be your goal. By applying the best practices in this book, the software you develop will be as free from security vulnerabilities as possible. The fewer the number of vulnerabilities, the harder it will be for an attacker to exploit a given application. By no means are we going to stop all threats through the use of software security best practices, but maximizing the reduction of the attack surface is our ultimate goal in that it makes our job as software security professionals easier and that of our adversaries more difficult. By implementing the practices outlined in this book, you will be able to a large extent mitigate most threats coming from non-state threat actors. (*Core Software Security*, pp. 325–326)[*]

In this section, we will break down the threats into three major categories, specifically, strategic, tactical, and user specific. We will then provide examples of attacks in each category. The SDL best practices outlined in this book will assist you in developing software that is resistant to these threats and attack methodologies.

5.2.3.1 Strategic, Tactical, and User-Specific Software Attacks

Now that we have described secure software development practices, it is important to finish this book by reminding the reader of the importance of using these practices to protect against today's cyber threats. After a few quotes from industry leaders, we will give a high-level overview of the type of cyber threats that secure software development practices provide as a baseline protection against at the core.

Organizations are implementing policies to address secure software development practices, and beyond using software scanning tools, finding it important to integrate secure software practices into the culture of the organization. Some firms have found that using judicious secure software development processes can reduce vulnerabilities associated with mission critical software by 70%.[†]

– Jeff Snyder, Vice President, Cyber Programs
Raytheon Company, 2012

Cyber attacks take advantage of software errors, such as not properly validating user input, inconsistencies in the design assumptions among system components, and unanticipated user and operator actions. Software errors can be introduced by disconnects and miscommunications during the planning, development, testing, and maintenance of the components. Although an application development team may be expert in the required business functionality, that team usually has limited or no applicable security expertise. The likelihood of disconnects and miscommunications increases as more system components have to satisfy security requirements. The necessary communications and linkages among the life-cycle activities, among multiple development teams, and between

[*] Ransome, J. and Misra, A. (2014). *Core Software Security: Security at the Source*. Boca Raton (FL): CRC Press/ Taylor & Francis Group.

[†] Snyder, J. (2012). "Growing Cyber Threats Demand Advanced Mitigation Methodologies." Retrieved from http:// www.raytheon.com/capabilities/rtnwcm/groups/iis/documents/content/rtn_iis_cyber_whitepaper_wcs.pdf

the system development and eventual usage should be reflected in project management. Project managers should consider the additional communications requirements, linkage among life-cycle activities, and the potential usage environment as these items relate to security needs.[*]

– Robert J. Ellison, "Security and Project Management," 2006

By promoting the best software security practices industry-wide, there is a significant opportunity to improve the overall security of the technology ecosystem.[†]

– Howard Schmidt, Former U.S. Cybersecurity Czar, 2013

The importance of an organization understanding its application security maturity level and the impact it has on their overall IT security profile is critical. **Research has shown that the application layer is responsible for over 90 percent of all security vulnerabilities**, *yet more than 80 percent of IT security spending continues to be at the network layer, primarily focused on perimeter security. The findings of this study reveal the need for making greater investment in application security programs to reduce overall organizational exposure to cybercrime.*[‡]

– The State of Application Security—A Research Study by
Ponemon Institute LLC and Security Innovation, 2013

Strategic attacks are typically planned and controlled to target information assets including specifications, technologies, plans, capabilities, procedures, and guidelines to gain strategic advantage. They are typically conducted by state sponsors (or by entities supported by states), organized crime, or competitors. Tactical attacks are typically random and opportunistic; they target information assets for prestige or financial reward through the use of malware, exploits, hackers, surrogates, insider threat, and chat rooms, and they are conducted by professional hackers, script kiddies, and insiders. As you can see, one of the key differentiators between tactical and strategic attacks is motive: Tactical attacks target network assets for prestige or financial reward, whereas a strategic attack is the coordination of multiple tactical attacks (and on a much larger scale) against multiple target networks for strategic advantage or to preempt an adversary from getting one. The targets of tactical attacks are random and opportunistic, taking advantage of software vulnerabilities and user ignorance, whereas strategic attacks target a higher-level process and are intelligence driven and carefully planned and orchestrated. For example, strategic attacks may include infiltrating strategic infrastructure, targeting telecommunications infrastructure, and aggregating information in specific technology areas such as stealth technology. The ability to understand strategic attacks requires an understanding of (1) the business functions and processes supported by individual networks; (2) the business relationships between networks; and (3) the sharing of tactical attack data among contractors, suppliers, and target entities. The information gleaned by threats to these business relationships is used to guide and direct strategic attacks.[§]

---

[*] Ellison, R. (2006). "Security and Project Management." Retrieved from https://buildsecurityin.us-cert.gov /articles/best-practices/project-management/security-and-project-management

[†] Acohido, B. (2013, February 27). "Former Cybersecurity Czar Pursues Safer Software." Retrieved from http:// www.usatoday.com/story/tech/2013/02/27/howard-schmidt-executive-director-safecode/1952359

[‡] Ponemon Institute and Security Innovation. (2013, August 27). "The State of Application Security—A Research Study by Ponemon Institute LLC and Security Innovation," p. 21. Retrieved from https://www .securityinnovation.com/uploads/ponemon-state-of-application-security-maturity.pdf

[§] Gilbert, L., Morgan, R., and Keen, A. (2009, May 5). "Tactical and Strategic Attack Detection and Prediction." U.S. Patent 7530105. Retrieved from http://www.freepatentsonline.com/7530105.html

User-targeted specific software attacks can be strategic, tactical, or opportunistic. They may involve an attack targeting a privilege escalation of a specific user that exploits a vulnerability in software to gain access to resources and information that would normally be unrestricted to the user—including data on the specific user machine or resources that the user can access. Strategic attacks are a superset that leverage tactical and/or user-specific attacks.

5.2.3.1.1 Strategic Attacks

In general, strategic software targets are applications which are essential to critical infrastructure functions of the government, economy, or society at large. Components of the critical infrastructure include highways, airports and aircraft, trains and railways, bus lines, shipping and boat lines, trucking systems, and supply networks for basic goods, electric power plants and lines, along with oil and gas lines and utilities of all kinds, including water and sewer systems, land and cell phone systems, computer networks, television, and radio (not only that which is publicly accessible, but that controlled by private or government entities in special networks or on special frequencies), banks and other financial institutions, and security, fire, hospital, and emergency services. Each element of the critical infrastructure is so vital that if it were removed from the equation, even temporarily, the entire nation would experience monumental repercussions. Even when the infrastructure of a particular area is threatened, the results can be disastrous. This can include telecommunications, energy, banking and finance, transportation, water systems, and emergency services.[*] Of course, strategic targets also include critical elements of the government such as defense, intelligence, and other agencies considered of high value to an adversary.

Strategic software attacks are highly repeatable and use general targeting such as against a broad industry (military, finance, energy, etc.) or groups of individuals (politicians, executives), and must have long-term staying power. Strategic attacks are less sophisticated in comparison to tactical threats and typically are lower in cost to develop and maintain. These types of attacks can be categorized in three major areas: espionage, criminal, and socio-political.

5.2.3.1.2 Espionage

Cyber spying, or cyber espionage, is the act or practice of obtaining secrets without the permission of the holder of the information, from individuals, competitors, rivals, groups, governments and enemies for personal, economic, political or military advantage using methods on the Internet, networks or individual computers through the use of cracking techniques and malicious software including Trojan horses and spyware. It may wholly be perpetrated online from computer desks of professionals on bases in far away countries or may involve infiltration at home by computer trained conventional spies and moles or in other cases may be the criminal handiwork of amateur malicious hackers and software programmers. Cyber spying typically involves the use of such access to secrets and classified information or control of individual computers or whole networks for a strategic advantage and for psychological, political and physical subversion activities and sabotage.[†]

Cyber espionage is highly strategic in nature; key targets include critical infrastructures, industrial attacks, manufacturing, research and development, pharmaceuticals, finance, and

---

[*] Encyclopedia of Espionage, Intelligence, and Security (2013). *Espionage Encyclopedia: Critical Infrastructure.* Retrieved from http://www.faqs.org/espionage/Cou-De/Critical-Infrastructure.html

[†] Linktv.org. (2013). "Cyber Espionage." Retrieved from http://news.linktv.org/topics/cyber-espionage

government. Government targets may also include the defense industrial base (DIB), which includes defense contractors, research organizations, and political and other high-ranking individuals.

Examples of espionage attacks are Aurora (GhostNet), Shady RAT, Titan Rain, and Night Dragon. Note that some of these attacks can be counted both as espionage and as cyber warfare. They may have multiple utilities depending on how they are deployed. It might be helpful to think of cyber espionage as one part of cyber warfare.

Operation Aurora and GhostNet. The 2012 USCC Annual Report on China contains the following statement:

> *China's cyber capabilities provide Beijing with an increasingly potent tool to achieve national objectives. In a strategic framework that leans heavily on cyber espionage, a diverse set of Chinese hackers use pilfered information to advance political, economic, and security objectives. China's pursuit of intellectual property and trade secrets means that much of this espionage targets private enterprises.*[*]

The information security community has been aware of cyber espionage activities for some time now. However, the extent and impact of such activities surprised many of us. In 2009, researchers at Information Warfare Monitor gave the name "GhostNet" to large-scale cyber espionage operations conducted by the Chinese government. These operations, associated with advanced persistent threats (APTs), raised awareness of APT attacks in the security community and among the general public. GhostNet enabled infiltration of high-value political, economic, and media targets spread across 90+ countries around the world. Though its command and control centers were based in China, there was plausible deniability for the Chinese government, as there was no way to associate it with actual operations. Note that successful cyber espionage operations will have this trademark, allowing governments to disassociate themselves from the actual groups carrying out these attacks.[†]

The attackers would "social engineer" targets to open a document or a link infected with malware. After that, malware would be installed on the target's system (without raising any red flags for most users). Once this happened, malware would provide almost unrestricted access to the attackers. Code was obfuscated, and multiple Trojans were used to avoid detection by many popular antivirus/antimalware software.

Operation Aurora was a cyber attack conducted from China. Attacks began in 2009 and continued until the end of the year. The targets for these attacks were multinational companies including Google®, Adobe®, and Rackspace®. Some companies chose to disclose publicly that they had been the targets of attacks, while others remained under suspicion but never came out publicly. According to McAfee®, the primary goal of the attack was to get access (and modify) source code of these multinational companies. One should note that many of these companies have development offices in Asia (including China). Thus, protecting their bread and butter—source code—is of paramount importance to them, though it was not considered "severe" enough by some companies before this attack. This trend is changing, but not fast enough. If anything, it has resulted in chaos, especially in China, and suspicion of employees working in

---

[*] U.S.–China Economic and Security Review. (2012). "2012 Report to Congress of the U.S.–China Economic and Security Review Commission," One Hundred Twelfth Congress, Second Session. Retrieved from http://www.uscc.gov/sites/default/files/annual_reports/2012-Report-to-Congress.pdf

[†] Information Warfare Monitor. (2009). "Tracking GhostNet: Investigating a Cyber Espionage Network." Retrieved from http://www.scribd.com/doc/13731776/Tracking-GhostNetInvestigating-a-Cyber-Espionage-Network

off-shore offices. This complicates any SDL activities a security group would like to implement in a global enterprise.[*]

Operation Shady RAT. Dimitri Alperovitch of McAfee reported Operation Shady RAT in 2011. Like Operation Aurora, Operation Shady RAT consists of ongoing cyber attacks and has targeted 70+ countries as well as the United Nations and the International Olympic Committee. RAT is an acronym for Remote Access Tool, and though it is not confirmed who is behind these operations, suspicions point to China in this case as well—especially due to the targeting of Olympic organizations around the time of the Beijing Olympics in 2008.[†] Among other targets were Associated Press offices, the U.S. Energy Department, and U.S. defense companies. In this case, as in GhostNet, attackers would "social engineer" users of selected organizations into opening documents, spreadsheets, and other innocent-looking files that actually contained malware. Once the end user complied, malware would be installed and would try to connect to its remote server (hard coded into the malware) and provide attackers with a remote shell.[‡]

Night Dragon. In 2011, McAfee reported that well-organized and targeted cyber attacks were taking place on key international oil and energy companies. These attacks seem to have started in 2009 (though, as for many attacks in this class, there is no sure way of knowing this definitively). Based on investigations by McAfee, fingers point again to China (or China-based hackers). Targeted companies were spread across many different countries, including the United States, Greece, and Taiwan. Information that was stolen included specifics on companies and their operations, bidding data, as well as financial information on projects. Attackers exploited vulnerabilities in Windows® operating systems, applications (including SQL injection), and active directory infrastructure. Remote Access Tools (RATs) were used to harvest and steal sensitive information. First, the companies' external-facing infrastructure (e.g., Web servers) was compromised through SQL injection attacks. This allowed attacks to execute remote commands to target and compromise internal desktops and servers within the enterprise. Additional information was harvested (e.g., passwords), allowing attackers to access sensitive information inside the infrastructure. Attackers were able to establish direct connections from infected systems to the Internet and infiltrated sensitive information including from senior executives' systems.[§,¶]

Titan Rain. APT class attacks were launched against infrastructure in the United States and its allies by hackers believed to be working on behalf of the Chinese government. Attackers were able to get access to many sensitive systems of defense contractors and federal agencies. The purpose of these attacks was to obtain sensitive information, thus putting Titan Rain into

---

[*] McAfee Labs and McAfee Foundstone Professional Services. (2010). "Protecting Your Critical Assets—Lessons Learned from 'Operation Aurora.'" Retrieved from http://www.mcafee.com/us/resources/white-papers/wp-protecting-critical-assets.pdf

[†] Nakashima, E. (2011, August 02). "Report on 'Operation Shady RAT' Identifies Widespread Cyber-Spying." *The Washington Post.* Retrieved from http://articles.washingtonpost.com/2011-08-02/national/35269748_1_intrusions-mcafee-china-issues

[‡] Symantec (2011, August 4). "The Truth Behind the Shady Rat." Symantec Official Blog. Retrieved from http://www.symantec.com/connect/blogs/truth-behind-shady-rat

[§] Hsu, T. (2011, February 10). "China-Based Hackers Targeted Oil, Energy Companies in 'Night Dragon' Cyber Attacks, McAfee Says." *Los Angeles Times.* Retrieved from http://latimesblogs.latimes.com/technology/2011/02/chinese-hackers-targeted-oil-companies-in-cyberattack-mcafee-says.html#sthash.d7PrG6Iy.dpuf

[¶] McAfee Foundstone Professional Services and McAfee Labs (2011, February 10). "Global Energy Cyberattacks: 'Night Dragon.'" Retrieved from http://www.mcafee.com/us/resources/white-papers/wp-global-energy-cyber-attacks-night-dragon.pdf

the espionage category rather than warfare, although it could be easily used for cyber warfare as well.[*,†,‡,§]

5.2.3.1.3 Organized Crime

Along with the evolution of the Internet, cyber crime has evolved from the domain of individuals and small groups to traditional organized crime syndicates and criminally minded technology professionals working together and pooling their resources and expertise. This has been largely due to the speed, convenience, and anonymity that modern technologies offer to those wanting to commit a diverse range of criminal activities. Consequently, just as brick-and-mortar companies moved their enterprises to the World Wide Web seeking new opportunities for profits, criminal enterprises are doing the same thing. The global nature of the Internet has allowed criminals to commit almost any illegal activity anywhere in the world, making it essential for all countries to adapt their domestic offline controls to cover crimes carried out in cyberspace. These activities include attacks against computer data and systems, identity theft, the distribution of child sexual abuse images, Internet auction fraud, money laundering, the penetration of online financial services, online banking theft, illicit access to intellectual property, online extortion, as well as the deployment of viruses, botnets, and various email scams such as phishing. Organized crime groups typically have a home base in a nation that provides safe haven, from which they conduct their transnational operations. In effect, this provides an added degree of protection against law enforcement and allows them to operate with minimal risk. The inherently transnational nature of the Internet fits perfectly into this model of activity and the effort to maximize profits within an acceptable degree of risk. In the virtual world there are no borders, a characteristic that makes it very attractive for criminal activity; yet when it comes to policing this virtual world, borders and national jurisdictions loom large—making large-scale investigation slow and tedious at best, and impossible at worst.[¶,**,††] Some of the more noteworthy groups are the European crime rings, state-sponsored criminal groups and proxies, U.S. domestic crime groups, and Mexican cartels.

As payoff from cyber crime grows, it is no surprise that organized crime groups seek a share in it. Cyber crime allows organized syndicates to finance their other illicit activities in addition to providing hefty profits. Criminal syndicates are involved in everything from theft to extortion, piracy, and enabling online crime in the first place. They are providing a new meaning to the "as-a-service" term. In addition to exploiting cyber infrastructure for monetary gains, they are enabling cyber attacks by providing vulnerabilities, creating tools, and offering resources to people who will pay for it. These services include selling vulnerabilities (proactively looking for

---

[*]   Graham, B. (2005, August 25). "Hackers Attack via Chinese Web Sites." *The Washington Post.* Retrieved from http://www.washingtonpost.com/wp-dyn/content/article/2005/08/24/AR2005082402318.html.

[†]   Thornburgh, N. (2005, August 25). "Inside the Chinese Hack Attack." *Time Magazine.* Retrieved from http://content.time.com/time/nation/article/0,8599,1098371,00.html

[‡]   Onley, D. and Wait, P. (2006, August 17). "Red Storm Rising." *GCN.* Retrieved from http://gcn.com/Articles/2006/08/17/Red-storm-rising.aspx?Page=2&p=1

[§]   Sandlin, S. (2007, October 14). "Analyst, Sandia Settle Suit."*Albuquerque Journal.* Retrieved from http://www.abqjournal.com/news/metro/602547metro10-14-07.htm

[¶]   Interpol (2013). "Cybercrime." Retrieved from http://www.interpol.int/Crime-areas/Cybercrime/Cybercrime

[**] Williams, P. (2013). "Organized Crime and Cyber-Crime: Implications for Business." CERT Coordination Center (CERT/CC). Retrieved from www.cert.org/archive/pdf/cybercrime-business.pdf

[††] Williams, P. (2013). "Organized Crime and Cybercrime: Synergies, Trends, and Responses." Retrieved from http://www.crime-research.org/library/Cybercrime.htm

them in new software products and infrastructure), creating and selling exploits for existing vulnerabilities, spam services, infrastructure (botnets, hosting), as well as malware.[*]

5.2.3.1.4 Socio-Political Attacks

Socio-political attacks are often intended to elevate awareness of a topic but can also be a component or a means to an end with regard to political action groups, civil disobedience, or part of a larger campaign, and they may be an indicator and warning of bigger things to come.

Evidence is growing that more cyber attacks are associated with social, political, economic, and cultural (SPEC) conflicts. It is also now known that cyber attackers' level of socio-technological sophistication, their backgrounds, and their motivations are essential components to predicting, preventing, and tracing cyber attacks. Thus, SPEC factors have the potential to be early predictors for outbreaks of anomalous activities, hostile attacks, and other security breaches in cyberspace.[†]

Some well-known examples of socio-political attacks have been the result of efforts by Anonymous, WikiLeaks, and Edward Snowden (also an example of an insider threat), and attacks by radical Muslim groups or jihadists (e.g., Al Qaeda).

Anonymous. Anonymous is a group of activists that over the last few years has become well known for its attacks on government and corporate infrastructure. It has a decentralized command structure and can be thought of more as a social movement. This movement has targeted everyone from religious institutions (Church of Scientology) to corporations (Visa®, MasterCard®, PayPal®, Sony®) and government institutions (the United States, Israel, Tunisia). Some of the most famous attacks launched by Anonymous are Project Chaology and Operation: Payback Is a Bitch. After a video of Tom Cruise was posted on a blog, the Church of Scientology responded with a cease-and-desist letter for copyright violation. The project users organized a raid against the church, including distributed denial-of-service (DDoS) attacks. In 2010, they targeted the RIAA and MIAA, bringing down their websites.[‡] This action was a protest to protect their rights to share information with one another—one of their important principles, in their opinion.

WikiLeaks published classified diplomatic cables in November 2010. Under pressure from the U.S. government, Amazon.com removed WikiLeaks from its servers, and PayPal, Visa, and MasterCard stopped providing financial services for WikiLeaks. This resulted in attacks against PayPal, Visa, and MasterCard, disrupting their websites and services.[§,¶,**]

---

[*] Samani, R. and Paget, F. (2011). "Cybercrime Exposed—Cybercrime-as-a-Service." McAfee—An Intel Company White Paper. Retrieved from http://www.mcafee.com/us/resources/white-papers/wp-cybercrime-exposed.pdf

[†] Gandhi, R., Sharma, A., Mahoney, W., Sousan, W., Zhu, Q., and Laplante, P. (2011, February). "Dimensions of Cyber-Attacks: Cultural, Social, Economic, and Political." *IEEE Technology and Society Magazine*, Vol. 30, No. 1, pp. 28–38. Retrieved from http://www.researchgate.net/publication/224223630 _Dimensions_of_Cyber-Attacks_Cultural_Social_Economic_and_Political

[‡] Vaughan-Nichols, S. (2012, January 20). "How Anonymous Took Down the DoJ, RIAA, MPAA and Universal Music Websites." *ZDNet*. Retrieved from http://www.zdnet.com/blog/networking/how-anonymous -took-down-the-doj-riaa-mpaa-and-universal-music-websites/1932

[§] Tucker, N. (2008, January18). "Tom Cruise's Scary Movie; In Church Promo, the Scientologist Is Hard to Suppress." *The Washington Post*. Retrieved from http://www.highbeam.com/doc/1P2-15129123.html

[¶] *The Economist* (2008, February 2). "Fair Game; Scientology. (Cyberwarfare Against a Cult) (Anonymous)." Retrieved from http://www.highbeam.com/doc/1G1-174076065.html

[**] BBC (2010, December 9). "Anonymous Hacktivists Say Wikileaks War to Continue." Retrieved from http:// www.bbc.co.uk/news/technology-11935539

Anonymous also launched a number of activities in support of the "Arab spring" movement and has targeted websites hosting child pornography. After San Francisco's Bay Area Rapid Transit (BART) blocked cell service to prevent a planned protest, Anonymous targeted the BART website and shut it down.[*]

Jihadists. Threats posed by jihadists are increasing. In one sense, this is part of cyber warfare, though there is a difference from most such activities in that there is a fundamental religious ideology driving these actors. Cyber attacks by terrorists/jihadist organizations started at least as far back as November 2001 (not long after 9/11), though these early attacks were relatively unsophisticated. A terrorist suspect told interrogators that Al Qaeda had launched low-level computer attacks, sabotaging websites by launching denial-of-service (DoS) attacks.[†]

5.2.3.1.5 Cyber Warfare

The term cyber war gives the impression that the war is happening only in cyberspace, when in fact a more accurate interpretation is cyber weapons are used in the digital theater of war that can be strategically aligned with traditional (physical) warfare activities.[‡]

Cyber warfare has been defined by government security expert Richard A. Clarke as "actions by a nation-state to penetrate another nation's computers or networks for the purposes of causing damage or disruption."[§] *The Economist* describes cyber warfare as "the fifth domain of warfare."[¶]

William J. Lynn, U.S. Deputy Secretary of Defense, states that "as a doctrinal matter, the Pentagon has formally recognized cyberspace as a new domain in warfare—[which] has become just as critical to military operations as land, sea, air, and space."[**]

From some of the quotes above you can see that there is an acceptance that when we speak of war, cyber and physical are not separate from each other; they are merely different theaters of war. Like other theaters of war, they all have commonalities but typically have different weapons, tactics, and command structure, as well as different rules of engagement, different forms of targets and different methods to identify a target, different expectations of collateral damage, and different expectations of risk. Cyber attacks can have a great impact, but not necessarily focused or highly targeted, such as disrupting communications, affecting processing of information, and disrupting portions of systems that inhibit normal functions.

In contrast to this, when the government or military use the term "cyber war," they are typically thinking of highly targeted and impactful eventualities, such as shutting down power, phones, air traffic control, trains, and emergency services. Cyber attacks are not limited to cyberspace; there is both intended and unintended collateral damage outside the realm of cyber. For example, manipulating a SCADA (supervisory control and data acquisition) system

---

[*] Swallow, E. (2011, August 14). "Anonymous Hackers Attack BART Website." *Mashable.* Retrieved from http://mashable.com/2011/08/15/bart-anonymous-attack

[†] Kingsbury, A. (2010, April 14). "Documents Reveal Al Qaeda Cyberattacks—The Attacks Were Relatively Minor but Show the Group's Interest in Cyberwar." *U.S. News & World Report.* Retrieved from http://www.usnews.com/news/articles/2010/04/14/documents-reveal-al-qaeda-cyberattacks

[‡] Tiller, J. (2010, June 10). "Cyberwarfare: It's a New Theater of War, Not Just a New Form of War." *Real Ssecurity.* Retrieved from http://www.realsecurity.us/weblog/?e=104

[§] Clarke, R. A. (2010). *Cyber War.* New York: HarperCollins.

[¶] The Economist. (2010, July 1). "Cyberwar: War in the Fifth Domain." *The Economist.* Retrieved from https://www.economist.com/briefing/2010/07/01/war-in-the-fifth-domain

[**] Lynn, W. J., III. (2010, Sept./Oct.) "Defending a New Domain: The Pentagon's Cyberstrategy." *Foreign Affairs*, pp. 97–108.

in a chemical plant or a critical infrastructure facility may cause an intended or unintended explosion, possible area contamination, or a toxic chemical spill or floating toxic cloud.

It is no secret that foreign cyberspace operations against U.S. public- and private-sector systems are increasing in number and sophistication. U.S. government networks are probed millions of times every day, and successful penetrations have led to the loss of thousands of sensitive files from U.S. networks and those of U.S. allies and industry partners. Moreover, this threat continues to evolve, as evidence grows of adversaries focusing on the development of increasingly sophisticated and potentially dangerous capabilities.*

The potential for small groups to have an asymmetric impact in cyberspace creates very real incentives for malicious activity. Beyond formal governmental activities, cyber criminals can control botnets with millions of infected hosts. The tools and techniques developed by cyber criminals are increasing in sophistication at an incredible rate, and many of these capabilities can be purchased cheaply on the Internet. Whether the goal is monetary, access to intellectual property, or the disruption of critical systems, the rapidly evolving threat landscape presents a complex and vital challenge for national and economic security.

To counter this threat, the U.S. Department of Defense has announced five strategic initiatives it is taking. They are worth reviewing here. First, treat cyberspace as an operational domain of war, just like land, sea, air, and space. Hence, the "fifth domain" of war is recognized as an operational theater. Second, evolve new defense concepts to combat cyber attacks. This entails taking four basic steps, as shown below:

1. Enhance cyber best practices to improve its cyber security.
2. Deter and mitigate insider threats, strengthen workforce communications, workforce accountability, internal monitoring, and information management capabilities.
3. Employ an active cyber defense capability to prevent intrusions onto networks and systems.
4. Develop new defense operating concepts and computing architectures.

The third initiative is to begin to partner with other U.S. government departments and agencies and the private sector to enable a government-wide cyber security strategy. The fourth initiative is to build robust relationships with U.S. allies and international partners to strengthen collective cyber security. Finally, leverage the nation's ingenuity through an exceptional cyber workforce and rapid technological innovation. The most significant thing to note in all of the aforementioned in relation to this book is the first step: recognition of cyber best practices that need to be developed to improve cyber security, which of course includes securing the core by building security into the development process as described in this book.

Examples of cyber warfare threats that strong secure development practices protect against include the cyber attacks on Estonia in 2007 and attacks on assets in Georgia during the Russia–Georgia conflict in 2008.

Cyber Attacks on Estonia. Estonia and Russia have a long (and unstable) relationship. Estonia, one of the Baltic States, was part of the USSR from 1940 to 1991. Estonia became part of NATO in 2004. In 2007, the Estonian government moved the Bronze Soldier—a memorial honoring the Soviet liberation of Estonia from Nazi Germany—to a different location. This resulted in rioting by the Russian-speaking minority community in Estonia, which viewed the move as an effort to further marginalize their ethnic identity. At the same time, DDoS attacks started to target the country's cyber infrastructure. Attacks were able to shut down websites of the government, banks, and political institutions. Estonians accused Russia of waging cyber

---

* "U.S. Department of Defense Strategy for Operating in Cyberspace," July 2011, p. 3.

war and considered invoking Article 5 of the NATO treaty, although it chose not to do so in the end. One should note that cyber war can lead to much wider military conflict in such situations—something we might not have seen so far but which remains a real possibility. Estonia was the first case of a country publicly claiming to be a victim of cyber war.[*,†,‡]

Georgia–Russia Conflict of 2008. In the fall of 2008, hostilities broke out between Russia and Georgia over South Ossetia. At the same time, coordinated cyber attacks against Georgian assets started as well. The Georgian government accused Russia of being behind these attacks (though the Kremlin denied it). Note that this was the first time that cyber warfare actually accompanied a military war. The official website of Georgia President Mikheil Saakashvili was under the control of attackers before Russian armed intervention started, and so were the websites of other government agencies. Commercial websites were also hijacked. Visits to websites in Georgia were routed through Russia and Turkey, where traffic was blocked, preventing people from accessing them. When Germany intervened and traffic was routed through German servers, attackers again took control to route traffic through servers based in Russia.[§]

5.2.3.1.6 Tactical Attacks

Tactical cyber threats are typically surgical by nature, have highly specific targeting, and are technologically sophisticated. Given the specific nature of the attack, the cost of development is typically high. Repeatability is less significant for tactical attacks than for strategic attacks. Tactical attacks can be adjuncts to strategic attacks; in some cases they serve as a force multiplier or augment other activities such as a military campaign or as a supplementary action to a special-interest action group. Given the surgical nature of these attacks, they are also popular for use in subversive operations. Given the cost of these attacks, they are typically financed by well-funded private entities and governments that are often global in nature and popularity—a country, a business, or a special-interest group.

An example of tactical cyber attack (which was leveraged for strategic purposes) is the Stuxnet worm. The U.S. and Israeli governments, aiming to subvert nuclear power plants in Iran, likely designed the Stuxnet worm. However, it ended up infecting more than just the intended target, Iran: It impacted a host of countries, including India, the United States, and Great Britain. By September 2010, more than 100,000+ unique hosts had been infected by this worm.[¶] Stuxnet was unique in the way it was designed. It propagated through more than one medium (e.g., flash drives and Internet connections). It affected Windows systems and exploited known patched and unknown vulnerabilities in the operating system. However, these

---

[*] Herzog, S. (2011, Summer). "Revisiting the Estonian Cyber Attacks: Digital Threats and Multinational Responses." *Journal of Strategic Security*, Vol. 4, No. 2, Strategic Security in the Cyber Age, Article 4. Retrieved from http://scholarcommons.usf.edu/cgi/viewcontent.cgi?article=1105&context=jss

[†] RIA Novosti. (2007, September 6). "Estonia Has No Evidence of Kremlin Involvement in Cyber Attacks." Retrieved from http://en.rian.ru/world/20070906/76959190.html

[‡] Rehman, S. (2013, January 14). "Estonia's Lessons in Cyberwarfare." *U.S. News Weekly*. Retrieved from http://www.usnews.com/opinion/blogs/world-report/2013/01/14/estonia-shows-how-to-build-a-defense-against-cyberwarfare

[§] Swaine, J. (2008, August 11). "Georgia: Russia 'Conducting Cyber War.'" *The Telegraph*. Retrieved from http://www.telegraph.co.uk/news/worldnews/europe/georgia/2539157/Georgia-Russia-conducting-cyber-war.html

[¶] Falliere, N., Murchu, L., and Chien, E. (2011, February). "W32.Stuxnet Dossier, Version 1.4—Symantec Security Response." Retrieved from http://www.symantec.com/content/en/us/enterprise/media/security_response/whitepapers/w32_stuxnet_dossier.pdf

Windows systems were not the actual targets of this worm. After infecting a host, it would look for a specific industrial control system, the Programmable Logic Controller made by Siemens. Apparently, this controller was being used by Iran in its nuclear power plants. If it did not detect the particular controller software, it would not do anything but would wait to propagate around to other hosts. If it did find the controller software, it would infect and change it.[*]

5.2.3.1.7 User-Specific Attacks

User-specific cyber threats can be strategic, tactical, or personal in nature, and target personal devices that may be either consumer- or enterprise-owned. The use of strategic, tactical, or publicly available methods to exploit specific individuals or general populations of users for monetary, political, or personal gain can be specifically targeted to a user as a primary target or as a means to get to another target or random exploitation of a user as a target of opportunity.

In many ways, most strategic and tactical attacks are a form of user attack. The difference between these attacks and user-specific attacks are those of scale. An example of this type of attack is to target a user by installing a key-logger on his system with the intent to use it for immediate financial benefit (e.g., to get passwords to log onto bank accounts), unauthorized access to someone else's e-mail account (for spying on a spouse or celebrities), or to target a quiz with the intention to get around actual results. All these attacks are of benefit to a handful of individuals. Examples of attacks in these categories are ransomware, credit card harvesting, targeting of specific individuals for monetary gains (bank accounts, Social Security numbers, and so on), unauthorized access to social media sites, e-mails, and other online information with intent to blackmail, exploit, or embarrass individuals, identify theft, phishing attacks, and exploitation of "smart home" products. Readers will be familiar with most of these attacks. Ransomware is a kind of malware that tricks users into believing that there is no way out for them except to pay to get rid of a nuisance. An example of such an attack would be locking a user's desktop and asking for a payment to unlock it. Such attacks were initially found in Russia but have spread to other countries over the last couple of years.[†] (*Core Software Security*, pp. 326–339)

5.3 Security Tools, Automation, and Vendor Management

The goal of DevOps is to give development teams more ownership in deploying and monitoring their software products. Automation is at the heart of DevOps and helps the development teams move faster and ship higher-quality products. As part of this process, security must be part of the development process that is automated as much as possible to not slow it down. This also includes security policies and standards designed so that they don't slow the process down. This holistic approach to automation will not only help the development teams to ship their code faster with higher quality but also more securely. Automating the manual processes in CI/CD has helped the previously disparate operational and development teams to work as one single team.

> *Automation in DevSecOps is the common denominator. It empowers development, security, and operations roles in the unified DevSecOps team to collaborate and scale their perspectives across*

---

[*] Schneier, B. (2010, October 7). "Stuxnet." *Schneier on Security—A Blog Covering Security and Security Technology*. Retrieved from https://www.schneier.com/blog/archives/2010/10/stuxnet.html

[†] Dunn, J. (2012, March 9). "Ransom Trojans Spreading Beyond Russian Heartland: Security Companies Starting to See More Infections." *Techworld*. Retrieved from http://news.techworld.com/security/3343528/ransom-trojans-spreading-beyond-russian-heartland

the SDLC regardless of the deployment framework—on-premises, private cloud, public cloud, or hybrid. It accelerates security by making it a frictionless part of an organization's new culture. . . . Although automation in DevSecOps is critical, it is not a substitute for all manual efforts. You still need to focus on the design of applications and on infrastructure support of application and security controls. It is important to identify potential weaknesses that may increase your system's susceptibility to an attack, including where your design violates secure design patterns, your system omits security controls, or those security controls suffer from misconfiguration, weakness, or misuse.[*]

– Steve Cohen, Synopsys, 2018

Integrating security and audit capability should be a built-in component of your DevOps processes and pipeline by incorporating automated security testing and compliance. As more and more of your tests and processes are automated, you have less risk of introducing security flaws due to human error. This provides an automated pipeline a closed-loop process for testing, reporting, and resolving security concerns. Through automation and integrating security tools and tests as part of the pipeline used by development and operations, security becomes an enabler of the process rather than a boat anchor.

Security as Code is about building security into DevOps tools and practices, making it an essential part of the tool chains and workflows. This requires the addition of security checks, tests, and gates without introducing unnecessary costs or delays. Security tools and testing are moved directly into Continuous Integration and Continuous Delivery (CI/CD) in order to verify security as soon as changes are made. Some considerations for key security tools to be used for continuous security and integration within the DevOps development pipeline are briefly discussed below. (Sections 5.3.1–5.3.4 are discussed at length in Chapter 3.)

5.3.1 Static Application Security Testing (SAST)

SAST tools are used to examine source code for security defects. It is one of the several checks designed to identify and mitigate security vulnerabilities early in the DevOps software development process. Automating these capabilities drive efficiency, consistency, and early detection. Within GitLab, SAST will automatically generate a summary of fixes and unresolved vulnerabilities following every code commit before your code is merged to the target branch. Tools that allow SAST reports to sit within the developer's work interface enable ease of remediation and streamline testing procedures within the development phase.[†]

5.3.2 Dynamic Analysis Security Testing (DAST)

Black box DAST tools and services are useful for testing Web and mobile apps, but they don't always play nicely in continuous integration or continuous delivery. As with SAST, DAST should auto-run, so that the developer doesn't have to take measures to initiate the test. In other situations, DAST can also be used to continuously monitor live Web applications for issues like cross-site scripting or broken authentication flaws. Test results should inform developers of potential vulnerabilities and serve as a catalyst for ongoing updates. GitLab's DAST tool runs live attacks on a review app during QA, meaning developers can iterate on new apps and updates earlier and faster.[‡]

[*] Cohen, S. (2018, October 12). "Automation: One of the Keys to DevSecOps." Synopsys—Software Integrity Blog. Retrieved from https://www.synopsys.com/blogs/software-security/automation-in-devsecops/

[†] Wegner, V. (2019). "DevOps Zone: Why You Need Static and Dynamic Application Security Testing in Development Workflows." Retrieved from https://dzone.com/articles/why-you-need-static-and-dynamic-application-securi

[‡] Ibid.

5.3.3 Fuzzing and Continuous Delivery

Fuzz testing is important in embedded systems development for which the costs of mistakes are high and are also commonly used by security researchers to hunt for bugs. Some newer fuzzing tools are designed to run (or can be adapted to run) in CI/CD. They let you seed test values to create repeatable tests, set time boxes on test runs, detect duplicate errors, and write scripts to automatically set up/restore state in case the system crashes.[*]

5.3.4 Unit and Functional Testing

DevOps teams use test-driven development (TDD) frameworks and continuous integration (CI) tools to automate unit testing. Security can write code and add custom security unit tests to the pipeline, in particular, testing for edge cases, exceptions, and negative cases that could catch security problems.

5.3.5 Integration Testing

Integration testing is when you test more than one component and how they function together. The purpose of this level of testing is to expose faults in the interaction between integrated units. As with unit testing, Security should add custom security integration tests to the pipeline.

5.3.6 Automate Red Team Testing

You should always try to beat your adversaries in attacking your systems. Red teaming in this context means looking at your infrastructure and code from the viewpoint of an attacker allows for a better security understanding of the weaknesses and strengths of a software product. There are a few test frameworks that are designed for ease of use and behave well for automated attacks against your systems in a CI/CD environment. They provide the ability to set up and run a basic set of targeted automated pen tests against your system as part of your automated test cycle. See Chapter 3 for a more in-depth discussion regarding red and purple teams.

5.3.7 Automate Pen Testing

Out-of-band pen testing is still appropriate use in satisfying mandatory compliance requirements or for validating the strengths or weaknesses of your security program. However, the pace and velocity of delivery is too fast in CI/CD for traditional manual pen testing that will take too long to set up, run, and review. There are new tools and services available that deliver a continuous and on-demand Penetration Testing as a Service that can be fully integrated into a DevOps environment by executing end-to-end security testing for your product, thereby ensuring that speed, reliability, and consistency of your development process are maintained.

---

[*] Bird, J. (2016). *O'Reilly Media Online—DevOpsSec: Chapter 4. Security as Code: Security Tools and Practices in Continuous Delivery.* Retrieved from https://www.oreilly.com/library/view/devopssec/9781491971413/ch04 .html

5.3.8 Vulnerability Management

Managing vulnerability risk in an Agile, DevOps, and cloud environment is complicated. Constant configuration changes, code and container vulnerabilities, cloud sprawl, and evolving compliance requirements make this task difficult and challenging.

Automated vulnerability monitoring enables you to check for vulnerabilities in your software without interrupting the flow of delivery. These systems do this by looking for two main types of vulnerabilities. Applying continuous monitoring practices for vulnerability scanning can enhance your vulnerability management program, keeping your pipeline constantly under surveillance. It will help you detect vulnerabilities earlier and determine the effectiveness of your remediation practices. Security teams need to detect and manage vulnerabilities in a number of categories across the development process. They should search for vulnerabilities that may be present in code, in containers, and in the cloud.[*] For a more detailed discussion regarding the management of pipeline issues and A/B testing, please refer to Chapter 3.

Products are evolved quickly to address the specific requirements of vulnerability management within the CI/CD DevOps environments as well as being interoperable with current CI/CD development tools. Vulnerability management solutions are at the core of a DevSecOps process in which all tools are required to spool their data into those solutions so that it can be centrally managed, triaged, tracked and remediated. It is important to create or purchase a developer dashboard program that combines technical aspects of vulnerability management with individual accountability to help instill a security mindset among the company's developers.

5.3.9 Automated Configuration Management

Code-driven configuration management tools make it easy to set up standardized configurations across hundreds of servers using common templates, minimizing the risk that hackers can exploit one unpatched server and letting you minimize any differences between production, test, and development environments. All of the configuration information for the managed environments is visible in a central repository and under version control. This means that when a vulnerability is reported in a software component such as OpenSSL, it is easy to identify which systems need to be patched. And it is easy to push patches out, as well. These tools also provide some host-based intrusion-detection capabilities and give you control over configuration drift: They continuously and automatically audit runtime configurations to ensure that every system matches the master configuration definition, issue alerts when something is missing or wrong, and can automatically correct it.[†]

5.3.10 Software Composition Analysis

Software Composition Analysis (SCA) analyzes applications for third parties and open source software to detect illegal, dangerous, or outdated code as well as check for vulnerabilities arising from missing security patches. Depending upon the number and severity of vulnerabilities to either continue running the pipeline or fail to fix the vulnerabilities. It will be important that you pick a tool/solution that can

[*] Verma, A. (2020). "DevOps Automation for the Secure Cloud: Vulnerability Management." Retrieved from https://www.whizlabs.com/blog/vulnerability-management-for-devops/

[†] Bird, J. (2016). *O'Reilly Media Online—DevOpsSec: Chapter 4. Security as Code: Security Tools and Practices in Continuous Delivery.* Retrieved from https://www.oreilly.com/library/view/devopssec/9781491971413/ch04.html

integrate with continuous integration tools to provide users with visibility into all direct and indirect open source libraries in use, known and unknown vulnerabilities in those libraries, and how they impact applications, without slowing down development velocity.

5.3.11 Bug Bounty Programs

Bug bounty programs can strengthen your operational security in any part of the DevOps pipeline and create a synergy between your security team and your developers. Using an extended community of security researchers will provide you with skills that you would not likely be able to afford to hire internally. Although this isn't an automated process, it can help test the efficacy of both the automated tools and manual assessments you are using to identify security issues in your software. This includes information on where your security needs to improve to include design, threat modeling, security reviews, testing, coding, and configuration management.

5.3.12 Securing Your Continuous Delivery Pipeline

Continuous delivery and continuous deployment effectively extend the attack surface of your production system to your build and automated test and deployment environment. It is important to secure the continuous delivery tool chain and build and test environments to have confidence in the integrity of delivery and the chain of custody, not just for compliance and security reasons but also to ensure that changes are made safely, repeatably, and traceably. Your continuous delivery tool chain is also a dangerous attack target itself since it provides a clear path for making changes and pushing them automatically into production. It can provide a path, if compromised, for attackers to have an easy way into your development, test, and production environments. Threat modeling the continuous delivery pipeline should be required to assess any weaknesses in the setup and controls, and gaps in auditing or logging.[*] The SDL threat modeling requirement is also discussed in Chapter 3.

Of most importance in the CI/CD DevOps environment is how quickly you get your code production. For security to effectively be part of the pipeline, it must be automated, embedded early, continuous, and fully integrated into the development lifecycle and DevOps pipeline. Automation, where possible, is key to the success of security within the DevOps pipeline. It has become a key characteristic for organizations with highly developed DevOps practices, as shown in the 2018 Sonatype Survey[†] of nearly 2,300 IT, where 57% of respondents indicated that they ran automated security tests throughout the entire development lifecycle and that mature DevOps practices are 338% more likely to integrate automated security. Integrating security into DevOps practices through automation results in two significant advantages:

1. It ensures that flaws and weaknesses are exposed early on through monitoring, assessment, and analysis, so remediation can be implemented far earlier than traditional efforts.
2. By failing fast with security testing, organizations reduce the risk of a security incident and decrease the cost of rework.

The bottom line is that if security embraces automation in the DevOps environment, it can make itself much more integral to the DevOps development pipeline. For example, they could

---

[*] Ibid.
[†] Sonatype. (2018). *DevSecOps Community Survey 2018*. Fulton (MD): Sonatype, p. 9.

- Inject code analysis tools into the development process and enforce fixes prior to deployment;
- Automate attacks against preproduction code and prevent that code from reaching production if they're successful;
- Continually test the production environment for weaknesses in an automated fashion; and
- Embrace next generation automated security tools to secure their enclave.[*]

As stated in Chapter 2, Section 2.3.3, vendor risk management (VRM) and third-party risk management are important parts of both your DevOps and company overall risk profile. The principles for vendor management present in that section will be the same for this section.

5.3.13 Vendor Management

Vendor management is very important to ensure the efficiency, performance, and value of the third-party security tools in your development environment. Some of the consequences of the mismanagement of vendors include the following:

- A significant number of missed bugs can result from a poor understanding of software requirements by the testing team.
- Incoherent bug description may become a problem, if you don't talk over a conventional bug reporting procedure or bug tracking tools with your vendor.
- Excessive costs can ensue. This issue may arise if the testing strategy is unbalanced, implies unreasonable testing types or human resources allocation, lacks relevant test automation, or your vendor reports the activities that were performed only partially (or not performed at all) as completed.
- A vendor doesn't improve their performance. If they don't get your feedback stating that there is space for performance improvement (optimizing testing teams, providing more coherent bug reports or introducing the relevant testing types), they may not even consider it.
- Vendor lock-in may be a nasty side effect in case your vendor uses legacy software testing tools and neglects testing documentation.
- Difficulties with contract management may arise if vendor management processes and vendor performance assessment criteria aren't agreed upon in the contract, so it's highly complicated for your vendor to live up to relevant key performance indicators (KPIs) without even knowing them.[†]

To help prevent the above and other issues from happening, vendor management should include the following best practices:

- Monitor the testing team's performance and output using the conventional bug tracking and project management tools.
- Ensure that the service-level agreement (SLA) terms and requirements are followed and met. SLAs can provide solid legal ground for regular vendor performance assessment and comprehensive management.
- Organize updates of software requirements.
- Provide judgment in disputable situations able to hinder the testing performance.
- Mediate the problem-solving process.

[*] Brown, J. (2020). *Mythbusting: DevOps and Security*. Retrieved from https://www.wired.com/insights/2013/10 /mythbusting-devops-and-security/

[†] Dracup, B. (2019). "QA Vendor Performance Management." Retrieved from https://www.devopsonline.co.uk /qa-vendor-performance-management/

- Provide the testing team with continuous feedback on their performance.
- Suggest the possibilities to improve vendor performance. The feedback provided to your quality assurance (QA) vendor should be based on performance assessment results. It's essential to evaluate the vendor performance regularly to be sure that software testing outsourcing meets your expectations.
- Conduct periodic vendor performance assessment, the results of which will help to find the ways to enhance their performance; decide on a vendor replacement or a multivendor strategy in case of need. Vendor performance management and reporting is important, as your vendor needs to receive constant feedback in order to meet your expectations and improve their performance.[*]

5.4 DevOps Security Incident Response

The FIRST.org PSIRT Services Framework webpage clearly defines the role and function of a Product Security Incident Response Team (PSIRT):

> A Product Security Incident Response Team (PSIRT) is an entity within an organization which, at its core, focuses on the identification, assessment, and disposition of the risks associated with security vulnerabilities within the products, including offerings, solutions, components, and/or services which an organization produces and/or sells.
>
> A properly deployed PSIRT is not an independently operating group, disconnected from the development of the organization's products. Instead it is part of the organization's broader secure engineering initiative. This structure ensures that security assurance activities are integrated into the Secure Development Lifecycle (SDL).
>
> Product security incident response is often associated with the maintenance phase of the SDL because most product security vulnerabilities are reported as quality escapes after the product has been released to the market. However, PSIRT can be impactful in the earlier requirements gathering of architecture, design, planning, and risk-modeling phases. PSIRT functions may also add value by providing guidance and oversight for the handling of internally found security issues.[†]

Building upon what was discussed in Chapter 2, the following sections will describe what it takes to evolve to the next level of PSIRT support in a DevOps environment.

5.4.1 Organizational Structure

The mature PSIRT responsibilities and organization were described in Chapter 2. Ideally, that was actually where you should be right now, but the future will require a more integrated partnership and integral set of tools to alleviate any security bugs in the shortest amount of time possible to maximize the reduction of externally discovered security vulnerabilities in your software products. In addition, the single most important thing a PSIRT needs is executive leadership buy-in and support. Without it, PSIRT will not be able to be effective in fulfilling its role.

As stated earlier, part-time security champions should be replaced by full-time security engineers who are also developers. They will still retain security responsibilities, such as helping lead security activities, developing security strategies and processes, proactively monitoring security, helping evaluate security issues in conjunction with security architects, scoring vulnerabilities, and reviewing exceptions

---

[*] Ibid.
[†] FIRST.org (2020). "PSIRT Services Framework." Retrieved from https://www.first.org/standards/frameworks/psirts/psirt_services_framework_v1.0

to policies. This will also include working with and being an extension to the centralized product security response function. This will result in a much more streamlined and efficient process than in the past, as well as better credibility and buy-in with the development team. The security engineer will be a PSIRT evangelist, trainer, and response lead for the development team that they represent.

5.4.2 Proactive Hunting

The value of red teams, as mentioned previously, provides the ability of your organization to get ahead of the hackers to identify the defects in your products before they do. Establishing a proactive approach to the hunting and testing of your software, along with the automating tools described earlier in the chapter, optimizes your ability to surface software weaknesses that can be exploited by an adversary. By increasing internal security testing and making it proactive, an organization benefits because remediation guidance becomes immediately actionable and integrated with business processes. This is typically done through the use of internal red teams, bug bounty programs, and automated tools. For a detailed discussion of red teaming and proactive hunting, please refer to Chapter 3.

5.4.3 Continuous Detection and Response

There is an increasing focus on incidence response and reporting, as many regulatory standards require the ability to rapidly respond to incidents and report them in a timely manner. To ensure the efficacy of this process, all data surrounding the incident must be captured to allow for proper investigation. Given the dynamic environment most code software is deployed in, to include the cloud, the ability to capture data, and analyze and react in a rapid manner is almost impossible to do using traditional manual methods. This is only exacerbated by the automation of various management services as well as autoscaling that can result in instances being turned on or off in minutes. Autoscaling is the process of dynamically allocating resources to match performance requirements.

Next generation PSIRT in DevOps will require continuous detection, comparison, correlation, and response to mitigate software vulnerability shortcomings derived from gating processes and paper-based controls. This goes beyond established detection and response practices. Security in DevOps requires a more continuous approach that feeds back into automation and red team processes to increase the speed by which internal teams learn about external discovery and exploitation attempts. Traditional PSIRTs believe in lockdown-affected product production and having all requests funnel through a ticket system. The principles of automation of DevOps must be applied to security, and we should expect better tools that will support this PSIRT function in the not so distant future. This will minimize human intervention and improve efficiency and response times resulting in improving customer satisfaction and minimal software development pipeline interruptions.

The cognitive tools/technologies of machine learning (ML) and artificial intelligence (AI) are impacting the cybersecurity ecosystem in a variety of ways. Applied AI machine learning and natural language processing are being used in cybersecurity by both the private and public sectors to bolster situational awareness and enhance protection from cyber threats.[*]

Security Orchestration, Automation and Response (SOAR) solutions currently used in Computer Security Incident Response (CSIRT) offer automating some of the functions in PSIRT. Industry isn't there yet, but the functions being provided look promising for reuse or modification or use on the product side. These technologies enable organizations to collect security threat data and alerts from different sources, where incident analysis and triage can be performed leveraging a combination of human and

---

[*] Brooks, C. (2020, April 13). "SOAR Cybersecurity: Reviewing Security Orchestration, Automation and Response." Retrieved from https://cybersecurity.att.com/blogs/security-essentials/security-orchestration -automation-and-response-soar-the-pinnacle-for-cognitive-cybersecurity

machine power to help define, prioritize, and drive standardized incident response activities according to a standard workflow. Tools allow an organization to define incident analysis and response procedures or plays in a security operations playbook in a digital workflow format, such that a range of machine-driven activities can be automated.

5.4.4 Software Bill of Materials

A software bill of materials (SBOM) is a nested inventory of a list of ingredients that make up software components. Having a detailed description of the software components in any software-based product is necessary to identify cyber vulnerabilities and, ultimately, help reduce cybersecurity risks. The SBOM applies to digital products and identifies and lists the pieces of software, information about those components and supply chain relationships between them. Over the last few years, the United States Department of Commerce—National Telecommunications and Information Administration has been working with industry stakeholders to strengthen the use and requirements of the SBOM to enhance software vulnerability management and response.

Since 2018, the NTIA has been working in conjunction with government and industry stakeholders through the Framing; Practices & Use Cases; Formats & Tooling; and Healthcare working groups—meeting weekly or biweekly to create a framework and draft key documents, information, or practices around the use of an SBOM. According to the NTIA, the parties are guided by the goal of "exploring how manufacturers and vendors can communicate useful and actionable information about the third-party and embedded software components that comprise modern software and IoT devices, and how this data can be used by enterprises to foster better security decisions and practices."[*] The Framing working group created the Framing Software Component Transparency document,[†] which defines a minimum viable SBOM to guide parties that make, select, and operate software.

> The value of quickly gathering this minimum set of baseline information for a majority of software components will significantly improve the ability for each industry to better manage the components that they use," the document states. "Starting with a baseline set of information allows this process to be adopted by a variety of stakeholders quickly and then be built upon over time. This is one of the major drivers for establishing such a basic set of information as a starting point, rather than requiring a more robust set of data elements that may require more time and resources to collect and maintain." Friedman suggests that the government, the military or any other entity purchasing software or software services demand to know what is a part of the digital code, and they ask for a software bill of materials from their suppliers. "Software powers our entire world, everything and everyone is involved in the software world," he notes. "If you make cars, well that's a software product. You make tanks; it's a software product. And now it is about pushing a market demand for good quality software components upstream. So that the organization, whether it's government or private sector, can ask its software suppliers, 'Hey, are you using the freshest ingredients or are you using toxic ingredients?' That's really what we're trying to do is drive the demand for better, higher-quality software ingredients in the supply chain.[‡]

An SBOM helps perform spot checks of applications and code whenever a vulnerability is disclosed or a core library, such as OpenSSL, releases a new version. This would have been a significant help for the companies affected by Heartbleed in April 2014 to determine whether OpenSSL was included in

---

[*]   NTIA (2020). "Roles and Benefits for SBOM Across the Supply Chain." Retrieved from https://www.ntia.gov /files/ntia/publications/ntia_sbom_use_cases_roles_benefits-nov2019.pdf

[†]   Ibid.

[‡]   Underwood, K. (2020). "Using a Software Bill of Materials to Unveil Vulnerabilities." Retrieved from https:// www.afcea.org/content/using-software-bill-materials-unveil-vulnerabilities

their software inventory. The PSIRT and development teams would have had a quick reference as to whether they had a vulnerable version of OpenSSL and whether they needed to have taken remedial action. SBOM can help answer whether your software is affected by a recently discovered software vulnerability, whether you need to act, and, if so, the course of action you need to take.

Today's software is typically a complex mixture of code pulled from various software libraries, reuse of old lines of existing code, and in many cases, predominantly third-party code. This is exacerbated by attackers increasingly targeting vulnerabilities in third-party libraries as part of their attacks because this gives them more targets than just a single application since libraries can call other components and easily go more than two levels deep. This highlights the need to check the efficacy and security of all dependencies and components discussed in Chapter 3. Ultimately, your organization is responsible for any software product that you produce that has revealed a vulnerability, whether it is a third-party component or not. The SBOM should describe the components included in the application, the version and build of the components in use, the license types for each component, details such as the location within the source code where that component is being called, the list of all tools used to build the application, and relevant build scripts.

When a customer is buying software, they only have a limited view of the components, whether it is commercial or open source. If your SBOM is complete, your customer will be able to decide whether they want to risk using an application containing an old, possibly unsupported, component or update to the latest version, if the product is still being produced. One of the biggest pet peeves we have is development organizations that have end-of-life products with no support but still sell them to customers with PSIRT and development teams still expected to address customer complaints. This is a recipe for disaster since the development team members with knowledge of the product are likely no longer at the company that developed it, and it gets handed off to an inexperienced triage team to fix. Most importantly, a customer will want a complete SBOM so they have visibility into the components you use in your software products to assess whether there are any potential security and licensing problems. It also helps the customer decide whether they want to put temporary mitigations in place for a reported vulnerability in your product that has been discovered while they wait for an update to fix the problem.

Over the last few years, there has been a move by organizations to require software suppliers to provide an SBOM in order to discover potential security and licensing problems or whether the software product is using an outdated version of the library. In 2019, the Underwriters Laboratories rolled out a voluntary Cybersecurity Assurance Program (UL CAP) for the Internet of things (IoT) and critical infrastructure vendors to assess the security vulnerability and weaknesses in their products against a set of security standards. The UL CAP aims to minimize risks by creating standardized, testable criteria for assessing software vulnerabilities and weaknesses in embedded products and systems. This helps reduce exploitation, address known malware, enhance security controls, and expand security awareness.[*]

In short, having a detailed SBOM provides the ability for PSIRT, the development teams, and customers to track ingredients for better security. This will save a significant amount of time and money as well as your reputation, compared to the old way of doing things.

5.4.5 Organizational Management

There are also some organizational management functions and capabilities that should be in place for PSIRT to evolve to the next level. The following checklists from FIRST.org[†] will help you define your requirements to build your PSIRT operational readiness levels at an Intermediate or Advanced level:

---

[*] UL (2020). "UL Cybersecurity Assurance Program (UL CAP)." Retrieved from https://www.ul.com/resources /ul-cybersecurity-assurance-program-ul-cap
[†] FIRST.org (2020). "Product Security Incident Response Team (PSIRT) Maturity Document, Annex7: Sample Checklist." Retrieved from https://www.first.org/standards/frameworks/psirts/psirt_maturity_document

Maturity Level 2 (Intermediate)

- ☐ Operational Foundations
- ☐ Establish charter
- ☐ Build organizational model
- ☐ Ensure management & stakeholder support
- ☐ Identify additional staffing requirements
- ☐ Identify additional resources and tools
- ☐ Ensure branch/version support policies and lifecycles are understood
- ☐ Create baseline metrics
- ☐ Establish a product registry with dependency mapping
- ☐ Stakeholder Ecosystem Management
- ☐ Identify internal stakeholders who will be key to vulnerability management
- ☐ Identify downstream stakeholders
- ☐ Establish incident communications and coordination
- ☐ Vulnerability Discovery
- ☐ Establish process for discovering unreported vulnerabilities
- ☐ Vulnerability Triage
- ☐ Identify finders who repeatedly come to you with quality reports
- ☐ Develop internal vulnerability reproduction capability
- ☐ Remediation
- ☐ Formalize security remedy management plan
- ☐ Vulnerability Disclosure
- ☐ Create system to notify stakeholders
- ☐ Establish vulnerability metrics
- ☐ Training & Education
- ☐ Provide training to the PSIRT team members
- ☐ Provide feedback mechanisms

Maturity Level 3 (Advanced)

- ☐ Operational Foundations
- ☐ Build out organizational policies
- ☐ Determine cost of vulnerability management
- ☐ Stakeholder Ecosystem Management
- ☐ Begin direct engagement with the finder community
- ☐ Community & organizational engagement (i.e., join organizations such as FIRST.org)
- ☐ Create stakeholder metrics
- ☐ Vulnerability Discovery
- ☐ Monitor for product component vulnerabilities
- ☐ Identify new vulnerabilities (i.e. monitor feeds, forums, and external sites)
- ☐ Establish vulnerability discovery metrics
- ☐ Remediation
- ☐ Define advanced incident handling
- ☐ Develop vulnerability release metrics
- ☐ Vulnerability Disclosure
- ☐ Build playbook for stakeholder/industry coordination
- ☐ Training & Education
- ☐ Train development teams
- ☐ Establish continuing education of all stakeholders

The Intel Security (McAfee) Product Security Maturity Model (PSMM) is another model that can be used for your organization. Harold and James presented a public version of the model at the session of the CERT vendor meeting on the 29th of February, in 2016. It can be found at http://toomey.org/harold /resume/Presos/160229_CERT_Vendor_Meeting_2016_Intel's_PSMM_Toomey_29_Feb_2016.pptx. James, Brook, and Harold developed the PSMM while at McAfee® and Intel®. The model has been used by numerous other companies to manage and assess the maturity of their PSIRT and Product Security organizations.

5.5 Security Training Management

Continuous education and training are extremely important for DevOps, in particular for security. Constant changes in DevOps and security to include the addition of new tools and technologies requires innovative, flexible, and constantly updated training. It must also be malleable enough to meet the needs of individuals and teams that are at different stages of growth and levels of knowledge. The fail fast, fail often, and making changes quickly tempo in the Agile development process pushes out software faster than in the past, and your training must adapt to the environment. Building security in requires that your training program has both top down support and buy-in from senior management and bottoms up from the development teams. The requirements and suggestions on how to take a security training program to the next level in a DevOps environment are divided into three distinct areas in this section: People, Process and Technology.

5.5.1 People

Product security is primarily about people, not technology, and principally focused on changing the mindset of how they approach the security of individuals who develop software code. Everybody should have the security mindset to include the managers who ultimately make go/no-go product release decisions, and technology acquisition decisions, as well as interface with others to make strategic decisions about security, product security, and programmatic changes.

As discussed earlier in this chapter, evolving to the next step of security in DevOps goes beyond the software security champions mentioned in Chapter 2 and in *Core Software Security*. It is very important to have fully dedicated security engineers who have been developers as the security experts in each team. Security can no longer be an unfunded mandate. It is too important to be unfunded because nearly all technology incorporates software to include hardware and has a malleable layer of software responsible for processing, storage, and networking on top of it that makes everything work together. Of course, all applications are software. The bottom line is that developers ultimately control the security of the software and systems they are creating. Security is still rarely part of a computer sconce curriculum; therefore, we need to mentor and teach developers until security is in their DNA and just part of developing quality code.

There is significant emphasis in the development community for the developers to think like hackers and adversaries that may target your specific class of products. This is an important skill set to know so that the developers can interface with red teams, bug bounty teams, and external researchers as well as operating with blue team skills, when needed. However, what is overlooked is that they also need to think like security people (defense, not just offense). Development is your first line of defense, and they need to be taught these skills as well.

Security tends to want to tell developers what and how to do something. What they need to know is why they need to do it. When the development engineers don't know why, the what and how really won't make sense and goes against the grain of how engineers process tasks. It is important to keep this in mind when you are developing your training program.

Each organization is going to have different requirements, but the training must be holistic in most cases, starting with foundational concepts rather than with advanced topics so that you can ensure that your audience has a context within which to work. One of the key things to consider is that developers think about and test the software as to what it should do, but security training must change their mind-set to what they shouldn't do. This will require them to go back to security basics when thinking about the security of their products—specifically, in terms of confidentiality (who is allowed to have access to the data in the product); integrity (who is allowed to modify the data in the product); and availability (how does the customer have access to their data).

From a DevOps perspective, probably the most important human challenge you will have is how you will change the culture and build your security community within the development organization. It is important that you determine how you will be able to break down the historical resistance and silos to do this.

5.5.2 Process

True security culture change comes through behavior changes and not process. However, the process by which you deliver your training program will be key to the security cultural changes required in a DevOps environment. Behavior is something you can teach. Security behavior is a manner of behaving that decreases risk or threats. Security habits and skill sets are learned behavior, and your current culture will dictate how you adjust your security training program to facilitate this.

Some key things to consider as you plan your software security training program:

- Keep the training relevant by using your own product and code issues.
- Use your own people to train others, when possible. This can be done via recordings or in person at Scrum team meetings. These should be 15 minutes or less, if possible, and relevant to the code your team is working on. It is much easier to make your security relevant to your development teams if you grow your own. Use your security engineers and security architects as trainers and mentors, when possible.
- For general externally sourced security training, you should avoid training, where possible, that requires the use of your corporate Learning Management Software (LMS) system. This is a very expensive route requiring unnecessary resources compared to cloud-delivered training. You should also make sure that any external training is relevant to your environment and codebase, can change with your changes, and can quickly modify its training to support your environment. Additionally, levels of certification for training should be assessed as to whether they are of interest to you such as belt programs with some vendors. If the vendor you are considering has used their training program to help build a security community and facilitate culture change in DevOps, this is a bonus. Gamification is also a technique used by some vendors that may be attractive to some development cultures.
- Whether you create your own internal or outsource (or combination of both) your external security training program, hands-on training with your own code, where possible, should be a priority. This maximizes the value of your program, from a developer standpoint.
- Threat modeling training, security code review training, and mentoring must be a priority.
- Your developers should be trained to be blue team competent, where appropriate. A blue team is an internal security team that defends against both real attackers and red teams. This can be facilitated by having the red team and bounty program members train the security engineers and other appropriate development team members in the art of thinking like an attacker and the tools that they use to discover and exploit software vulnerabilities.
- It is critical that not only the security engineer but the entire product team be trained in the process that PSIRT adheres to when they respond to an externally discovered incident. Most

importantly, the security engineer and development teams must be trained on their responsibilities during a PSIRT event and the dos and don'ts for communications outside the group during the process. Your relevant partners such as legal and IT should also be trained in this process.

- If appropriate for your organization, consider supported third-party DevSecOps certifications for the appropriate security and development team personnel.
- Keep in mind that in a DevOps environment, your training program should be continuous, embedded, and built into the integrated development environment (IDE), where possible, while also sitting above the reference architecture to go across all areas that are integrated together. This will provide for a holistic but organizationally focused and relevant security training program designed to empower and help development teams learn and implement best practices for secure coding.

5.5.3 Technology

Training should always be part of your contracts when you buy security tools. Many of the security tools are not that intuitive and will only frustrate those not training on how to use them. With many security tools, you must learn to walk before you can run. For example, when you buy and deploy a security tool such as one for a static analysis, you should pick one that has that suite of checks that are high fidelity and provide a low false-positive rate. Your development team will then see how this tool can be used successfully in that it found a problem, there will presumably be a low number of items identified, and that they can typically be fixed in a reasonable amount of time. This will earn the development teams trust in contrast with what usually happens where you have likely spent seven figures for a tool, turn it on, and a 100,000+ issues are identified, many of which are false positives. This is typically so daunting that the team says they ran the tool then put it on the shelf and never use it again until compliance or QA finds out it isn't being used consistently. The lesson here is that proper training on security tools must occur, and the use should strive for continuous improvement rather than trying to boil the ocean with its first use.

It is important that you train the teams that they need to understand what they are trying to defend against before selecting a proper security tool to use. Things like threat modeling and value stream mapping are important to understand your attack surface before you select the tool to use. For example, if you scan for Python and you have no Python in the code being scanned, then you are wasting time. Since management is typically involved in making the tool-selection decision, this highlights the need to have continuous education reach include the managers as well. This way they know the value of the tool and how to make a better impact with it.

In some cases, security tools may have certification training available either through the vendor or a third party. Consider funding appropriate team members to obtain these certifications, but always try to leverage the vendor, when possible and appropriate, to include these costs in your contract when you purchase the tools.

Successful DevOps implementations generally rely on an integrated set of solutions or a "toolchain" to remove manual steps, reduce errors, increase team agility, and scale beyond small, isolated teams.[*]

---

[*] IBM (2020). "IBM DevOps." Retrieved from https://www.ibm.com/cloud/devops?p1=Search&p4 =p50367844197&p5=b&p1=Search&p4=p50367844197&p5=b&p1=Search&p4=p50367844197&p5 =b&cm_mmc=Search_Bing-_-1S_1S-_-WW_NA-_-%2Bdevops%20%2Btools_b&cm_mmca7 =71700000060884999&cm_mmca8=kwd-81226564053017:loc-71278&cm_mmca9=CLDXw-_Dw -gCFRKrxQIdmvwPhQ&cm_mmca10=81226482883101&cm_mmca11=b&&utm_source=bing&utm _medium=cpc&utm_campaign=Search%7CDeveloper%20Tools%7CMid%7CWW%7CNA%7CGeneric %7CEN%7CBMM&utm_term=%2Bdevops%20%2Btools&utm_content=DevOps_DevOps_Generic _BMM_NULL&gclid=CLDXw-_Dw-gCFRKrxQIdmvwPhQ&gclsrc=ds

Your security tools are part of the DevOps toolchain and are a critical part of the DevOps development pipeline. They need to be managed accordingly, and part of that management is to ensure that all people using the security tools used in their environment are trained and mentored appropriately.

5.6 Security Budget Management

For the next step of evolution for security budget management in DevOps, the recommendations and overview remain the same as described in Chapter 2, Section 2.6. In particular, this includes those sections that discuss preparing and delivering the budget message and other things to consider when preparing the budget.

In DevOps, security is intertwined with every area of the organization, from basic tasks to driving strategic goals. Security budgeting cannot operate in a vacuum and should be a critical part of the DevOps process. It is imperative that there is agreement between the two sides. Security must be at the table with development and operations teams to ensure that security is built into DevOps initiatives. If security hasn't been built into DevOps, the budget-allocation process will be problematic. A typical annual budgeting process, predicting and locking in funding and allocating resources 12 months in advance, is an antithesis to the DevOps process. As with everything that is migrating and transforming into the dynamic and responsive DevOps environment, budgeting must evolve and adapt its culture in this change.

Mustafka Kapadia provides three budgeting-process options for DevOps in a 2018 DevOps.com article "Transforming the Annual Budgeting Process for DevOps"[*]:

1. **Shorter Cycles and Frequent Reviews**
   Some organizations are moving to a shorter budgeting and review cycle. The traditional construct of annually funding projects remains, but plans and allocations are revisited quarterly or on a rolling basis. Both business and DevOps are continuously reprioritizing what features to fund and jointly collaborating on making go/no-go decisions. The benefit of such a system is that it allows teams to allocate funds dynamically within the project—it forces teams to think in terms of a minimum viable product, and mistakes in allocations can be quickly corrected. However, there are two major drawbacks. First, funds cannot be reallocated across projects, forcing executives to still wait for the annual cycle. And second, if the quarterly review process is not streamlined, it can create a climate of constant budgeting, where managers end up spending more time jockeying for funds instead of doing real work.

2. **Product-Based Funding**
   In this approach, applications and the associated resources are grouped into product teams and are given a share of the total budget. This budget is primarily managed by the chief product owner, which then further distributes it to the product owners. Just like in the last model, the chief product owner collaborates with the business to decide on go/no-go activities. In addition, it also allows chief product owners to reallocate funds across both products and projects within their portfolio. And the product owners are responsible for executing on the minimum viable feature sets within their allocated funds. The benefit of this model is in its simplicity. Instead of making bets on projects, CFOs just have to decide on how the budgets are spread across various product groups. Chief product owners and product owners have freedom to allocate their share as they see fit. As a result, budget decisions are pushed as close to the front line as possible, allowing for greater flexibility and improved market response times. To get around this, some

[*] Kapadia, M. (2018. June 16). "Transforming the Annual Budgeting Process for DevOps." Retrieved from https://devops.com/transforming-the-annual-budgeting-process-for-devops/

organizations force teams to reserve a piece of the budget for maintenance and paying down technical debt.

3. **Venture-Based Funding**

This is a model that mirrors Silicon Valley–style venture capitalists (VCs) in that an executive board will fund ideas for minimal viable products. Based on the effectiveness of the product, additional funding is granted to the teams. This model is to seed lots of ideas and fund only the ones that work. The benefit is greater transparency and reduced financial risk. The drawback is that most companies are not wired like VC firms.

5.7 Security Governance, Risk, and Compliance (GRC) Management

For the next step of evolution for security governance, risk, and compliance (GRC) management, the recommendations and overview remain the same as described in Chapter 2, Section 2.7. In particular, this includes those sections that discuss SDL Coverage of Relevant Regulations, Certifications, and Compliance Frameworks; Third-Party Reviews; Post-Release Certifications; Privacy; Privacy Impact Assessment (PIA) Plan Initiated; Privacy Implementation Assessment; Final Privacy Review; and Post-Release Privacy Response. Some further comments are compiled below from Anders Wailgren's article "DevSecOps: 9 Ways DevOps and Automation Bolster Security, Compliance":

> *You must always fix things quickly as possible, but in an DevOps environment this is more important. DevOps accelerates your lead time, so that you can develop, test, and deploy your patch/update more quickly. This will be particularly important if you have to resolve an issue such as Heartbleed. The meticulous tracking provided by some DevOps platforms into the state of all your applications, environments, and pipeline stages greatly simplifies and accelerates your response when you need to release your update. When you know exactly which version of the application, and all components in its stack, is deployed on which environment, you can quickly pinpoint the component of the application that requires the update, identify the instances that require attention, and quickly roll out your updates in a faster, more consistent, and repeatable deployment process by triggering the appropriate workflow. Your DevOps tools and automation can be configured to enable developers to be self-sufficient and "get things done," while automatically ensuring access controls and compliance. DevSecOps enables organizations to achieve speed without risking stability and governance. Security and compliance controls should be baked in as an integral part of DevOps processes that manage the code being developed all the way through to production. By implementing DevOps processes that incorporate security practices from the start, you create an effective and viable security layer for your applications and environments that will serve as a solid foundation to ensure security and compliance in the long run, in a more streamlined, efficient, and proactive way.**

In Chapter 3, we discussed A/B testing of updated components. To stay true to the DevOps way of thinking, our SDL accounts for this type of automated updating.

5.8 Security Metrics Management

The security metrics and discussion in Chapter 2, Section 2.8, for metrics management are still relevant, but further discussion and metrics are important to address to take you to the next level in support

---

* Wailgren, A. (2020). "DevSecOps: 9 Ways DevOps and Automation Bolster Security, Compliance." https://techbeacon.com/devops/devsecops-9-ways-devops-automation-bolster-security-compliance

of DevOps. Measuring the success of security in a DevOps environment should be measured quantitatively by the efficiency of continuous development, quality of code, threat detection, and release cycles. You need the right metrics to determine the effectiveness of your security, performance, and overall operation. Without measurements demonstrating that the effort is effective, it's hard to justify your success and budget to senior management and those that you support. Once you know the security challenges you want to address within DevOps, you can determine what metrics to use. Once that has been done, you can decide which metrics will be most useful in helping you measure how well you are dealing with these challenges. Some key metrics to establish success should include:

- Deployment frequency
- Lead time
- Test coverage
- Detection of threats, security defects, and flaws
- Mean time to repair
- Mean time to recovery[*]

It is also important to use effective metrics to show how the changes are improving business operations. A few of the metrics relevant to a DevOps environment are below:

- *Number of Continuous Delivery Cycles Per Month*: This is an important baseline metric to show you how quickly you can deploy code changes in your production environment. Part of DevOps is delivery cycles your organization can manage, and your security approach should increase this number.
- *Number of Software Defects Per Lines of Code*: It is important to measure the amount of vulnerabilities discovered via static and dynamic security code analysis to see how effective your security practices are. This will help ascertain whether you are getting better at detecting flaws before your custom code is moved to production.
- *Percent of Policy Adherence to Center for Internet Security (CIS) hardening standards on operating systems that support containers*: Although containers have clear advantages due to their size and efficiency, they also introduce a new set of security challenges that must be addressed. The percentage of compliance with these standards can be a useful tool to measuring how safe your environment is.[†]

When using cloud-provided virtual environments in which the cloud vendor is responsible for the hardening, the last metric listed above becomes meaningless. Once one gets into the cloud environment, it's important to understand the package rather than "servers," "hosts," or "OS." It becomes important to determine what is weak/vulnerable in the custom code (at whatever level, from guest OS through containers to serverless).

One of the best ways that security can provide meaningful advice to developers about their daily implementation of security principles is by using metrics. A few metrics that can be valuable in keeping DevOps teams continuously improving their security are below. These metrics are derived from an article written by Ericka Chickowski covering a 2018 RSA Conference panel composed of Shannon Lietz, Caroline Wong, and Paula Thrasher[‡]:

---

[*] Berg, A. (2017). "DevSecOps: Incorporate Security into DevOps to Reduce Software Risk." Retrieved from https://www.agileconnection.com/article/devsecops-incorporate-security-devops-reduce-software-risk

[†] Schilling, J. (2018). "Diving into DevSecOps: Measuring Effectiveness & Success." Retrieved from https://www.armor.com/resources/diving-devsecops-measuring-effectiveness-success/

[‡] Chickowski, E. (2018). "Seven Winning DevSecOps Metrics Security Should Track." Retrieved from https://businessinsights.bitdefender.com/seven-winning-devsecops-metrics-security-should-track

- *Defect Density:* One of the simplest benchmarks to set, defect density can be used to measure progress across an organization, within teams, and within specific applications or services by recording the number of bugs and dividing them by a set number of code.
- *Defect Burn Rate:* This focuses on the quantity of defects and is a good measure of how quickly those defects are addressed by the team and a good measure of how efficiently and quickly you are fixing defects found internally and securing your software.
- *Critical Risk Profiling:* One of the biggest issues that development teams have with security personnel is that they typically provide the DevOps teams a large list of vulnerabilities without any prioritization. The security team should conduct an analysis to characterize defects by criticality and put together matrices for developers to give them easy visibility into the order in which they should fix those defects.
- *SLA Performance:* This sets up SLAs based on criticality and tracking the SLA performance consistently.
- *Top Vulnerability Types and Top Recurring Bugs:* This will help developers make long-term improvements in the way they code such as customized training planning and forecasting skill sets needed.
- *Number of Adversaries per Application:* This helps improve the developers' risk awareness and interest in security. This is going to have the software developer look for the adversary and gain an interest in what they're actually doing to their application.
- *Adversary Return Rate:* This helps developers think about how applications are being attacked and how often an adversary is coming using the same tactics, techniques, and procedures. It can also be used for prioritization of bug fixes and training.

5.9 Mergers and Acquisitions (M&A) Management

The mergers and acquisitions (M&A) management discussion in Chapter 2 (Section 2.9) is still relevant, but additional information is provided in this section to take you to the next level in support of DevOps.

The number of significant software security breaches reported over the last few years from subsidiaries or parts of a company that were independent entities not long before the breach occurred should be a telltale sign that security should have been part of the M&A process. A significant example of lessons learned for M&A security due diligence is Yahoo's acquisition by Verizon whereby the public nature of the breach at Yahoo led to the value of the acquisition being cut by $350M.[*]

As discussed previously, the acquisition of open source software should have a particular focus and rigor from a security perspective in a DevOps environment. Most importantly, security should not only be part of the process to vet any security risks but also be empowered and have a seat at the table with the decision makers. Over the years, we both have seen cases where security is part of the process and has made significant documented warnings that should have been show stoppers for moving forward, but the M&A takes place anyway. Some issues carried over to the new company were fixed before a public or private security issue occurred and some were not. Private security issues are those in which a customer(s) finds the security issue, demands the issue to be fixed, but the issue is not made public. These issues typically remain private when both parties could be embarrassed, receive negative press, and possibly lose market share. Not having security as part of the M&A decision-making process is like playing Russian Roulette with your company's reputation. These risks do not go away in a DevOps environment and arguably only accelerate faster if not addressed properly. Matt Rose quotes some

---

[*] Law.com-ALM Media. (2018, June 22). "Cybersecurity Due Diligence in M&A Transactions." Retrieved from https://finance.yahoo.com/news/cybersecurity-due-diligence-m-transactions-151002419.html

pertinent survey results in the Dark Reading article, "Security Matters When It Comes to Mergers & Acquisitions,"* which highlights continued security issues in relation to M&A:

> *A report by West Monroe[†] surveyed 100 senior global executives in early 2017 and found that cybersecurity continues to be a major issue in relation to M&A, both in due diligence and after the deal closes. Fifty-two percent reported discovering a cybersecurity problem after closing the deal. It was also found that security was the No. 2 reason M&A deals were abandoned, and the second most common reason buyers regretted closing a deal. When evaluating the entire M&A process, respondents shared that the top three reasons deals often fail are security concerns (23%), financial and tax issues (23%), and problems with compliance (18%). While these are relatively low, the most anxiety appears to come after the deal is done. The study found that two in five respondents said problems during post-merger integration (41%) was their main worry when thinking about issues related to security.*

Key questions to consider:

- Does the target company/product have unresolved data privacy, cybersecurity, or regulatory compliance issues?
- Does the target company have enough money in escrow to address any potential security or privacy investigatory or compliance concerns with regard to action, both under state and federal law?

Key tasks to consider:

- Ensure the target company prepares the necessary documentation to show that their security and privacy comply with regulatory and industry requirements.
- Ensure that the target company identifies any software products that are internally developed, and how they may cause risk.
- The security review should include any issues, from electronic records to network infrastructure. Buyers have a view into existing vulnerabilities and potential security concerns.
- Has the company had any security breaches? If so, these problems will not disappear when an enterprise is absorbed into a larger one without remediation before or after acquisition.
- During the merger and acquisition due-diligence process, the acquiring team's first goal is to assess and understand the value of the acquired company. Assessing the value of a company or its products during the M&A is achieved by a full and thorough investigation of the company's financials, technology, litigations, sales, and other relevant pieces of information.
- Evaluating risks for software is typically the most time-consuming part of the M&A evaluation process and will require the target company to provide their code inventory reports and describe their development and deployment environments, third-party libraries, patch tools, and licenses. This will include proprietary code, third-party libraries, and open source components.
- As mentioned in Chapter 2, unmanaged use of open source software can delay processes, reduce the value, or jeopardize acquisition. WhiteSource™ describes a three-step Open Source Due Diligence Checklist[‡] on how to prepare, which is summarized below:

---

[*]   Rose, M. (2019). "Security Matters When It Comes to Mergers & Acquisitions." Retrieved from https://www.darkreading.com/application-security/security-matters-when-it-comes-to-mergers-and-acquisitions/a/d-id/1333548

[†]   westmonroe. (2017). "Harnessing Potential: Mid-Market Integration and Managing Change." Retrieved from https://www.mergermarket.com/assets/West-Monroe-Mid-market_Report_Final-LR2.pdf

[‡]   WhiteSource. (2019). "On the Verge of an M&A? Don't Ignore Open Source Due Diligence." Retrieved from https://resources.whitesourcesoftware.com/blog-whitesource/on-the-verge-of-an-m-a-don-t-ignore-open-source-due-diligence

1. Create an open source inventory list, including all dependencies. With this exercise, you will be able to identify the relevant licenses, security vulnerability, and quality issues relevant to your products.
2. List all the identified open source licenses and check compliance. Once you've identified all the open source components that you're using, you are required to identify all the licenses that your components have, and their dependencies. At this point, you'll have to carefully check what it is that each license requires you to do and whether your company meets these requirements.
3. Identify vulnerable and outdated components. Security vulnerabilities might exist in your software without you even being aware of them. Uncovering these issues during an M&A process can damage your process, as security vulnerabilities can be exploited by malware or hackers. Monitoring and revealing security vulnerabilities require substantial time and effort, and their inheritance increases the risk to the acquiring team.

5.10 Legacy Code Management

Companies and individuals continue to use outdated versions of various critical software programs, including those that connect to the Internet. Even with the high number of data breaches arising from the use of unpatched and/or unsupported software with exploitable vulnerabilities, many companies struggle to see the need to replace/upgrade to newer systems. The legacy code management discussion in Chapter 2 (Section 2.10) is still relevant, but some further emphasis below regarding security and legal/compliance issues is important to address as a reminder to take you to the next level in support of DevOps.

5.10.1 Security Issues

Legacy software results in a number of security issues resulting from the inability to patch or upgrade older versions of software. This makes a particularly attractive target for adversaries to exploit due to the bugs and vulnerabilities that go unpatched. Even more concerning is legacy software, in particular, custom software, because the employees or contractors that developed the code have likely left the company or are retired. Another problematic issue is that legacy software could result in issues applying or having higher premiums for cybersecurity/cyber-liability insurance.

5.10.2 Legal and Compliance Issues

Companies that use legacy software increase their liability and risk of regulatory investigations, scrutiny, and fines—both domestically and globally—as a result of vulnerable legacy software and unauthorized personal information/personal data disclosures occurring because of a failure to meet minimum security safeguards. In addition, public companies may have to disclose cyber-liability risks that are inherent in legacy software that exist in their product or component.

Many frequently identified potential impacts of a cybersecurity incident will apply to data breaches arising from unpatched legacy software, including the following: the compromise of confidential customer or employee information; unauthorized access to proprietary or sensitive information/destruction or corruption of data; lost revenues due to a disruption of activities, which incur remediation costs; litigation, fines, and liability for failure to comply with privacy and information security laws; reputational harm affecting customer and investor confidence; diminished competitive advantage and negative impacts on future opportunities; operational delays, such as production downtimes or plant and utility outages; inability to manage the supply chain; inability to process customer transactions or otherwise service customers; disruptions to inventory management; loss of data from research and development activities; and devaluation of intellectual property.[*]

5.11 Chapter Summary

The criticality of software security as we move quickly toward this new age of tasks previously relegated to the human mind and now being replaced by software-driven machines cannot be underestimated. It is for this reason we have written this book. In contrast and for the foreseeable future, humans will continue to write software programs. This also means that new software will keep building on legacy code or software that was written prior to security being taken seriously or before sophisticated attacks became prevalent. As long as humans write the programs, the key to successful software security is to make the software development program process more efficient and effective. Although the approach of this book includes people, process, and technology approaches to software security, the authors believe the people element of software security is still the most important part to manage. This will remain true as long as software is developed, managed, and exploited by humans. This book has outlined a step-by-step process for software security that is relevant to today's technical, operational, business, and development environments. We have focused on what humans can do to control and manage a secure software development process in the form of best practices and metrics. Although security is not a natural component of the way industry has been building software in recent years, the authors believe that security improvements to development processes are possible, practical, and essential.

Software is only as secure as the quality and relevance of the best practices that the software development team uses. Software security must be built in from the very beginning. It must be a critical part of the design from the very beginning and included in every subsequent development phase all the way through fielding a complete system. Correcting vulnerabilities as early as possible in the SDLC through the adoption of security-enhanced processes and practices is far more cost effective than attempting to diagnose and correct such problems after the system goes into production. This will greatly reduce the need to patch the software to fix security holes discovered by others after release of the product, which will degrade the reputation and credibility of the vendor and adversely impact it financially. Today, we are seeing an increased need for security in software development in that security requirements, design, and defensive principles have to be worked into the traditional SDLC and, most important, in choosing security development practices that embrace this need throughout all the activities of the SDLC. Although security is not a natural component of the way industry has been building software in years past, we believe that security improvements to development processes are possible, practical, and essential in the DevOps pipeline. Finally, software executives, leaders, and managers must support the robust coding practices and required security enhancements as required by a business-relevant security as well supporting the staffing requirements, scheduling, budgeting, and resource allocations required for this type of work to be successful in the DevOps environment.

Unlike legacy models wherein security, operations, and development teams typically worked as distinct and separate organizations (Figure 5.5), these teams must now evolve into an holistic DevOps organization working as a single unit (Figure 5.6).

In closing this chapter, it is important to repeat the first line of the chapter introduction: "Within software development, the weakest link is still the human and, in particular, the managers of those humans and processes and tasks they are expected to carry out." This chapter was all about what managers can do to help them deliver secure software at Agile speed. The sections are a repeat of those covered in

---

[*] Lifshitz, L. (2018). "Time to Say Goodbye: Dealing with Legacy Software." Retrieved from https://www.canadian lawyermag.com/news/opinion/time-to-say-goodbye-dealing-with-legacy-software/274988

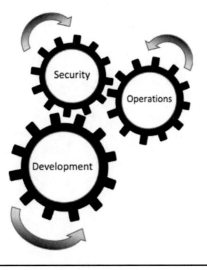

Figure 5.5   Development, Operations, and Security Working as Separate Units.

Chapter 2, but focused on adopting a new model proposed earlier in the book (Chapter 3)—specifically, a future state where security tools, technology, and people are integral to the DevOps pipeline and are used to fully integrate software security into the DevOps environment. Throughout the discussion, the methodologies, tools, human talent, and metrics to overcome the challenges to make software secure while managing security in a DevOps environment were highlighted. Most importantly, just having the tools and techniques is not enough, we also discussed that security in a DevOps environment requires a cultural change that promotes the "secure by default" culture.

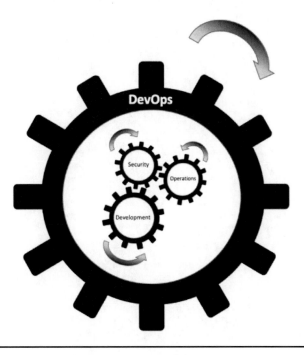

Figure 5.6   DevOps Organization Working as a Single Unit.

Chapter 6

Culture Hacking

6.1 Introduction

"Continuous improvement" has been a modern, organizational objective for many years. A Google® Ngram™ search shows the curve of author discussion of "continuous improvement" starting around 1939. There was a small peak in the mid-1950s; then, in the 1990s, continuous improvement gained enormous attention, which peaked around 1995. The term has settled down to a long-term plateau since around 2003 to the present (2019*). By now, "continuous improvement" has become one of management's guiding principles. In every organization that we've worked at, we have been urged to strive for "continuous improvement" of our programs, our effectiveness, our leadership styles, you name it. The assumption in "continuous improvement" or the Japanese productivity objective of Kaizen, which is sometimes credited as the originator of modern continuous improvement,[†] is that everything can be made "better," more effective, if teams reflect upon what they've done with an eye towards improvement and removing blocks to effectiveness. In fact, continuous improvement is built into the fabric and rituals of Agile Scrum (please see the description of Agile Scrum in Chapter 2). Continuous improvement has by now become a foundational assumption for many organizations, including software security practice.

The main thrust of this book has been that we must improve our software security practices or we will continue to offer attackers plenty of opportunity, too much opportunity, so much attacker leverage that we, makers of software, operators of software, users of software, interact in a hostile context that is not survivable. In some sense, I think we might sum up our thrust with a traditional commandment: "change or die."[‡] Software development has changed. Security must meet those changes or become

---

[*] Ngram queries do not include the current year, which was 2020 at the time of the query.

[†] Please see "What Is Continuous Improvement?" Retrieved from https://kanbanize.com/lean-management/improvement/what-is-continuous-improvement#:~:text=In%20Lean%20management%2C%20continuous%20improvement,automobile%20manufacturer%20on%20the%20planet

[‡] The origins of "change or die" are unclear. First published in a sermon in 1710, it did not take on its current meaning until the 19th century. Please see Wisnioski, M. (2012, December 12). "'Change or Die!': The History of the Innovator's Aphorism." The Atlantic. Available at https://www.theatlantic.com/technology/archive/2012/12/change-or-die-the-history-of-the-innovators-aphorism/266191/

irrelevant. Attackers will probably celebrate should security fail to meet the development changes we have described in previous chapters. Or we can use the techniques described herein and methods yet to be invented so that security will be fully integrated into the software that we build. We must combine security practices with the way that software is developed and operated today and into the foreseeable future.

James and Brook were discussing the nature of security with a friend and former colleague who is a well-regarded Agile Scrum coach, Jorgen Hesselberg (cofounder of Comparative Agility). Jorgen wryly noted that security is a process of "becoming better." In thinking about his statement and our collective security needs, we might simply say that "security is the art of constantly becoming." There is no end-state at which we might arrive. The environment in which we work is highly dynamic. As each of the authors has written and said numerous times, attackers are adaptive and creative. Though new exploit techniques are not born every hour, or even every day, every year sees a few new ones added. New exploitation methods require us to adjust defenses, perhaps even to create new ones. Yesterday's defense in depth will not protect us from tomorrow's entirely new exploitation technique.

Added to the constantly evolving threat landscape is a firehose of new technologies and techniques for producing software: new languages, new operations, new deployers, new execution environments, and so forth. Just as threats constantly evolve with the occasional revolution produced by an entirely new attack type, so, too, the targets of exploitation evolve through revolutionary methods and/or technology. As security people, we must constantly renew and revise.

New methods and technologies most certainly require us to revise our security assumptions and methods. At the same time, it is imperative to learn the new technologies and methods themselves. For instance, when microservices appear, the astute security person must dive into how microservices work and how architecture changes, as well as learn about the tools used to deliver and operate microservices. It's almost never sufficient to apply yesterday's defenses to tomorrow's software development and delivery mechanisms. We cannot defend what we do not understand, and at a fairly deep level. "Renew." Repeatedly, regularly.

The organizations that develop software have gone through a revolution in methods to write, deploy, and run software. These sea changes must be part of software security practice's "becoming," as well. Yesterday's software security is out of sync with today's DevOps development. A failure to recognize that software security may be out of step with development risks missing key security activities. And disconnects, discontinuities between security and development, increase interfunction friction, which is an organizational problem, not a technical one. Unless software security practitioners meet this revolution, we risk becoming irrelevant. We hope that we have made a strong enough case about the importance of software security to a digital future!

Each of the challenges named above requires organizations, developers, and security to make cultural shifts. Our friend, Noopur Davis, Executive Vice President, Chief Product and Information Security Officer for Comcast, Inc., calls the cultural aspects of security, "culture hacking." That's an apt term because cultures are inherently conservative; cultures maintain themselves. Once gelled, an organization's culture is resistant to change. Change agents, which software security practitioners must consider themselves, have to provide incentives for change and make the path of change easier and more rewarding than remaining the same.

In this chapter, we consider the cultural aspects of a software security program and what can be done to "hack" an organization's culture such that programs like those described herein will be successful and effective.

6.2 Culture Must Shift

As our software security programs have matured, both authors (alone and together) have observed a shift in the way that software security is perceived.

Before a software security program, or after a past security effort, has foundered (which is often when we get hired!), security is typically viewed as "something else," something distinct, a result produced magically or at least opaquely by a function distinct from development, something done "to" software versus a set of qualities that software possesses and behavior that it exhibits.

If software security could be delivered from outside, built around software, then, of course, there's no need for culture change.

But we hope that, by now, you clearly understand that software security cannot be delivered without deep integration as a key part of the creation, realization, and operation of software. Appropriate software security emerges as a direct result of the efforts of developers, often with the help and support of software security experts. That is, security is "built in" not "bolted on," to trot out a trite bit of security wisdom.

The needed changes, we've found, require considerably more than merely embedding security practices in development teams—which is often seen as more or less a "solution," in and of itself. We haven't ever seen mere embedding deliver. Developers have to believe that their job includes security thinking. They have to hold security in their bones, as a deep part of a holistic development practice. Which leads us to culture hacking the organization to shift belief and practice towards the goal.

This chapter contains our tricks and tips for shifting organizational perspectives from "security done to software" to "development producing security." This is a paradigm shift that goes beyond telling people what to do and how to do it (i.e., an SDL).

The required shifts cannot happen solely through concerned executive declarations, though that is one part of a total culture hack: It's easier when one has substantive executive support. It's not impossible with executive indifference. (We'll note just this once that presented with active executive sabotage, we'd find ourselves a new organization to help.)

The shift will not occur because documents are drafted demanding it (policy) and describing how to enact it (the SDL). Documentation is important; please make no mistake. Enactors may have questions or forget how a particular thing is done, when to do it, or what to expect. Plus, there is always churn: people leave. New people are brought in. Process, in our experience, has tremendous entropy in that over successive personnel generations, the justification for a process gets lost, which then can lead to people wondering (quite rightly) just why is it that they are required to perform some sequence of actions? Documentation supported through regular training and reinforcement addresses staff churn and process entropy. This is also an important component of culture hacking.

Smart people, in our experience, don't change because they're told to. They change their thinking based upon obvious value derived from the change: Better software! Increased skills. Enhanced job prospects. Potential for premium compensation. Pride from delivery. These motivators work together and complement each other. Obvious value must follow from the changes: Clear contributions to organizational goals must result. And people should also gain from the intended changes.

As we noted above, "culture hacking" was our colleague's pithy way of summarizing intentional organizational change. Perhaps neither of us set out to be culture hackers, though each of us, before we first worked together, had already arrived at some sense of ourselves as organizational change agents.

As we built and then led our software security programs (each in our respective roles: organization and management dynamics guru, and technical leader), we noticed that there were culture shifts occurring. One just needs to be a bit observant and then reflect on one's observations to see patterns in the dynamics.

Plus, and this is a big plus for those considering jumping into the change agent stew, we've had each other to explore hypotheses with, to share our successes and the inevitable failures. Through ongoing interaction, we've been able to identify that which works more than once versus the lucky break. We've been sharing in this way for more than 10 years, whether working together or separately. The results of our ongoing analysis comprise the contents found in this book and, especially, this chapter. At the same time, our friend, Noopur, gave us a phrase with which to tie our efforts together, a banner under which we can now deliver: "culture hacking."

In this chapter, we will share with you "culture hacks" that have produced a shift towards a culture of software security.

6.3 Hack All Levels

Through the dint of hard experience, we've come to understand that in order to build effective software security programs, the change agent (i.e., us or you) must work through and with parallel levels in an organization:

- Executives
- Mid-management
- Throughout the development organization:
  - Technical leadership
  - Line management
  - All levels of developer experience: junior to senior

Brook wrote about interacting with the various levels in his *Secrets of a Cyber Security Architect*[*]:

6.3.1 Executive Support

Executives of course are important; without executive buy-in and support even the best intentioned and run effort will fail: Eventually, there will be resistance somewhere in the organization. Designing and building security costs money, time, resources, focus, and effort. Somewhere along the way, some teams will meet resource challenges, trade-offs between security work and some, usually many, other competing requirements. While elsewhere in this work [*Secrets of a Cyber Security Architect*], *Core Software Security*,[†] and *Securing Systems*[‡] I've presented various ways to deal with those challenges, nevertheless, it is inevitable that there will be resistance to security—perhaps, down-right rebellion. This must be expected.

When it is not obvious what should be done, when agreement cannot be reached as to whether to put off a security requirement against something more pressing, the usual approach will be to escalate. Those escalations sometimes end up in front of executives, and that is the point at which one finds out whether the executives are only giving lip service to security or if they will stand up for it.

This is not to say that supportive executives will decide in favor of security every time. I've never seen that. Sometimes, there are very good business reasons to put off security. That is always an executive prerogative.

However, if said executive always decides against security, then one knows where one really stands—nowhere, to be exact. A supportive executive will consider, will hear all sides, will take all the risk factors into account. Sometimes, it will be a matter of when to complete required

---

[*] Schoenfield, B. S. E. (2019). *Secrets of a Cyber Security Architect*. Boca Raton (FL): Auerbach Publications/ Taylor & Francis Group.

[†] Ransome, J. and Misra, A. (2014). *Core Software Security: Security at the Source*. Boca Raton (FL): CRC Press/ Taylor & Francis Group.

[‡] Schoenfield, B. S. E. (2015). *Securing Systems: Applied Security Architecture and Threat Models*. Boca Raton (FL): CRC Press/Taylor & Francis Group.

security, not whether to do it at all. Sometimes, the executive will decide to prioritize security against other risk factors. That is as it should be. I don't expect to win—winning is not the attitude to cultivate for these escalations. Security risk needs to be fully acknowledged and validated. That's all I'm looking for in these situations. That's enough; I consider that executive support. When security is consistently undermined or disregarded, that is a clear lack of support. Without that support, much of an organization will follow suit. It may be time to look for a different organization.

Executive support is more than communicating how important security is to an organization. It's also standing up for security, making time for the hard decisions, making those hard decisions based upon the best information that can be had at that moment. (*Secrets*, pp. 105–106)

6.3.2 Mid-Management Make or Break

I learned fairly early on after assuming a technical leadership security role that mid-management were going to make or break my efforts. Typically, minor, low, even medium risks will be decided by mid-management—in most organizations, the directors or equivalents. If the risk is not catastrophic to the entire organization or is confined to a particular set of functions or teams, mid-management will often handle the issue.

Plus, directors often set priorities for their groups. If a director wishes to undermine security initiatives, at least for their teams, they can do it. In large, complex organizations, mid-management may have wide degrees of influence. Knowing whether they support, don't care, or are actively resisting is crucial, which is why one of the first things I do at a new organization is to have a chat with each of the relevant directors. Plus, I observe what they do as security requirements and security tasks are introduced.

Critical questioning is fine; that equals engagement. Engagement is a sign of support, although it might not feel that way when one is subject to a sharp director interrogation. As long as the inquiry seems to be about making the work better, about making security work with all the other factors that go into producing good software, that rings as support to me.

Again, just like executives, if, when push comes to shove, teams are consistently allowed to put security tasks off, to deprioritize security requirements, then that's either passive aggression or active resistance. I want to identify resisters. I can't meet their issues without actively uncovering them.

So that's one of my hacks: Find out what the issues are, perhaps what is being protected, and then I can start to craft solutions that don't ruin what's already been built. A great deal of the time, in functional organizations, resistance is about protecting one or more "things" that are working well.

One cannot always predict what one might threaten when one begins a program of culture change. Resistance is an invitation to investigate, to learn. Mid-management has the power to change, but also to resist. It is in this layer that I have often uncovered processes or methods that I must take into account in order to be successful[,] . . . looking beyond resistance to what need[s] to be accomplished in order to be successful for all involved. (*Secrets*, pp. 106–107)

6.3.3 Accept All Help

We covered empowerment of developers, as well as skill building, so that the SDL as described in this book can be executed. At this point, we hope that readers are intimately familiar with a "developer-centric" security view, what that means, and how to go about enacting it.

Obviously, some people will offer greater security expertise and/or domain expertise than others. When security has been deeply integrated into the fabric of software creation, distinctions between central team experts and developer (architect, what have you) security experts mostly disappear, especially when solving problems, as members of a thriving software security community of practice.* When contribution is more about value than team membership, role, or hierarchy, that is a sign that the program is working.

We've covered experts elsewhere. The following excerpt from *Secrets of a Cyber Security Architect* addresses including help from those who haven't been assigned official SDL roles.

> I accept assistance or support from everyone and anyone at any level. Sometimes management and, especially, executives don't have a full understanding of what my friend Dr. James Ransome calls "ground truth"—that is, what is actually going on in development teams. To move a software organization toward a culture of security, ground truth is critical. Without it, I guarantee that executive pronouncements, mid-management directives, strategy statements, security development lifecycle (SDL) documents, policies, standards, processes, and methods will flounder.
>
> One of the most important things that I can do is to talk to developers and observe how they are actually developing software, because if the SDL directly contradicts or interferes with the development process, it cannot work. Smart developers will find a way around anything that slows them down or that they perceive as lacking value.
>
> On the other hand, if something—anything—seems to help build better software, gets more bugs out quicker, the vast majority of developers with whom I've worked will embrace that task, that tool, that activity rapidly and with little resistance. It often comes down to perceived utility.
>
> [S]ecurity has to fit into the development process. But that fit cannot be accomplished by one expertise or the other; it must be accomplished by working together. This is why security must interact with grassroots developers directly. We must understand the entire project or effort process. Whatever security tasks (the SDL, essentially) need to be accomplished must fit within the processes and methods that will be used to build the software. (*Secrets*, pp. 107–108)

6.4 Trust Developers

Repeatedly in this book, we have extolled the importance of empowering developers to enact security. But that brings up concerns for some security folk. Some security information is sensitive, some highly so. If attackers know what's weak and where to get at the weaknesses, we've given them more than a leg up; we've given them a big advantage, perhaps handing our adversaries victory on a silver platter, as it were.

Developers may feel insulted simply because the question has been posed? After all, tens of thousands of developers labor away regularly to protect project plans, credentials, architectures, innovative ideas, administrative access, proprietary code, intellectual property, the panoply of data items that may be encompassed within a software development effort.

---

* There are, of course, differences in roles. These may come into play over security strategy, training, skill building, facilitating the software security program, and, most especially, during difficult executive risk decision making, where the central team can relieve pressure and tension from development security experts who may have to conflict with their own management. In the day-to-day execution of SDL activities, including refinements and reviews, though, these differences more or less disappear, which is an objective. When practitioners don't really care about which team one is on, but rather, what value they add, that is a sign that the entire program is working as designed.

On the other hand, there have been documented occurrences of the breach of undisclosed projects, development data, code, etc. It does happen from time to time, often unintentionally. Due diligence demands that we defend against such an event, even if the incidence is rare. The impact from lost code or concept disclosure can be significant.

Throughout this book, we have used the phrase: "Trust and verify." We trust developers; we empower them to enact security to the best of their abilities. We will take up "verify" after the following quote about trusting developers with the oftentimes very sensitive output from threat modeling taken from Brook's *Secrets of a Cyber Security Architect.*

> I will admit to you, the reader, that it's true that the results of the threat model, the security requirements, especially those requirements not yet built or perhaps delayed for later implementation, may be quite sensitive. That's the reason that many security practices hold threat models close, treat them as highly sensitive, and thus not sharable to development teams. I'd be willing to bet that this is the argument put forth by that past administration on why they didn't want to share threat models or the process of deriving models.
>
> [James] and I have talked about this problem a great deal. . . . The chink in the armor of protectionism around threat models is that the development team have and hold the code! Please consider this carefully: They don't need the threat model in order to destroy the software for which development teams are responsible. If the team were to go rogue, they could usually insert all manner of awful things into the code, like backdoors or malicious code.
>
> There are checks against collusive teams doing bad things (please see some of my public talks on secure development or take a look at my chapter in *Core Software Security*). Still, even the best run governance process ultimately relies on people, some of whom may not have the organization's best interests at heart. As James likes to say, "If you can't trust developers with the code, who can you trust?" It's a truism.
>
> The way that we have handled this problem is to remind developers of their awesome responsibility to the company, that their success is tied to keeping the company's intellectual property from leaking out, including any sensitive security situations. Repeat regularly, through different media and presentation channels, but don't be such a nag that the message becomes part of the background noise of the job.
>
> Nothing's perfect; someone will post some code or a sensitive project name probably for no other reason than that person is inexperienced or wildly proud of what they're doing. Handling these mistakes is part of security's role. (*Secrets*, pp. 87–88)

Alongside empowering continued trust in everyone involved in development and then reiterating the awesome responsibility that trust entails, people have to have methods for identifying lapses and mistakes. That's the "verify" in "trust and verify."

In our programs, verify isn't just invested in security, or development, or any other group: Verify is everyone's responsibility, just as security is. "Trust <u>and</u> verify" shifts culture away from "security is someone else's job" to "security is my job." How does that "and" work?

We've already extensively covered software verification methods; static and dynamic analyses, fuzzing, and penetration testing are integrated into the SDL. We've never shown a preference for who performs these tests (except for independent, third-party testing).

In practice, verification requires skill. Some methods (SAST and DAST) are easier than others. Fuzzing often requires some up-front training and a bit of practice before it starts to produce results. Obviously, manual penetration testing requires a significant investment of learning, and then practice. That's kind of the point: "skilled manual testing." Even for the more relatively straightforward scanning techniques and scanning tools, there are levels of expertise. Few of the available tools (as of this writing) are trivial. Some of them are quite complex.

The way skill levels seem to play out in a developer-centric program is that the lower-skilled verification must be handed over to developers. Developers should take on as much verification as humanly possible, while still achieving useful results. Doing so is the essence of "trust <u>and</u> verify."

• Identify appropriate verification approaches
• Ensure that the correct verification tools and training are available
• Provide expertise that supports developer efforts
• Augment developers' skills and methods, whenever needed

With today's complex array of build, deploy, and operate tools, it's easy to make a mistake that opens a security hole, even for highly experienced people. Of course, we all make mistakes, at whatever level of skill we may attain. We have mentioned configuration management tools in passing. These become particularly important for software that will run on clouds—expressly, public or commercial clouds.

Configuration scanners, especially those that include security checks, have become increasingly important. Part of that increase is related to cloud use: Every week sees another data breach because the cloud storage was mistakenly configured to allow public access (that is, everyone on the Internet) versus what the storage should have been: private to the software accessing and processing the data. Build and deploy chain configuration is equally critical.

We find that these scans are best performed by the people who configure and manage the tool set. They need information about what they're doing, as well as a way to spot the inevitable mistakes. They have to have tools ("trust") that they can use to verify their work. Again, as in any verification, the scanners ought to be supported by people who they can safely ask if they have questions as to results and findings.

But how do we verify for information disclosure? There are commercial services and scan products for this problem, as well. There are products that sit on the edge of organization networks. There are protection products that watch corporate storage and/or endpoints. There are several solutions to the problem. Finding the right mix is beyond the scope of this book. Suffice it to say that intellectual property protection is a part of "trust and verify," since this is an area of developer responsibility that will need to be verified, as well.

This part of the puzzle is perhaps best left to an independent team, outside of development. Security should periodically scan for intellectual property leaks across public properties.

A finding doesn't necessarily indicate a compromise or fraudulent behavior. Again, people make mistakes. Still, the scanners aren't easy to use. And the scan is for everyone who might be charged with keeping organizational secrets. In addition, if an employee has been trying to steal secrets, it's usually important that they aren't also involved in identifying themselves.

Our one caveat to a security (or other independent) intellectual property scan or intellectual property data protection (IDP) mechanism is that we warn security people not to assume dishonest behavior when investigating a potential leak.

One investigation of which we were a part involved credit card numbers being emailed to an employee every week. It looked bad to the investigators.

The truth of the matter was quite different from the appearance. The person receiving the credit card numbers had worked on the development of the system. During development, the data for testing were fake card numbers. He asked for emails of the test data to verify system behavior as a part of the system's pre-flight validation. Just before the system went into production use, he told the administrators to kill the email. The system went live. Every week he repeated his request to stop the email (he had all the emails going back to Week 1), pointing out to the administrators that the weekly card number email was a serious breach of security. He duly deleted and then securely overwrote each email, week after week after week. By the time of the investigation, he was at his wits end, having talked with the administrator's management, and their management. Nobody would put a stop those horrid emails, which also made him look dishonest. Obviously, with the power of a security breach investigation, the administrators finally killed the email. All to the good. This investigation was a powerful lesson in keeping an open mind while discovering the facts of a matter.

6.5 Build a Community of Practice

One of our favorite culture hacks is cross-team learning coupled to independent review. As we stated in the "Nimble Governance" section in Chapter 3, include someone independent of the materials under review, especially for design and threat model reviews, where significant craft is required alongside engineering skill. We noted benefits for the review in that earlier section. Here we will mention skill-building aspects, while focusing particularly on creating a community of practice.

One of the downsides of development teams, in general, and particularly so when developers are segmented into Agile Scrum teams, is isolation. This is because in order for a team to be effective, it has to remain relatively stable long enough to cohere into a functioning unit with its own subculture, jargon (sub-dialect), style, and often, even, a distinct type of humor. The software that the team works on may shift from time to time. But quite often, a Scrum team will be assigned complete responsibility for a portion of a larger system. This is often true in larger projects, at larger development organizations fielding multiple large software projects (often called "epics" in Scaled Agile® terminology).

Each team may not have a complete picture of the entire system. That view may be held by senior architects who are structuring (architecting) the system and the components that have been assigned to individual Scrum teams. The team will understand its portion exceedingly well, but it may have only enough knowledge about how the entire system fits together as is necessary to be experts in what they work on.

The result of parceling out pieces of a large project, which then are owned, worked on, and delivered by small, tightly focused teams, will be that team members become experts in bits and pieces but only have a sense of shared experience with their own team members and team culture. For developers confined to tight task teams (Scrum), each person may feel very little "culture," or sense of shared experience, with the entirety of those working on a particular system, much less all of engineering or the company. We do not make this up, by the way. We have seen precisely this lack of shared experience at organizations with which we've worked. Lots of individual teams, each of whom is tightly focused on their area of expertise, but have no sense that "we"—development, and even more so, development and security—are pulling towards something together.

By pulling in a member of another team (a person who is senior and who probably isn't in the Scrum team, either), we cross-pollinate. Considering problems not one's own is an incredible skill accelerator. Brook has written about the benefits of working on unfamiliar problems in Chapter 4, *Secrets of a Cyber Security Architect*, should readers want more detail.

Beyond the learning aspects of cross-team inclusion, doing so builds community. Creating and maintaining a community of practice has been a primary aspect of Brook's practice for nearly 30 years (as a technical leader even before he focused on security). The software security programs he and James have built always include community building around execution of the SDL as one of their first objectives and main culture hacks.

We include Brook's ruminations on the importance of communities of practice and how he goes about facilitating these from *Secrets of a Cyber Security Architect*, below. That book was focused on security architecture. However, there is no difference between communities built around SDL; the same techniques work, irrespective of the focus. The same benefits ensue.

> As learners build skill while interacting with new people, they build trust in each other. New lines of relationship get formed. The network of shared practices increases. This instills a sense of shared purpose, builds a community of practice. Working across project lines shouldn't be the only vector of shared practice. Still, sharing across knowledge areas builds upon other

community practices you may introduce. The sense of contribution and execution together is a powerful community builder.

Inviting team outsiders to review isn't the only method for creating a community of practice. What are other methods? And why is a community of practice important?

A sense of community fosters belief in the shared purpose. For those who are motivated to contribute to something worthy of their time, something of substance, contribute to something that serves a grander purpose, a belief in a shared purpose can be very motivating and sustaining. Others may be more motivated by that very sense of shared purpose and support. I also find that when people see something happening, things actually being accomplished, joining becomes very attractive. Building community scratches each of these itches.

Communities also offer significant opportunities to increase skill and to integrate new skills through sharing with others. This aspect of "learning the trade" shouldn't be overlooked when creating an environment that fosters learning and creativity. While not every engineer likes to share, some can be encouraged to share what they know. The act of explaining to someone else why something does or doesn't work and how it can be accomplished is a key method for the integration of knowledge already acquired.

One of my main strategic initiatives is the creation of community. This is another powerful culture hack. Total team learning accelerates through the dynamics of shared sense of purpose and community. But also, as my friend Vinay Bansal (Vinay Bansal is a Distinguished Engineer at Cisco Systems, Inc.) once said to me, "Brook, we could move mountains together." Just the simple knowledge that others are going to support you when you're challenged or make a mistake, that you trust others to help you find the best solution to complex problems, that you can share your trials and tribulations, your joys and successes, makes most of us more resilient and oftentimes stronger.

But community doesn't simply spring forth without putting in some directed effort. It may be that engineers, many of whom tend toward introversion, can be a fairly difficult population with which to form community. Participants will have to stop working with their computers in order to interact. Following is a list of many of the techniques that I've used to foster a sense of community:

- Create a space for a community.
- Make sharing a safe activity.
- Share both successes and failures.
- Problem solve together.
- Allow diverse and even conflicting opinions.
- Meet regularly and predictably.
- Communicate to the community through multiple channels.
- Offer regular improvement training as a part of the space for the community.
- Model active listening.
- Give the community decision-making power over items which affect the community.

The community space can be virtual; I've created virtual community spaces five times, as of this writing. A community space can really help to establish trust, relationships, and a bond of shared experience. It helps to meet face to face from time to time. However, in-person meetings will usually be rare treats; most people in software development and security, at least currently, are used to working with people who are remote and are comfortable with virtual meeting environments. So long as the meetings commonly offer value to attendees, people will attend regularly. The key is that the community space exists and recurs predictably.

How does one create a sense of value in a recurring meeting? I won't claim that I have a patentable technique that always works. And, regrettably, sometimes at the virtual team meetings, one just has to take care of administrative business, which can be a community disintegrator (unfortunately). When I have significant business on the agenda, I always try to balance it with something of interest.

A great technique that I learned from another sphere entirely is to begin meetings with a short skill-building presentation or exercise. Nearly always, threat modeling a piece of a team's software draws lots of interest. If my community members are at least partially drawn from development teams, then one of their current projects makes a great subject of wide interest.

The team will present their architecture. Then, the entire community gets to analyze the architecture for attacks and defenses. These discussions become quite interactive, sometimes conflictual, which is fine so long as polite and professionally focused on the work at hand. Lots of participants have an opportunity to analyze and to speak. Dialogues between two people who don't agree should quickly be ended in favor of letting others try their hand at the analysis.

The presentations could also be about new pilots or experiments, new technologies, new processes that teams have invented, including strengths and pitfalls of the processes. If these presentations are kept short and to the point, they will be of interest to at least part of the community.

It's hard to find subjects that are of interest to everyone. Presentations about new process mandates and existing process or tool changes are often of reasonably broad interest, generally receiving strong engagement—the point being that by offering some opportunity for skill building and knowledge transfer, while every presentation will not be of interest to every participant, over time and through variety, many of the presentations are likely to be significantly engaging.

Shared problems are another important community builder. But, long reports of everything that each team is doing are boring, disengaging, and ultimately community killing. My strong advice is to avoid agendas packed with each team reporting in. Engineers go through plenty of those on multi-team projects in which periodic reports must be a part of the process. They don't need to do that in the security architecture community space.

Instead, open a regular and predictable time for any member to bring an issue for which they'd like help. This agenda item should be relatively unstructured.

If there's an organizational history of emotional baggage around speaking up, or even negative consequences from bringing up problems, then the facilitator will have to address that history directly. I don't mean going over the history; I mean soliciting contributions, and then honoring these in some meaningful manner.

Dialoging—that is, when two or three participants go back and forth, essentially disagreeing with each other, or repeating the same, conflictual points—must be interrupted, usually with a simple act of thanking the speakers for bringing up the problem and then asking others for opinions. If everyone else remains quiet, then I will ask if anyone else cares about the issue. If the speakers or just a few participants are the only ones concerned, then the facilitator can move the agenda item or problem to a meeting just with those concerned, taking the conflict out of the community space. Or, if other participants remain silent, ask them why. This never fails to illicit contributions beyond those who've been taking up all the verbal space in the meeting. Sometimes, when quiet folks speak up, the group gets to hear an entirely new view that creatively opens a problem/solution set up. Responses to, "Why are you not participating?" can be very revealing.

However one chooses to facilitate conflicts and grandstanding, it's important that the facilitator remembers that the larger goal is not necessarily to solve problems, but rather, to create community trust and solidarity. Solutions may actually be better generated by a smaller group.

If a small group is going to be spun off to work on a particular problem, I make sure that the problem scope is understood. I also try to ensure that every viewpoint, even those quite divergent, is represented in the makeup of the group—as well as a couple of members who don't have a strong stake in any particular perspective. The group can then report back to the entire community when it has a proposal. The proposal will then be discussed, and perhaps eventually agreed to (or amended) by the entire community.

As I wrote above, any decision which affects the way that software is developed or the way that security is to be achieved should get community input and agreement. This establishes a shared sense of purpose, as well as some sense of control over how the work should be done.

I will note that even if I believe a particular way of executing a task is less than perfect, or maybe might not work as believed, I will still let the community decide and try. There's nothing like grappling with the consequences of a decision for learning. Plus, meeting the challenge as a community builds that necessary sense of shared task and shared responsibility: "We are all in this together."

There is one caveat to the dreamy, people-oriented strategic description I've laid out just above. If your management is not 100% on board with the strategy, problems will ensue. As soon as I've received a technical leadership role, I go over my long-term community-building strategy with my direct management and their managers. Everyone needs to support the strategy or significant problems, likely misunderstandings, will occur. My first task is to ensure that we are aligned both with the strategy and the fact that along the way, there will be inevitable errors.

- Are we all willing to take those risks?
- At what level of risk should I use my influence to avert impacts?
- What level of poor decision making can we tolerate?
- What should I prevent with my leadership power and influence?

Once we have collectively answered these questions, I'm better armed to lead as well as to facilitate. I then have guidance on when to listen, when to let the community proceed, and when I need to step in and prevent negative impacts. Answering the above questions with my management allows the strategy to unfold rather more smoothly than might otherwise happen." (*Secrets,* pp. 131–134)

6.6 Threat Model Training Is for Everyone

After we opened up threat modeling training to anyone, with any role connected to software development and operations, we began to see a profound cultural shift. Though, as you can see from this chapter, there are numerous "culture hacks" that we employ, the one hack the drives security awareness deep into development is threat modeling.

This is not to indicate that everyone in development becomes an expert threat modeler. That's not needed and far from realistic. We introduce people to threat modeling, and then build skills with those who will be responsible for building and maintaining models. These are most often more senior engineers and architects, though certainly not always.

There is something indefinable about considering attacks and defenses. Most people (there is no "all" or "always" in training and culture change), after they've had time to think through a few credible attacks and then figure out how a system might then be defended properly, arrive at a deeper and more integrated understanding of what software security is about and why it is important.

We know of no other method that delivers software security awareness as broadly and consistently as an introduction to threat modeling that involves attendees actually trying to identify attacks that might work, and then defenses that help protect or prevent. Certainly, there are security awareness programs, which often include something about software security. Those who must generate code must (as our SDL requires) take secure coding training. But secure coding training doesn't help non-coders.

Threat modeling is something everyone does at some level, anyway. Driving a car involves some threat modeling (as well as much reactive threat response!). Purchasing a big-ticket item, such as appliances, a home, a vehicle, all involve a bit of threat modeling. It's a matter of focusing on digital threats and digital defense mechanisms. This culture hack brings software security "home" to attendees in a clearly perceivable way (at least for most participants).

Encouraging everyone to become familiarized with at least the intent of threat modeling and to be acquainted with its techniques internalizes the importance of software security and the SDL. It's a powerful culture hack toward a "culture of security."

In addition, once everyone understands threat modeling, at least at some high level, each just might contribute an important piece of the model's puzzle. The following excerpt from *Secrets of a Cyber Security Architect* highlights the importance of inclusion when building models.

To my point, introduce threat modeling and a project's threat model to everyone. At the same time, remind them that the model and, especially, its unimplemented results are confidential and not to be shared with those who don't need to know—particularly, outside the organization. Attackers can have a field day with a threat model, so it needs to be protected from inadvertent release.

What we discovered running around our global development centers is that when you include everyone, you get better threat models. One reason for this should be obvious but is often missed: Threat models are best when done holistically. A single missed or passed-over detail might very well miss an important attack vector or important impacts.

Let me offer an example from real life. We were examining a gateway product. The team had already done a rather thorough threat model. All I had to do was to review the results. Because I included everyone at that review, one of the more junior members of the team mentioned that the underlying operating system that had been chosen for this gateway, which would be delivered along with the product, had its SSH server running. The SSH server came with a published, default password. This is the way that the operating system was configured by its vendor in order to make debugging during development easier.

Because the team was highly focused on the functionality of the product, they'd forgotten to think about the entire runtime stack (which is a point I make repeatedly in *Securing Systems*: One must include the runtime or risk leaving attack surfaces undefended). This gateway might have been shipped with exactly the problem that allowed the Mirai Botnet to be formed and which had resulted in the famous DYN attack. That is, cameras deployed all over the world had SSH running with a published default password. The rest is history.

If we hadn't had everyone in the room, it's quite likely that during the review we would have missed this key piece of information—this readily available attack point that needed to be defended. In my presentations I like to say, "A threat model is a crossroads of many different domains and a collection of subject matter experts. Absence of any one of these can mean that the threat model is incomplete." That gateway's threat model is a perfect example of exactly this point.

Just as important as the completeness of the threat model is the culture hack that inclusivity offers us. Here's where the "magic" comes in.

Based upon hundreds of threat model classes taught at sites spanning the globe, I have observed that, once participants play at mentally attacking a system and identifying defenses against those attacks, they come away with an integral sense of why software security is so critical. Participants gain an appreciation of the importance of the entire security development lifecycle (SDL), however that SDL may be expressed within their organization. For most participants, the shift towards a culture of security is profound, as long as they've gotten the chance to participate in the threat modeling process. As I noted above, if there's any magic in software security, it is allowing everyone to participate in building threat models, in learning the process, and in making threat models accessible throughout the development process and to everyone involved, even nontechnical roles.

To add to my exhortation to include even nontechnical roles, I spoke at an internal security architecture event for Daimler, AB. Carsten Scherr runs Daimler's security architecture program, and Luis Servin is one of the technical leaders. They invited the security architects from throughout their supply chain to attend. Brilliant!

Inviting the architects from throughout their supply chain aligns security architecture practice of the third parties on whose security Daimler's products must depend. The inclusion of these key people means that each of the companies that attended now understand what Daimler expects from products whose security posture must affect the overall posture of products as they go into service. As we have seen in examples in this book, a threat model must be taken holistically, without respect to whomever may be responsible for any particular portion of an integration.

Carsten and Luis have realized that they cannot bring Daimler's products to their "desired defensive state," cannot bring their highly integrated products to the required security posture without the full participation of each of the suppliers whose products' security postures are going to contribute or detract from the overall posture.

So why not include everyone who must be involved in any discussions on how things must be done? I've never seen any company take such holistic care for their supply chain before. To my mind, this sort of out-of-the-box, inclusive thinking is what we, the industry, need to climb out of the design problems that we apparently keep creating. Include *everyone*! Really!

Participatory threat modeling is culture hacking—hacking development culture toward a culture of security." (*Secrets*, pp. 88–89)

6.7 Audit and Security Are Not the Same Thing

Inclusion means divergence. One cannot have the first without the result. It may be overly trite to state the obvious: The greater our diversity, the greater the diversity in opinions, which inevitably leads to disagreement and, perhaps, outright conflict.

Study after study has shown that diverse teams whose different perspectives are valued outperform "the smartest guys in the room" over and over again, provably so. Brook took this topic up from various angles in *Secrets of a Cyber Security Architect* in Chapters 4 through 6. We refer readers to that work for greater depth than we can give the subject here.

Still, in a chapter on culture hacking, we felt that we had to at least touch upon a subject that is quite dear to both the authors' hearts, and on which we each and together have spent significant amounts of our professional lives.

Diversity strengthens. But what to do when confronted with strongly held, opposing views? The following from *Secrets* shares a story about just such a situation and how it unfolded.

The story also makes a tangential point about the place of compliance in software security. The two, compliance and security, are not equivalent and do not necessarily deliver equal results, as the following will explain.

The larger the organization, the more likely it is that one is going to run into pretty divergent perspectives. Sometimes, my security architect's perspective might run smack dab up against a conflicting, maybe even incompatible, view. This is perhaps one of the biggest challenges facing those of us who pursue organizational transformation—those of us who are culture hackers.

Let me give an example. One of my dear friends (who shall not be named to protect her privacy), a recognized expert in her field, comes out of a compliance background. We disagree greatly about the nature of compliance and security. She believes that achieving strong compliance delivers appropriate security. I do not find this to be true, because standards and regulations often make assumptions about the nature of the problem space, assumptions about whom the standard applies to, about how the target organizations are structured, about whom the standard addresses, and about solutions sets. Because of the amount of time it takes to create, draft, and ratify a standard (years), the threat landscape and solution sets may have moved significantly since the codification of the language in the standard: These are rarely up to date.

Imagine a standard that assumes that software security is about building applications. Already, organizations that create embedded software or clouds might readily believe that "application security" doesn't include the software that these other organizations are building. Further, imagine that the standard always addresses information technology (IT) whenever the implementing organization is named. Many organizations do not build product software in their IT function, but rather, in their research and development or engineering functions. May they then believe that the standard is not intended for their software?

I didn't make the above up. In fact, draft 1 of ISO® 27034 had exactly the problems described in the preceding paragraph. These issues crept in despite the fact that ISO 27034 was intended to cover software security in general, not just IT software delivery, not confined to applications only. Oops? I think so.[*]

The truth is, writing general standards is hard. Assumptions that change the scope can creep in rather too easily. Standard drafters might assume that everyone already knows what "penetration testing" is, so there's no need to define it. That's what the first and second revisions of the Payment Card Industry Data Security Standard (PCI) did. But, unfortunately, there is no standard definition of penetration testing, and PCI didn't point to a particular definition as the one to which the standard refers. In fact, companies pass PCI audits of their penetration testing requirement with a wide range of testing, all the way from periodic vulnerability scans, through application vulnerability testing, to manually driven attempts to break in (which is the common, industry-accepted definition of "penetration testing"). The three test examples I just gave vary greatly in the results that they deliver.

To achieve compliance, the goal is to meet a specific set of predetermined requirements: what's been codified into the language of the standard or regulation. These could be for regulation such as GDPR[†] or HIPAA,[‡] or a standard such as ISO® 27001 or SOC 2®.

Unfortunately, some requirements of a standard might very well be irrelevant to the situation to be secured. In fact, this happens a lot. Or, as in GDPR, the requirement might be so vague as to be essentially meaningless. As an example, take Article 32, which purportedly describes what security measures are required:

"ARTICLE 32: Security of Personal Data—Security of Processing
"Article 32 of the GDPR, which requires 'controller and the processor shall implement appropriate technical and organizational measures to ensure a level of security appropriate to the risk'
"(a) the pseudonymization and encryption of personal data;
"(b) the ability to ensure the ongoing confidentiality, integrity, availability, and resilience of processing systems and services;
"(c) the ability to restore the availability and access to personal data in a timely manner in the event of a physical or technical incident;
"(d) a process for regularly testing, assessing and evaluating the effectiveness of technical and organizational measures for ensuring the security of the processing."[§]

---

[*] Retrieved from http://www.iso27001security.com/html/27034.html
[†] European Union Global Data Protection Regulation.
[‡] Health Insurance Portability and Accountability Act.
[§] Gen. Data Protection Regulation 2016/679, Article 32. European Union: http://www.privacy-regulation.eu/en/article-32-security-of-processing-GDPR.htm

If we take (c), anyone who's practiced any security knows that the point is CIA: Confidentiality, Integrity, and Availability. This statement is so general as to be essentially meaningless.

Like California's SB 1386, the encryption line doesn't set forth any of the implementation patterns for encryption to provide real protection. Would it be enough to implement transparent, hard disk encryption, where the keying material is available to the logged-in user?

As I remember, one of the dodges that less than fully honest and forthright companies started to use in order to protect themselves from breach notification under SB 1386 was to use transparent disk encryption. Any legal reader of the storage would get decrypted information: That's what "transparent" means. However, although this measure provides near zero runtime security benefit, it meets the legal definition of "data must be encrypted." We might start to see organizations try similar legal dodges in the GDPR space, as well. Line (a) doesn't tell us anything about the difficulties that must be met for robust, protective encryption. One could legally claim that simply having some sort of encryption meets the intent of the law. But is it security? No.

My friend insisted that being compliant automatically delivered appropriate security. I hope I've proved to you in the examples above that this is not at all true. Still, we had to not only work together, but to be effective together. Somehow, we had to find a way that our differences didn't hinder effectiveness.

How does one go about that?

I can't tell you that I have a never-fail secret to share to meet the challenge of wildly divergent perspectives such as compliance versus security. I struggle with this probably is much as any other person who routinely works with a wide range of smart and often rather opinionated people.

What I look for are places in which we are attempting to reach the same goal, only from varying routes. I listen carefully for areas of resonance, for areas of alignment. It may be when actually trying to get something done that a conflicting philosophy is irrelevant. It may be that it's merely a matter of semantics or articulation. I try really hard not to get too hung up about the way things are expressed so long as security requirements are met.

In the case of my friend, if she insisted upon expressing things with a line from some regulation or standard, so long as implementers understood the security needs to be met, what does it matter?

By being malleable around expression, I can focus on the objective. Only in a case in which there's a conflict in what must actually be accomplished do I want to enter into a need for conflict resolution, negotiation, and compromise. Often enough, all roads actually do lead to the Rome of appropriate security implementation. Or, if a regulatory requirement really is inappropriate, or worse, irrelevant, there is always the "out" of carefully documenting the insignificant likelihood and impact from failing to comply. Most of the standards and regulations allow for a statement of noncompliance given in business risk terms. Done well enough, risk assessments offered in place of compliance will usually pass audit.

There's also usually a possibility for "compensating controls." Compensating controls are alternative defenses that achieve a CIA protection similar to those that a standard requires. For instance, a compensating set of controls for encryption of data at rest would be something like the following set of controls:

- Highly restricted network segment.
- Access requires multifactor authentication.
- Strict, need-to-know only restrictions for privileged access.
- When access has been granted it would only be allowed for a limited period.
- The grant occurring through a formalized process employing separation of duties between grantor and grantee.

- Any access to the storage requires that all high privileged actions will be logged and then monitored by an independent group (not the grantee).

The above controls would compensate for encryption of data at rest. If properly documented, these are likely to pass an audit and to be defensible in court as "encryption of personal data" and an "ability to ensure the ongoing confidentiality, integrity," as GDPR requires. (*Secrets,* pp. 100–103)

We've given you a short survey of some of our favorite "culture hacks"—things we do that might not be "official," or, at least, not officially part of the management of a program (though, certainly, a community of practice has been universally a strategic initiative). The following sections comprise ways that the organization has to be officially and very consciously "hacked"—that is, changed in shape and form to meet the challenges of a DevOps, cloud-run, and developer-empowered security approach. Indeed, some readers may feel that we are suggesting that organizations change the way that they are structured, the "organization chart," if you will. Make no doubt about it; we are, most certainly, declaring that in order to achieve an SDL that integrates deeply into software development's warp and woof, organizations will very likely have to consciously change who reports to whom, change some roles, and invest differently.

The following sections outline organizational structures and investments that support the changes that we've outlined through this book.

6.8 An Organizational Management Perspective

From an organizational management perspective, we believe there are four key areas that differentiate the move of security into DevOps that go beyond the normal DevOps discussion of automation and tools: (1) Security Cultural Change; (2) Security Incident Response; (3) Security Training; and (4) Security Technical Debt (Legacy Software). These are also areas that were covered in both Chapters 2 and 5 and are key takeaways of what we have presented from an organizational management perspective.

6.8.1 Security Cultural Change

First and foremost are the cultural changes required to build security in DevOps in a way that properly facilitates building security at Agile speed. This will require a very controversial change in that it requires a move from a nearly universal status quo of an unfunded mandate for security with part-timers (security champions) only in the development groups, to a funded mandate that has full-time, dedicated security engineers and architects who have development experience and are part of the development teams and groups, respectively.

As discussed previously in this book, DevOps requires a cultural change that merges operations with development while facilitating collaboration. This book has been about merging security into the same DevOps process. Most importantly is that development, operations, and security should all be collaborating and engaged from the beginning of a product development project. This will ultimately result in the early identification of vulnerabilities, the eliminate of silos, a reduction in lead time, and an increase the frequency of delivery.

Another key component of DevOps that we have discussed is that the teams must strive for continuous integration and delivery. A key advantage of security being built in is that it can now provide for the efficiency of continuous development, threat detection, and release cycles. Collaboration will enhance security issue detection gains achieved through threat modeling, code reviews, and red teaming discussed early in this book. Another security advantage resulting from these cultural changes is that it encourages more frequent code check-in and version control.

Key business values achieved through the cultural changes discussed above include increased efficiency of operations, cost savings, quality, and automated testing, which will all result in a declining number of security threats.

Some key elements of cultural change should include the following:

- *Security in DevOps is also about investing in people, improving the lines of communication between development, operations, and security, and automating where you can automate to give humans the ability to focus on what we do best. You maximize success with DevOps when you invest in people, which, in turns, also improves your processes and tools. Some of this involves delivering remediation guidance back to developers, integrating security knowledge and secure coding practices into your DevOps teams, and having security teams obtain a greater appreciation for development by doing coding themselves if they haven't already.[*]*
- *Using automated security review of code and automated application and product security testing. Automate core security tasks by embedding security controls early on in the software development lifecycle. Continuous monitoring and remediation of security defects across the application lifecycle should be implemented including development and maintenance.[†]*
- *Continuous process improvement by establishing strategic drivers for DevOps teams to meet changing business requirements without excluding security and compliance needs. This should include continuous enablement to initiate culture change to foster collaboration between developers, security teams, and operations. Security in DevOps requires continuous improvement to achieve desired efficiency.[‡]*
- *Promote change and collaboration within their respective domains, resulting in a cultural shift in the practices of the individuals implementing them. This must be a transformational shift which incorporates secure culture, practices, and tools to drive visibility, collaboration, and agility of security into each phase of the DevOps pipeline.[§]*
- *Every employee and team are responsible for security, and that decisions need to be reached efficiently and put into action without sacrificing security. Getting new code out to production faster is a goal that often drives new business—however, in today's world, that goal needs to be balanced with addressing security.[¶]*
- *Enables organizations to provide consumers with increasingly secure products at an accelerated rate. Less gridlock during the application of late-stage security practices can make a major difference in freeing up time for DevSecOps engineers to make improvements during other segments of the product development cycle.[**]*

The ultimate goal is to enable DevOps teams to implement security efficiently and automatically, where possible, as part of their everyday processes. DevOps and security have a shared framework to

---

[*] Weeks, D. (2018, August 13). "DevSecOps: Overcoming the Culture of 'No.'" Retrieved from https://dzone .com/articles/devsecops-overcoming-the-culture-of-no

[†] Moore M. and Bovoso, A. (2018). DevSecOps: Embedded Security Within the Hyper Agile Speed of DevOps . DEVOPS Enterprise SUMMIT. Retrieved from https://www2.deloitte.com/content/dam/Deloitte/global /Documents/About-Deloitte/DevSecOps-Explained.pdf

[‡] Ibid.

[§] GSA (2020). "Understanding the Differences Between Agile & DevSecOps—from a Business Perspective." GSA Tech Guides. Retrieved from https://tech.gsa.gov/guides/understanding_differences_agile_devsecops/

[¶] RAPID7™ (2020). "DevSecOps: Definition and Deep Dive." Retrieved from https://www.rapid7.com /fundamentals/devsecops/

[**] Ibid.

work with as transformation that will lead to the elimination of the friction that has existed between security and DevOps teams in the past. The following behaviors will result through a successful cultural change:

- *Security teams trust DevOps teams to take ownership for security,*
- *Security empowers DevOps with the right tools to adopt DevSecOps,*
- *Culture change happens organically,*
- *Security partners with DevOps to adopt DevSecOps,*
- *Security adopts a trust, but verify posture, and*
- *A process of continuous improvement strengthens the security posture.*[*]

6.8.2 Security Incident Response

Security incident response, specifically, the traditional responsibilities and organizational structure of the product security incident response team (PSIRT) will have to change to meet the Agile speed and collaborative nature of DevOps. PSIRT must distribute their traditional monolithic structure; evolve from their veil of secrecy for secrecy's sake; and break down traditional response stovepipes to an organization that is distributed, practices open communications, where possible, and creates a collaborative environment in which the events become learning experiences to prevent future bugs and vulnerabilities.

The Observe, Orient, Decide, and Act (OODA) was described earlier in the book. This process is also important to the PSIRT and should be applied as follows:

- ***Observe:*** *Use security monitoring to identify anomalous behavior that may require investigation.*
- ***Orient:*** *Evaluate what's going on in the cyber threat landscape & inside your company. Make logical connections & real-time context to focus on priority events.*
- ***Decide:*** *Based on observations & context, choose the best tactic for minimal damage & fastest recovery.*
- ***Act:*** *Remediate & recover. Improve incident response procedures based on lessons learned.*[†]

An incident response process is a collection of procedures aimed at identifying, investigating, and responding to potential security incidents in a way that minimizes impact and supports rapid recovery. An incident response process is the entire lifecycle (and feedback loop) of an incident investigation, whereas incident response procedures are the specific tactics you and your team will be involved in during an incident response process. This should include how you are going to meet with and interface with executive leadership. This should include what your PSIRT will do to include expectations on your team's role, industry trends, key areas of concern, and your recommendations, as well as what to expect in terms of communications, metrics, and contributions. Find out the best way to work with the legal, HR, IT, public relations, internal communications, and procurement teams to fast track requests during essential incident response procedures. The incident response team members will need ample instruction, guidance, and direction on their roles and responsibilities. Post incident security policy reviews will identify the most important lessons to learn after an incident occurs regarding how to prevent a similar incident from happening in the future. In addition to potential updates to your security

---

[*] Venkataraghaven, V. (2020, May 11). "Bridging the DevOps and Security Divide with DevSecOps." Retrieved from https://blog.paloaltonetworks.com/2020/05/cloud-devsecops/

[†] AT&T Business™ (2020). *Insider's Guide & Incident Response: Chapter 2—Incident Response Process and Procedures.* Retrieved from https://cybersecurity.att.com/resource-center/ebook/insider-guide-to-incident-response/incident-response-process-and-procedures

policy, expect incidents to result in updates to your security education and awareness program. This is one of the important reasons why we have included security training in the following section.[*]

6.8.3 Security Training

In order to meet the needs of DevOps, security training must be relevant, succinct, adaptable, and Agile:

- **Relevant:** Use your own code and have your training internally focused on security issues that your development teams are currently facing, where possible. Prioritize using internal resources as instructors, when available.
- **Succinct:** Your developer's time is valuable and attention spans are short regarding security, TED-like, short 15- to 20-minute duration talks, updated on a regular basis, should be the norm when exercises for training, such as threat modeling and extensive code reviews, are not needed.
- **Adaptable:** Change as your development environment, priorities, and goals change.
- **Agile:** Your training should be nimble enough to meet the needs of your organization, whether it is internal, outsourced externally, or a combination of both. For externally sourced training, the old LMS-based training is expensive, the overhead costs are prohibitive and it has limited flexibility, and, in many cases, classes that are not relevant. If you outsource any of your training, it should be cloud based and only include training that is relevant to your environment.

Building security into DevOps requires the appropriate education and training for every part of the organization. This will require best practices around product security training, metrics, skills, and how they fit into the DevOps scope. DevOps specialists should be security aware, and they should be applying best security development and deployment practices. This should result in a quality assurance mindset with security as a top priority when looking for or remediating vulnerabilities.

Some other things you should consider as you develop and mature your security training and awareness program include:

- **Security as a shared responsibility:** DevOps teams need to learn that security is a responsibility that they must share with the security team. Without it, security is impossible, and without security, DevOps will not be secure. It's one thing to say that security is everyone's responsibility; it's another to arm everyone with the knowledge and tools needed to actually make that so.[†]
- **Security awareness:** Development and operations specialists should understand application vulnerabilities, their different categories, and best practices to avoid making applications vulnerable. Without this training, developers and operations specialists likely won't fully grasp just how important security is and the effects it can have on the business.[‡]
- **TED-like readily available training classes:** These can be self-developed or they can come as part of your product security testing and management solutions.
- **All training and education must be up to date and appropriate for the environment:** Be wary of outdated material and teaching methods provided by vendors. Make sure that the training and awareness you put in place is current and appropriate to your environment.
- **Security training and education is a two-way street:** Security practitioners who have not come through the software development ranks should be trained on how developers operate and the constraints they face.

---

[*] Ibid.
[†] Feiman, J. (2019, October 18). "5 Tips for DevSecOps Education and Training." Retrieved from https://dzone.com/articles/5-tips-for-devsecops-education-and-training
[‡] Ibid.

6.8.4 Security Technical Debt (Legacy Software)

Legacy applications can leave massive security holes and must be dealt with, no matter how critical they are. Technical debt includes the cost to renew legacy systems for current requirements and maintain software quality for acceptable risk and performance. Companies that postpone efforts to remediate it will eventually incur heavy technical debt. Excuses vary, but the reason for the delay to resolve technical debt is commonly that it is time consuming and expensive and will take away from other, presumably higher-priority, projects. Technical debt becomes a huge boat anchor for any company, but for development groups in a DevOps environment, it is totally unacceptable and arguably an antithesis to both DevOps and Agile delivery. In addition to security typically being an unfunded mandate, legacy software and security support for it is almost certainly an unfunded mandate most of the time. Moving forward, this needs to change, in particular, within a DevOps environment.

Taking a concerted and aggressive approach to managing technical debt and not allowing any accrued "debt" and "interest" should be a key element of the security cultural change in DevOps. Despite all the advantages of building security into DevOps, challenges like technical debt still remain. DevOps is not a solution in itself for reducing technical debt as it may produce its own, characteristic forms of technical debt. In fact, if technical debt is carried over into the DevOps process, it will be incorporated into the beginning of the process and all later changes to that process may be affected by that debt.[*]

> *It may be that DevOps' real strength in relation to technical debt is its fundamental dynamism. DevOps assumes that nothing is static, that everything will change and should change, and it casts itself as the appropriate framework for change. This means that existing technical debt, whether in the application code or in the process, will (at least in theory) eventually be eliminated by the same dynamic process of self-renewal that is at the core of DevOps itself. But no DevOps team can afford to assume that it is free of technical debt.*[†]

The following cultural changes should be considered in your development process to address and manage technical debt effectively:

- **Build it into the plans and Sprints.** Take the time to remove both small and large technical debt for the greater good of the team.
- **Refactor often.** If things are difficult or painful to modify in the code, consider redesign and/or re-implementation.
- **Take the long-term approach.** The goal here is to measure impact rather than activity. It's not about Source Lines of Code (SLOC) or team metrics (capacity, burndown, velocity), but rather the overall impact these changes can create in the long term.[‡]

By embracing security practices, quite the opposite can occur. Security practices inherently take the pressure off of the back end of the project timeline by making security a priority at all points in the development lifecycle. This enables the team to become aware of security issues early on in the process, saving time and heartache down the road.[§]

---

[*] Churchman, M. (2016, February 12). "Technical Debt and Its Impact on DevOps." Retrieved from https://www.sumologic.com/blog/technical-debt-impact-on-devops/

[†] Ibid.

[‡] Blea, S. (2020, March 5). "Technical Debt—The Anti-DevOps Culture." Retrieved from https://devblogs.microsoft.com/premier-developer/technical-debt-the-anti-devops-culture/

[§] Fitzpatrick, S. (2018, April 4). "Why Legacy Security Practices Are Incompatible with DevSecOps." Retrieved from https://www.twistlock.com/2018/04/04/legacy-security-incompatible-devsecops/

6.9 Summary/Conclusion

We believe that part of delivering "built-in" software security requires significant organizational and organizational culture changes, what we've termed "culture hacks." Some of these are subtle and operate largely at a personal behavior level. Some of the hacks we've described are quite overt: changes to an organization's very structure and investment strategies. Rest assured, every technique mentioned in this chapter is consciously undertaken.

We use the culture hacks outlined in this chapter to move our organizations towards a culture of software security, wherein security is one of the key considerations and sets of tasks (SDL) throughout development and during the operation of software. We've divided the hacks into two main categories: execution hacks and organization structure hacks.

Execution Hacks:

- Gain the support of, and identify resistance from, every level of the organization:
  ○ Executives
  ○ Mid-management
  ○ Senior technology leaders
  ○ Everyone else willing to help
- Trust developers to do the right thing. Consistently message what the "right things" are, as well as communicating responsibility for and empowering to deliver.
- Trust AND verify: Remember that everyone makes mistakes. Provide tools and training so that developers can find errors before they're released.
- Build a community of practice to support learning and motivation through a shared sense of purpose.
- Introduce threat modeling to everyone who contributes in any way to development.
- Remember that achieving a desired risk posture (the CIA of security) will lay a foundation for compliance with standards and regulations. But compliance alone will not necessarily deliver appropriate security.

Structure Hacks:

- Investing in people goes far beyond hiring the right people. Investing in effective communication skills and channels, appropriate automation, and supportive critical analysis (particularly risk analysis) are also part of people investment.
- Automation has become critical. Every DevOps shop will use a great deal, through a variety of tools. At the same time, some problems are better handled by humans. This is especially true for complex analyses.
- Establish clear strategic objectives that coordinate people's efforts.
- Empower and invest in a strong, effective product security incident response team (PSIRT).
- Train, then practice, refresh, remind, renew, and practice more. Consider what's working. Identify challenges and potential solutions. Review success. And then retrain.
- Address technical debt.

In this, the last chapter of the book, we've addressed those organizational and cultural shifts that we believe must be made to foster Agile, DevOps developer-centric software security. Culture hacking provides a closing bookend to our book, because without culture change, a generic SDL, and the organization and management of its supporting software security program, cannot be entirely effective. Software security remains, at its essence, a people problem, requiring people-driven solutions. Humans live in cultures, whether we consider a wider, regional culture; a nation's particulars; or each organization's unique expectations, habits, and style.

Having declared at the outset of this book that "software security is a people problem," it made sense to us to leave the cultural aspects to last, after we had laid out the problem, then provided the solution (a generic SDL), particulars about secure design (which really requires its own book to fully explain), and organizational and management aspects that allow a program to run and be run with intention and focus. Each of the broad aspects given throughout this book must be brought together into a whole for success. Failure to attend to one or more aspects, in our experience, will inhibit results, often profoundly.

In this chapter, we have closed the circle back to people and how empowering people and giving them the right tools and the right incentives (in the right structure and empowerment), through workable methods, will lead to better software security and a culture of security that prizes building security from the start, and through the development process, as a key part of the warp and weft of developing software.

We stand behind this book's contents with a conviction built from creating programs, reflecting on what works and what has not, upon how we might change what we're doing, or add something new, and perhaps different, even unique. Sometimes, it's painful to acknowledge that a course we had thought should deliver has not. Then, quite literally, James and Brook will go into an office or a conference room, or have a phone call, meet for lunch or coffee to honestly and forthrightly confront the problem. We may try to tweak what we're doing, or switch to something different, or even change the approach entirely. Alternatively, we may double down on what we believe will work: Perhaps the execution has simply been flawed? The confidence expressed in this book has been built on success and failure. Our hope is that you, our readers, don't have to make the same mistakes and that you will benefit from the more effective results that we've been able to draw forth from ours.

May we meet the security challenges that lie before us. We pray that what we've written here can speed you and your organization on its path to appropriate and relevant software security.

Appendix A

The Generic Security Development Lifecycle

A.1	Begin Threat Model
Purpose	Begin a threat model to deliver a secure design based upon the security objectives for the software. Security objectives are based, in part, on the attacks the system must resist and the security expectations of the system's stakeholders, i.e., the system threat model.
Preconditions	The threat model may be started when there is an idea or concept to be realized through software. The threat model must be initiated when more than one structural element has been conceived as a solution to deliver the objectives of the software. When no threat model has been started for an architecture that is nearing or has been completed, and for mature systems, start the threat model immediately.
Definition of Done	Not Applicable—the threat model will be refined throughout development.
Results & Outputs	At concept time, output high-level security requirements and features. Identify additional security requirements and those structural elements/components and implementations that will deliver the security requirements.
Triggers for review or refinement	As architecture elements are added or conceived, refine the threat model. When security features are identified, refine the threat model. When new attack techniques or avenues of attack are discovered (threats), refine the threat model.

A.2	Refine Threat Model
Purpose	Refine a threat model to more clearly represent the attacks that the unfolding system will need to resist and to identify new security requirements, as well as to ensure that existing requirements remain synchronized with the architecture and the implementation of the software.
Preconditions	There must be an existing threat model. There must be at least some architecture (structural elements) that can be analyzed.
Definition of Done	The threat model is complete enough when all relevant attack scenarios have been considered, when scenarios have been risk rated, and when every attack scenario with potential for significant impact, as well as likelihood of exploitation, has sufficient security defenses to bring the system to the risk tolerance of the system's stakeholders.
Results & Outputs	A set of risk-rated attack scenarios and a set of defenses (including already-implemented and to be built) that together comprise an appropriate "defense in depth."
Triggers for review or refinement	Refine the threat model when there is a change to the architecture, when new exploitation types have been discovered, and when new defenses become available. Architectural changes might be any of the following: • Components or functions • Assets • Use cases • Lines of communication or data flows • Trust boundaries or levels of trust/distrust • Shifting the exposure of potentially vulnerable components

A.3	Conduct Privacy Impact Assessment (PIA)
Purpose	An analysis of the software to identify requirements (security and other) needed to protect the privacy of personal data and to comply with those privacy regulations to which the software will be subject. An essential part of the analysis will be threat modeling for privacy and data attacks. (Please see Begin Threat Model & Refine Threat Model activities, as well.)
Preconditions	There is a need to collect human entities' data. The data elements that are/will be collected must be known, as must the reasons for collecting the data. There must be an existing threat model. There must be at least some architecture (structural elements) that can be analyzed.
Definition of Done	The PIA is complete when all the privacy requirements (security and other) have been identified and the privacy-focused portions of the threat model are finished. (Please see Refine Threat Model activity.)
Results & Outputs	• A set of risk-rated attack scenarios and a set of defenses (including defenses already implemented and defenses to be built), which together comprise an appropriate "defense in depth" for privacy protection and privacy regulation compliance. • A set of non-security requirements to achieve privacy typically include legal, user interface, and privacy engineering needs.
Triggers for review or refinement	• Changes to the human entities' data elements • Use cases • Lines of communication or data flows • Trust boundaries2 or levels of trust/distrust • Shifting the exposure of potentially vulnerable components that handle privacy-related data

A.4	Threat Model Build, Package, Release, and Deploy Mechanisms
Purpose	To extend attack and defense analysis beyond the software development to include all mechanisms used to generate, run, and maintain the running software. Although a "comprehensive" threat model should include these aspects, particularly in DevOps where much of these functions will also be "coded," we call this threat modeling subtask out separately, since it is often skipped. But attackers don't skip it and compromise can allow the attacker to spoof or otherwise manipulate the software to their ends.
Preconditions	There must be build, package, release, and deploy mechanisms, code, and software components planned and existing.
Definition of Done	The threat model is complete enough when all relevant attack scenarios have been considered, when scenarios have been risk rated, and when every attack scenario with potential for significant impact, as well as likelihood of exploitation, has sufficient security defenses to bring build, release, deploy, and operations to the risk tolerance of the system's stakeholders.
Results & Outputs	A set of risk-rated attack scenarios and a set of defenses (including already implemented and to be built) that together comprise an appropriate "defense in depth."
Triggers for review or refinement	Refine the threat model when there is a change to the architecture, when new exploitation types have been discovered, and when new defenses become available. Architectural changes might be any of the following: • Components, functions, or tools • Assets used for build, release, deployment, and operating • Use cases • Lines of communication or data flows • Trust boundaries or levels of trust/distrust • Shifting the exposure of potentially vulnerable components

A.5	Assess Security of Hosting Infrastructure
Purpose	When unknown, any hosting infrastructure that will be used must have its security capabilities, security posture, and security practices assessed. Every infrastructure has security strengths and limitations. Software making use of an infrastructure must understand what it will gain and must take responsibility for the software's overall security posture. Threat modeling the infrastructure will be one of the foundational tasks of the assessment, but not the only one, since the software system to be deployed on the infrastructure may need to consume security services from the infrastructure. (Please see Begin Threat Model and Refine Threat Model activities.)
Preconditions	• A hosting infrastructure (planned, internal, external, commercial cloud, hybrid cloud, etc.) will be used by the software. • No previous infrastructure assessment has been undertaken, nor have significant changes occurred to the infrastructure.
Definition of Done	All services to be used or currently employed have been threat modeled and assessed for security tolerance, security posture, and security practices.
Results & Outputs	• A set of security requirements that the software will need to meet in order to run on the infrastructure and meet the software's security needs and objectives. • A set of the additional risks (if any) that running on the infrastructure adds to the operation and maintenance of the software.
Triggers for review or refinement	Review the assessment whenever unassessed infrastructure is added or changed (e.g., change of vendors or locations or services, etc.).

A.6	Review Threat Model
Purpose	To validate that a threat model is comprehensive enough, and that it is sufficiently complete for the state of development at this review moment.
Preconditions	A threat model that is believed to have been sufficiently completed. Each review should be made by a threat model practitioner who is independent of the target system and development and a reviewer who has more experience than those who generated the model. (In the case of the most senior threat modeler, peer review by other senior practitioners is sufficient.)
Definition of Done	The reviewers agree that the model is complete and comprehensive enough.
Results & Outputs	A risk-rated set of reviewed security requirements, including defensive measures and mitigations against attack scenarios.
Triggers for review or refinement	Whenever a threat model has been refined and the refiners believe that refinements are finished.

A.7	Secure Coding Training
Purpose	To prepare programmers (and other related staff) for generating code without security issues.
Preconditions	A need to generate or change software programming code.
Definition of Done	Demonstration of attendance and ability to apply the techniques that have been learned.
Results & Outputs	Programmers have been through appropriate training and can demonstrate secure coding practices.
Triggers for review or refinement	N/A

A.8	Manual Code Review
Purpose	Manual code review is used to find security issues that have been coded, as well as to ensure that security functionality has been coded correctly.
Preconditions	Code has been generated or changed.
Definition of Done	• Peer review has been performed and acknowledged by the programmer. • For security critical code, expert review has been performed and acknowledged. • Issues that have been agreed upon have been fixed. Code has been resubmitted for review and potential commit to build.
Results & Outputs	The security issues or incorrect implementations that have been identified are acknowledged and fixed.
Triggers for review or refinement	Code has been generated or changed.

A.9	Static Analysis Testing
Purpose	Static analysis for security testing (SAST) is employed to identify security errors that are contained in program source code.
Preconditions	Code has been generated or changed.
Definition of Done	• SAST has been performed over code modules containing changes and over all dependent and interacting modules. • Issues that have been found to offer potential attacker leverage ("true positives") have been fixed. Code has been resubmitted for analysis and potential commit to build.
Results & Outputs	The security issues or incorrect implementations that have been identified are acknowledged and fixed.
Triggers for review or refinement	Code has been generated or changed.

A.10	Assess Third-Party Code
Purpose	Third-party code assessment ensures that included code generated by external or outside parties (e.g., commercial and open source) meets similar SDL requirements as code produced under the organization's SDL.
Preconditions	Third-party code will be included.
Definition of Done	Third-party software security practices have been found to be sufficient so that inclusion of the code will not degrade the software security of the system or software. That is, the third-party execution of their SDL is similar to and meets the requirements of the organization's SDL.
Results & Outputs	An assessment as to whether third-party code may be included or must be avoided.
Triggers for review or refinement	• Third-party code proposed for inclusion/use. • Changes have been made to third-party used/included code.

A.11	Patch (Upgrade or Fix) Issues Identified in Third-Party Code
Purpose	Issues in third-party code become issues in the entire system or software. The task is to apply software upgrades ("patches") that fix issues in software produced by external parties.
Preconditions	Third-party software must be included or employed. And security issues (vulnerabilities) have been found or announced within the third-party software.
Definition of Done	All existing vulnerability patches whose issues may cause significant harm have been fixed or the risk has been accepted by risk decision makers.
Results & Outputs	Software patches have been applied or risk decisions recorded.
Triggers for review or refinement	• Announcement of issues in included/used third-party code. • Discovery of issues in included/used third-party code.

A.12	Functional Security Testing
Purpose	Functional testing of security functions and features ensures that these functions behave as intended and that they can handle error conditions and edge cases well.
Preconditions	• Completed realizations of security functions and features. • A set of tests designed to exercise the full range of behavior and error handling that is expected from each function or feature.
Definition of Done	Tests have completed successfully. All identified issues have been fixed.
Results & Outputs	Incorrect software behavior and improper handling of errors.
Triggers for review or refinement	• Tests must be rerun each time a feature or function has been changed. • Tests must be rerun to prove that issues have been fixed and new issues have not been introduced.

A.13	Web Protocol and Services Dynamic Testing
Purpose	Web protocol and services dynamic testing uses specialized tools to identify vulnerabilities and security weaknesses.
Preconditions	• Web protocol and services are included in the software, and the code has been completed sufficiently to execute in the intended execution environment or its simile. • The availability of tools (scanners, etc.) built to test the particular protocols and services that have been built.
Definition of Done	Tests have completed successfully. All identified issues have been fixed.
Results & Outputs	Incorrect software behavior. Vulnerabilities and weaknesses in the software.
Triggers for review or refinement	• Tests must be rerun each time changes are introduced. • Tests must be rerun to prove that issues have been fixed and new issues have not been introduced.

A.14	Other Inputs Security Testing (e.g., Fuzzing)
Purpose	Other inputs security testing uses fuzzing and potentially other specialized tools to identify incorrect software behavior when malformed data are input.
Preconditions	• Non-Web inputs are included in the software, and the code has been completed sufficiently to execute in the intended execution environment or its simile. • The availability of fuzzers capable of sending malformed data to each particular program input.
Definition of Done	Tests have completed successfully. All identified issues have been fixed.
Results & Outputs	Incorrect software behavior. Vulnerabilities and weaknesses in the software.
Triggers for review or refinement	• Tests must be rerun each time changes are introduced. • Tests must be rerun to prove that issues have been fixed and new issues have not been introduced.

A.15	Attack and Penetration Testing
Purpose	• Manual attack and penetration testing is used to find security issues whose discovery is not easily automated by commercial and open source vulnerability discovery tools. • Attack and penetration testing also proves/disproves the security assumptions and the sufficiency of the security requirements identified in the threat model.
Preconditions	Software capable of execution in its intended environment and the intended execution environment or an accurate simile.
Definition of Done	Tests have completed successfully. All identified issues have been fixed.
Results & Outputs	Vulnerabilities and weaknesses in the software. Proof of issue presence is provided by successful compromise.
Triggers for review or refinement	• Tests must be rerun each time changes are introduced. • Tests must be rerun to prove that issues have been fixed and new issues have not been introduced.

A.16	Assess and Threat Model Build/Release/Deploy/Operate Chain
Purpose	• Ensure that tools and administrative access do not offer attacker leverage to meet security posture needs. • Ensure that the software that is released contains only intended software.
Preconditions	Methods, processes, and technology used to build, package, release, deploy, and operate software.
Definition of Done	A comprehensive set of defenses has been identified (i.e., a completed threat model. (Please see Begin Threat Model and Refine Threat Model activities.)
Results & Outputs	A set of security requirements and controls that, when implemented, close or mitigate potential attacker leverage (threats).
Triggers for review or refinement	• Tool or technology changes. • Change to the number of administrators/administrative access types/points.

Index